JUDY GORMAN'S
Vegetable Cookbook

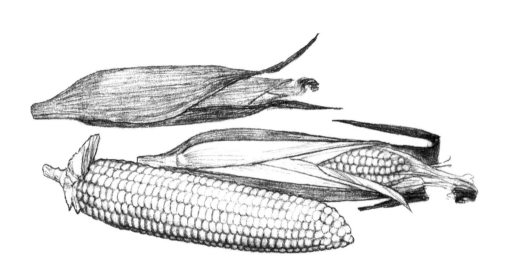

JUDY GORMAN'S VEGETABLE COOKBOOK

MJF BOOKS

NEW YORK

Notice: This book is intended as a reference volume only, not as a medical manual. If you suspect that you have a medical problem, we urge you to seek competent medical help. Keep in mind that nutritional needs vary from person to person, depending on age, sex, health status and total diet. The foods discussed and recipes given here are designed to help you make informed decisions about your diet and health. They are not intended as a substitute for any treatment prescribed by your doctor.

Published by MJF Books
Fine Communications
Two Lincoln Square
60 West 66th Street
New York, New NY 10023

Copyright © 1986 by Yankee Publishing Incorporated

Cover photographs by Ralph Copeland
Design and illustrations by Jill Shaffer
Food styling on cover by Kristie Scott

Library of Congress Catalog Card Number 94-75369
ISBN 1-56731-042-7

Published by arrangement with Rodale Press, Inc.
Manufactured in the United States of America

MJF Books and the MJF colophon are trademarks of Fine Creative Media, Inc.

10 9 8 7 6 5 4 3 2 1

To My Mother and Father,
who planted and tended the garden.
And who, as often as necessary,
insisted that I help.

Contents

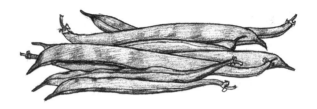

Introduction

D URING THE YEARS of my childhood that I remember most vividly, my family lived on a tobacco
farm. And since there was always a plot of unused land
available, we planted an annual garden. It sounds blissful,
but the memories are not all happy ones. I detested that
garden. Out in the hot sun to hoe; up at the crack of dawn
to harvest — clearly, this was not the life for me.

Now, I often think about that garden. For as much as
I disliked the work, I loved the taste of those fresh vegetables. What I would give today to be able to pick a vine-
ripened tomato still warm from the sun or pull a handful
of baby beets no bigger than marbles. But that isn't possible. So I scout the supermarket produce stand instead.
Always on the lookout for a vegetable at its peak of
freshness, I plan the day's menu around whatever delicacy
I find.

What I hope to share in this book is an enthusiasm
for fresh vegetables, tempered with the understanding
that, for many of us, a backyard garden is out of the
question. The text is divided into alphabetical entries.
Under each heading, I've described the characteristics vital
to selecting the freshest, most flavorful vegetables of each
type, and given suggestions for successfully storing them.
Each entry also lists general methods of preparation.

The recipes that follow the information on selection,
storage, and preparation reflect my own personal taste.
Consequently, they rely to a great extent on the use of fresh
herbs. And the measuring of fresh herbs often poses a
problem or two, so I would like to offer you the following
words of explanation. Recipes customarily call for a certain

amount of chopped herbs. But in some instances — specifically, thyme and rosemary — the leaves may be left whole to create a more aesthetically pleasing effect. Dill leaves and oregano leaves, if tiny, may also be left intact. It is very much a matter of personal preference.

When measuring fresh herbs, do not feel obliged to pack the leaves too tightly. The best approach is to remove the herb leaves from the woody stem, if there is one, and then chop the leaves or keep them whole. Push the leaves into a small pile and scoop them up with a measuring spoon, leveling it off so that the leaves sit loosely. Keep in mind, of course, that because herbs play such an important role in flavoring, you can always feel free to adjust the amount you use to suit your personal taste.

Another frequent culinary directive is to store certain vegetables in a "cool, dry, well-ventilated place." Unfortunately, that is not as easy as it sounds. Many homes today don't have cool, well-ventilated places because modern insulation does such a good job of keeping out the heat or the cold. An unheated cellar or a garage is probably the best storage environment during the winter. Absolutely avoid storing vegetables in the kitchen cupboard under the sink. It is not only damp there, but the heat from the hot-water tap or nearby dishwasher makes that space quite warm.

Since the focus of this book is on fresh vegetables, dried varieties of shell beans, dried mushrooms, and sun-dried tomatoes have not been included. And while I hope that vegetarian cooks might find useful information here, this is not meant to be a strictly vegetarian book. Rather, it is a celebration of the wonderful variety of tastes, textures, colors, and shapes that make fresh vegetables a feast for the eye as well as the palate.

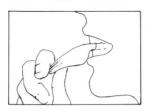

Artichokes

A GLOBE ARTICHOKE is actually the large green bud of a flower — a thistle to be exact. The question of how to eat a whole artichoke often prevents people from trying this delightful vegetable. But the procedure is quite simple once you get the hang of it. When served one, begin by snapping off an outer leaf with your fingers. If a dipping sauce is provided, dunk the base of the leaf into the mixture. Holding the tip of the leaf, bite down on the fleshy part at the base and pull it through your teeth.

Proceed in this manner, around and around the artichoke. If the artichoke is stuffed, the filling may be eaten with a fork. When all the outer leaves have been peeled away, you'll find a tightly closed cone of purple-tipped, pale green leaves (unless these have been removed, which is usually the case with a stuffed artichoke). Remove these thin leaves by pulling the cone away with a sharp twist of your wrist. Set them aside. Scoop out the fuzzy core with a spoon or pluck the fibers away with your fingers. Finish by eating the bottom of the artichoke with a knife and fork. Artichokes can be purchased year round, but are at their best in the spring and fall.

Snap off an outer leaf and bite down on the fleshy part at the base while you pull it through your teeth.

TO SELECT:

Artichokes come in three basic sizes and two basic shapes, both having more to do with how artichokes grow than with quality. Artichokes grow on a branching plant. The bud at the very top of the main stalk is the largest artichoke; lower branches produce slightly smaller buds. In the crook between the branches where new growth forms are the tiny buds called baby artichokes, or hearts. (These are usually what you get when you buy canned or frozen artichoke hearts.) The artichokes harvested in the spring are round buds with tightly packed leaves; those harvested in the fall are more elongated with slightly opened leaves. Whichever you buy, look for artichokes that feel firm and resilient when you squeeze gently. Avoid any that are soft, spongy, or have loose, spreading leaves.

The outer leaves of artichokes bruise and mar easily. This is not so much an indication of poor quality as it is of careless handling. If an artichoke feels heavy for its size and otherwise seems fresh, don't hesitate to select one with a few brown scratches. Artichokes harvested in the fall are apt to be "winter kissed." When the outer leaves are subjected to frost, the skin blisters and breaks, causing a bronze discoloration. This doesn't affect the quality of the vegetable; in fact, some cooks prefer these artichokes for their meatier flesh.

TO STORE:

Artichokes need humidity to keep fresh. Transfer them, without washing, to a plastic bag and seal tightly. Or wrap each individual bud in plastic wrap. They can be refrigerated for up to 4 or 5 days.

TO PREPARE:

Most cooks prefer to trim artichokes in order to remove the prickly tips of the leaves.

Wash artichokes by soaking them for 5 to 10 minutes in tepid water. For each artichoke, trim the stem off at the base if you want the bud to sit upright; otherwise, you can leave a portion of the stem attached and peel it with a swivel-blade peeler. Snap off any coarse or discolored outer leaves. Turn the artichoke on its side and cut off the top quarter of the leafy portion. Then, using scissors, cut off the notched or prickly ends of the remaining leaves. Cook immediately or keep in acidulated water (to prevent discoloration) until ready to use.

Cook the artichokes until tender, then submerge them in cold water. Drain thoroughly by turning them upside down on absorbent paper. Spread the center leaves apart and reach in with your fingers to remove the pale, purple-tipped cone of thin leaves. Scoop out the fuzzy choke with a melon baller or the sharp edge of a metal spoon. (You may also remove the thin leaves and choke before cooking if the artichoke is to be baked and served hot, but the method described above is easier, so it is the recommended technique for preparing artichokes to be served cold.)

Baby artichokes may be eaten raw or cooked briefly and served cut in half. Large artichokes may be prepared as discussed above, then quartered and fried in a batter coating, or trimmed of all the leaves and served as artichoke bottoms (also frequently called artichoke hearts). The meaty pulp may be scooped from the leaves and used as a purée or transformed into soup.

Artichoke Fritters

SERVES 4 TO 6

These artichoke tidbits are coated with a light, puffy batter and deep-fried. Serve as an appetizer or a side dish.

4 medium artichokes
1 tablespoon lemon juice
1 cup all-purpose flour
1 teaspoon baking powder
½ teaspoon salt
½ cup water
2 large egg whites
½ cup club soda
Vegetable oil for deep-
    frying
4 lemon wedges

1. Wash and trim the artichokes as described earlier (see TO PREPARE) and drop into a large pot of boiling, salted water. Add the lemon juice and cook, uncovered, at a gentle bubble for 30 to 40 minutes or until the stem ends are tender when pierced. Lift out with a slotted spoon and drain on absorbent paper.

2. Cut the artichokes into quarters lengthwise and remove the fuzzy chokes with a metal spoon. Cut each quarter in two, again lengthwise.

3. In a large bowl, combine the flour, baking powder, and salt. Whisk to blend thoroughly. Beat the water and egg whites in another bowl until frothy, then add to the dry ingredients. Add the club soda and stir to blend. Dip the pieces of artichoke into the batter and fry, a few at a time, in deep fat heated to 375°. Drain on absorbent paper and serve immediately with wedges of lemon.

Greek-Style Artichokes

Artichokes, marinated in a savory broth, are served chilled or at room temperature. Offer as an appetizer or part of a salad.

4 medium artichokes
2 cups water
2 cups white wine
½ cup lemon juice
1 tablespoon coriander seed
1 teaspoon dried thyme
2 bay leaves
½ teaspoon salt
12 black peppercorns

1. Wash and trim the artichokes as described earlier (see TO PREPARE), removing the thin inner leaves and fuzzy choke.

2. In a wide saucepan, combine the water, wine, and lemon juice. Stir in the coriander, thyme, bay leaves, salt, and peppercorns. Bring to a boil and drop in the prepared artichokes. Cook, uncovered, at a gentle bubble for 30 to 40 minutes or until the stem ends are tender when pierced.

3. Remove from the heat and allow the artichokes to cool in the liquid. Lift them out with a slotted spoon and cut into quarters. Place in a large bowl and pour on enough of the cooking liquid to cover by 1 inch. Refrigerate for at least 24 hours, then drain to serve.

Artichoke Soup

I first tasted artichoke soup at The Stanford Court in San Francisco, and I found its flavor elusive yet captivating. This version incorporates a small amount of mustard to intensify the artichoke flavor.

4 large artichokes
3 tablespoons butter
1 medium onion, coarsely chopped
1 garlic clove, minced
2 tablespoons all-purpose flour
4 cups chicken broth
½ teaspoon Dijon mustard
3 tablespoons Madeira
½ cup medium or whipping cream
Salt and freshly ground black pepper
Freshly grated nutmeg

1. Rinse the artichokes and drop them into a large pot of boiling, salted water. Cook, uncovered, at a gentle bubble for 20 minutes or until tender. Lift them out and immediately submerge in cold water. When cool enough to handle, pull off the leaves and remove the choke from the heart. Cut the heart into quarters and set aside. Using a metal spoon, scrape the flesh from the meaty leaves and place it in a bowl.

2. Melt the butter in a large saucepan. Add the onion and garlic and toss to coat evenly. Stir over medium heat until the onion is tender. Sprinkle on the flour and continue stirring over medium heat until the mixture foams. Stir in the chicken broth and bring to a boil. When the mixture is slightly thickened, pour it into the container of a blender or processor. Add the artichoke flesh and the quartered hearts. Whirl until smooth. Return to the saucepan and blend in the mustard and Madeira. Add the cream and place over medium heat. Warm the soup gently, but do not allow it to boil. Season with salt and pepper and ladle into soup bowls. Sprinkle with nutmeg and serve hot.

Baked Artichoke Hearts with Feta Cheese SERVES 4

Fresh herbs and shallot blended with feta cheese make a wonderful filling for the meaty bottom portions of artichokes.

2 cups water
1 cup chicken broth
½ cup olive oil
Juice of 1 lemon
2 garlic cloves, sliced
1 teaspoon dried thyme
1 bay leaf
8 medium artichokes
1 large package (8 ounces)
  cream cheese
1 large egg yolk, beaten
4 ounces feta cheese,
  crumbled
1 shallot, minced
1 tablespoon chopped fresh
  basil
1 tablespoon chopped fresh
  thyme
¼ teaspoon salt
Freshly ground black
  pepper

1. In a large saucepan, combine the water, chicken broth, oil, lemon juice, garlic, thyme, and bay leaf.

2. Wash and trim the artichokes as described earlier (see TO PREPARE). Cut off the stem at the base and pull away all the leaves until you come to the inner cone of pale, purple-tipped leaves. Slice off the cone at its base, creating a flat, round portion of artichoke. Smooth the outer surface by shaving it with the blade of a paring knife. As you finish each artichoke, drop it into the prepared liquid.

3. Place over high heat and bring the liquid to a boil. Reduce the heat and simmer, uncovered, for 20 to 30 minutes or until tender when pierced. Lift out the artichoke hearts with a spoon and allow them to cool.

4. Preheat the oven to 400°. Generously butter a shallow baking dish. Scoop any traces of the fuzzy chokes away from the hearts with a metal spoon. In a small mixing bowl, blend together the cream cheese and egg yolk. Add the feta cheese, shallot, basil, thyme, salt, and pepper. Mix well and spoon into the cavity of each artichoke. Place in the prepared pan. Bake for 8 to 10 minutes or until the cheese is slightly puffed and browned.

After cutting off the stem at the base of the artichoke, pull away all the leaves until you reach the inner cone of pale, purple-tipped leaves. Slice off the cone at its base.

Smooth the outer surface of the artichoke heart by shaving it with the blade of a knife. Then, using a spoon, scrape away the fuzzy chokes.

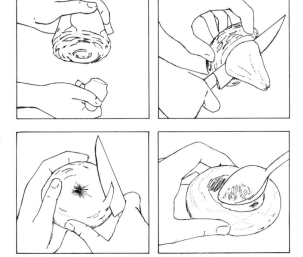

Baked Stuffed Artichokes

Chopped fresh mint combined with garlic makes an aromatic stuffing to intersperse between artichoke leaves.

4 medium artichokes
4 tablespoons butter
1 garlic clove, minced
2 anchovy fillets, minced
1½ cups unseasoned bread crumbs
4 tablespoons chopped fresh mint
2 tablespoons chopped fresh parsley
½ teaspoon salt
Pinch of cayenne
1 cup dry white wine
½ cup olive oil

1. Wash and trim the artichokes as described earlier (see TO PREPARE), removing the thin inner leaves and fuzzy choke.

2. Melt the butter in a large skillet. Add the garlic and anchovies, then stir over medium heat for 30 seconds. Stir in the bread crumbs and blend well so that the crumbs absorb the melted butter. Remove from the heat and mix in the mint, parsley, salt, and cayenne.

3. Preheat the oven to 375°. Spread apart the leaves of each artichoke and stuff with the bread crumb mixture. Spoon some of the stuffing into the center cavity. Pour the wine and olive oil into a shallow baking dish. Set the artichokes in the liquid and cover the dish with aluminum foil. Bake for 30 minutes. Uncover and continue baking for an additional 15 minutes. Serve the artichokes hot or at room temperature.

Arugula (a-ROO-guh-la)

ARUGULA, also called rocket, is a leafy green related to the mustard family, a kinship that becomes immediately apparent when you bite into it. The sharp, mustardy flavor of arugula adds a zesty accent to soups and salads composed of milder tasting greens. It is available throughout the year at specialty grocers, but is at its best in spring and early summer.

TO SELECT:

Arugula comes in small clumps of 4 or 5 leafy stems attached at the root. (It is also sold bereft of its root and packed in small plastic pouches, but it is apt to be less fresh than greens that are still attached to a root.) This green is assertively flavored, so 1 clump will do for a salad serving 4 people, which is fortunate because arugula is expensive. Choose arugula with bright green, fresh-looking leaves; avoid any that is wilted or tinged with yellow. The smaller the leaves, the less pungent the flavor will be.

TO STORE: Arugula is delicate and bruises easily. Gently place the unwashed greens in a plastic bag and seal with a wire twist. Refrigerate and use within 1 or 2 days.

TO PREPARE: Separate the leafy stems at the root and trim off the brownish ends. Rinse briefly under a cool gentle stream from the tap and distribute the leaves over a clean kitchen towel in a single layer. Pat dry with a paper towel. Then gently roll up the towel and the leaves like a jelly roll. Chill for 2 to 3 hours. To serve, tear the leaves into bite-size pieces and combine with gently flavored greens like Boston, Bibb, or ruby lettuce. The lower portion of the stem may be thinly sliced as you would chives and sprinkled over a green salad, chicken salad, or an array of sliced tomatoes.

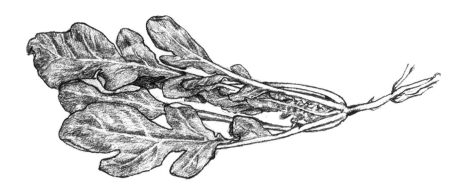

Arugula Salad

SERVES 4

1 large bunch arugula
8 red radishes, thinly sliced
8 mushrooms, thinly sliced
2 tablespoons lemon juice
¼ teaspoon dry mustard
6 tablespoons olive oil
¼ teaspoon salt
Pinch of cayenne
1 garlic clove, minced or
  pressed

Arugula and radishes team up to create a zesty salad. Serve as a separate course to fully appreciate the interplay of flavors.

1. Rinse the arugula and pat dry on absorbent paper. Arrange on 4 salad plates, adding the sliced radishes and mushrooms in an attractive pattern.

2. Whisk together the lemon juice and mustard until the mustard is dissolved. Add the oil, salt, and cayenne and whisk to blend. Stir in the garlic, then pour the dressing over the salad and serve.

Arugula • 17

Fettuccine with Arugula and Mushrooms   SERVES 4

Sautéing arugula in olive oil mollifies its sharp flavor and transforms it into something quite different.

1 small bunch arugula
2 tablespoons olive oil
3 tablespoons butter
16 mushrooms, sliced
Salt and freshly ground
  black pepper
1 cup light cream
2 large egg yolks
½ cup freshly grated
  Parmesan cheese
½ pound fettuccine, boiled
  and drained

1. Rinse the arugula and pat dry on absorbent paper. Stack the leaves and cut them across into thin shreds. Heat the oil in a small skillet. Add the arugula and stir over high heat for 30 seconds or until wilted and intensely green. Transfer to a plate and set aside.

2. Melt the butter in a large skillet. Add the mushrooms and toss to coat. Stir over medium heat until tender, but do not allow them to brown. Sprinkle with salt and pepper. Remove from the heat and stir in the arugula.

3. In a small bowl, whisk together the cream and egg yolks. Add the mixture to the mushrooms and return to medium heat. Sprinkle on the Parmesan cheese and stir constantly until the cheese is melted and the sauce is slightly thickened. Add the drained fettuccine and toss over medium heat to coat and to warm the noodles. Serve immediately.

Asparagus

FOR MANY FOOD LOVERS, the early spears of asparagus are a true sign that spring has finally arrived. Poking their tightly budded heads through otherwise barren soil, these brave stalks are among the first green shoots of the new season.

Asparagus from California and Florida is available as early as February, but the season in colder regions begins later in the year and coincides with the first cool weeks of spring. Asparagus is a good source of vitamins A and C and of potassium.

TO SELECT:

Asparagus, like sweet corn, is at its absolute best when picked and then cooked immediately. That's because the natural sugar in harvested asparagus quickly converts to starch, causing the asparagus to lose flavor and begin to develop a woody texture.

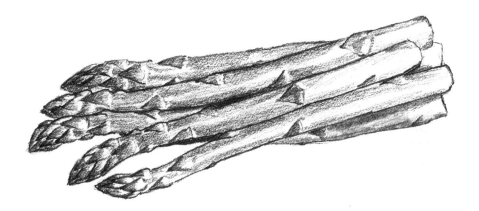

Because most of us do our harvesting at the supermarket, we have to judge freshness by the outward appearance of this vegetable. If possible, shop where you can choose the spears you want from a loose display. Pick only those stalks that have tightly closed buds; open heads with tiny sprouts showing between the leaves are a sign of age. Stalks about ½-inch in diameter are the optimum size. (While it is possible for fat asparagus to be tender and flavorful, anything thicker than your index finger is usually quite stringy.) Asparagus should be a vibrant green, the color of lush moss, and the stems should feel brittle enough to snap between your fingers.

There is a variety of ultrathin asparagus available that looks promisingly delicate. The stalks are about the width of a lollipop stick, but they are somewhat of a disappointment. When cooked, their flavor is often harsh and they are apt to be stringy.

White asparagus, also newly available in supermarkets, is produced by the same plant as green asparagus, except that during cultivation the shoot is protected from the sun by a mound of earth so that no chlorophyll develops. White asparagus is considered a delicacy and therefore is expensive.

TO STORE: Treat asparagus as you would cut flowers. When you get asparagus home, slice off the stale ends of the stems and stand the stalks in 1 inch of cool water. (Depending on the number of stalks, any tall, cylindrical container is fine.) Refrigerate, uncovered, and prepare as soon as possible.

TO PREPARE:

Wash asparagus by gently sloshing it up and down in a basin of cool water. If the stems are sandy, rub them clean with your fingers.

To peel or not to peel is a matter of great debate. I almost always peel asparagus — the exception would be stalks of impeccable freshness. Peeling takes less time than you might think: about 2½ minutes to do a pound, once you're experienced. It eliminates strings and evens the cooking process by making the lower stalk as tender as the tip.

Cradling the tip end of the asparagus in one hand, use light strokes to peel down the length of the stalk.

Trim about 1½ inches off the bottom of each stalk, removing the white or pale green woody portion. Cut the stalks to all the same length if you wish. Cradle the tip of a stalk in your hand and apply a swivel-blade peeler just below the tip. Using light strokes, peel down the length of each stalk.

Asparagus may be served raw. It may also be boiled, steamed, microwaved, baked, or stir-fried. My favorite method of boiling asparagus is in an uncovered skillet. This preserves the color and enables you to closely monitor the tenderness of the stalks. Bring a large amount of water to a boil in a teakettle. Pour the boiling water into a 12-inch, nonreactive skillet to a depth of 2 inches. Set the heat on high and when the water returns to the boil, add the asparagus and more water if necessary to cover the stalks. Cook at a medium bubble for 5 to 20 minutes, depending on the thickness of the stalks and the degree of tenderness you desire. Some cooks prefer the bright green stage at which the stalks are crisp-tender. Others choose to cook asparagus until it turns a pale green and yields to the blade of a paring knife. Just be sure not to overcook the stalks; properly cooked asparagus should bend slightly or fall in a graceful arc, but it should never be so soft that it droops over on itself.

Chilled Asparagus Spread

¾ cup water
4 tablespoons butter
1 pound asparagus,
 trimmed, peeled, and cut
 into 1-inch lengths
4 green onions, white and
 green portion, sliced
½ teaspoon dried thyme
½ teaspoon salt
1 small package (3 ounces)
 cream cheese
½ cup sour cream
1 tablespoon lemon juice
Several drops Tabasco sauce
Lemon zest strips for
 garnish

Offer this pale green, subtly flavored spread with crisp wheat crackers or tortilla wedges that have been heated under the broiler until crisp.

1. Heat the water and butter in a large skillet. When the butter is melted, add the asparagus and onions and bring to a boil. Sprinkle on the thyme and salt. Cover the pan and reduce the heat. Cook at a gentle bubble for 5 minutes. Remove the cover and stir the asparagus over high heat until all the moisture is evaporated.

2. Combine the cream cheese and sour cream in the container of a blender or processor. Add the asparagus mixture, lemon juice, and Tabasco. Whirl until smooth, then transfer to a serving bowl. Cover and refrigerate until thoroughly chilled. Garnish with strips of lemon zest.

Asparagus with Tangerine Mayonnaise

Pencil-thin spears of asparagus are cooked until crisp-tender. When lightly chilled, they are served with an elegant tangerine-flavored dipping sauce.

1 pound very thin asparagus
¾ cup mayonnaise,
 preferably homemade
2 tablespoons tangerine
 juice
½ teaspoon Dijon mustard
1 shallot, minced
1 tablespoon grated
 tangerine zest

1. Preheat the oven to 325°. Cut the asparagus stalks to measure 5 inches in length. (Pencil-thin stalks need not be peeled, but thicker ones should be.) Rinse the stalks and arrange them in a 7x11-inch baking dish with the water that clings. Sprinkle on enough additional water so that you can see numerous droplets. Cover with aluminum foil and bake for 20 minutes. At that point, the stalks should be crunchy and sturdy enough for dipping. Immediately submerge the asparagus in cold water. When cool, arrange the stalks on a clean kitchen towel and gently roll up. Refrigerate until serving time.

2. In a small mixing bowl, blend the mayonnaise, tangerine juice, and mustard until well mixed. Stir in the shallot and tangerine zest. Cover and chill. Just before serving, spoon the dipping sauce into a decorative bowl and serve surrounded by the chilled asparagus.

Iced Asparagus Soup

Tarragon lends a subtle flavor to this smooth essence of asparagus.

3 tablespoons butter
2 medium onions, coarsely
    chopped
2 tablespoons all-purpose
    flour
6 cups water
1½ pounds asparagus,
    trimmed, rinsed, and cut
    into 1-inch lengths
1 teaspoon dried tarragon
2 tablespoons lemon juice
½ cup medium or whipping
    cream
Salt and freshly ground
    white pepper
Fresh tarragon for garnish

1. Melt the butter in a large saucepan. Add the onions and toss to coat. Stir over medium heat until the onions are tender. Sprinkle on the flour and continue stirring over medium heat until the mixture foams. Stir in the water and bring to a boil. Add the asparagus and tarragon and reduce the heat. Cover and cook at a gentle bubble for 10 minutes or until the asparagus is tender.

2. Transfer the asparagus with its cooking liquid to a food mill and process to eliminate the asparagus strings, then press through a sieve to smooth out the consistency. Stir in the lemon juice. Cover and refrigerate until thoroughly chilled. Just before serving, blend in the cream and season with salt and pepper. Ladle into glass soup bowls and garnish with sprigs of fresh tarragon.

Asparagus Vinaigrette

Chilled asparagus in a shallot vinaigrette is a refreshing salad for a hot summer's night.

1 pound asparagus,
    trimmed and peeled
Salt and freshly ground
    black pepper
3 tablespoons lemon juice
½ teaspoon dry mustard
6 tablespoons olive oil
1 shallot, minced
1 teaspoon dried chervil

1. Boil, steam, or bake the asparagus until crisp-tender (see steps 1 and 2 of Baked Asparagus). Immediately submerge the stalks in cold water. When cool, drain and transfer to absorbent paper. Pat the stalks dry and arrange them in a 9x13-inch glass baking dish. Sprinkle with salt and pepper.

2. In a small mixing bowl, whisk together the lemon juice and mustard until the mustard is dissolved. Whisk in the olive oil. Stir in the shallot and chervil. Pour the mixture over the asparagus and turn to coat the stalks. Cover the dish with plastic wrap. Refrigerate until thoroughly chilled, turning the asparagus occasionally. To serve, arrange the asparagus spears on glass plates and spoon some of the dressing over the top.

Baked Asparagus

This simple method of preparing asparagus requires no fuss and produces asparagus with excellent color and flavor.

4 tablespoons butter
1 pound asparagus
Salt and freshly ground
  black pepper
4 lemon wedges

1. Preheat the oven to 325°. Place 2 tablespoons of the butter in a 7x11-inch glass baking dish. Set the dish in the oven until the butter melts, then remove it, tilting to coat the bottom evenly.

2. Trim and peel the asparagus. Then rinse under cool running water and place in the dish with whatever water clings to the stalks. Sprinkle on enough additional water so that you can see numerous droplets. Cover the dish with aluminum foil and bake for 30 minutes to 1 hour, depending on the degree of doneness you desire. At 30 minutes, the stalks will be bright green and crisp-tender; at 1 hour, they will be pale green and very tender.

3. Slide the remaining 2 tablespoons of butter over the hot asparagus and season with salt and pepper. Serve immediately with wedges of lemon.

Asparagus with Penne

SERVES 6

1 pound asparagus,
  trimmed and peeled
½ cup olive oil
3 carrots, cut into julienne
  strips
6 green onions, white and
  green portion, sliced
  diagonally
3 tablespoons lemon juice
2 tablespoons chopped
  fresh parsley
1 tablespoon chopped fresh
  basil
1 pound penne, boiled and
  drained
½ teaspoon salt
Freshly ground black
  pepper
2 tablespoons pine nuts (or
  substitute slivered
  almonds)

Penne, or quill-shaped pasta, is lightly coated with olive oil and tossed with asparagus and thin carrot strips.

1. Boil, steam, or bake the asparagus until crisp-tender (see steps 1 and 2 of Baked Asparagus). Drain and transfer to absorbent paper. Pat the stalks dry and cut on the diagonal into 1-inch lengths.

2. Heat 3 tablespoons of the oil in a large skillet. Add the carrots and green onions and toss to coat. Stir over medium heat until the onions are limp. Add the remaining oil, the lemon juice, parsley, and basil. Add the penne and toss to coat with oil. Season with salt and pepper. Scatter the asparagus and pine nuts over the mixture and toss to combine. Stir over low heat until warmed through, then serve.

Asparagus in Red Wine Sauce

SERVES 4

Asparagus spears cloaked with a rosey-hued sauce may be served as a luncheon dish or an elegant first course. For an extra-special touch, garnish each plate with a thin slice of Westphalian ham folded into a cornucopia.

1 pound asparagus,
  trimmed and peeled
½ cup red wine
2 tablespoons butter
1 teaspoon dried tarragon
1 cup mayonnaise,
  preferably homemade
Salt and freshly ground
  black pepper

1. Boil, steam, or bake the asparagus until crisp-tender (see steps 1 and 2 of Baked Asparagus). Transfer to a heated platter and keep warm in an oven set at 200°.

2. In a small saucepan, combine the wine, butter, and tarragon. Cook over medium heat until reduced by half. Remove from the heat and gradually whisk in the mayonnaise. Stir over low heat to warm gently. Sprinkle the asparagus spears with salt and pepper, then pour the sauce over the spears. Serve immediately.

Asparagus Mousse

SERVES 4

Individual servings of Asparagus Mousse look particularly attractive when garnished. Reserve 4 cooked asparagus tips and set them aside at room temperature. Just before serving, place 1 asparagus tip on each mousse and lay a curl of lemon zest alongside.

1 pound asparagus,
  trimmed and peeled
2 large eggs, separated
¼ teaspoon dried tarragon
Pinch of freshly grated
  nutmeg
½ teaspoon salt
Freshly ground white
  pepper
Lemon zest curls for garnish

1. Boil, steam, or bake the asparagus until tender (see steps 1 and 2 of Baked Asparagus). Drain and transfer to absorbent paper, reserving 4 tips for garnishing, if desired. Pat the stalks dry and cut into 1-inch lengths. Transfer to the container of a blender or processor and whirl until smooth. Add the egg yolks, one at a time, then blend in the tarragon, nutmeg, salt, and pepper. Pour into a large mixing bowl.

2. Preheat the oven to 350°. Generously butter 4 ramekins or individual soufflé molds. In a separate bowl, whisk the egg whites until soft peaks form and fold into the asparagus purée. Pour into the prepared baking dishes and loosely cover each with aluminum foil. Arrange the baking dishes in a shallow pan, then pour in boiling water to the depth of 1 inch. Bake for 25 to 30 minutes or until the slender blade of a paring knife inserted in the center comes out clean. Garnish with asparagus tips and lemon zest curls and serve immediately.

Asparagus and Gruyère Custard

SERVES 4

A smooth, rich custard dotted with tender morsels of asparagus. Pair with a green salad and serve for luncheon or offer as a vegetable side dish.

1 pound asparagus, trimmed and peeled
4 tablespoons butter
1 medium onion, finely chopped
2 tablespoons all-purpose flour
1½ cups light cream
4 ounces Gruyère cheese, grated
½ teaspoon salt
Freshly ground black pepper
1 tablespoon lemon juice
4 large eggs, beaten
Freshly grated nutmeg

1. Boil, steam, or bake the asparagus until crisp-tender (see steps 1 and 2 of Baked Asparagus). Drain and transfer to absorbent paper. Pat the stalks dry and cut into 1-inch lengths.

2. Preheat the oven to 350°. Melt the butter in a large saucepan. Add the onion and toss to coat. Stir over medium heat until the onion is tender. Sprinkle on the flour and cook until the mixture foams. Gradually stir in the cream and continue cooking until thickened. Remove from the heat and stir in the Gruyère cheese, salt, pepper, and lemon juice. Blend in the beaten eggs.

3. Generously butter a round casserole or soufflé dish. Gently mix the asparagus into the cheese mixture and pour into the prepared dish. Sprinkle the surface with nutmeg and bake for 30 to 40 minutes or until the blade of a knife inserted in the center comes out clean.

Stir-Fried Asparagus with Chicken

SERVES 4

2 teaspoons cornstarch
2 tablespoons water
4 tablespoons soy sauce
2 tablespoons lemon juice
½ teaspoon sugar
1 garlic clove, minced or pressed
3 tablespoons vegetable oil
1 pound asparagus, trimmed, peeled, and sliced diagonally
1 large chicken breast, boned, skinned, and cut into ½-inch-wide strips
1 tablespoon toasted sesame seed

Slices of asparagus are stir-fried until crisp-tender and then combined with lightly cooked strips of chicken and toasted sesame seeds.

1. Dissolve the cornstarch in the water, then blend in the soy sauce and lemon juice. Stir in the sugar and garlic. Set aside.

2. Heat the oil in a wok or large skillet. Add the asparagus and stir-fry over high heat for 30 seconds or until bright green and crisp-tender. Transfer to a large plate.

3. Pour more oil into the pan if necessary, then add the chicken. Stir-fry until firm. Return the asparagus to the pan. Stir-fry briefly to heat through and pour in the soy sauce mixture. Continue stirring over high heat until the sauce bubbles and thickens. Sprinkle on the sesame seed and serve.

Florida avocado

Hass avocado

Fuerte avocado

Cut in half to show seed

Avocados

IF AVOCADOS are on your shopping list, don't give up when at first you can't find them. A surprising number of supermarket managers insist on sticking by the principle that avocados are fruit, so with fruit they shall be displayed. This strikes me as a stubbornly narrow point of view. They would sell many more avocados if they would display them with the lettuce and tomatoes and other salad ingredients.

It is true, however, that the avocado is actually a fruit; in fact, in some areas it is known as the avocado pear. Smooth and buttery, the texture of its flesh might be compared with that of a firm, ripe banana. Avocados are available year round and are an excellent source of potassium and vitamin C.

TO SELECT:

There are three basic types of avocados — the bright green, thin-skinned Fuerte is about the same size and shape as a pear; the Hass variety, which is also pear shaped, possesses a thick, dark purple-green skin with a pebbly surface; and the Florida avocado, which is larger and round, has a medium green skin that is frequently pitted. All have an equally delicious nutty flavor, but many cooks develop a preference for one type over the others.

Avocados ripen only after they have been picked, so it's not at all unusual to find that those on the produce stand are hard as rocks. Some stores hold them in the back room until they soften a bit, but that's not as common a practice as it should be. A ripe, ready-to-eat avocado will yield slightly to gentle pressure; it will feel similar to a firm, ripe banana.

Because avocados are easily damaged, there's a certain wisdom in purchasing them while they're still hard, then ripening them at home where they won't be poked at by every customer who goes by. Look for evenness of texture — an avocado should feel uniformly hard or soft over its entire surface. Avoid any with soft spots or bruises.

TO STORE:

Unsoftened avocados can be brought to ripeness by placing them in a brown paper bag. Roll the top down loosely and set the bag in a cool spot for 4 to 5 days. The object is to hasten the softening process by enclosing the ripening gases. Do not use a plastic bag because a certain amount of air circulation is necessary to prevent spoilage. Since avocados ripen best at 60° to 70°, avoid placing them in direct sunlight.

As avocados ripen, those with bright green skins often develop brown patches. That's acceptable because it's an indication that they are almost ripe. Test by pressing gently on the flesh; however, keep in mind that the dark purplish green avocados possess a thicker, unyielding skin and are therefore less responsive to this touch test. When avocados have ripened, they will keep, refrigerated, for 2 to 3 days.

TO PREPARE:

Begin by laying the avocado on its side. Holding it steady with one hand, insert the tip of a paring knife at the narrow end. (First, remove the small, hard stem depression if necessary.) Cutting through to the opposite side, draw the knife down the length of the avocado. When the tip of the knife meets the large center stone, ease the knife around the stone to the end of the avocado. Proceed around the end to the other side until you meet the initial cut just above the stone. Cradle the halves in your hands and twist sharply in opposite directions. One half will come away from the stone. (See illustrations on next page.) If you plan to use only half the avocado, leave the stone in the cavity of the other half, for it will protect the cavity from turning brown.

Peel the outer skin away from the flesh. (You'll notice a great difference in the way the purplish green variety peels — it tends to break away in pieces rather than lifting off smoothly.) The flesh of an avocado should be a pale, creamy

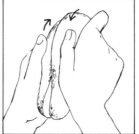

*Cut into and around the avo-
cado, easing the knife along
the stone inside. Holding the
halves in your hands, twist
sharply in opposite directions.
One half will pull away from
the stone.*

yellow. If you find dark spots or blemishes, cut or scrape them off.

Once it is peeled, you can cut the avocado into long thin slices or small chunks, or mash the flesh with a fork. The important thing to remember is that avocado flesh darkens quickly when exposed to the air, so plan to prepare avocados as close to serving time as possible, and brush their surfaces with lemon juice, lime juice, or vinaigrette dressing to retard browning.

Unused avocado can be refrigerated for 1 to 2 days. To protect it against browning, apply an acidic juice (or stir it into mashed avocado), then seal out the air by laying plastic wrap directly on the flesh or on the surface of a purée. Any browning that does appear can be cut or scraped from the surface, and the remainder may be used.

Avocado Dressing

SERVES 4

1 large avocado
1 garlic clove, sliced
2 green onions, white
   portion only, sliced
2 tablespoons vegetable oil
3 tablespoons lemon juice
¼ teaspoon ground cumin
½ teaspoon salt
Freshly ground black
   pepper
1 green chili, minced

*Serve this lovely pale green dressing over romaine leaves, and
spoon a portion of chilled crabmeat salad to one side.*

1. Combine the avocado, garlic, and onions in the container of a blender or processor, then whirl until smooth. Add the oil, lemon juice, cumin, salt, and pepper and whirl briefly. Stir in the green chili. Refrigerate and pour over 4 individual salads.

Guacamole

Guacamole may be served in the traditional way — that is, as a dip for tortilla chips — but it is also wonderful on grilled hamburgers, spooned into tomato shells, or spread on bacon and tomato sandwiches. If I have any leftover Guacamole, I put it into the bottom of a salad bowl and thin it with a little Italian dressing to produce a fresh-tasting avocado dressing in seconds.

2 avocados, peeled, seeded, and sliced
2 garlic cloves, pressed
1 shallot, minced
2 tablespoons lemon juice
½ teaspoon Worcestershire sauce
½ teaspoon salt
Several drops of Tabasco sauce
1 tablespoon chopped fresh cilantro

1. Place the avocado slices on a large plate and mash them with a fork. (This method creates a consistency that is smooth yet texturally interesting.) Blend in the garlic, shallot, lemon juice, Worcestershire sauce, salt, and Tabasco. Mix in the chopped cilantro. Transfer to a bowl and lay a sheet of plastic wrap directly on the surface to retard browning. Refrigerate for 2 to 3 hours or until lightly chilled.

Avocado Yogurt Soup

2 cups chicken broth
1 medium onion, sliced
4 medium avocados, peeled and cut into chunks
1 tablespoon lime juice
1 tablespoon chopped fresh cilantro
½ teaspoon chili powder
½ teaspoon salt
Pinch of cayenne
2 cups unflavored yogurt
Freshly chopped chives for garnish

This quick and easy soup is a perfect prelude to a meal of barbecued chicken or ribs.

1. In the container of a blender or processor, combine the chicken broth and onion and whirl until smooth. Add the avocados, lime juice, cilantro, chili powder, salt, and cayenne. Process briefly to incorporate, but do not over-liquefy.

2. Transfer to a large bowl. Blend in the yogurt and cover. Refrigerate until thoroughly chilled. Serve cold, sprinkled with freshly chopped chives.

Avocado Salad with Lime Vinaigrette

SERVES 4

Tufts of spiky-leaved chicory are a mildly bitter counterpoint to the bland creaminess of sliced avocado.

6 tablespoons olive oil
2 tablespoons lime juice
½ teaspoon salt
Pinch of cayenne
1 garlic clove, minced or pressed
2 large avocados, peeled, seeded, and cut in half
1 head chicory
1 small red onion, finely chopped
2 tablespoons chopped fresh cilantro

1. In a small bowl, whisk together the oil, lime juice, salt, and cayenne. Stir in the garlic.

2. Cut each avocado half into 6 slices. Lay the slices in the dressing and turn them to coat all sides. Brushing off the excess dressing with a pastry brush, divide the avocado slices among 4 glass plates. Arrange the slices in a fan-shaped design to the right side of each plate.

3. Gather a few leaves of chicory together in a clump and set them on the left side of the plate. Scatter the onion over the avocado slices, then sprinkle on the cilantro. Pour the remaining dressing over all. Chill briefly or serve at once.

Avocado Pâté with Chilled Lobster

SERVES 10

This delightful pâté may be made in a regular loaf pan, but for a more elegant presentation, chill the mixture in an 11x4-inch galantine mold, which produces a slim, straight-sided pâté.

1 package unflavored gelatin
¼ cup cold water
½ cup chicken broth
1 shallot, minced
4 large avocados, peeled, seeded, and mashed
1 cup heavy cream
2 large egg yolks
1 tablespoon Cognac
½ teaspoon salt
Several drops of Tabasco sauce
1 pound lobster meat, cut into bite-size pieces
3 tablespoons lemon juice

1. Preheat the oven to 325°. Generously butter a 9x5-inch loaf pan or a galantine mold. Sprinkle the gelatin over the water in a small bowl and allow it to soften. Heat the chicken broth in a small saucepan. Add the gelatin mixture and the shallot. Stir over medium heat until the gelatin dissolves.

2. In a large mixing bowl, combine the avocados, cream, and egg yolks. Add the Cognac, salt, Tabasco, and the gelatin mixture and blend well. Pour into the prepared mold and set inside a shallow roasting pan. Add hot water to a depth of 1 inch and bake for 45 to 55 minutes or until a knife inserted in the center comes out clean.

3. Cool on a rack for 30 minutes, then refrigerate. When thoroughly chilled, unmold onto a serving plate. Toss the lobster with the lemon juice and spoon it around the pâté. Cut the pâté into slices and serve with a portion of the lobster meat.

Fettuccine with Avocado

2 lemons

2 tablespoons chopped
   fresh parsley

1 large garlic clove, minced

1 cup heavy cream

4 tablespoons butter

6 thin slices prosciutto, cut
   into julienne strips

2 large avocados, peeled,
   seeded, and cut into ½-
   inch chunks

¾ pound fettuccine, boiled
   and drained

Salt and freshly ground
   white pepper

½ cup freshly grated
   Parmesan cheese

½ cup alfalfa sprouts,
   loosely packed

Fettuccine is tossed with chunks of avocado in a light creamy sauce sparked with lemon.

1. Squeeze the juice from the lemons and set aside. Remove the zest with a swivel-blade peeler and chop finely. Place in a small bowl and add the parsley and garlic. Toss to combine.

2. Gently heat the cream in a small saucepan. Meanwhile, melt the butter in a large skillet. Add the lemon juice, prosciutto, and avocados and toss to coat. Sprinkle on the lemon zest mixture and stir over medium heat for 1 minute. Add the hot, drained fettuccine, salt, and pepper, then pour on the warm cream. Toss to combine and transfer to a serving dish. Sprinkle with Parmesan cheese and scatter the sprouts over the surface.

Ramekins of Avocado, Shrimp, and Eggs

3 tablespoons butter

2 tablespoons all-purpose
   flour

1 teaspoon dry mustard

½ teaspoon salt

1½ cups milk

Pinch of cayenne

1 teaspoon dried tarragon

½ cup freshly grated
   Parmesan cheese

2 medium avocados, peeled,
   seeded, and cut into ½-
   inch cubes

24 medium shrimp, cooked,
   peeled, and deveined

6 large hard-boiled eggs,
   quartered

½ cup unseasoned bread
   crumbs, mixed with 2
   tablespoons melted
   butter

Serve these individual casseroles with a tossed green salad and toasted rounds of French bread.

1. Preheat the oven to 350° and generously butter 6 ramekins. Melt the 3 tablespoons butter in a small saucepan. Sprinkle on the flour, mustard, and salt. Stir over medium heat until the mixture foams. Remove from the heat and whisk in the milk. Return to medium heat and stir until thickened. Remove from the heat and blend in the cayenne, tarragon, and Parmesan cheese.

2. Spoon a small amount of sauce into each ramekin. Divide the avocados, shrimp, and eggs among the ramekins. Spoon on the remaining sauce, then sprinkle on the buttered bread crumbs. Bake, uncovered, for 25 to 30 minutes or until bubbly and nicely browned.

Avocado Bread

Slice this pecan-studded bread thinly, then spread with softened cream cheese blended with lemon juice and grated lemon zest. Serve for afternoon tea or with fruit salad for lunch.

2 cups all-purpose flour
¾ cup sugar
1½ teaspoons baking powder
½ teaspoon baking soda
½ teaspoon salt
1 large egg
½ cup mashed avocado (1 medium avocado)
½ cup buttermilk
½ cup chopped pecans

1. Preheat the oven to 375°. Generously grease a 9x5-inch loaf pan. Combine the flour, sugar, baking powder, soda, and salt in a large mixing bowl. Whisk to blend thoroughly.

2. In a separate bowl, beat together the egg and avocado. Stir in the buttermilk. Add to the dry ingredients and blend well. Stir in the pecans. Pour into the prepared pan and bake for 50 minutes to 1 hour or until a wooden pick inserted in the center comes out clean.

Avocado Mousse

A light, refreshing dessert. To serve, spoon into stemmed goblets or small glass bowls.

1 package unflavored gelatin
2 tablespoons cold water
½ cup light cream
½ cup sugar
2 large avocados, peeled, seeded, and sliced
4 tablespoons light rum
2 tablespoons lemon juice
1 cup heavy cream
Freshly grated nutmeg
Additional whipped cream for garnish

1. Sprinkle the gelatin over the water in a small bowl and allow the gelatin to soften. Heat the light cream in a small saucepan and add the gelatin mixture. Stir over medium heat until the gelatin dissolves. Stir in the sugar and remove from the heat.

2. In the container of a blender or processor, combine the avocados, rum, and lemon juice. Whirl until smooth. Blend in the gelatin mixture, then transfer to a large mixing bowl. Cover the bowl and refrigerate for 6 hours or until the mixture is lightly set.

3. Whip the heavy cream in a small bowl, adding the nutmeg just before soft peaks form. Fold into the avocado mixture and spoon into stemmed goblets. Top with additional whipped cream and freshly grated nutmeg.

Avocado Ice Cream

A cool, refreshing, not-too-sweet dessert. Serve with crisp lemon wafers.

2 large avocados, peeled, seeded, and sliced
4 cups medium or whipping cream
3 tablespoons tequila or light rum
3 large egg yolks
2 tablespoons all-purpose flour
¾ cup sugar
Pinch of salt
1½ teaspoons vanilla

1. Combine the avocados and 1 cup of the cream in the container of a blender or processor. Add the liquor and whirl until smooth. Refrigerate for 2 hours.

2. Beat the egg yolks with another cup of the cream. In a saucepan, combine the flour, sugar, and salt and whisk to blend thoroughly. Slowly whisk in the remaining 2 cups of cream and stir over medium heat until slightly thickened. Whisk half the hot mixture into the egg yolks. Pour the mixture back into the pan and stir over medium heat for 1 minute. Remove from the heat, stir in the vanilla, and chill for 2 hours.

3. Combine the avocado mixture and the egg yolk mixture in the container of an ice cream machine and process according to the manufacturer's instructions.

B

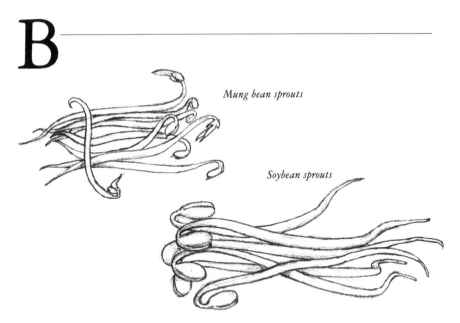

Mung bean sprouts

Soybean sprouts

Bean Sprouts

THE TERM "bean sprouts" is usually associated with the delicate shoots of mung beans, although soybean shoots are also considered bean sprouts. (For a discussion of alfalfa and radish sprouts, see Sprouts.) Mung bean sprouts, sometimes called small-bean sprouts, measure about 1½ to 2 inches in length. They bear a small light yellow seed head, a silvery white shoot, and a pale brown tail. Soybean sprouts, also called big-bean sprouts, grow 3 or 4 inches long. They have much larger, more conspicuous seed heads (about the size of navy beans), which are medium yellow or light green. Bean sprouts of both types may be stir-fried or blanched in hot water, but it is important to note that although mung bean sprouts may be eaten raw, soybean sprouts are slightly toxic when raw. Therefore, they should be cooked to avoid intestinal upset.

Bean sprouts have a subtle, nutty flavor, and much like celery, they possess a high water content, which makes them refreshingly juicy. Available all year, bean sprouts are a good source of protein and vitamin C. One pound served as a side dish or salad is enough for 4 to 6 people.

| **TO SELECT:** | Mung bean sprouts are sold loose or prepackaged in plastic bags. When they are sold loose, you'll usually find mung bean sprouts in a jumbled heap; loose soybean sprouts are frequently displayed in neat rows or tied in bundles with the seed heads bunched together like a bouquet. Mung bean sprouts come in two varieties — the short, fat type is more flavorful than those that are long and slender. Soybean sprouts are less tender and delicate than mung bean sprouts. |

If possible, buy bean sprouts where they are sold loose, because prepackaged sprouts deteriorate more quickly — a result of the moist environment inside their plastic bags. When purchasing bean sprouts, look for firm, white shoots. Avoid limp, wilted sprouts. If you must buy them prepackaged, examine the plastic bag carefully, passing up those that appear to have a great deal of moisture inside. This is an indication that the sprouts are on the verge of spoiling.

TO STORE: It's best to use bean sprouts as soon as possible, because they are extremely delicate and don't keep well. If you have purchased them in a plastic bag, transfer the sprouts to a sieve and rinse thoroughly under cold running water. Distribute over a kitchen towel and pat dry. Place them in a clean plastic bag and secure with a wire twist. Use within 2 to 3 days. Bean sprouts purchased loose should be scattered, without washing, on a clean kitchen towel. Roll the towel up loosely, place in the refrigerator, and use the sprouts within 2 to 3 days.

TO PREPARE: Rinse bean sprouts thoroughly by sloshing them up and down in a big bowl of cold water or by placing them in a sieve held under cold water from the tap. Pick them over, removing any dark green hulls and discarding any sprouts that are not firm and crisp. The entire sprout is edible, so there is no need to remove the seed or tail; however, tails that appear excessively hairy may be pinched off.

Drain the washed sprouts and pat them dry with absorbent paper if you're going to stir-fry them. This eliminates the excess spatter that can occur when wet sprouts hit hot oil. It's also important to dry sprouts when they are to be used in a salad.

Bean Sprouts and Romaine Salad

SERVES 4

Thin strips of romaine tossed with crisp mung bean sprouts are coated with an Oriental dressing. Serve with grilled meat or deep-fried shrimp.

½ pound mung bean
  sprouts
16 large romaine leaves
2 tablespoons soy sauce
1 tablespoon rice vinegar
1 teaspoon sesame seed oil
  (dark)
1 teaspoon sugar
3 green onions, white and
  green portion, thinly
  sliced

1. Bring a kettle of water to a boil. Rinse the bean sprouts and pick them over. Place in a large bowl. Pour in enough boiling water to cover the sprouts by 2 inches. Allow them to stand for exactly 1 minute. Immediately drain in a colander and rinse with cold water. Scatter over a clean kitchen towel and pat dry. Roll up the towel and place in the refrigerator.

2. Rinse the romaine and pat dry. Stack the leaves and slice thinly across to shred. Transfer to a salad bowl.

3. In a small bowl, combine the soy sauce, vinegar, oil, and sugar. Blend thoroughly. Add the bean sprouts and the onions to the romaine and toss to combine. Pour on the dressing and serve immediately.

Stir-Fried Bean Sprouts

SERVES 4

1 tablespoon soy sauce
1 tablespoon rice vinegar
1 tablespoon dry sherry
1 tablespoon honey
3 tablespoons vegetable oil
1 red bell pepper, cut into
  narrow strips
4 green onions, white and
  green portion, sliced
  diagonally
2 tablespoons water
1 pound mung bean or
  soybean sprouts, rinsed
  and picked over

Stir-fried bean sprouts retain their crisp juiciness. Serve with grilled shrimp or barbecued pork.

1. In a small bowl, combine the soy sauce, vinegar, sherry, and honey. Whisk to blend and set aside.

2. Heat the oil in a wok or large skillet. Add the red bell pepper and onions and toss to coat. Stir over high heat for 30 seconds. Sprinkle on the water and continue to stir over high heat until the pepper is crisp-tender.

3. Add the bean sprouts, stirring continuously. When the bean sprouts are slightly wilted, pour on the soy sauce mixture and stir over high heat for 30 seconds. Serve immediately.

Bean Sprouts with Celery and Mushrooms

SERVES 4 TO 6

1 tablespoon cornstarch
¼ cup Madeira
¾ cup chicken broth
2 tablespoons soy sauce
2 tablespoons red wine
  vinegar
2 tablespoons dark brown
  sugar
1 garlic clove, minced or
  pressed
Several drops Tabasco sauce
3 tablespoons vegetable oil
3 ribs celery, sliced
  diagonally
8 medium mushrooms,
  sliced
1 teaspoon finely chopped
  fresh ginger
1 medium onion, cut into 8
  wedges and separated
  into layers
1 red bell pepper, cut into
  ½-inch squares
½ pound mung bean or
  soybean sprouts, rinsed
  and picked over

Bean sprouts combine with stir-fried celery and mushrooms to create this wonderful Oriental-style vegetable side dish.

1. In a small bowl, combine the cornstarch and Madeira and stir until the cornstarch is dissolved. Blend in the chicken broth, soy sauce, vinegar, brown sugar, garlic, and Tabasco. Set aside.

2. Heat the oil in a wok or large skillet. Add the celery, mushrooms, and ginger and toss to coat. Stir over high heat for 30 seconds. Add the onion, red bell pepper, and bean sprouts and continue stirring. (If the vegetables begin to stick to the pan, sprinkle on 1 or 2 tablespoons of water.)

3. When the bean sprouts are slightly wilted, pour on the chicken broth mixture and stir over high heat until the sauce bubbles and thickens. Serve immediately.

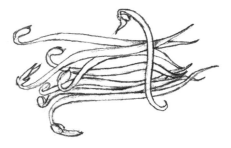

Beans: Green and Yellow

GREEN STRING BEANS and yellow wax beans are both commonly referred to as snap beans. I suppose that has to do with the familiar method of testing for freshness. When pressed between the thumb and first two fingers, a fresh green or yellow bean will break sharply, producing a distinct snapping sound. Green and yellow beans are available all year, but are at their best from July to September. Beans of both colors are nearly identical in nutritional value, except that green beans contain more than twice as much vitamin A.

TO SELECT:

If possible, shop for green and yellow beans at a produce stand that offers them in a loose display. That way, you can pick out beans of the same size, which promotes even cooking. Produce managers don't take too kindly to shoppers snapping beans in half to find the freshest ones, but you can judge freshness by appearance almost as well. Look for slim beans, about as thin as a drinking straw, with smooth pods. As beans mature, the seeds inside grow fatter, so pass up any pods that have a series of bulges caused by large seeds. Feel the skin of the pod; it should not feel tough or leathery. Avoid green or yellow beans that are limp or spotted with brown. Green beans should be of an intense

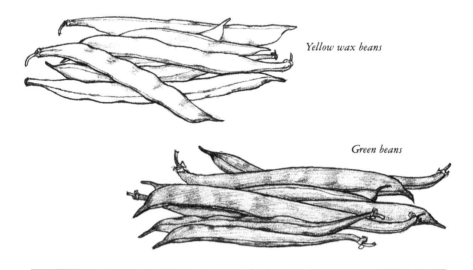

Yellow wax beans

Green beans

color; yellow beans that are young and tender are often tinged with light green. One pound will feed 4 people.

TO STORE: Snap beans are highly perishable, so your best bet is to use them on the day of purchase. If necessary, they may be placed, without washing, in an airtight plastic bag and refrigerated for 3 or 4 days. However, cold temperatures over an extended period of time will cause the development of pits and brown spots.

TO PREPARE: Wash snap beans in cool water. Drain well and cut off the stem ends. The pointed tails may be left on or removed. Most varieties of green and yellow beans are now virtually stringless, so the tedious chore of stringing snap beans is no longer necessary.

It is best to cook green and yellow beans whole because sliced beans cooked in water lose much of their flavor. I prefer boiling snap beans briefly to just the crisp-tender point (they should still offer some resistance to the teeth), because this produces a more beautiful color and crisper texture. Green and yellow beans may also be steamed whole, or stir-fried, either whole or sliced into pieces.

Dilly Beans

SERVES 8 TO 10

Dilled green beans make marvelous tidbits to nibble as appetizers.

2 pounds green beans,
    whole
1 cup water
¾ cup white vinegar
½ cup sugar
2 garlic cloves, sliced
1 teaspoon dried tarragon
1 bay leaf
1 teaspoon salt
1 tablespoon mustard seed
2 tablespoons chopped
    fresh dill leaves

1. Drop the beans into a large pot of boiling, salted water and cook, uncovered, at a gentle bubble for 6 to 8 minutes or just until crisp-tender. Drain in a colander set under cold running water. Shake to remove as much water as possible.

2. In a large saucepan, combine the water, vinegar, and sugar. Add the garlic, tarragon, bay leaf, and salt. Stir in the mustard seed and bring the liquid to a boil. Stir to completely dissolve the sugar. Remove from the heat. Add the dill leaves and pour the mixture into a large rectangular baking dish. Add the cooked beans, arranging them so that they are well coated. Cover the dish with waxed paper, then with aluminum foil. Refrigerate for at least 24 hours. Serve chilled or at room temperature.

Green Bean and Basil Soup

3 tablespoons butter
2 medium leeks, thinly
   sliced
1 garlic clove, minced or
   pressed
4 cups chicken broth
2 medium mealy potatoes,
   peeled and cut into cubes
1 pound green beans, cut
   into 1-inch lengths
½ cup fresh basil leaves
   (loosely packed), coarsely
   chopped
1 tablespoon lemon juice
½ teaspoon salt
Pinch of cayenne
1 tablespoon chopped fresh
   savory
½ cup medium or whipping
   cream
Sliced raw mushrooms for
   garnish

Puréed green beans and fresh basil combine to form a compelling and sophisticated soup.

1. Melt the butter in a large saucepan. Add the leeks and garlic and toss to coat. Stir over medium heat until the leeks are tender. Pour in the chicken broth. Add the potatoes and green beans. Bring to a gentle bubble. Cover the pan and cook for 20 minutes or until the potatoes and green beans are tender. Stir in the basil and cook, uncovered, for 5 minutes.

2. Pour into the container of a blender or processor and whirl until smooth. Return to the saucepan and blend in the lemon juice. Add the salt, cayenne, and savory. Blend in the cream and place over medium heat. Warm gently, but do not allow the soup to boil. Ladle into soup bowls and garnish with slices of raw mushroom.

Green Bean Salad

Shallots, lightly cooked in bacon fat, complement the flavor of fresh green beans.

1 pound green beans, whole
¼ pound sliced bacon
1 shallot, minced
2 tablespoons white wine
   vinegar
1 tablespoon chopped fresh
   tarragon
1 teaspoon sugar
Salt and freshly ground
   black pepper
1 tablespoon chopped fresh
   chives

1. Drop the beans into a large pot of boiling, salted water and cook, uncovered, at a gentle bubble for 6 to 8 minutes or just until crisp-tender. Drain in a colander set under cold running water. Distribute the beans over absorbent paper and pat dry. Place in a shallow serving dish.

2. Fry the bacon until crisp, then drain on absorbent paper. Reserve the bacon fat.

3. Pour off all but 2 tablespoons of the bacon fat. Add the shallot and stir over medium heat until tender. Blend in the vinegar, tarragon, sugar, salt, and pepper. Remove from the heat, stir in the chives, and pour over the green beans. Crumble the bacon over the beans and serve at room temperature.

Yellow Bean Salad with Chervil

SERVES 6

Chilled wax beans paired with fresh chervil make a refreshing salad. Arrange the beans around a glass plate with their pointed tails outward to create a striking visual effect.

1 pound yellow wax beans, whole
2 green onions, white and green portion, sliced
6 tablespoons olive oil
2 tablespoons white wine vinegar
¼ teaspoon salt
Pinch of cayenne
1 tablespoon chopped fresh chervil

1. Rinse and trim the beans, but leave the pointed tails intact. Drop them into a large pot of boiling, salted water and cook, uncovered, at a gentle bubble for 6 to 8 minutes or until crisp-tender. Drain in a colander set under cold running water. Drain thoroughly and transfer to a large bowl. Sprinkle on the onions and toss to combine.

2. In a small bowl, whisk together the oil, vinegar, salt, and cayenne. Pour over the beans and toss to coat. Cover the bowl and refrigerate, stirring occasionally, to ensure even marinating.

3. When thoroughly chilled, arrange the beans on a glass plate, sprinkle with chervil, and pour on the dressing that remains in the bowl. Chill briefly or serve at once.

Green Beans Vinaigrette

SERVES 8

These are marvelous to take along on a picnic. For extra glamour, package them in tiny bundles "tied" with pimiento strips.

3 cups water
½ cup dry white wine
¼ cup olive oil
½ teaspoon dried thyme
½ teaspoon salt
¼ teaspoon fennel seed
12 black peppercorns
1 bay leaf
3 green onions, white and green portion, sliced
½ cup chopped celery leaves
2 sprigs fresh parsley
2 one-inch strips lemon zest
1 pound green beans, whole
1 teaspoon dried tarragon
2 tablespoons lemon juice
2 canned pimientos, cut into narrow strips

1. In a wide saucepan, combine the water, wine, and oil. Stir in the thyme, salt, fennel seed, peppercorns, and bay leaf. Add the onions, celery leaves, parsley, and lemon zest, then bring to a boil.

2. Drop the beans into the boiling liquid and cook, uncovered, for 6 to 8 minutes or until crisp-tender. Lift them out with a slotted spoon and place them in a deep rectangular dish. Continue to boil the liquid until it is reduced by half. Stir in the tarragon and lemon juice, and pour over the beans. Cover the dish with waxed paper, then with aluminum foil. Refrigerate for 24 hours.

3. Remove the beans from the liquid and divide into 8 small portions, lining them up like bundles of sticks. Wind a narrow strip of pimiento around each bundle and overlap the ends. Serve immediately, or if packing for a picnic, enclose each bundle in a piece of plastic wrap.

Sautéed Yellow Wax Beans with Pecans

SERVES 4

Yellow wax beans are sautéed until crisp-tender and tossed with butter-toasted pecans.

3 tablespoons vegetable oil
1 pound yellow wax beans, cut diagonally into 1-inch lengths
1 teaspoon sugar
½ cup water
3 tablespoons butter
½ cup coarsely chopped pecans
Salt and freshly ground black pepper

1. Heat the oil in a wok or large skillet. Add the beans and toss to coat. Stir over high heat for 30 seconds. Sprinkle the beans with sugar, then pour on the water. Reduce the heat and cover the pan. Simmer for 3 to 5 minutes or until crisp-tender.

2. Meanwhile, melt the butter in a small skillet. Add the pecans and cook over medium-low heat for 1 minute. Do not allow the butter to turn brown.

3. Uncover the beans and increase the heat. Cook, stirring, until all the liquid is evaporated. Add the pecans and melted butter. Season with salt and pepper and toss to combine. Serve immediately.

Green Bean Purée

SERVES 6

Sparked with fresh cilantro, puréed green beans are a smashing accompaniment for roast chicken.

1 pound green beans, whole
1 large mealy potato, peeled and quartered
4 tablespoons butter, cut into pieces
1 tablespoon lemon juice
1 tablespoon chopped fresh cilantro
Salt and freshly ground black pepper
1 tablespoon chopped fresh chives for garnish

1. Drop the beans into a large pot of boiling, salted water. Add the potato and cook, uncovered, at a gentle bubble for 10 minutes or until the beans are tender. Remove the potato with a slotted spoon. Drain well and transfer to the container of a blender or processor. Break the potato apart with a fork to release the steam.

2. Drain the beans in a colander set under cold running water. Shake to remove as much water as possible. Transfer the beans to the blender or processor and whirl with the potato until smooth. Return to the pan. Blend in the butter, lemon juice, and cilantro and stir over medium heat to warm through. Season with salt and pepper and transfer to a serving bowl. Sprinkle the surface with chives.

Yellow Wax Beans with Chives

SERVES 4

Crisp yellow beans receive a lively accent from chopped fresh chives.

1 pound yellow wax beans,
    whole
4 tablespoons butter
Salt and freshly ground
    black pepper
2 tablespoons freshly grated
    Parmesan cheese
2 tablespoons chopped
    fresh chives

1. Drop the beans into a large pot of boiling, salted water and cook, uncovered, at a gentle bubble for 6 to 8 minutes or until crisp-tender. Drain in a colander set under cold running water. Shake to remove as much water as possible.

2. Melt the butter in a large skillet. Add the beans and toss to coat. Season with salt and pepper. Sprinkle on the Parmesan cheese and the chives, then stir over medium heat until warmed through. Serve immediately.

Buttered Green Beans with Almonds

SERVES 4

The unassuming combination of buttered green beans and toasted almonds has no doubt retained its popularity because it looks wonderful and tastes so good.

1 pound green beans, whole
4 tablespoons butter
¼ cup slivered almonds
Salt and freshly ground
    black pepper
4 lemon wedges

1. Drop the beans into a large pot of boiling, salted water and cook, uncovered, at a gentle bubble for 6 to 8 minutes or just until crisp-tender. Drain in a colander set under cold running water. Shake to remove as much water as possible.

2. Melt the butter in a large skillet and add the almonds. Stir over medium-low heat until the almonds turn golden. Add the beans and toss to coat. Gently stir over medium heat until warmed through. Season with salt and pepper and serve with wedges of lemon.

Beans: Long

THESE EXTRAORDINARY green pods are some-times called yard-long beans, because they can grow to the remarkable length of 4 feet. Their usual size, however, is more often 12 to 16 inches. Nearly identical in taste to green snap beans, long beans cook up with a slightly chewier texture. They are available year round in Oriental food stores and large supermarkets.

TO SELECT:

Long beans resemble green snap beans in appearance, and you can use almost the same guidelines to judge their quality. Choose pods that have a smooth surface because, like snap beans, bulges created by the presence of large seeds indicate that the beans are overly mature. Don't be dismayed to find that long beans are pliable instead of snappy-crisp; rigidity is the one characteristic they do not share with snap beans. Select long beans with firm, tender skin; avoid any that are shriveled, leathery, or spotted with brown. One pound will feed 4 people as a vegetable side dish.

TO STORE:

Treat long beans as you would snap beans. Use on the day of purchase if at all possible, or place, without washing, in an airtight plastic bag in the refrigerator for 3 to 4 days.

TO PREPARE:

Wash long beans in cool water and remove the stem ends. There is no need to remove any strings. Cut the beans into 2-inch lengths and steam or stir-fry. Or for a more dramatic presentation, cook whole long beans in gently boiling water until tender. Then serve them coiled into nests or curved gracefully around a roast.

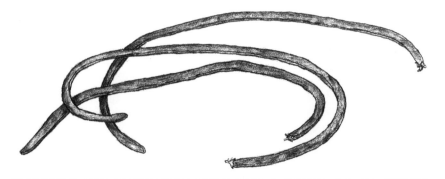

Stir-Fried Long Beans

SERVES 4

¾ cup chicken broth
2 tablespoons soy sauce
2 tablespoons rice vinegar
2 tablespoons Chinese
  barbecue sauce
1 teaspoon sugar
2 teaspoons cornstarch
2 tablespoons cold water
3 tablespoons vegetable oil
1 pound long beans, cut
  diagonally into 2-inch
  lengths
4 green onions, white and
  green portion, thinly
  sliced diagonally
1 garlic clove, minced
1 tablespoon finely chopped
  fresh ginger

Chinese barbecue sauce, which is also marketed as satay sauce, contains chili peppers and ground shrimp, among other ingredients. Here it contributes a spicy flourish to stir-fried green beans.

1. In a small bowl, blend together the chicken broth, soy sauce, rice vinegar, barbecue sauce, and sugar. In a separate bowl, combine the cornstarch and water and stir to dissolve.

2. Heat the oil in a wok or large skillet. Add the beans and toss to coat evenly. Add the onions, garlic, and ginger and stir over high heat for 30 seconds. Pour on the chicken broth mixture and reduce the heat. Cover the pan and simmer for 2 to 3 minutes. When the beans are crisp-tender, pour on the dissolved cornstarch. Increase the heat and stir until the sauce is slightly thickened. Serve at once.

Long Beans with Herb Butter

SERVES 4

1 pound long beans
6 tablespoons butter
1 shallot, minced
1 tablespoon chopped fresh
  chives
1 tablespoon chopped fresh
  cilantro
Salt and freshly ground
  black pepper

Cook these long beans whole, then serve them coiled into 4 nestlike mounds. Or twist the beans into a rope and lay them around a roast, as shown below.

1. Trim the beans and drop them into a large pot of boiling, salted water. Reduce the heat and cook, uncovered, at a gentle bubble for 8 to 10 minutes or until tender. Drain in a colander set under cold running water. Shake to remove as much water as possible.

2. Melt the butter in a large skillet. Add the shallot and stir over medium heat until tender. Add the chives, cilantro, salt, and pepper. Transfer the beans to the skillet and toss as you would spaghetti to coat with the herb butter. Continue until the beans are heated through. Arrange the beans on a serving plate and pour on the herb butter that remains in the pan.

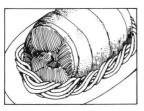

Long beans cooked whole and placed around a roast.

Beet Greens

THE EDIBLE TOPS of red beets may be eaten cooked or raw. Also called spinach beet, these greens possess a mild tangy flavor that is best preserved by brief cooking techniques, such as stir-frying. Served uncooked in a salad, they are a perfectly natural partner for grated raw beets or cold sliced, cooked beets (see Beets). Beet greens are available most of the year and are an excellent source of vitamin A and calcium. One pound serves 3 to 4 people.

TO SELECT: Beet greens come either attached to red beets or trimmed of their roots and stuffed in a plastic bag. Which kind to buy depends on how young and fresh the greens look. Many times the greens sold separately will be younger, and therefore more tender, than those attached to fairly mature beets. Look for pale red, slender stems running through the center of relatively small leaves. Avoid limp, wilted greens and examine those in plastic bags for slimy spots, a sign of deterioration caused by excessive moisture.

TO STORE: Cut the beet greens from fresh beets, leaving about 2 inches of stem attached to the beets. Without rinsing, place the greens in a plastic bag and secure with a wire twist. They

may be refrigerated this way for 2 or 3 days. If you purchase packaged beet greens, open them immediately and pick them over, discarding any leaves that are yellow or wilted. Rinse under cold running water and pat dry with absorbent paper. Scatter the leaves over a clean kitchen towel, roll the towel up loosely, and place inside a plastic bag. Secure the bag with a wire twist, refrigerate, and use the greens within 1 or 2 days.

TO PREPARE: The stems of mature beet greens are apt to be tough, so remove them by gently tearing the stem out of the center of each leaf. If the leaves have not been washed, rinse them under cold running water and drain in a colander or pat dry with absorbent paper. Boiling and steaming tend to drain beet greens of their flavor. Consequently, quick-cooking techniques, such as sautéing or stir-frying, produce the best results. Beet greens may also be served raw in chilled salads.

Beet Green Salad with Beets

SERVES 4

An orange vinaigrette lightly coats the tender beet greens. Tiny cooked beets and chopped walnuts complete this simple but arresting salad.

1 pound beet greens with tiny beets attached
3 tablespoons orange juice
½ teaspoon Dijon mustard
6 tablespoons olive oil
1 shallot, minced
1 tablespoon chopped fresh parsley
Salt and freshly ground black pepper
2 tablespoons coarsely chopped walnuts

1. Cut the beets from the beet greens and drop them into a pot of boiling, salted water. Cook, uncovered, for 3 to 5 minutes or until crisp-tender. Immediately submerge the cooked beets in cold water.

2. In a small mixing bowl, combine the orange juice and mustard and stir to blend. Whisk in the oil, then stir in the shallot and parsley. When the beets are cool enough to handle, remove their skins and place the beets in the dressing. Toss to coat.

3. Pull the center ribs from the beet greens and discard. Rinse the leaves and pat them dry, then tear into bite-size pieces. Transfer to a large salad bowl. Using a slotted spoon, remove the beets from the dressing and set to one side. Pour the dressing over the greens, sprinkle with salt and pepper, and toss to coat evenly. Place a portion of dressed greens on each of 4 salad plates. Divide the beets among the plates, arranging them on top of the leaves. Sprinkle on the chopped walnuts and serve.

Stuffed Beet Greens

24 large beet leaves, rinsed
1 large egg
1 pound ground veal
½ cup unseasoned bread
  crumbs
1 tablespoon chopped fresh
  dill leaves
1 teaspoon grated lemon
  zest
½ teaspoon ground allspice
Salt and freshly ground
  black pepper
2 cups chicken broth
1 garlic clove, minced or
  pressed
1 tablespoon all-purpose
  flour
1 cup sour cream
2 tablespoons lemon juice

Beet leaves are wrapped around ground veal and braised in a flavorful liquid.

1. Cut off the beet green stems at the base of the leaves and discard. Place the leaves in a large bowl. Pour on enough boiling water to cover the leaves by 1 inch and allow them to stand for 5 minutes. Pour off the water and transfer the leaves to an absorbent kitchen towel. Pat dry.

2. Generously butter a large skillet. In a mixing bowl, beat the egg, then add the veal. Stir to combine. Blend in the bread crumbs, dill leaves, lemon zest, allspice, salt, and pepper. Take up by tablespoonfuls and shape into 24 cylinders. Place each cylinder on a beet leaf near the stem end and roll up, tucking in the sides to form a neat bundle. Place, seam side down, in the prepared skillet. Pour on the chicken broth and add the garlic. Cover the pan and cook at a gentle bubble for 30 minutes.

3. Using a slotted spoon, transfer the stuffed beet leaves to a serving platter. Increase the heat under the skillet and cook the liquid until it is reduced to ½ cup. Remove from the heat. Blend the flour into the sour cream and stir into the reduced liquid. Add the lemon juice and return to the heat. Cook, stirring, until slightly thickened. Pour over the stuffed leaves to serve.

Place the veal filling near the stem end of the beet leaf, then roll up, tucking in the sides to form a neat bundle.

Sautéed Beet Greens

Brown sugar and lemon juice accentuate the flavor of coarsely chopped beet greens.

2 pounds beet greens, rinsed
2 tablespoons bacon fat
2 tablespoons lemon juice
1 tablespoon light brown
  sugar
Salt and freshly ground
  black pepper

1. Submerge the beet greens in a large pot of boiling, salted water and cook briefly, uncovered, until the greens are limp. Drain in a colander set under cold running water. When cool enough to handle, take up the greens by handfuls and squeeze gently to press out the excess water. Chop the greens coarsely and set aside on absorbent paper.

2. Melt the bacon fat in a large skillet. Add the beet greens and stir over medium heat for 1 minute.

3. Meanwhile, combine the lemon juice and brown sugar in a small saucepan and heat until the sugar dissolves. Season the beet greens with salt and pepper, then transfer them to a serving bowl. Pour on the lemon juice mixture and toss lightly to combine. Serve immediately.

Beets

IT HAS BEEN SAID that two-thirds of all the beets consumed in the United States are canned. That's a shame, because although canned beets are certainly satisfactory, they can never compare with the wonderful, earthy flavor of fresh beets.

This round, deep red root vegetable, also known as beetroot, is one of the best bargains at the produce counter: for the price of a single vegetable, you get two — the red-fleshed root and the delicately bitter greens. Beets are available most of the year and are an excellent source of potassium.

TO SELECT:

The average-size beet sold in the market runs 1½ inches to 2 inches in diameter. These are small enough to be tender and sweet, but occasionally (if you're lucky) you'll come across bunches of tiny beets the size of walnuts. Grab them and run. These are called thinnings, because the farmer has pulled them from the garden row so the remaining beets will have room to grow. Some farmers feed thinnings to the

pigs, but there are still those who will send them to the local produce stand. In any event, choose beets with size in mind (the smaller the better), and accept only those that have stems and greens attached. Even if you don't plan to use the greens, their presence is a guide to freshness. The surface of the beet (or root) should be firm and smooth with unbroken skin, and the tail (or taproot) should be intact. Avoid beets with wilted greens. For best results in cooking, choose beets that are all the same size. Plan on 3 or 4 average-size beets per person.

TO STORE: Cut the greens from the beets, leaving about 2 inches of the stem attached. Reserve the greens for another use (see Beet Greens). Do not remove the tail. Without washing, place the beets in a plastic bag and secure it with a wire twist. They may be kept this way, refrigerated, for up to a week.

TO PREPARE: Beets may be boiled, baked, steamed, fried, grilled, or microwaved. They may also be served raw. Microwaving is far and away the best cooking method. Not only is it easy and quick, but more flavor and color are retained by this technique than by any other. Without removing the tail or 2-inch portion of the stem, wash the beets carefully under cold running water. Rub the surface gently with your hands; don't use a stiff brush because it is apt to break the skin. It is generally best to leave the skin intact to prevent the loss of flavor, color, and nutrients during cooking. On the other hand, if your recipe calls for peeled beets, you can wash them with a brush, then remove the skin with a swivel-blade peeler, which does the job more easily and quickly than a paring knife.

Beet Consommé

This intensely flavored, clear broth makes the perfect starter for a festive meal.

2 pounds beets, peeled and
    quartered
6 ribs celery
4 cups beef broth
Salt and freshly ground
    black pepper
1 tablespoon lemon juice

1. Place the quartered beets in a large saucepan. Thinly slice 4 ribs of the celery and add to the beets. Pour in enough cold water to cover the vegetables by 1 inch. Bring to a gentle bubble and cook, uncovered, for 20 minutes or until the beets are tender.

2. Transfer to the container of a blender or processor and whirl until smooth. Return to the saucepan and add the beef broth, salt, and pepper. Cut the remaining 2 ribs of celery into 2-inch lengths. Slice the lengths into julienne strips and add to the consommé. Cover and cook over low heat until the celery is tender. Remove from the heat and stir in the lemon juice. Ladle into clear glass bowls and serve hot.

Summer Borscht

Unlike the classic borscht, which is a meat-based hearty soup, this chilled version is light in both flavor and texture. Whisking the beet broth and sour cream together produces a beautiful pink hue, making it a lovely addition to a wedding luncheon in June.

2 tablespoons butter
2 medium onions, coarsely
    chopped
4 ribs celery, coarsely
    chopped
2 teaspoons sugar
4 cups chicken broth
8 medium beets, peeled and
    quartered
Salt and freshly ground
    white pepper
2 tablespoons lemon juice
1 cup sour cream
2 teaspoons prepared
    horseradish

1. Melt the butter in a large saucepan. Add the onions and celery and toss to coat. Sprinkle on the sugar and stir over medium heat until the onions are tender. Pour in the chicken broth. Add the beets, salt, and pepper. Cover the pan and cook at a gentle bubble for 20 minutes or until the beets are tender.

2. Transfer to the container of a blender or processor and whirl until smooth. Pour into a large mixing bowl. Blend in the lemon juice and cover the bowl. Refrigerate until thoroughly chilled.

3. Just before serving, whisk the sour cream and horseradish in a large bowl to lighten the mixture. Gradually whisk in the chilled borscht. Ladle into glass soup bowls and serve.

Beet Salad in Lettuce Cups

SERVES 6

3 tablespoons red wine
vinegar
½ teaspoon salt
1 teaspoon dry mustard
½ cup olive oil
1 large shallot, minced
Pinch of cayenne
2 pounds beets, peeled and
shredded
1 tablespoon chopped fresh
chives
Iceberg lettuce

Raw shredded beets make a delightful salad when tossed with a shallot vinaigrette. For best results, use firm, crisp leaves of iceberg lettuce to create the lettuce cups.

1. In a small bowl, whisk together the vinegar, salt, and mustard until the mustard is dissolved. Gradually whisk in the oil and stir in the shallot and cayenne.

2. Place the shredded beets in a mixing bowl and pour on the dressing. Scatter the chives over the top and toss to combine. Place a cup-shaped lettuce leaf on each of 6 salad plates and divide the beet mixture among them. Chill briefly or serve at once.

Baked Beets

SERVES 4

One of the easiest ways to prepare beets is to wrap them in aluminum foil and bake them whole as you would potatoes.

8 medium beets, unpeeled
4 tablespoons butter
2 tablespoons dry red wine
2 teaspoons chopped fresh
chives
Salt and freshly ground
black pepper

1. Preheat the oven to 375°. Wrap each beet in a square of aluminum foil and place directly on the oven rack. Bake for 1 to 1½ hours or until tender when pierced. Peel the beets and cut them into quarters.

2. Melt the butter in a wide saucepan. Stir in the wine and chives. Add the beets and toss to coat evenly. Season with salt and pepper and heat until warmed through.

Harvard Beets

SERVES 4

Harvard Beets, an old American favorite, make wonderful picnic food. Pack some to nibble with cold fried chicken.

8 medium beets, unpeeled
½ cup sugar
2 teaspoons cornstarch
¼ cup white vinegar
¼ cup cold water
2 tablespoons butter

1. Drop the beets into a large pot of boiling, salted water and cook, uncovered, at a gentle bubble until tender. Drain in a colander set under cold running water. When the beets are cool enough to handle, peel them and slice into ¼-inch-thick rounds.

2. In a wide saucepan, combine the sugar, cornstarch, vinegar, and water. Stir to dissolve the cornstarch and place

over medium heat. Cook, stirring, until the mixture boils and thickens. Add the beet slices and stir gently to coat each one. Add the butter and stir until melted. Serve lightly chilled or at room temperature.

Baked Shredded Beets

Shredded beets are enrobed in a lightly thickened citrusy sauce.

½ cup orange juice
1 tablespoon lemon juice
¼ cup honey
4 tablespoons butter
1 tablespoon cornstarch
1 tablespoon cold water
1½ pounds beets, peeled and shredded
Salt and freshly ground black pepper

1. Preheat the oven to 350°. Generously butter a 1½-quart baking dish. In a small saucepan, combine the orange juice, lemon juice, honey, and butter. Heat until the butter is melted. Remove from the heat. Dissolve the cornstarch in the cold water and stir into the orange juice mixture.

2. Place the shredded beets in the prepared baking dish and season with salt and pepper. Pour on the orange juice mixture and stir to combine. Cover the dish and bake for 20 minutes. Remove the cover and bake for 10 to 15 additional minutes or until the beets are tender.

Grilled Beets with Ginger Butter

The most convenient way to grill beets is in a grilling basket. However, if you don't have one, they may also be placed directly on the grill as you would potatoes.

12 medium beets, unpeeled
4 tablespoons butter
2 tablespoons honey
1 tablespoon finely chopped fresh ginger
1 tablespoon soy sauce

1. Boil, steam, or microwave the beets until partially tender. Transfer them to a colander set under cold running water. When cool enough to handle, peel the beets, but leave them whole.

2. In a saucepan, combine the butter, honey, ginger, and soy sauce and heat until the butter and honey are melted. Brush the ginger mixture over the beets and place them in a grilling basket or set them directly on a hot grill. Basting frequently, cook the beets for 8 to 10 minutes or until tender. Transfer them to a serving dish and pour on any flavored butter that remains in the saucepan.

Sweet and Sour Beets

The tangy flavor of these julienned beets makes them a wonderful companion to hearty roasts, such as pork or game.

8 medium beets, unpeeled
3 tablespoons butter
Salt and freshly ground
   black pepper
¼ cup red wine vinegar
1½ tablespoons sugar

1. Drop the beets into a large pot of boiling, salted water and cook, uncovered, at a gentle bubble until tender. Or microwave the beets by enclosing each one in plastic wrap and arranging them in a circle inside the oven. Cook on high power for 15 to 18 minutes, turning the beets every 5 minutes.

2. Transfer the cooked beets to a colander set under cold running water. When they are cool enough to handle, peel and slice into ¼-inch-thick rounds. Cut the rounds into narrow strips.

3. Melt the butter in a large skillet and add the beets, tossing to coat evenly. Season with salt and pepper. Pour in the vinegar and sprinkle on the sugar. Cook, stirring, over medium heat until the liquid is evaporated. Serve at once.

Beet Purée

If you have oversize beets, which tend to be woody, use them to make this delightful ruby red purée.

4 or 5 large beets, unpeeled
3 tablespoons butter
2 tablespoons light brown
   sugar
Salt and freshly ground
   black pepper
Freshly grated nutmeg

1. Drop the beets into a large pot of boiling, salted water and cook, uncovered, until tender when pierced. Drain in a colander set under cold running water. When cool enough to handle, peel the beets and cut them into small chunks. Place the chunks in a blender or processor and whirl until smooth.

2. Melt the butter in a wide saucepan. Stir in the brown sugar and heat until the sugar is dissolved. Add the beet purée and stir over medium heat until warmed through. Season with salt and pepper and blend in the nutmeg. Mound in a serving dish and top with a generous dollop of butter.

Belgian Endive

PRONUNCIATION disputes aside, Belgian endive is a vegetable of exceptional merit. Smooth, creamy white, spear-shaped leaves with a pleasantly bitter taste comprise the chicons, or slender shoots, of Belgian endive. Measuring 4 to 6 inches in length, these small, elongated heads weigh no more than 3 or 4 ounces apiece. Belgian endive is available from September through May, with December through February being the peak of the season.

TO SELECT:

Individual heads of Belgian endive used to be presented for sale wrapped with the beautiful blue tissue paper in which they had been shipped. Today, however, it is more common to find them displayed loose and unwrapped or packaged inside plastic film. I'm told that the traditional blue tissue paper has been cast aside because the marketing segment of the supermarket industry thought it was perplexing to customers. This is unfortunate because that paper wrapping served the purpose of shielding out light, which causes Belgian endive to turn green and excessively bitter.

If you cannot find heads of Belgian endive wrapped in protective tissue paper, be sure to select only creamy white heads with pale yellow tips. Good-quality Belgian endive should be soft yet firm to the touch, and have unblemished leaves. Belgian endive is a source of vitamin A. Plan on a medium head per person.

TO STORE:

At home, individually wrap each head of Belgian endive in plastic wrap. Then place the wrapped heads in a brown paper bag to protect them from the light. Refrigerated, they will keep this way for up to 5 days.

Individual leaves of Belgian endive make an attractive appetizer or salad when used whole and arranged around a serving plate.

To shred Belgian endive, first remove the central core with a paring knife, then cut the head crosswise into thin slices.

TO PREPARE:

Heads of Belgian endive are so tightly packed that the interior leaves seldom need washing. Briefly rinse the outer leaves with cool water and pat the heads dry. Cut off the darkened end of the head. To serve raw, simply pull off as many leaves as you need and tear them into bite-size pieces. Or leave them whole and arrange attractively on a salad plate. An alternative is to remove the central core with a paring knife and then slice the head crosswise into thin rounds.

Some cooks also remove the center core as a preliminary step to cooking Belgian endive. However, leaving the core in place helps the head to keep its shape. Belgian endive may be braised, steamed, or boiled whole; it may also be coarsely chopped and sautéed. Braising is the best technique for cooking this vegetable and is often employed as a preliminary step in other preparations, such as Belgian endive au gratin. Steaming endive causes it to become waterlogged and lose its elegant coloring. Boiling may be accomplished without discoloration if acidulated water and a stainless-steel pan are used, but you aren't left with any flavorful juices as when you braise the Belgian endive.

Belgian Endive with Shrimp Mousse   SERVES 10 AS AN APPETIZER

A light, fluffy shrimp mousse is easily scooped up by spears of crisp Belgian endive.

1 package unflavored
 gelatin
½ cup dry white wine
½ pound shrimp, cooked,
 peeled, and deveined
1 small onion, sliced
2 tablespoons lemon juice
1 large package (8 ounces)
 cream cheese
½ teaspoon salt
Several drops of Tabasco
 sauce
1 tablespoon chopped fresh
 dill leaves
1 cup heavy cream, whipped
4 or 5 small heads Belgian
 endive

1. In a glass measuring cup, sprinkle the gelatin over the wine and allow it to soften. Set the cup in a small saucepan and pour water into the pan to a depth of 1 inch. Place over high heat and stir the gelatin until it is dissolved. Remove from the heat and set aside.

2. In the container of a blender or processor, combine the shrimp, onion, and lemon juice and whirl until smooth. Add the cream cheese and whirl to incorporate. Transfer to a large mixing bowl. Add the dissolved gelatin, salt, Tabasco, and dill and beat until light. Fold in the whipped cream. Cover and refrigerate until thoroughly chilled.

3. Trim the Belgian endive and separate the leaves. Beat the shrimp mixture to lighten it, then spoon into a decorative bowl. Set the bowl in the center of a large plate or tray and surround with spears of Belgian endive.

Belgian Endive Soup   SERVES 6

3 tablespoons butter
2 medium leeks, white
 portion only, thinly sliced
2 tablespoons all-purpose
 flour
6 cups chicken broth
6 medium heads Belgian
 endive, sliced across into
 thin shreds
1 teaspoon dried thyme
Salt and freshly ground
 white pepper
½ cup medium or whipping
 cream
Chopped fresh chives for
 garnish

This is a lovely, delicately flavored soup to serve before a dinner of wild game.

1. Melt the butter in a large saucepan. Add the leeks and toss to coat. Stir over medium heat until the leeks are tender. Sprinkle on the flour and continue stirring over medium heat until the mixture foams. Stir in the chicken broth and bring to a boil. Add the Belgian endive and thyme. Reduce the heat, cover, and cook at a gentle bubble for 10 minutes or until the endive is tender.

2. Pour into the container of a blender or processor and whirl until smooth. Return to the saucepan. Season with salt and pepper and blend in the cream. Place over medium heat and warm gently. Ladle into soup bowls and garnish with chopped fresh chives.

Belgian Endive Braised with Lime

SERVES 4

Delicate heads of Belgian endive are simmered slowly in butter dashed with lime.

5 tablespoons butter
8 small heads Belgian
 endive
¾ cup boiling water
Juice of 1 lime
1 teaspoon sugar
Salt and freshly ground
 white pepper

1. Melt 3 tablespoons of the butter in a large skillet and remove from the heat. Trim the Belgian endive and arrange the heads in a single layer in the melted butter. Add the boiling water and lime juice. Sprinkle on the sugar. Bring to a gentle bubble. Cover the pan and reduce the heat. Simmer for 10 minutes. Turn the Belgian endive over and season with salt and pepper. Cover the pan and cook for 10 to 15 additional minutes or until tender.

2. Transfer the Belgian endive to a serving plate. Increase the heat and reduce the braising liquid until it barely coats the bottom of the pan. Add the remaining 2 tablespoons of butter and swirl to melt. Pour over the Belgian endive and serve as a vegetable side dish.

Belgian Endive and Scallops with Fettuccine

SERVES 4

3 medium heads Belgian
 endive
3 tablespoons butter
1 teaspoon sugar
Salt and freshly ground
 white pepper
1 cup dry white wine
1 pound bay scallops
1 bay leaf
1 teaspoon dried thyme
1 cup heavy cream
¾ pound fettuccine, boiled
 and drained
¼ cup freshly grated
 Parmesan cheese

Tender noodles, coated with a silken sauce, are tossed with shredded Belgian endive and tiny scallops. Serve as a luncheon or light supper.

1. Trim the Belgian endive and slice the heads into thin rounds. Separate the rounds into shreds. Melt the butter in a large skillet. Add the Belgian endive and toss to coat evenly. Cover the pan and cook over low heat for 3 to 5 minutes or until limp. Sprinkle on the sugar, salt, and pepper. Add the wine, scallops, bay leaf, and thyme. Increase the heat and bring to a gentle bubble. Cook until the scallops are firm and the liquid is reduced by half.

2. Stir in the cream and simmer for 30 seconds. Remove the bay leaf. Add the hot, drained fettuccine and toss to combine. Serve sprinkled with Parmesan cheese.

Sautéed Belgian Endive

Shredded Belgian endive is cooked briefly in butter and wine, then softened with cream. Coarsely chopped pecans contribute a distinctive flavor and lend textural interest.

4 medium heads Belgian endive
4 tablespoons butter
1 cup dry white wine
2 tablespoons chopped fresh parsley
Salt and freshly ground white pepper
½ cup heavy cream
½ cup coarsely chopped pecans

1. Trim the Belgian endive and slice the heads into thin rounds. Separate the rounds into shreds.

2. Melt the butter in a large skillet. Add the Belgian endive and toss to coat evenly. Pour in the wine and bring to a gentle bubble. Cover the pan and reduce the heat. Simmer for 10 minutes. Add the parsley, salt, and pepper and increase the heat. Stirring constantly, cook the Belgian endive until most of the liquid is evaporated. Blend in the cream and cook until it is absorbed. Stir in the pecans and serve immediately.

Bok Choy

THERE IS much confusion in the labeling of bok choy and various other Chinese cabbages. This is partly because a number of varieties exist, and some are called by several different names. It is also due to carelessness on the part of supermarket personnel who hang identification tags in a haphazard manner. To be confident of what you're purchasing, it's essential to know the distinguishing features of each type of cabbage. (See also Napa.)

The type of bok choy most commonly available in supermarkets consists of a loose bunch of broad white stems bearing dark green leaves. Measuring 10 to 12 inches long, a bunch of bok choy closely resembles Swiss chard. (Incidentally, bok choy is also called Chinese chard.) The brilliant white stems are sturdy and rigid, with the feel of celery. The leaves are soft and crisp, similar to those of spinach.

A medium-size bunch of bok choy will serve 4 people. It is an excellent source of vitamin A.

Oriental markets frequently offer a thinner, dark-leaved bok choy with edible yellow flowers labeled choy sum. It is more tender and delicately flavored than common bok choy. There is also a long, slender version of bok

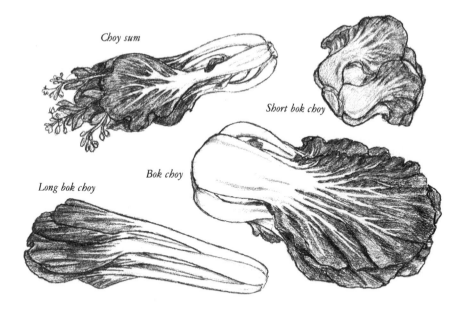

Choy sum

Short bok choy

Bok choy

Long bok choy

choy with light green leaves, and a short variety that rather resembles Boston lettuce. Bok choy is available all year, but is at its best when harvested during cool weather.

TO SELECT:

Look for bunches with plump, juicy-looking stems and handsome green leaves. The stems should feel firm; the leaves should feel resilient and fresh. Avoid any bok choy that exhibits brown spots or has patches of yellow on the leaves. The smallest bunches will be the most tender and delicate.

TO STORE:

Without washing, tightly enclose bok choy in plastic wrap or place in a plastic bag and secure with a wire twist. Refrigerate and use within 3 to 4 days.

TO PREPARE:

Bok choy has a subtle flavor, mildly evocative of cabbage. The leaves may be served raw in a salad as you would spinach. The stems may be cut into lengths and served raw with a dipping sauce, like celery; whole leaves may be shredded and made into coleslaw.

Separate the bunch of bok choy by pulling the stems apart. Trim the ends of the stems and peel if necessary. (The outer stems often bear a tough skin that should be removed with a swivel-blade peeler or paring knife.) Wash the bok choy and pat dry. Since the leaves cook much faster than the stems, you may want to remove the leaves so you can cook them for a shorter period of time. Bok choy is at its most delectable when it is sliced on the diagonal and stir-fried or sautéed briefly. It may also be steamed, blanched whole, or coarsely chopped and added to soups.

Bok Choy Salad

SERVES 6

1 medium bunch bok choy
6 tablespoons vegetable oil
8 mushrooms, sliced
3 green onions, white and green portion, sliced
¼ cup water
2 tablespoons rice vinegar
2 tablespoons soy sauce
1 teaspoon sesame seed oil (dark)
6 ounces Chinese noodles, boiled and drained
¼ cup unsalted cashews, coarsely chopped
1 tablespoon chopped fresh cilantro

The concept of cold pasta salad needn't be limited to Italian-style noodles. In this recipe, cold Chinese noodles are combined with bok choy and unsalted cashews to create a delightful luncheon entrée.

1. Trim the stem end and thinly slice the bunch of bok choy. Heat 3 tablespoons of the vegetable oil in a wok or large skillet. Add the bok choy and toss to coat evenly. Stir over high heat until the bok choy is limp. Add the mushrooms and onions and pour on the water. Continue stirring over high heat until the water is evaporated. Remove from the heat.

2. Whisk together the remaining 3 tablespoons of vegetable oil, the vinegar, soy sauce, and sesame seed oil. Pour over the bok choy and toss to coat. Add the drained noodles, cashews, and cilantro. Toss to combine. Refrigerate until thoroughly chilled and serve on glass salad plates.

Bok Choy with Ginger Butter

SERVES 8

Blanched bok choy is tossed in ginger-flavored butter and sparked with cilantro.

2 medium bunches bok choy
6 tablespoons butter
1 tablespoon minced fresh ginger
2 tablespoons soy sauce
1 garlic clove, pressed
1 tablespoon chopped fresh cilantro
Salt and freshly ground black pepper

1. Trim the stem end of each bunch of bok choy, and slice across into 1-inch strips. Drop into a large pot of boiling, salted water and cook, uncovered, for 2 to 3 minutes or until crisp-tender. Transfer to a colander set under cold running water. Drain thoroughly.

2. Melt the butter in a large skillet. Add the ginger, soy sauce, garlic, and cilantro. Stir briefly over medium heat. Add the bok choy and toss to coat. Continue stirring until heated through. Season with salt and pepper and serve while hot.

Broccoli

THE BEST APPROACH to broccoli is to regard it as a two-part vegetable. By that I mean you should prepare the stalks and flowerets in two entirely different ways. Whether you serve both stalks and flowerets at the same meal is a matter of choice; it is possible, and quite appealing, to present the flowerets whole and cooked crisp-tender surrounded by a border of stir-fried, shredded stalks. On the other hand, many cooks prefer to serve the stalks and flowerets at separate meals. Good-quality broccoli is available almost year round. In fact, broccoli ships so well that it is often one of the best fresh vegetables on the produce stand during the winter months. Broccoli is an excellent source of vitamins A and C and of potassium. One large bunch (1½ to 2 pounds) will provide enough stalks and flowerets for 2 meals, each serving 4 people.

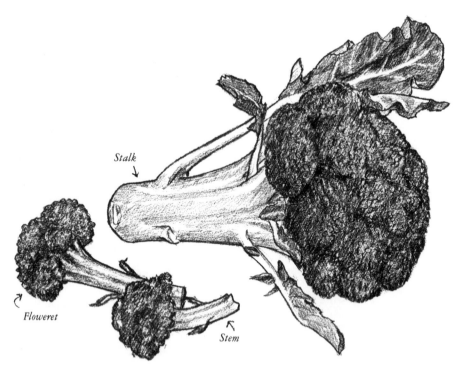

Stalk

Floweret

Stem

TO SELECT: Broccoli is offered for sale in bunches of 2 or 3 stalks. The tops may or may not be covered loosely with clear plastic to protect the buds, but broccoli should not be entirely wrapped in such a way as to prevent air from circulating. Look for firm heads of tightly closed buds. Heads, or flowerets, that are limp or loosely packed indicate aging. Broccoli of good quality will be colored a deep, rich green, and the very tops of the buds will exhibit a bluish purple cast. Avoid any heads that have buds opening to reveal yellow flowers; they are overly mature and will taste cabbagy. The stalks should be relatively thin and feel firm to the touch; a spongy, pulpy texture is a clue that broccoli is past its prime.

TO STORE: Broccoli has an exceptionally high respiration rate, which means that, like you and me, it takes in oxygen and gives off moisture and carbon dioxide. Consequently, this particular vegetable should have plenty of air circulation. Storing it in a closed plastic bag causes it to decay rapidly because humidity builds up inside the bag. The best way to store broccoli at home is to spray it lightly with cold water using a plant mister. Wrap the broccoli in a damp kitchen towel, refrigerate, and use within 2 to 3 days. As an alternative, you may place unwashed broccoli in a perforated plastic bag (a paper punch makes good-size holes), refrigerate, and use within 2 to 3 days.

TO PREPARE: Commercially sold broccoli is washed thoroughly at the processing plant and therefore seldom needs more than a quick rinse under cold running water. If you buy it at a farmer's stand, however, you may want to soak broccoli in warm salted water for 15 to 20 minutes to float out any insects lurking inside. Rinse and drain in a colander.

Cut the flowerets from the stalks so that only 1½ to 2 inches of stem are attached to the flowerets. Reserve the stalks for another use. Using a paring knife or swivel-blade peeler, remove any traces of tough outer skin from the stems of the flowerets. If you wish, cut the larger flowerets in half to even out the cooking time. (You may also steam or blanch them longer, removing the smaller flowerets with a slotted spoon as they become tender.) To prepare the stalks, remove the fibrous skin with a swivel-blade peeler, cutting deeply enough so you are left with nearly white stalks. You may then cut the stalks in a variety of ways or even shred them. They will cook up tender and mildly flavored.

Broccoli may be boiled, steamed, blanched, microwaved, stir-fried, or deep-fried in a batter coating. It may also be served raw (although some cooks prefer to blanch it for 30 seconds to mellow its flavor). My favorite way to prepare broccoli is to blanch it just to the crisp-tender stage. This method preserves the vegetable's bright green color yet slightly softens its flavor. To retain broccoli's full, natural flavor, steam or microwave it. And keep in mind that broccoli easily absorbs water and turns to mush, so always drain cooked broccoli immediately and do not over-expose it to steam.

Broccoli Buttermilk Soup

SERVES 6

Buttermilk lends an unexpected tang to this flavorful, creamy soup.

1 medium bunch broccoli
  (about 1½ pounds)
3 tablespoons butter
1 medium onion, coarsely
  chopped
2 ribs celery, coarsely
  chopped
4 cups chicken broth
2 mealy potatoes, peeled
  and cut into cubes
Salt and freshly ground
  black pepper
2 tablespoons chopped
  fresh cilantro
2 cups buttermilk

1. Separate the broccoli into flowerets. Reserve about 1½ cups of the smallest flowerets and set aside. Cut the stalks into 1-inch lengths.

2. Melt the butter in a large saucepan. Add the onion and celery and toss to coat. Stir over medium heat until the onion is tender. Pour in the chicken broth. Add the broccoli, potatoes, salt, pepper, and cilantro. Cover the pan and cook at a gentle bubble for 20 minutes or until the broccoli is tender.

3. Transfer to the container of a blender or processor and whirl until smooth. Return to the saucepan and stir in the reserved flowerets. Cover and cook slowly until the flowerets are crisp-tender. Remove from the heat and allow the soup to cool for 10 minutes. Blend in the buttermilk and place over medium heat. Warm gently, but do not allow the soup to boil. Serve hot.

Broccoli Salad

Chilled broccoli with an Oriental dressing makes an excellent accompaniment for barbecued chicken or pork.

1 medium bunch broccoli
½ cup rice vinegar
½ cup soy sauce
¼ cup honey
1 garlic clove, pressed
1 tablespoon minced fresh
    ginger
Salt and freshly ground
    black pepper
1 tablespoon toasted sesame
    seed

1. Separate the broccoli into flowerets, cutting any large flowerets in half to promote even cooking. Reserve the stalks for another use. Boil the flowerets gently in salted water until crisp-tender. Or microwave by placing the flowerets in a covered casserole with ¼ cup of water and cooking on high power for 5 to 8 minutes. Transfer the broccoli to a colander set under cold running water. Drain thoroughly and shake to remove as much water as possible. Place in a large bowl.

2. In a saucepan, combine the vinegar, soy sauce, and honey. Stir over medium heat until the honey melts. Add the garlic and ginger and bring the mixture to a boil. Remove from the heat and pour over the broccoli. Toss to coat evenly. Cover with plastic wrap and refrigerate for 6 to 8 hours, stirring occasionally. Season with salt and pepper and sprinkle on the toasted sesame seed before serving.

Broccoli with Minted Curry Butter

Crisply tender flowerets of broccoli are bathed in curry butter with a whisper of mint.

1 medium bunch broccoli
5 tablespoons butter
1 teaspoon curry powder
2 teaspoons chopped fresh
    mint
Salt and freshly ground
    black pepper

1. Separate the broccoli into flowerets, cutting any large flowerets in half to promote even cooking. Reserve the stalks for another use. Drop the flowerets into a large pot of boiling, salted water and cook, uncovered, for 3 to 5 minutes or until crisp-tender. Drain in a colander set under cold running water. Shake to remove as much water as possible.

2. Melt the butter in a large skillet. Stir in the curry powder, then add the mint. Stir for 30 seconds over medium heat. Add the broccoli and toss to coat evenly. Cook over medium heat until warmed through. Season with salt and pepper, then transfer to a serving dish.

Broccoli Stalks with Herbed Cheese SERVES 4

When peeled and cut into discs, the stalks of broccoli are transformed into tender, delicate morsels. Melted Boursin cheese provides a flavorful sauce.

1 medium bunch broccoli
3 tablespoons butter
Salt and freshly ground
   black pepper
1 cup water
1 package (6 ounces) herbed
   Boursin cheese

1. Separate the flowerets from the stalks and reserve the flowerets for another use. Peel the stalks with a swivel-blade peeler, then cut them into ½-inch lengths.

2. Melt the butter in a wide saucepan and add the broccoli, tossing to coat. Season with salt and pepper and add the water. Cover the pan and simmer for 10 to 12 minutes or until the broccoli is tender. Uncover the pan and continue stirring until all the liquid is evaporated.

3. Push the broccoli to one side of the pan and spoon in the Boursin cheese. As the cheese begins to melt, mix in the broccoli and heat until bubbly. Serve hot.

Baked Broccoli and Butternut Squash SERVES 6

Golden chunks of squash tossed with bright green broccoli flowerets are baked in a cardamom-scented butter sauce.

1 medium bunch broccoli
1 medium butternut squash
½ cup water
6 tablespoons butter
1 cup chicken broth
Salt and freshly ground
   black pepper
1 teaspoon ground
   cardamom
Juice of half a lemon

1. Separate the broccoli into flowerets, cutting any large flowerets in half to promote even cooking. Reserve the stalks for another use.

2. Meanwhile, bake the uncut squash at 350° for 20 minutes (or microwave on high for 3½ minutes) to soften it slightly. When cool enough to handle, cut the squash in half and scoop out the seeds. Peel the squash and cut the flesh into small chunks.

3. Put the water and 2 tablespoons of the butter in a 13x9-inch glass baking dish. Add the broccoli and the squash, then cover the pan with aluminum foil. Bake at 350° for 15 minutes. Uncover the pan, stir the broccoli and squash, and pour on the chicken broth. Season with salt and pepper. Cover the pan and continue baking for 20 to 25 additional minutes or until the vegetables are crisp-tender.

4. Melt the remaining 4 tablespoons of butter in a saucepan and stir in the cardamom. Transfer the broccoli

and squash to a serving dish, using a slotted spoon. Pour any remaining liquid in the baking dish into the saucepan and blend with the butter. Just before serving, pour the butter over the vegetables and drizzle on the lemon juice.

Broccoli Timbales

SERVES 6

Cream cheese gives these individual broccoli custards a refined flavor and extraordinary smoothness.

1 medium bunch broccoli
6 ounces cream cheese, softened
4 large eggs
½ cup medium or whipping cream
½ teaspoon salt
Pinch of cayenne
¼ cup grated Gruyère cheese
4 tablespoons butter, cut into small pieces
6 lemon wedges for garnish

1. Separate the broccoli into flowerets, cutting any large flowerets in half to promote even cooking. Reserve the stalks for another use. Boil or steam the flowerets until crisp-tender. Transfer to a colander set under cold running water. Drain well and scatter over absorbent paper. Blot dry. Chop the broccoli coarsely and set aside.

2. Preheat the oven to 350°. Generously butter 6 timbale molds or individual soufflé dishes. In a large mixing bowl, beat together the cream cheese, eggs, and cream. Stir in the salt, cayenne, and Gruyère cheese.

3. Transfer the broccoli to a large skillet. Place over medium heat and stir gently to evaporate all traces of water. When the broccoli begins to stick to the bottom of the pan, remove it from the heat. Immediately add the butter and toss, allowing the melted butter to coat the broccoli.

4. Combine the broccoli with the cream cheese mixture and ladle into the prepared molds. Place in a shallow roasting pan. Add hot water to the depth of 1 inch. Cover the pan with aluminum foil. Bake for 25 to 30 minutes or until the blade of a knife inserted in the center comes out clean. Remove the timbales from the hot water and allow them to stand for 10 minutes. Run a knife around the perimeter of each timbale and unmold onto a serving plate. Garnish with lemon wedges.

Brussels Sprouts

BANISH ALL previous notions of Brussels sprouts as dreary, mushy, and cabbagy smelling. With the recent emphasis on cooking vegetables to the crisp-tender stage, this vegetable has acquired a whole new personality.

Available from August to April, Brussels sprouts possess a more delicate flavor if harvested in the cooler temperatures of late fall or spring. Summer heat tends to give them a stronger flavor, as does prolonged storage. Consequently, your best bet is to purchase Brussels sprouts at a produce stand where you know they've come straight from the field. One pound serves 4 people and is an excellent source of vitamin C and potassium.

TO SELECT:

Brussels sprouts are often sold in cardboard cups with cellophane wrappers. This helps to preserve their freshness, but it doesn't allow you to select heads of all the same size, which is important when it comes to cooking them evenly. If possible, buy Brussels sprouts where they are offered in a loose display. Choose only those with vibrant green, tightly packed heads. Smaller Brussels sprouts have a sweeter, more delicate flavor; 1 inch in diameter is a good size. Leaves that are limp or yellow and heads that feel spongy to the touch indicate that Brussels sprouts are past their prime. They will cook up with a mushy consistency and smell like stale cabbage.

TO STORE:

Since prolonged storage intensifies the flavor of Brussels sprouts, it's best to prepare them as soon after harvest as possible. However, if necessary, you may transfer them, unwashed, to a plastic bag, secure with a wire twist, and refrigerate; use within 2 or 3 days.

TO PREPARE:

Brussels sprouts grow on a tall, thick stalk protected by numerous broad leaves. For this reason, they should be free of garden soil. And because modern farming methods have reduced the likelihood of insects lurking between the leaves, it is usually sufficient to rinse the tiny heads under cold running water. (If you suspect the presence of bugs, soak the Brussels sprouts in warm, salted water for 15 to 20 minutes.) Pull off any loose or damaged leaves and trim the stem end with a paring knife. Then cut a shallow *x* in the stem end to speed the cooking of the dense center core.

Brussels sprouts may be boiled, steamed, stir-fried, or microwaved. When steamed, Brussels sprouts turn olive drab, but when boiled briefly in an uncovered pot, they retain their bright green color. Stir-frying and microwaving produce Brussels sprouts that are pleasantly crunchy and bright green in color without cooking away vitamins or minerals. And don't be reluctant to try Brussels sprouts raw. They may be halved or quartered and served with dipping sauce, or shredded and lightly dressed as a salad.

Brussels Sprouts Salad

1 pound Brussels sprouts
3 ribs celery, sliced
1 red bell pepper, cut into narrow strips
1 red onion, coarsely chopped
2 tablespoons red wine vinegar
2 tablespoons rice vinegar
1 teaspoon sugar
½ teaspoon salt
Freshly ground black pepper
6 tablespoons vegetable oil
1 tablespoon capers, drained
½ cup alfalfa sprouts

Chilled Brussels sprouts are tossed with celery slices and narrow strips of red bell pepper to create a dazzling salad.

1. Drop the Brussels sprouts into a large pot of boiling, salted water and cook, uncovered, for 12 minutes or until crisp-tender. Drain in a colander set under cold running water. Shake to remove as much water as possible. Transfer to a salad bowl. Add the celery, red bell pepper, and onion and toss to combine. Refrigerate for 1 hour or until lightly chilled.

2. In a small bowl, combine the red wine vinegar, rice vinegar, sugar, salt, and pepper. Stir to dissolve the sugar, then whisk in the oil. Pour over the chilled Brussels sprouts and toss to coat. Scatter on the capers and alfalfa sprouts and serve.

Brussels Sprouts with Dilled Lemon Sauce

SERVES 4

Brussels sprouts are stir-fried until crisp-tender, then coated with a zesty lemon sauce.

⅓ cup lemon juice
½ cup cold water
1 teaspoon cornstarch
¾ cup chicken broth
2 tablespoons honey
1 pound Brussels sprouts
3 tablespoons vegetable oil
1 tablespoon chopped fresh
  dill leaves

1. In a saucepan, combine the lemon juice, ¼ cup of the water, and the cornstarch. Stir until the cornstarch is dissolved and blend in the chicken broth. Add the honey and place over medium heat. Stir until the honey melts and the sauce thickens slightly. Remove from the heat and set aside.

2. Rinse and trim the Brussels sprouts. Heat the oil in a wok or large skillet. Add the Brussels sprouts and toss to coat evenly. Stir over high heat until the Brussels sprouts turn bright green. Pour on the remaining ¼ cup of water and reduce the heat to medium, stirring until the Brussels sprouts are crisp-tender and the liquid is evaporated.

3. Pour the lemon sauce over the Brussels sprouts. Sprinkle on the dill leaves. Stir until the sauce begins to bubble and serve at once.

Shredded Brussels Sprouts with Mustard-Caraway Cream

SERVES 4

Brussels sprouts can be quickly shredded by slicing them across with a serrated knife. They may also, of course, be shredded in a food processor.

1 pound Brussels sprouts
1 cup sour cream
1 tablespoon Pommery
  whole-grain mustard
2 teaspoons caraway seed
4 tablespoons butter
1 shallot, minced
½ cup dry white wine
Salt and freshly ground
  black pepper

1. Rinse and trim the Brussels sprouts. Then shred them by slicing each sprout thinly across its head. In a small bowl, blend together the sour cream, mustard, and caraway seed. Set aside.

2. Melt the butter in a large skillet. Add the shredded Brussels sprouts and the shallot and toss to coat evenly. Stir over medium heat until the Brussels sprouts become limp. Pour on the wine. Season with salt and pepper and continue stirring over medium heat until all the liquid is evaporated. Remove from the heat and stir in the sour cream mixture. Return to the heat and stir until warmed through, but do not allow the mixture to boil.

Brussels Sprouts Polonaise

SERVES 4

White and yellow borders of sieved hard-boiled egg make this dish of Brussels sprouts as attractive as it is delicious.

1 pound Brussels sprouts
6 tablespoons butter
1 tablespoon lemon juice
1 tablespoon chopped fresh chervil
¼ cup unseasoned bread crumbs
2 large eggs, hard-boiled and cooled

1. Preheat the oven to 250°. Generously butter a shallow baking dish. Drop the Brussels sprouts into a large pot of boiling, salted water and cook, uncovered, for 12 minutes or until crisp-tender. To microwave, place the Brussels sprouts in a glass casserole with ¼ cup of water. Cover and cook at high power for 2½ minutes. Stir, then cook for 2½ minutes more.

2. Transfer the cooked Brussels sprouts to a colander set under cold running water. Drain well and shake to remove as much water as possible. Spoon into the prepared baking dish. Melt 2 tablespoons of the butter in a small skillet and pour over the Brussels sprouts. Toss to coat then place in the oven to keep warm. Melt the remaining 4 tablespoons butter in the skillet and blend in the lemon juice and chervil. Add the bread crumbs and stir to moisten. Set aside.

3. Separate the egg yolks from the whites. Force them both through a sieve, allowing the yolks and whites to collect in separate piles. Take the Brussels sprouts from the oven and increase the heat to 350°. Scatter the bread crumbs over the Brussels sprouts and toss to combine. Distribute the sieved egg white in a border around the perimeter of the baking dish. Then next to it, make a row of sieved egg yolk. Return the dish to the oven and heat for 5 minutes.

Brussels Sprouts in Celery Sauce

SERVES 4

Celery, cooked until tender and then puréed, creates an elegant sauce for Brussels sprouts.

1 pound Brussels sprouts
8 ribs celery, thinly sliced
3 tablespoons butter
1 tablespoon all-purpose flour
1 cup medium or whipping cream
Salt and freshly ground white pepper
Freshly grated nutmeg
½ cup coarsely chopped pecans

1. Generously butter a shallow baking dish. Drop the Brussels sprouts into a large pot of boiling, salted water and cook, uncovered, for 12 minutes or until crisp-tender. Drain in a colander set under cold running water. Shake to remove as much water as possible and transfer to the prepared baking dish.

2. Place the celery in a wide saucepan and add enough water to cover by 1 inch. Cover the pan and place over medium heat. Cook for 8 to 10 minutes or until the celery is tender. Transfer to the container of a blender or processor and whirl until smooth. Return to the saucepan and cook, uncovered, until reduced by half.

3. Meanwhile, melt the butter in a small saucepan. Sprinkle on the flour and stir over medium heat until the mixture foams. Whisk in the cream and continue stirring over medium heat until bubbly and slightly thickened. Whisk in the reduced celery broth. Season with salt and pepper and stir in the nutmeg.

4. Preheat the oven to 350°. Pour the celery sauce over the Brussels sprouts and toss to coat. Scatter the pecans over the top and bake for 20 minutes or until heated through.

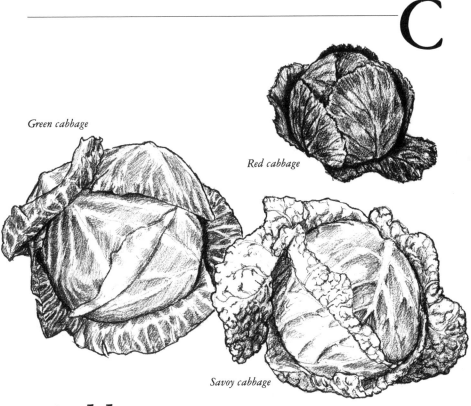

Green cabbage

Red cabbage

Savoy cabbage

Cabbage

PITY THE POOR CABBAGE. It is maligned by many as being strongly flavored and foul smelling. But that is a reputation unfairly earned.

There are a number of vegetables, cabbage among them, that contain organic sulfur compounds. Not only is cabbage high in these particular chemical elements, but it is also capable of producing more of them during the cooking process. When these volatile compounds are released, they create the characteristic smell and taste associated with cooked cabbage. However, they needn't be overwhelming. Lightly cooked cabbage possesses a mild, delicate flavor and pleasant aroma; overcooked cabbage develops a strong flavor and objectionable odor.

TO SELECT:	There are three kinds of heading cabbage — green, red, and Savoy — all of which are available year round, and are an excellent source of vitamin C. The green and red varieties have tightly packed heads and should feel heavy for their size. The crinkly, vein-laced leaves of the Savoy cabbage are rather loosely furled, so the head of this variety does not seem as weighty. Choose cabbage with fresh, firm leaves. If possible, select a head bearing a considerable number of its gracefully curved, darker-colored outer leaves. Since produce managers keep their stands looking fresh by repeatedly trimming away the outer leaves as they wilt, an abundance of these leaves is a clue to the freshness of the head.

Savoy cabbage is the best choice for rolling and stuffing, because its leaves have a more delicate, pliable texture. On the other hand, the same characteristic makes it a poor candidate for coleslaw. Green and red cabbages are the ones to choose for shredding. You can judge the quality of the interior fairly accurately by the condition of the outside leaves. Avoid any heads that show traces of sandy slime or insect holes. Purchase a medium-size head to serve 4 people. |
| **TO STORE:** | Cabbage loses moisture rapidly, so place the untrimmed head in a plastic bag and seal with a wire twist. You may refrigerate a whole head for 5 to 7 days, but cut cabbage does not store well. Plan to use a cut head within 1 day. |
| **TO PREPARE:** | Cut off the stem end and remove the outer leaves. Rinse the outside of the head under cold running water and pat dry. To cook the head in one piece, remove the center core by making a cone-shaped incision with a paring knife. To cook wedges, slice the head into quarters, then trim the center core from each piece. When shredding cabbage, first divide the head into quarters. Then cut away the core if you wish, or leave it in place as something to hold on to during the shredding procedure.

Cabbage may be served raw and is customarily shredded or chopped, and then tossed with dressing. It may also be cooked in several ways. Steaming, stir-frying, and braising are far superior methods to boiling, which inevitably results in mushy, watery leaves with a strong, overcooked cabbagy flavor. But the best way to cook cabbage is to microwave it. Cut into wedges and sprinkled with water, microwaved cabbage retains its color and possesses a mild flavor and a firm, al dente texture. |

Cabbage and Fresh Pineapple Salad

SERVES 6

1 large egg yolk
1 teaspoon Dijon mustard
2 tablespoons lemon juice
1 tablespoon white wine
vinegar
½ cup olive oil
1 medium-size green
cabbage, shredded
2 teaspoons sugar
½ teaspoon salt
Freshly ground black
pepper
1 fresh pineapple, peeled
and coarsely chopped
1 tablespoon chopped fresh
mint

Tiny bits of fresh pineapple add lively contrast to this chilled cabbage salad.

1. In a small mixing bowl, whisk the egg yolk, mustard, lemon juice, and vinegar. Whisk in the oil.

2. Place the shredded cabbage in a large bowl and sprinkle on the sugar, salt, and pepper. Toss to combine and then pour on the dressing. Stir to coat evenly. Cover the bowl and refrigerate until thoroughly chilled.

3. Just before serving, mix in the chopped fresh pineapple and mint.

New England-Style Coleslaw

SERVES 6

1 large egg
1 cup sour cream
1 tablespoon all-purpose
flour
6 tablespoons cider vinegar
1 tablespoon sugar
1 medium onion, quartered
½ cup celery leaves, loosely
packed
1 bay leaf
1 medium-size green
cabbage, shredded
Salt and freshly ground
black pepper

This tangy salad is a traditional favorite for picnics.

1. Whisk the egg and sour cream in a small saucepan. Add the flour and stir over medium heat until the mixture bubbles and thickens slightly.

2. Meanwhile, combine the vinegar, sugar, onion, celery leaves, and bay leaf in another saucepan and boil, uncovered, at a gentle bubble for 5 minutes. Strain the liquid, then whisk it into the sour cream mixture.

3. Place the shredded cabbage in a large mixing bowl. Pour on the dressing and toss to combine. Season with salt and pepper. Cover the bowl and refrigerate until thoroughly chilled.

Red Cabbage Slaw with Raisins

SERVES 6

1 large red cabbage,
  shredded
1 cup raisins
Salt and freshly ground
  black pepper
1 cup sour cream
2 tablespoons white wine
  vinegar
½ cup slivered almonds,
  toasted

Serve this with fried chicken or cold baked ham.

1. In a large mixing bowl, combine the shredded cabbage and raisins. Sprinkle with salt and pepper and toss to combine.

2. Whisk together the sour cream and vinegar and pour over the cabbage. Mix thoroughly. Cover the bowl and refrigerate until thoroughly chilled. Just before serving, mix in the toasted almonds.

Hearty Cabbage Soup

SERVES 6

Slices of spicy kielbasa enliven this thick, hearty soup. Serve with warm pumpernickel bread.

4 tablespoons vegetable oil
4 tablespoons butter
3 medium onions, sliced
4 mealy potatoes, cubed
1 teaspoon sugar
1 teaspoon salt
Freshly ground black
  pepper
8 cups water
1 medium-size green
  cabbage, shredded
1½ pounds kielbasa
1 teaspoon dried thyme
¼ teaspoon ground allspice

1. Heat the oil and butter in a Dutch oven or large soup pot until the butter is melted. Add the onions and potatoes and toss to coat evenly. Sprinkle on the sugar, salt, and pepper and cover the pan. Cook slowly for 15 to 20 minutes or until the potatoes are tender. Scoop out half the potato mixture and place it in the container of a blender or processor to cool.

2. Pour the water into the soup pot, and add the cabbage. Prick the kielbasa in several places and drop it into the liquid. Stir in the thyme and allspice. Cover the pan and cook slowly for 20 to 30 minutes or until the cabbage is tender and the kielbasa is firm. Remove the kielbasa and peel it if you wish. Slice it into ½-inch-thick rounds and return the pieces to the soup.

3. Ladle about 1 cup of the broth into the potato mixture in the blender or processor and whirl until smooth. Gradually stir it into the soup. Cook, uncovered, for 10 minutes, and serve piping hot.

Green Cabbage and Apples

2 tablespoons bacon fat
1 medium onion, coarsely
  chopped
2 tart apples, coarsely
  chopped
1 tablespoon all-purpose
  flour
1 cup water
½ cup red wine vinegar
2 tablespoons sugar
1 medium-size green
  cabbage, shredded
1 bay leaf
Salt and freshly ground
  pepper

Green cabbage, sautéed in bacon fat, makes a hearty cold-weather dish that goes well with venison or roast goose.

1. Melt the bacon fat in a large skillet. Add the onion and apples and toss to coat. Stir over medium heat until the onion is limp. Sprinkle on the flour and continue stirring until the mixture foams. Pour in the water and vinegar. Increase the heat and bring to a boil. Stir in the sugar.

2. Add the cabbage, stirring to coat, then drop in the bay leaf. Reduce the heat and cover the pan. Simmer for 25 to 30 minutes or until the cabbage is crisp-tender. Remove the bay leaf and season with salt and pepper. Serve at once.

Glazed Red Cabbage

Serve small portions of this savory cabbage as an accent to wild game or roast pork.

4 tablespoons butter
1 large red cabbage,
  shredded
½ cup water
Salt and freshly ground
  black pepper
4 tablespoons red wine
½ cup red currant jelly

1. Melt the butter in a large skillet. Add the cabbage and toss to coat. Stir over medium heat until the cabbage is limp. Pour on the water and cover the pan. Reduce the heat and cook slowly for 20 to 25 minutes or until the cabbage is crisp-tender.

2. Season with salt and pepper and stir over high heat until all the liquid is evaporated. Add the red wine and jelly. Continue stirring until the jelly melts and glazes the cabbage. Spoon into 12 small mounds surrounding a roast or present in a decorative glass bowl.

Butter-Braised Cabbage with Fennel and Red Peppers

SERVES 4

Narrow strips of red bell pepper contribute color and flavor to lightly braised green cabbage. Serve with grilled bratwurst or veal sausage.

6 tablespoons butter
1 tablespoon fennel seed
1 medium onion, thinly sliced
1 medium-size green cabbage, shredded
1 cup dry white wine
1 red bell pepper, cut into narrow strips
Salt and freshly ground black pepper

1. Melt the butter in a large skillet. Add the fennel seed and stir over medium heat for 1 minute or until toasted. Add the onion, tossing to coat, then stir in the cabbage. Pour on the wine. Cover the pan and reduce the heat. Simmer for 10 minutes.

2. Stir in the red bell pepper strips and season with salt and pepper. Continue cooking, covered, for 15 to 20 minutes or until the cabbage is crisp-tender. Increase the heat and cook, stirring, until all the liquid is evaporated. Transfer to a serving dish.

Colcannon

SERVES 6

This traditional Irish dish is composed of shredded cabbage and buttery mashed potatoes blended with thinly sliced green onions and chopped fresh parsley.

4 large mealy potatoes, peeled and cut into quarters
¼ cup medium or whipping cream
8 tablespoons butter
1 medium-size green cabbage, shredded
8 green onions, white and green portion, sliced
½ cup water
Salt and freshly ground black pepper
2 tablespoons chopped fresh parsley

1. Drop the potatoes into a large pot of boiling, salted water and cook, uncovered, at a gentle bubble for 20 to 30 minutes or until tender when pierced. Drain well and transfer to a large bowl. Immediately break up the potatoes with a fork to release the steam. Add the cream and 4 tablespoons of the butter and beat until smooth.

2. Melt the remaining 4 tablespoons of butter in a large skillet and add the shredded cabbage. Stir over medium heat until wilted. Add the onions and water. Continue stirring until the cabbage is tender and the liquid is evaporated. Season with salt and pepper. Mix in the potatoes and parsley. Continue stirring over medium heat until the potatoes are heated through. Transfer to a serving bowl and serve piping hot.

Cabbage Strudel

4 tablespoons vegetable oil
12 tablespoons butter
1 medium onion, coarsely
  chopped
1 medium-size green
  cabbage, shredded
¾ cup dry white wine
1 tablespoon caraway seed
½ teaspoon salt
Freshly ground black
  pepper
½ cup unseasoned bread
  crumbs
Additional bread crumbs
12 sheets phyllo dough

A slice of Cabbage Strudel makes a perfect companion for roast veal or fresh noncured ham.

1. Heat the oil and 2 tablespoons of the butter in a large skillet until the butter is melted. Add the onion and toss to coat. Stir over medium heat until the onion is limp. Stir in the cabbage. Pour on the wine and add the caraway seed. Increase the heat and stir constantly until the cabbage is limp and the liquid is evaporated. Sprinkle with salt and pepper and set aside.

2. Preheat the oven to 400°. Generously grease a flat baking sheet. Melt 2 tablespoons of the butter in a small skillet. Add ½ cup bread crumbs and stir to evenly butter the crumbs. In a small saucepan, melt the remaining 8 tablespoons of butter.

3. Place a linen towel on a work surface so that the long edge is in front of you. Sprinkle the towel with unbuttered crumbs. Lay a sheet of phyllo on the crumbs with the long edge in front of you. Brush the surface with melted butter. Repeat until you have a stack of 6 buttered phyllo sheets. Sprinkle the top sheet with half the buttered bread crumbs. Then, spoon half the cabbage mixture down the length of the phyllo, about 4 inches in from the edge nearest you. Using the towel to help you, roll up the strudel as you would a jelly roll. Don't be too concerned about the ends. Tuck them in or pinch them closed. (You can slice off the ends before serving.) Place the strudel, seam side down, on the prepared baking sheet. Repeat the procedure using the remaining 6 sheets of phyllo dough to form another strudel. Brush the surface of the dough with melted butter and bake the strudels for 30 to 40 minutes or until golden brown. Slice into 1-inch-wide portions to serve.

Spoon half the cabbage mixture down the length of the sheet of phyllo.

Using the towel to help you, roll up the strudel in a jelly-roll fashion.

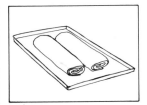

Place seam side down on a baking sheet and tuck under or pinch closed the ends.

Stuffed Savoy Cabbage

A spicy filling of rice and garbanzo beans lends Middle Eastern intrigue to these stuffed cabbage rolls.

1 large Savoy cabbage
2 cups cooked rice
1 tablespoon olive oil
½ teaspoon ground cinnamon
¼ teaspoon freshly grated nutmeg
⅛ teaspoon ground allspice
½ teaspoon salt
Freshly ground black pepper
1 cup canned garbanzo beans, drained
½ cup chopped fresh parsley
2 garlic cloves, minced
Juice of 2 lemons

1. Butter the bottom of a nonreactive Dutch oven or wide casserole. Separate the head of cabbage and select 12 well-formed leaves. Drop the leaves into a large pot of boiling, salted water and cook, uncovered, at a gentle bubble for 2 minutes. Lift them out and immediately submerge in cold water. Drain, underside up, on absorbent paper. Holding a sharp knife parallel to the leaf, slice off any protruding portion of the central rib. Invert each leaf so that it forms a cup.

2. In a large mixing bowl, combine the rice, oil, cinnamon, nutmeg, allspice, salt, and pepper. Add the beans and parsley and blend well. Spoon a generous table-spoon of filling onto a cabbage leaf at the stem end. Roll up the leaf, tucking in the sides to form a neat bundle. Repeat with the remaining leaves.

3. Transfer to the prepared Dutch oven, seam side down, and pack tightly so the leaves won't unroll. Pour on enough water to cover the rolls. Add the garlic and cover the pan. Simmer gently for 45 minutes. Add the lemon juice and cook, uncovered, for 10 minutes more. Lift out the bundles with a slotted spoon and serve hot or lightly chilled. Sprinkle with additional lemon juice, if you wish.

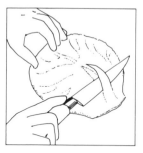

Hold the knife parallel to the leaf and slice off the protruding portion of the rib.

Invert the leaf so that it forms a cup. Spoon a portion of the filling onto the stem end.

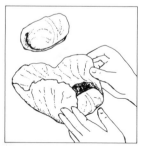

Roll up the leaf, tucking in the sides as you go, and set aside the bundle with its seam side down.

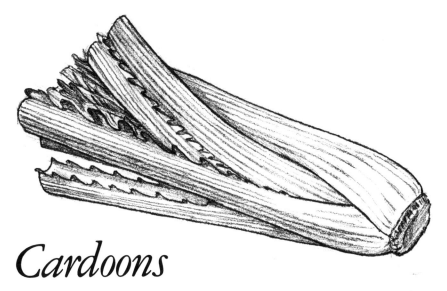

Cardoons

CARDOONS ARE a member of the same thistle family as globe artichokes, so it is not surprising that their flavors are often compared. Cardoons, however, are the celerylike stalks of the thistle plant, while artichokes are the edible flower buds.

Cardoons are available during the months of December through February, and they are sold in specialty food shops and Italian grocery stores. You're most apt to find them at Christmastime, and during annual Italian festivals held by large supermarket chains as an advertising promotion.

TO SELECT:

With their pale green stalks joined at the base, cardoons closely resemble bunches of celery, and they are often referred to as heads of cardoon. Their distinguishing feature is a row of small spiky leaves running down the outside of each ridged stalk. Look for firm, crisp, unblemished bunches that exhibit very little browning. Large, long stalks are apt to be bitter, so purchase the shortest bunches you can find. The amount of cardoons to buy depends on how you plan to serve them. Because the outer stalks are usually tough and bitter, they are not suitable for serving raw. Only the delicate inner stalks are the ones to offer as a crudité or salad component. Cooking tenderizes the outer stalks, however, and tempers their flavor, so you may want to divide cardoon bunches and serve them two different ways. In any event, purchase one-quarter pound per serving.

TO STORE:	Much like celery, cardoons may be placed in an airtight plastic bag and refrigerated. Plan to use them within 7 days.
TO PREPARE:	Pull the cardoon stalks apart, and discard any that seem limp or wilted. Trim off both ends and rinse thoroughly. To serve cardoons raw, remove the spiky leaves that run down the edge of the stalk by applying shallow strokes of a swivel-blade peeler. Then insert the tip of a paring knife under the inside curve of the stalk to pull away any tough white skin. Finish by removing the strings on the outside of the stalk. Cut the stalks into lengths. Rub the surface with lemon juice to retard discoloration, or submerge in acidulated water until serving time.
	When cooking cardoons, you may prepare the stalks as described above. However, it is much easier to boil them gently until tender, then remove the leaves and strings. Cooked cardoons are customarily finished with butter and Parmesan cheese, or baked in a rich cream sauce. They may also be batter coated and deep-fried. Another alternative is to simmer cardoons in a flavorful broth, and then serve them chilled as a salad or appetizer.

Cardoons with Asiago

SERVES 4

Cardoons, lightly sautéed until golden, are finished with a sprinkling of Asiago cheese.

1 bunch cardoons
3 tablespoons olive oil
3 tablespoons butter
1 garlic clove, minced
2 teaspoons grated lemon
  zest
Salt and freshly ground
  white pepper
½ cup grated Asiago cheese
  (or substitute freshly
  grated Parmesan cheese)

1. Wash and trim the cardoons as described earlier (see TO PREPARE). Cut into 2-inch lengths and drop into cold acidulated water.

2. Transfer the cardoons to a large pot of boiling, salted water and cook, uncovered, at a gentle bubble until tender. Drain in a colander. Shake to remove as much water as possible.

3. Heat the oil and butter in a large skillet until the butter is melted. Add the cardoons and stir over high heat until lightly golden. Distribute the garlic and lemon zest over the cardoons. Season with salt and pepper to taste and stir briefly over high heat. Sprinkle on the grated cheese and allow it to melt. Serve immediately.

Cardoons with Bagna Cauda

Raw cardoons are the classic partner for the anchovy-flavored dipping sauce known as Bagna Cauda. In this recipe, reduced cream takes the place of the traditional olive oil and creates an intensely rich, creamy result. Feel free to offer additional raw vegetables for dipping. Strips of red or green bell pepper, green beans, cherry tomatoes, or zucchini slices are all possibilities.

1 bunch cardoons
2 cups heavy cream
4 tablespoons unsalted butter
8 flat anchovy fillets, finely chopped
2 garlic cloves, minced or pressed
Pinch of cayenne

1. Wash and trim the cardoons as described earlier (see TO PREPARE). Cut into 2-inch lengths and drop into cold acidulated water. Cover the bowl and refrigerate until serving time.

2. In a saucepan, boil the cream gently until it is reduced to 1 cup. Meanwhile, melt the butter in a separate pan and add the anchovies. Stir over medium heat until the anchovies disintegrate. Whisk in the garlic and the reduced cream. Stir in the cayenne. Place over an alcohol burner to keep warm. Drain the cardoons and pat dry. Serve immediately. If necessary, thin the sauce with additional cream.

Carrots

CARROTS PLAY such an important role in everyday cooking that many cooks keep them on hand at all times to use in soups or stocks, or as a flavor base of sauces and gravies. Available year round, carrots are sold, trimmed of their tops, in 1-pound plastic bags or tied in bunches with their greenery attached. The variety that comes in plastic bags is noted for its keeping quality and long shelf life. Consequently, it's the best choice when you're purchasing carrots to use as a kitchen staple.

TO SELECT:

The sweetest, most delicate carrots are the ones the farmer pulls from the row at the beginning of the summer so that others will have room to grow. Often called spring carrots,

they are immature or baby carrots of a regular variety. Next best are the finger carrots, which are mature carrots of a dwarf variety. These are found in many supermarkets packaged in small plastic pouches. Baby carrots, on the other hand, can usually be found only at a farmer's stand.

The bunched carrots sold in supermarkets are quite adequate if they are fresh, which is indicated by the condition of the tops. If the greenery is perky and of good color, you know that the carrots were recently pulled. Look for slender, firm carrots with a smooth surface. Avoid any that are limp or cracked. When purchasing bagged carrots, buy only those that are colored bright orange. A deep orange, or red-orange, hue is a sign of age and a clue that the carrots probably have developed a woody core. Also, check their tops because bagged carrots can become moldy at the point where the greens were removed. One pound of trimmed carrots or a bunch of 7 or 8 medium-size carrots will serve 4 people.

TO STORE:

Since carrot greens draw moisture from the flesh, it's important to remove them as soon as you get the carrots home. (The greens are rinsed and used by some cooks in soups and stocks, although most people discard them.) Place the unwashed carrots in a plastic bag to supply them with humidity; refrigerate and use within 1 to 4 weeks, depending on their durability. Baby carrots should be eaten as soon as possible, but bagged carrots will keep for 4 weeks.

Carrots held in storage undergo a remarkable change in their character — their carotene content increases. Carotene is a yellow-orange pigment that not only gives carrots their color, it also converts to vitamin A when eaten. When the color of carrots deepens during storage, it is a sign that the carotene content is greater than that in freshly pulled carrots, which are pale, yellowish orange. A flavor change occurs, too. While carrots that have been recently harvested are sweet and delicately flavored, those that have been stored for some time give up their sweetness and take on a more assertive carroty flavor. This makes them a good candidate for hearty casseroles and stews where the taste of mildly flavored carrots would be overwhelmed.

TO PREPARE:

Rinse carrots under cold running water to remove any soil. If they are baby carrots, the skins will be so delicate that a gentle brushing will be sufficient. Finger carrots, however, are a mature variety and often have a fairly tough skin. These are most easily dealt with by cooking them whole, then rubbing the skin off under lukewarm tap water. Older carrots need to be peeled to look and taste their best. Cradle a carrot in your hand and apply a swivel-blade peeler with firm, away-from-you strokes. (Some cookbooks advise peeling toward you. Use whichever direction feels the most comfortable.)

Carrots that have been stored a long time develop woody cores. If, when you cut into a carrot, the center portion is noticeably light in color and feels a bit pulpy, the best approach is to cook all the flesh and purée it or cut the core away and use only the brighter orange portion.

The assortment of ways to cook carrots is endless. They may be steamed, boiled, baked, microwaved, grilled in foil, or stir-fried. They may be puréed and made into any number of dishes, including desserts such as cakes, pies, and soufflés. And of course they may be served raw. Carrots can be cooked whole or cut into slices, chunks, fancy ovals, or julienne strips. Just keep in mind that whole carrots and large chunks take longer to cook than thin slices and julienne strips.

Marinated Finger Carrots

Tiny carrots marinated in a spicy broth are delightful to munch as an appetizer or as part of a picnic lunch.

1 pound finger carrots
¾ cup white vinegar
½ cup water
3 tablespoons sugar
½ teaspoon salt
1 garlic clove, thinly sliced
½ teaspoon mustard seed
½ teaspoon dill seed
½ teaspoon crushed red
  pepper
1 tablespoon chopped fresh
  dill leaves

1. Steam or boil the carrots until crisp-tender. Immediately submerge them in cold water. Then rub the carrots under a gentle stream of cool tap water to remove their skins. Place them in a bowl.

2. Combine the vinegar, water, sugar, and salt in a saucepan. Stir over medium heat until the sugar is dissolved. Add the garlic, mustard seed, dill seed, and red pepper. Simmer, uncovered, for 20 minutes. Remove from the heat and stir in the dill leaves.

3. Pour the vinegar mixture over the carrots and toss to coat evenly. Cover the bowl and refrigerate for 6 to 8 hours. Stir occasionally to promote even marinating.

Gingered Carrot Soup

4 tablespoons butter
1 pound carrots, peeled and
  sliced
1 medium onion, sliced
4 cups chicken broth
Salt to taste
Pinch of cayenne
1 tablespoon finely chopped
  fresh ginger
Freshly grated nutmeg
1 cup fresh orange juice,
  chilled
2 tablespoons Cointreau
2 tablespoons chopped
  fresh mint for garnish

Fresh ginger and orange juice contribute their special flavors to this sophisticated soup.

1. Melt the butter in a large saucepan. Add the carrots and onion and toss to coat. Cover the pan and cook slowly for 10 minutes. Pour in the chicken broth. Add the salt, cayenne, ginger, and nutmeg. Simmer, uncovered, until the carrots are soft enough to mash against the side of the pan.

2. Transfer to the container of a blender or processor and whirl until smooth. Pour into a large mixing bowl. Blend in the orange juice and Cointreau. Cover the bowl and refrigerate until thoroughly chilled. Serve in clear glass bowls garnished with mint.

Shredded Carrot Salad

1 pound carrots, shredded
6 green onions, white and
  green portion, sliced
Salt and freshly ground
  black pepper
2 tablespoons lemon juice
1 tablespoon honey
1 teaspoon Dijon mustard
6 tablespoons vegetable oil
1 tablespoon grated fresh
  ginger

Shredded carrots are tossed with sliced green onions and dressed with a honey-mustard sauce. Serve chilled with batter-fried fish.

1. Place the carrots and onions in a large bowl and toss to combine. Season with salt and pepper.

2. In a small bowl, whisk together the lemon juice, honey, and mustard. Whisk in the oil and add the ginger. Pour over the carrot mixture and stir to combine. Cover the bowl and refrigerate for 4 to 6 hours before serving.

Sautéed Carrots with Oregano

Using a food processor makes it easy to prepare this simple yet elegant dish. Other fresh herbs, such as tarragon, parsley, or mint, may be substituted for the oregano.

3 tablespoons vegetable oil
1 pound carrots, cut into
  julienne strips
⅓ cup water
2 tablespoons butter
1 tablespoon chopped fresh
  oregano
Salt and freshly ground
  black pepper

1. Heat the oil in a wok or large skillet. Add the carrots, tossing to coat evenly. Cook over high heat, stirring constantly for 30 seconds.

2. Pour on the water and cover the pan. Reduce the heat and simmer for 3 to 5 minutes or until the carrots are crisp-tender. Add the butter and oregano and increase the heat. Cook, stirring, until all the liquid is evaporated from the pan. Season with salt and pepper and serve immediately.

Honey-Glazed Carrots

SERVES 4

Glazed carrot slices shimmer so beautifully in candlelight that they make an especially nice dinner-party vegetable.

1 pound carrots
1 teaspoon sugar
4 tablespoons butter
2 tablespoons honey
Salt and freshly ground
   black pepper
Freshly grated nutmeg

1. Cut the carrots diagonally into ¼-inch-thick slices. Transfer to a wide saucepan and add enough water to cover the carrots by 1 inch. Add the sugar and 2 tablespoons of the butter. Place over medium heat and cook, uncovered, at a gentle bubble for 10 to 12 minutes or until tender.

2. Add the honey and the remaining 2 tablespoons of butter. Increase the heat and cook, stirring constantly, until all the liquid is evaporated and the carrot slices are coated with a shiny glaze. Season with salt and pepper, then transfer to a serving dish. Sprinkle with freshly grated nutmeg.

Carrot Purée

SERVES 10

Fragrant with Cointreau, this Carrot Purée makes a dramatic addition to the Thanksgiving Day menu.

3 pounds carrots, cut into
   1-inch lengths
¼ cup sugar
8 tablespoons butter
⅓ cup Cointreau
½ teaspoon salt
Generous pinch of cayenne
½ teaspoon ground mace

1. Place the carrots in a wide saucepan. Add the sugar and 2 tablespoons of the butter. Pour in enough water to cover the carrots by 1 inch. Bring to a gentle bubble and cook, uncovered, for 25 to 30 minutes or until the carrots are tender. Increase the heat and cook, stirring, until all the water is evaporated.

2. Transfer to the container of a blender or processor and whirl until smooth. Return the purée to the saucepan and stir in the Cointreau. Add the salt, cayenne, mace, and 4 tablespoons of the butter. Place over medium heat and stir until the butter is melted and absorbed. Mound in a serving bowl and place the remaining 2 tablespoons of butter in a depression in the center to melt.

Carrot Fritters

SERVES 4

2 large eggs
2 tablespoons milk
1 tablespoon sherry
½ teaspoon baking powder
½ teaspoon salt
Pinch of cayenne
1½ cups unseasoned bread
  crumbs
1 pound carrots, shredded
1 medium onion, shredded
  or coarsely chopped
Vegetable oil

These distinctive carrot patties make an excellent partner for baked ham.

1. In a large mixing bowl, beat together the eggs, milk, and sherry. Blend in the baking powder, salt, cayenne, and bread crumbs. Stir in the carrots and onion and blend well.

2. Spoon the mixture onto a hot griddle brushed with vegetable oil and press down with the back of the spoon to shape into patties. Cook for 2 to 3 minutes, turning once to brown both sides. Serve on a napkin-lined plate.

Carrot Fettuccine with Cream

SERVES 4

1 pound carrots (slim ones
  work best)
3 tablespoons vegetable oil
1 cup medium or whipping
  cream
½ cup heavy cream
Salt and freshly ground
  white pepper
Freshly grated nutmeg
½ cup freshly grated
  Parmesan cheese

A swivel-blade peeler is used to create thin shavings of carrot, which remarkably resemble fettuccine. Lightly sautéed and simmered in cream, they are served with a sprinkling of Parmesan cheese. Carrot Fettuccine is particularly good with baked chicken or fish.

1. Using long, firm strokes, apply a swivel-blade peeler down the length of each carrot. Allow the shavings to fall in a heap. (See illustration.)

2. Heat the oil in a large skillet. Add the carrots and toss to coat evenly. Stir over medium heat for about 1 minute. Pour on the medium cream and heavy cream. Bring it to a gentle bubble. Stirring occasionally, cook, uncovered, until the cream is reduced by half and the carrots are tender. Season with salt and pepper and sprinkle with nutmeg. Transfer to a serving plate and sprinkle with Parmesan cheese.

Run the swivel-blade peeler down the length of the carrot to create long, thin shavings of "fettuccine."

Carrot-Raisin Muffins

MAKES 1 DOZEN

2 cups all-purpose flour
½ cup granulated sugar
¼ cup light brown sugar
2 teaspoons baking powder
½ teaspoon salt
2 large eggs
½ cup vegetable oil
¼ cup milk
1 teaspoon orange extract
1½ cups grated carrots
(about ½ pound)
½ cup raisins

Offer these savory muffins in place of dinner rolls as part of a festive holiday meal.

1. Preheat the oven to 400°. Generously grease 12 muffin tins. Combine the flour, granulated sugar, brown sugar, baking powder, and salt in a large mixing bowl. Whisk to blend thoroughly.

2. In a separate bowl, beat together the eggs, oil, milk, and orange extract. Add to the dry ingredients and blend well. Stir in the carrots and raisins. Pour into the prepared muffin tins and bake for 20 to 25 minutes or until a wooden pick inserted in the center comes out clean.

Carrot and Date Squares

MAKES 2 DOZEN

¼ cup water
6 tablespoons butter, cut into chunks
1 cup all-purpose flour
1 cup sugar
½ teaspoon baking soda
¼ teaspoon salt
1 teaspoon ground cinnamon
¼ teaspoon freshly grated nutmeg
¼ teaspoon ground ginger
1 large egg, beaten
¼ cup buttermilk
½ teaspoon vanilla
1 cup shredded carrots
(about 2 to 3 carrots)
½ cup coarsely chopped dates

These tasty squares provide a healthful snack or lunch-box dessert. They are also delicious when served with a scoop of vanilla ice cream.

1. Preheat the oven to 375°. Generously grease an 11x7-inch baking dish. Place the water and butter in a small saucepan and heat until the butter is melted.

2. In a large mixing bowl, combine the flour, sugar, soda, and salt. Add the cinnamon, nutmeg, and ginger and whisk to blend thoroughly. Gradually stir in the water and melted butter. Then add the egg, buttermilk, and vanilla. Blend well.

3. Stir in the carrots and dates and pour into the prepared pan. Bake for 25 to 30 minutes or until a wooden pick inserted in the center comes out clean. Cool briefly on a rack and serve warm, or cool completely and cut into squares. (Dust the cooled squares with sifted confectioners' sugar, if desired.)

Carrot Graham Bread

MAKES 1 LOAF

2½ cups graham flour
1½ teaspoons baking powder
½ teaspoon baking soda
½ teaspoon salt
½ teaspoon ground cinnamon
½ teaspoon ground ginger
2 large eggs
½ cup honey
¼ cup vegetable oil
½ cup milk
2 cups shredded carrots (about 4 to 5 carrots)
½ cup chopped walnuts

Graham flour is actually a coarsely ground version of whole wheat flour. Ask for it in health-food shops or substitute whole wheat flour instead.

1. Preheat the oven to 375°. Generously grease a 9x5-inch loaf pan. Combine the flour, baking powder, soda, salt, cinnamon, and ginger in a large mixing bowl. Whisk to blend thoroughly.

2. In a separate bowl, beat together the eggs, honey, and oil. Stir in the milk. Add to the dry ingredients and blend well. Stir in the carrots and walnuts. Pour into the prepared pan and bake for 50 minutes to 1 hour or until a wooden pick inserted in the center comes out clean.

Individual Carrot Puddings

SERVES 6

Studded with golden raisins, these spicy, steamed puddings make a wonderful dessert for a fall meal.

1½ cups all-purpose flour
1½ teaspoons baking powder
½ teaspoon baking soda
½ teaspoon salt
1 teaspoon ground cinnamon
½ teaspoon freshly grated nutmeg
¼ teaspoon ground ginger
3 large eggs
½ cup butter, melted
1 teaspoon vanilla
½ cup light brown sugar
½ cup golden raisins
4 medium carrots, grated
1 apple, grated
Whipped cream

1. Preheat the oven to 350°. Generously butter 6 individual pudding molds or soufflé dishes. In a large mixing bowl, combine the flour, baking powder, soda, and salt. Add the cinnamon, nutmeg, and ginger and whisk to blend thoroughly.

2. In a separate bowl, beat the eggs, melted butter, and vanilla. Stir in the brown sugar and raisins. Add to the dry ingredients and blend well. Stir in the carrots and apple. Pour into the prepared molds and level the batter with the back of a spoon. Cover each mold with a square of buttered aluminum foil and place in a shallow roasting pan. Add hot water to the pan to the depth of 1 inch and bake for 45 to 50 minutes or until a wooden pick inserted in the center of the pudding comes out clean. Remove from the pan of water and allow to cool for 10 minutes. Run a knife around the perimeter of each mold, then invert the puddings onto individual plates. Serve warm, topped with lightly whipped cream.

Cassava (Cuh-SAH-vuh)

LIKE THE TRUE YAM, cassava is an irregularly shaped tuberous root with white starchy flesh. Its appearance is similar to that of a yam, except a cassava is somewhat longer and more narrow, and bears a deeper-colored, charcoal brown skin. It is an excellent source of complex carbohydrates. (See also Taro Root and Yams.)

There are many varieties of cassava, but all may be divided into two groups — sweet cassava and bitter cassava. Sweet cassava has a pleasantly bland flavor, and when cooked, it develops a consistency similar to that of Irish potato. In fact, sweet cassava may be prepared in any of the ways you might fix potato. Sweet cassava is the type most frequently sold in this country and is used in the recipes that follow.

Bitter cassava is widely used in Latin America, the Caribbean, and Africa. The interesting point is that bitter cassava contains enough prussic acid to prove fatal if the cassava is eaten raw. (Sweet cassava also contains this toxic acid, but not in such great amounts.) The prussic acid, therefore, must be either pressed out of the cassava flesh or rendered inactive by cooking the cassava root.

Sweet cassava is available all year, but it is rarely sold outside ethnic markets. Look in specialty food shops that cater to Latin American, Puerto Rican, or African cookery.

TO SELECT:

Choose a firm cassava that has no soft spots. Pass by any that are shriveled. The dark brown, barklike skin should feel dry and rough.

TO STORE:

Place a whole cassava in a cool, dry, well-ventilated place. It will keep for 2 to 3 weeks. Cut or peeled cassava should be wrapped in plastic film and stored in the refrigerator for no more than 3 days.

TO PREPARE:

Cassava is an all-purpose starchy tuber. It may be boiled and used in soups or stews in place of potato; it may be sliced and fried like potato chips; or it may be mashed and substituted for potato in recipes for baked goods.

Remove the tough outer skin by peeling the cassava with a paring knife under cool running water. To boil, cut the root into 2-inch chunks. Place in a nonreactive pot and add enough water to cover by 2 inches. Add the juice of 1 lemon and bring to a gentle boil. Cook for 30 to 40 minutes or until tender. Drain thoroughly. If you plan to serve this vegetable in chunks, check each piece and remove any woody core that may have existed in the center of the cassava. Otherwise, purée the flesh through a food mill, which will mash the cassava and eliminate the hairy fibers at the same time. Raw sweet cassava may be grated in a food processor (and then drained of its juice), but puréeing cooked cassava in a processor results in an overly gluey texture.

Cassava Cakes

Shredded cassava and onion are bound together with a light batter and fried like potato pancakes.

2 pounds sweet cassava, peeled and shredded
Juice of 1 lemon
6 large eggs
½ cup all-purpose flour
½ teaspoon salt
Freshly ground black pepper
1 medium onion, grated
1 garlic clove, pressed
Vegetable oil for frying

1. Place the shredded cassava in a large bowl and add enough cold water to cover by 1 inch. Stir in the lemon juice.

2. In a large mixing bowl, beat the eggs until foamy. Add the flour, salt, and pepper and blend until smooth. Stir in the onion and garlic.

3. Drain the cassava in a sieve, pressing down to extract most of the water. Distribute the drained cassava over a clean kitchen towel. Draw up the sides of the towel and squeeze to extract all the remaining traces of liquid. Add the cassava to the egg mixture and stir in.

4. Pour enough oil into a large skillet to cover the bottom of the pan. Place over medium-high heat. When the oil is hot, spoon in the mixture. Press down with the back of the spoon to form small cakes, about 1½ inches across. Fry on both sides until golden brown and drain on absorbent paper. Serve hot.

Spicy Cassava and Beef Stew

SERVES 6

1½ pounds sweet cassava, peeled and cut into 1-inch chunks
Vegetable oil for frying
1½ pounds lean, boneless beef, cut into 1-inch chunks
2 medium onions, coarsely chopped
1 garlic clove, minced
2 tablespoons all-purpose flour
1 teaspoon ground turmeric
3 cups beef broth
1 can (28 ounces) whole, peeled tomatoes, drained
Salt and freshly ground black pepper
1 cup coconut milk
4 green chilies, finely chopped
½ cup chopped fresh cilantro

Chunks of cassava simmer in an African-style beef stew, absorbing all the spicy flavors from the broth.

1. Drop the cassava into a large pot of boiling, salted water and cook, uncovered, for 15 to 20 minutes or until tender when pierced.

2. Meanwhile, heat a thin layer of oil in a large skillet or Dutch oven. Add half the beef and stir over high heat until nicely browned. Transfer to a plate and repeat the procedure with the remaining beef.

3. Add more oil to the pan if necessary, and stir in the onions and garlic. Cover the pan and cook over low heat until the onions are tender. Sprinkle on the flour and turmeric and increase the heat to medium. Stir continuously until the mixture foams. Pour in the beef broth. Return the beef to the pan and add the tomatoes, breaking them up with your fingers. Season with salt and pepper. Partially cover the pan and cook at a gentle bubble for 30 minutes.

4. Drain the cassava and add to the simmering mixture. Continue to cook, partially covered, for 30 to 45 minutes or until the beef is tender. Stir in the coconut milk, green chilies, and cilantro. Simmer until heated through, then serve piping hot.

Cauliflower

I'VE BEEN TOLD that 25 percent of all fresh cauliflower is sold during the months of October and November. I suppose this has to do with some notion of cauliflower as a fall vegetable. Actually, good-quality cauliflower can be found all year, and there are many delightful ways to serve it during the spring and summer. The trick, however, is to purchase only the freshest head, because prolonged storage gives cauliflower a strong cabbagy taste and smell. An excellent source of potassium, cauliflower also contains a moderate amount of vitamin C.

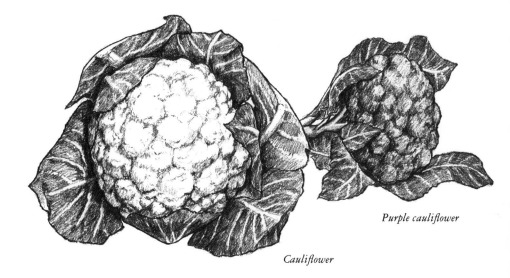

Purple cauliflower

Cauliflower

TO SELECT:

If possible, buy cauliflower nestled in a halo of crisp green-ery. This is not only a gorgeous sight, but it's also the best way to tell how fresh the cauliflower is. The creamy white head should be a mass of tightly packed flowerets. When you pick it up, it should feel heavy for its size and have a mild, pleasant smell. Reject cauliflower with wilted greens or whose white surface is marred by brown speckles.

Examine the surface of the cauliflower carefully, look-ing for an uncharacteristic smoothness that is made by the blade of a knife. It probably means someone along the way removed the brown spots that disclose the fact that the head has been stored too long. And don't attempt to economize by shopping at the bargain table. Old cauliflower is not worth buying at any price; it's bound to smell awful and taste even worse.

Cauliflower also comes wrapped loosely in clear plas-tic. In such instances, the head is usually trimmed of all its leaves, which is a disadvantage, because the crispness of the leaves is the only reliable indicator of freshness.

Occasionally, you may see purple cauliflower for sale. It is actually a cross between cauliflower and broccoli, and it possesses traits common to both. Its flowerets have longer stems with tough outer skin, like that on broccoli, which is best removed. Purple cauliflower tastes like cauliflower and loses its brilliant coloring when cooked.

The size of cauliflower is no help in gauging quality. Buy the size that you need, and because the density of this vegetable varies, it's better to rely on the diameter of the head rather than the weight. A medium, 7-inch head will feed 4 people.

TO STORE:

Since storage results in the development of a strong flavor and unpleasant odor, it is best to cook cauliflower as soon after purchase as possible. If necessary, you may refrigerate it unwashed for 1 or 2 days. Cauliflower bruises easily and needs oxygen, so wrap it gently and loosely with a sheet of plastic wrap. Above all, do not place it in a sealed plastic bag, because the humidity that accumulates inside will intensify the cabbagy character of cauliflower.

TO PREPARE:

Cut away the green leaves, if they are present, and discard them. Or set them aside to chop coarsely and then sauté, or to add to soup. If you plan to cook the head in one piece, place the whole cauliflower upside down in a large basin of warm salted water for 20 minutes to float away any insects. Rinse and pat the head dry, then transfer, core side up, to a soft kitchen towel folded into quarters. Using a paring knife, cut down and around the center core so you can lift it out. This will enable the center of the head to cook evenly.

To cook as flowerets, take the head apart by snapping the individual flowerets away from the center core. Rinse under cold running water and pat dry. Cut the largest flowerets in half, and trim off any portion of the center core that may still be attached. The flowerets of cauliflower have very short stems that are usually quite tender, but don't hesitate to apply a swivel-blade peeler to an occasional stem that looks like it might have tough skin.

Snap off individual flowerets from the central core of the cauliflower.

Flowerets may be crisped in ice water and served raw, but some cooks prefer to temper their flavor by blanching them for 30 seconds, or by placing them in a bowl and covering them with boiling water. After 10 minutes, they should be rinsed under cold running water. Raw or blanched flowerets may be stir-fried, coated with batter and deep-fried, pickled, or combined with a sauce and then baked. Flowerets may also be steamed, boiled, or microwaved until tender, and then served as is or puréed.

A whole head of cauliflower may be steamed, boiled, or microwaved and presented with a sauce. But whatever method you choose, avoid cooking cauliflower past the crisp-tender stage. Excessive cooking makes it mushy and waterlogged, and gives it an assertive cabbagy taste.

Cream of Cauliflower Soup   SERVES 6

Even if you think you don't like cauliflower, give this soup a try. The mild, engaging flavor will surprise you and just might change your mind.

4 tablespoons butter
3 tablespoons all-purpose flour
Salt to taste
Pinch of cayenne
6 cups chicken broth
1 medium cauliflower, divided into flowerets
2 tablespoons lemon juice
1 cup medium or whipping cream

1. Melt the butter in a large saucepan. Blend in the flour, salt, and cayenne and stir over medium heat until the mixture foams. Stir in the chicken broth and bring to a boil. Add the cauliflower and reduce the heat. Cover and cook at a gentle bubble for 20 minutes or until the cauliflower is tender. Lift out 6 of the most attractive flowerets and set aside. Stir in the lemon juice.

2. Transfer to the container of a blender or processor and whirl until smooth. Return to the saucepan and blend in the cream. Place over medium heat and warm gently, but do not allow the soup to boil. Ladle into soup bowls and garnish with the reserved flowerets.

Curried Cauliflower   SERVES 6 TO 8

Serve these flowerets as a summer salad or an appetizer.

1 medium cauliflower
3 tablespoons vegetable oil
½ teaspoon ground turmeric
½ teaspoon ground cumin
½ teaspoon ground coriander
½ teaspoon salt
Pinch of cayenne
1 tablespoon minced fresh ginger
½ cup water
1 medium tomato, peeled, seeded, and chopped
2 tablespoons chopped fresh parsley

1. Separate the cauliflower into flowerets and set aside.

2. Heat the oil in a large skillet. Add the turmeric, cumin, and coriander. Stir over medium heat until the spices are aromatic. Stir in the salt, cayenne, and ginger. Add the cauliflower and toss to coat. Pour on the water and cover the pan. Reduce the heat and simmer for 8 to 10 minutes or until the cauliflower is crisp-tender.

3. Increase the heat. Add the tomato and parsley and stir continuously until most of the liquid is evaporated. Transfer to a large bowl. Cover the bowl and chill thoroughly before serving.

Cauliflower Slaw

SERVES 6

1 medium cauliflower
4 ribs celery, coarsely
  chopped
4 green onions, white and
  green portion, coarsely
  chopped
1 cup sour cream
3 tablespoons white vinegar
1 teaspoon Dijon mustard
½ teaspoon salt
Freshly ground black
  pepper
1 teaspoon dried chervil

Raw, shredded cauliflower, mixed with coarsely chopped celery and green onions, is tossed with a sour cream dressing. Serve in place of coleslaw as part of a picnic supper.

1. Separate the cauliflower into flowerets. Shred the flowerets with a food processor or slice them thinly and cut into narrow strips. Transfer to a large salad bowl. Add the celery and onions and toss to combine.

2. In a small bowl, whisk together the sour cream, vinegar, mustard, salt, and pepper. Stir in the chervil. Pour over the cauliflower mixture and toss to coat evenly. Cover the bowl and refrigerate until thoroughly chilled.

Chilled Cauliflower with Lemon

SERVES 4 TO 6

Flowerets of cauliflower are cooked until crisp-tender and chilled in a garlic marinade. Just before serving, a creamy lemon dressing is applied.

1 medium cauliflower
2 tablespoons white wine
  vinegar
1 teaspoon Dijon mustard
6 tablespoons olive oil
1 garlic clove, minced
¾ cup sour cream
3 tablespoons lemon juice
2 tablespoons finely
  chopped lemon zest
¼ teaspoon salt
Freshly ground white
  pepper

1. Separate the cauliflower into flowerets and drop them into a large pot of boiling, salted water. Cook, uncovered, at a gentle bubble for 5 to 8 minutes or until crisp-tender. Or microwave the flowerets by placing them in a covered casserole with ¼ cup of water, then cooking them on high power for 4 to 6 minutes. Drain the cooked cauliflower in a colander set under cold running water. Shake gently to remove as much water as possible and transfer to a large bowl.

2. In a small bowl, blend together the vinegar and mustard. Whisk in the olive oil and add the garlic. Pour over the cauliflower and toss to coat. Cover the bowl with plastic wrap and refrigerate until thoroughly chilled. Stir occasionally to promote even marinating.

3. Just before serving, stir together the sour cream, lemon juice, 1 tablespoon of the lemon zest, the salt, and pepper. Drain the cauliflower and gently combine with the dressing. Sprinkle on the remaining tablespoon of lemon zest and serve.

Stir-Fried Cauliflower with Ham

Blanched flowerets are stir-fried with ginger and tossed with thin strips of smoked ham. Serve as a salad course or for a light supper.

1 medium cauliflower
½ cup chicken broth
1 teaspoon cornstarch
1 tablespoon sherry
1 tablespoon soy sauce
1 teaspoon oyster sauce
Several drops of Tabasco
  sauce
3 tablespoons vegetable oil
1 tablespoon minced fresh
  ginger
4 green onions, white and
  green portion, sliced
4 ounces sliced smoked
  ham, such as
  Westphalian, cut into
  julienne strips

1. Separate the cauliflower into flowerets and drop them into a large pot of boiling, salted water. Cook, uncovered, at a gentle bubble for 3 to 4 minutes or until partially tender. Drain in a colander set under cold running water. Drain thoroughly, and scatter the flowerets over absorbent paper to air-dry.

2. In a small bowl, combine the chicken broth and the cornstarch and stir to dissolve. Blend in the sherry, soy sauce, oyster sauce, and Tabasco. Set aside.

3. Heat the oil in a wok or large skillet. Add the ginger and stir briefly over high heat. Add the cauliflower and onions and stir continuously over high heat until the onions are wilted.

4. Pour on the chicken broth mixture and stir until it bubbles and thickens. Sprinkle on the ham and stir to incorporate. Serve immediately.

Cauliflower with Chive Butter

Fresh chives are a lively complement to the flavor of steamed cauliflower.

1 medium cauliflower
6 tablespoons butter
2 tablespoons lemon juice
½ teaspoon dry mustard
¼ teaspoon salt
Pinch of cayenne
1 tablespoon chopped fresh
  chives

1. Separate the cauliflower into flowerets. Place them in a basket set over boiling water and steam the cauliflower for 20 to 30 minutes or until crisp-tender.

2. Meanwhile, combine the butter, lemon juice, mustard, salt, and cayenne in a small saucepan. Heat until the butter melts. Stir to blend and add the chives.

3. Transfer the steamed cauliflower to a serving bowl and pour on the chive butter. Serve immediately.

Cauliflower and Ziti with Anchovies

1 medium cauliflower
3 tablespoons white wine
  vinegar
½ teaspoon salt
1 teaspoon dried oregano
1 shallot, minced
1 garlic clove, minced or
  pressed
1 tablespoon capers,
  drained
1 can (2 ounces) flat
  anchovy fillets
½ cup olive oil
½ pound ziti, boiled and
  drained
1 red bell pepper, cut into
  narrow strips
12 ripe black olives, pitted
  and sliced
1 tablespoon chopped fresh
  basil
1 tablespoon chopped fresh
  parsley

Strips of red bell pepper and sliced black olives lend vivid color to this cold pasta salad.

1. Separate the cauliflower into flowerets and drop them into a large pot of boiling, salted water. Cook, uncovered, at a gentle bubble for 5 to 8 minutes or until crisp-tender. Drain in a colander set under cold running water. Shake gently to remove as much water as possible, then set aside.

2. In a small mixing bowl, combine the vinegar, salt, and oregano. Stir in the shallot, garlic, and capers. Coarsely chop 4 of the anchovies and blend in. Gradually whisk in the oil.

3. Transfer the cauliflower to a large bowl. Add the drained ziti, red bell pepper, olives, basil, and parsley. Mix together. Pour on the dressing and toss to coat. Transfer to a serving plate lined with lettuce and garnish with additional anchovies if you wish.

Baked Cauliflower with Cheddar Cheese

SERVES 4

Sharp Cheddar cheese lends zest to an all-American favorite.

1 medium cauliflower
1 cup medium or whipping
  cream
2 large egg yolks
1 teaspoon Dijon mustard
½ teaspoon Worcestershire
  sauce
Salt to taste
Pinch of cayenne
4 ounces sharp Cheddar
  cheese, grated
2 tablespoons butter
4 soda crackers, crushed

1. Separate the cauliflower into flowerets and drop them into a large pot of boiling, salted water. Cook, uncovered, at a gentle bubble for 8 to 10 minutes or until crisp-tender. Drain in a colander and transfer to a large mixing bowl.

2. Preheat the oven to 350° and generously butter a shallow baking dish. In a small bowl, whisk together the cream, egg yolks, mustard, Worcestershire sauce, salt, and cayenne. Stir in the Cheddar cheese.

3. Melt the butter in a small skillet and add the soda crackers. Toss to coat evenly and set aside. Pour the cheese sauce over the cauliflower and stir to coat. Transfer to the prepared baking dish. Sprinkle on the buttered crumbs and bake for 35 to 45 minutes or until the sauce is bubbly and the crumbs are nicely browned.

Cauliflower Timbales

Parmesan cheese and nutmeg add subtle flavoring to these individual cauliflower custards. Serve as an accompaniment to roast beef or turkey.

1 medium cauliflower
4 large eggs
½ cup medium or whipping cream
½ teaspoon salt
Freshly ground white pepper
½ cup freshly grated Parmesan cheese
Freshly grated nutmeg

1. Separate the cauliflower into flowerets and drop them into a large pot of boiling, salted water. Cook, uncovered, at a gentle bubble for 8 to 10 minutes or until crisp-tender. Drain in a colander set under cold running water. Shake gently to remove as much water as possible, then transfer to the container of a blender or processor. Whirl until smooth. Measure out 1 cup of purée, reserving any that is left for another use.

2. Preheat the oven to 375° and generously butter 8 timbale or individual soufflé molds. In a large mixing bowl, whisk together the eggs and cream. Stir in the salt, pepper, and Parmesan cheese. Add the cauliflower purée and blend thoroughly. Pour into the prepared molds and cover each mold with a piece of buttered aluminum foil. Set the molds in a shallow roasting pan and add hot water to a depth of 1 inch. Bake for 25 to 30 minutes or until the blade of a knife inserted in the center comes out clean. Remove from the pan of water and allow the timbales to cool for 5 minutes. Run a knife around the perimeter of each mold and turn out. Generously sprinkle the top of each timbale with freshly grated nutmeg.

Celeriac (suh-LAIR-ee-ak)

I'M CONVINCED that people avoid this vegetable because it is so ugly. Certainly all but the most adventurous would be turned away by celeriac's gnarled, hairy appearance. Yet underneath its brown, knobby exterior is a crunchy, smooth white flesh similar to that of a raw potato. Celeriac is frequently called celery root, a practice that has led to some confusion: celeriac is not the root of the common celery plant, but rather an entirely separate vegetable. Celeriac is grown specifically for its edible root, and although it is a member of the celery family, its aboveground shoots consist of a skimpy bunch of undeveloped stems. Celeriac is available from October to April and is a good source of potassium.

TO SELECT:

Celeriac is sold both with and without its green stems. If the stems are present, their condition is a clue to the freshness of the root. Certain types of celeriac are quite hairy, and others

bear just a few straggly rootlets. Choose the smoothest celeriac you can find because those with convoluted, hairy skin are the most difficult to peel and result in the most waste. The best size to select is 8 to 10 ounces (or 3 to 4 inches in diameter); larger roots have a pithy fibrous core that must be discarded. Look for firm, dry celeriac and avoid any that feel spongy or light in weight for their size. Plan on purchasing 6 ounces per serving.

TO STORE: Because the green stems will continue to draw moisture from the root if left attached, trim them off when you get the celeriac home. Enclose the unwashed root in plastic wrap and refrigerate for no more than 1 week.

TO PREPARE: The trickiest thing about celeriac is its propensity for turning dark. Exposed surfaces must be covered immediately by acidulated water (3 tablespoons of lemon juice to 1 quart of water), so be sure to have this ready before you begin preparing the vegetable. Scrub the celeriac with a stiff brush under cool running water. Then cut the root into quarters and peel each quarter with a sharp knife. You may also use a swivel-blade peeler to shave away any pitted areas that lie under the skin. Drop the peeled celeriac into the acidulated water until the time for final preparation.

For dishes in which the celeriac is to be cooked, it is easier to boil the root without peeling it first. The heat deactivates most of the enzymes that can cause discoloration and softens the skin, making it less difficult to remove.

With its crisp, juicy texture and pronounced celery taste, celeriac is delicious served raw. Just be sure to keep the exposed flesh covered at all times with acidulated water, a dressing, or a sauce. Celeriac is also delightful when cooked. It may be boiled and treated in much the same way as the potato — mashed, sliced and baked au gratin, or cubed and sautéed in butter. It may also be added to soups and stews, or puréed to form a soup of its own.

Celeriac Pâté

Slices of this delicious pâté are topped with lemony yogurt.

4 medium celeriacs,
  unpeeled
2 large eggs, separated
½ cup medium or whipping
  cream
½ teaspoon salt
Freshly ground white
  pepper
4 ounces Gruyère cheese,
  grated
1 cup unflavored yogurt
3 tablespoons lemon juice
1 tablespoon chopped fresh
  parsley

1. Drop the celeriacs into a large pot of boiling, salted water and cook, uncovered, at a gentle bubble for 30 minutes or until tender when pierced. Drain in a colander. When cool enough to handle, peel the celeriac and cut into quarters. Place the quarters in the container of a blender or processor and whirl until smooth.

2. Preheat the oven to 350° and generously butter a glass 9 x 5-inch loaf pan. In a large mixing bowl, combine the celeriac purée, egg yolks, cream, salt, and pepper. Beat until well blended. Stir in the Gruyère cheese.

3. In a separate bowl, whip the egg whites until soft peaks form, then fold into the celeriac mixture. Pour into the prepared pan and cover the pan with aluminum foil. Bake for 40 to 45 minutes or until the blade of a knife inserted in the center comes out clean. Allow to cool for 5 minutes. Unmold onto a serving plate and serve warm. Or cover the pâté with plastic wrap and chill lightly. Just before serving, blend together the yogurt, lemon juice, and parsley. Spoon a dollop of the mixture on top of each slice of pâté.

Cream of Celeriac Soup

4 tablespoons butter
1 medium onion, coarsely
  chopped
2 leeks, white portion only,
  thinly sliced
4 medium celeriacs
4 cups chicken broth
½ cup coarsely chopped
  blanched almonds
¼ teaspoon ground mace
2 tablespoons lemon juice
Salt and freshly ground
  white pepper
½ cup medium or whipping
  cream

Blanched almonds are simmered gently in the liquid, then puréed to lend body to this rich, creamy soup.

1. Melt the butter in a large saucepan. Add the onion and leeks and toss to coat. Cover the pan and cook over low heat until tender. Meanwhile, peel and cut the celeriac into chunks. Pour the chicken broth into the pan. Add the celeriac and the almonds. Cover the pan and simmer for 20 minutes or until the celeriac is tender. Transfer to the container of a blender or processor and whirl until smooth.

2. Return the purée to the saucepan and blend in the mace and lemon juice. Season with salt and pepper and gradually stir in the cream. Place over medium heat and warm gently, but do not allow the soup to boil. Serve immediately.

Celeriac and Red Pepper Salad

SERVES 4

½ cup olive oil
3 tablespoons white wine vinegar
1 garlic clove, minced or pressed
1 teaspoon sugar
1 tablespoon coriander seed
½ teaspoon salt
Freshly ground black pepper
3 medium celeriacs
1 red bell pepper, cut into julienne strips
½ cup mayonnaise, preferably homemade

Shredded celeriac and strips of red bell pepper are chilled in a coriander marinade, then dressed with a spicy mayonnaise.

1. In a small saucepan, combine the oil, vinegar, garlic, sugar, coriander seed, salt, and pepper. Simmer, uncovered, for 10 minutes. Remove from the heat and pour into a large bowl. Allow to cool to room temperature.

2. Peel and shred the celeriacs and immediately transfer to the cooled mixture. Toss to coat evenly. Mix in the red bell pepper. Cover the bowl and refrigerate for 4 to 6 hours to marinate.

3. Using a slotted spoon, transfer the celeriacs and bell pepper to another mixing bowl. Strain the liquid that remains behind and then blend as much of it with the mayonnaise as needed to make a thin, creamy dressing. Pour over the vegetables, toss to coat, and serve.

Celeriac with Two-Mustard Sauce

SERVES 8

Smooth Dijon and grainy Pommery mustards unite to form a dramatic dressing for lightly cooked strips of celeriac.

4 medium celeriacs, unpeeled
¾ cup mayonnaise, preferably homemade
¾ cup sour cream
⅓ cup Dijon mustard
¼ cup Pommery whole-grain mustard
1 teaspoon sugar
3 tablespoons lemon juice
1 teaspoon dried tarragon
Salt and freshly ground white pepper

1. Drop the celeriacs into a large pot of boiling, salted water and cook, uncovered, at a gentle bubble for 20 minutes or until crisp-tender. Drain in a colander. When cool enough to handle, peel the celeriacs and slice thinly. Cut the slices into julienne strips and transfer to a large bowl.

2. In a small bowl, whisk together the mayonnaise, sour cream, Dijon mustard, and Pommery mustard. Blend in the sugar, lemon juice, and tarragon.

3. Sprinkle the celeriac with salt and pepper to taste. Then pour on the mustard mixture and toss to coat evenly. Cover the bowl and chill thoroughly. Spoon onto glass salad plates to serve.

Purée of Celeriac

SERVES 4

Smooth, rich celeriac purée makes a sophisticated partner for roast game hens or quail.

3 medium celeriacs
3 tablespoons butter, cut into pieces
2 tablespoons dark rum
¼ teaspoon freshly grated nutmeg
¼ teaspoon ground cloves
Salt and freshly ground white pepper
⅓ cup heavy cream (approximately)

1. Preheat the oven to 350°. Generously butter an ovenproof serving dish. Peel and quarter the celeriacs and drop them into a large pot of boiling, salted water. Cook, uncovered, at a gentle bubble for 20 minutes or until tender. Force through a food mill, allowing the purée to fall into a large bowl.

2. Add the butter and stir until melted. Blend in the rum, nutmeg, cloves, salt, and pepper. Gradually stir in as much of the cream as necessary to form a smooth, thick purée. Pour into the prepared dish and bake for 10 to 15 minutes to warm through.

Celery

ONE OF THE MOST common misunderstandings in culinary terminology has to do with celery. Celery emerges from the ground as a clump of tall stems with leafy tops. In some parts of the country, this clump is called a stalk, a bunch, or a head of celery. The individual stems should be referred to as ribs and should not be confused with the term "stalks."

TO SELECT:

Most supermarkets offer two types of celery year round — Pascal (also called green celery) and celery hearts (often called white celery). Pascal celery has long, tightly curved ribs that form loose bunches. It is usually sold untrimmed, sporting bright green, leafy tops. Pascal celery has a full-bodied flavor and possesses a crunchy, refreshing succulence when thoroughly chilled. Celery hearts, which are often sold in plastic bags, have shorter, wider, more open ribs. They bear pale yellowish green leaves that, for the most part, are removed before packaging. Celery hearts have a mild flavor,

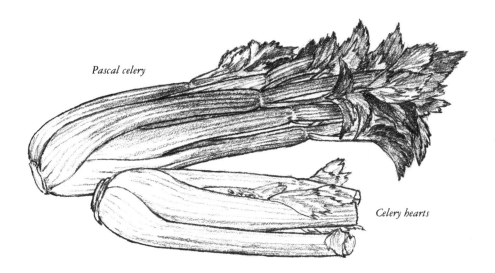

Pascal celery

Celery hearts

and a less juicy texture. In purchasing either type, look for full bunches of firm, unblemished stalks, selecting those that feel heavy for their size. One pound will serve 4 people as a vegetable side dish.

TO STORE:

Because celery needs to be protected from moisture loss, it's important to place it in an airtight plastic bag. Stored in the coldest section of the refrigerator, celery will keep this way for as long as 2 weeks.

TO PREPARE:

Separate the ribs and rinse under cool running water. Cut off the leafy tops, reserving them to use as a flavoring. Trim the base of the ribs. To remove the strings, position a paring knife parallel to the rib at the leaf end and make a shallow cut in the back of the rib. Lifting the knife toward you, pull the strings away from the rib. You may also remove the

Make a shallow cut in the back of the rib of celery and, lifting the knife toward you, pull the strings away from the rib.

strings by peeling the backs of the ribs with a swivel-blade peeler.

Celery may be braised, baked, microwaved, stir-fried, or simmered and then puréed. It may also be eaten raw. The leaves can be chopped and used in the same manner as chopped parsley — to flavor soups, stews, salads, casseroles, or stuffings. Since the inner ribs are more tender and delicately flavored, these are the best ones to serve raw; the outer ribs, which have a stronger flavor, are the ones to use in cooked preparations. When adding sliced celery to cold salads, such as tuna or shrimp, keep in mind that Pascal celery exudes more liquid than celery hearts, and thus can cause your salad to develop a watery consistency.

Celery Stuffed with Shrimp Pâté

SERVES 8

Ribs of Pascal celery are stuffed and then pressed together to re-form a bunch. When well chilled, the bunch is cut into slices and served as an appetizer or first course.

2 bunches Pascal celery
12 ounces shrimp, cooked, peeled, and deveined
4 ounces cream cheese, softened
4 tablespoons butter
2 tablespoons lemon juice
½ teaspoon Worcestershire sauce
½ teaspoon salt
¼ teaspoon sweet paprika

1. Separate the ribs of celery and select 9 of the greenest, most well-formed ribs, reserving the rest for another use. Cut off the wide ends and remove the strings from the ribs. Set aside.

2. In the container of a blender or processor, combine the shrimp, cream cheese, butter, lemon juice, Worcestershire sauce, salt, and paprika. Whirl until smooth. The consistency should be stiff, but soft enough to spread. If the mixture is too soft, refrigerate for 1 to 2 hours.

3. Spread some of the shrimp pâté into the cavities of each celery rib. Fill the ribs from one end to the other. Take up 3 of the stuffed ribs and press them together to resemble a bunch of celery. Add on the remaining 6 ribs, pressing them onto the bunch. As you work, fill in any openings with the remaining shrimp pâté.

4. Tightly wrap the re-formed bunch in plastic wrap and refrigerate for 12 hours or overnight. Just before serving, cut the bunch crosswise into 1-inch-thick slices. Arrange each slice on a plate with a few leaves of mâche or raw spinach.

Chilled Celery Bisque

6 tablespoons butter
2 bunches Pascal celery,
  plus the leaves, coarsely
  chopped
2 medium leeks, white and
  light green portion, thinly
  sliced
6 green onions, white and
  green portion, thinly
  sliced
2 cups water
4 cups chicken broth
1 tablespoon chopped fresh
  tarragon
Salt and freshly ground
  black pepper
½ cup heavy cream
2 tablespoons lemon juice
Sprigs of celery leaves for
  garnish

The captivating flavor of celery transforms this chilled soup into elegant fare.

1. Melt the butter in a wide saucepan. Add the celery, leeks, and onions and toss to coat evenly. Cover the pan and cook over low heat for 20 minutes or until the vegetables are tender.

2. Pour in the water and chicken broth. Add the tarragon and season with salt and pepper. Bring to a gentle bubble and cook, uncovered, for 10 minutes or until the vegetables are soft enough to mash against the side of the pan. Transfer to the container of a blender or processor and whirl until smooth. Pour into a large bowl and blend in the cream. Cover the bowl and refrigerate until thoroughly chilled.

3. Just before serving, stir in the lemon juice and pour into glass soup bowls. Garnish with sprigs of celery leaves if you wish.

Italian Celery Salad

2 bunches Pascal celery,
  sliced
2 red bell peppers, roasted
  (see page 254), then cut
  into thin strips
4 ounces provolone cheese,
  cut into thin strips
1 tablespoon chopped fresh
  basil
1 tablespoon chopped fresh
  parsley
6 tablespoons olive oil
2 tablespoons red wine
  vinegar
½ teaspoon salt
Pinch of cayenne
3 eggs, hard-boiled and then
  sliced

A colorful mélange of green celery, red bell peppers, and pale yellow cheese. Serve as an appetizer or as an accompaniment to grilled hamburgers.

1. In a large salad bowl, combine the celery, roasted red bell peppers, and provolone cheese. Sprinkle on the basil and parsley and toss to combine.

2. In a small bowl, whisk together the oil, vinegar, salt, and cayenne. Pour over the salad and toss to coat. Cover the bowl and chill for 2 to 3 hours. Just before serving, toss again, then arrange the egg slices around the perimeter of the salad bowl.

Celery Hearts in Raspberry Cream SERVES 4

Raspberry vinegar contributes complementary flavor tones and paprika adds a faint pink blush to the creamy dressing that accompanies this chilled braised celery.

2 bunches celery hearts
1 cup chicken broth
½ teaspoon salt
½ teaspoon dried thyme
4 black peppercorns
1 bay leaf, broken in half
3 tablespoons raspberry
   vinegar
½ teaspoon sweet paprika
3 tablespoons vegetable oil
¾ cup heavy cream
2 tablespoons chopped
   fresh parsley for garnish

1. Generously butter a wide, flameproof casserole dish. Trim the bottoms of the celery and remove any coarse outer ribs, but leave the bunches intact. Cut off the leafy ends so that each bunch measures 6 inches long. Cut each bunch in half lengthwise and transfer, cut side down, to the prepared baking dish.

2. Add the celery leaves and trimmings to the dish. Pour on the chicken broth and add as much water as necessary to cover the celery. Add the salt, thyme, peppercorns, and bay leaf to the liquid. Cover and cook at a gentle bubble for 10 to 12 minutes or until the celery is crisp-tender. Lift out with a perforated spatula and arrange on a flat serving plate. Cover tightly with plastic wrap and chill.

3. In a small bowl, blend together the vinegar and paprika. Whisk in the oil until well combined. Whisk in the cream. Pour the dressing around the celery and sprinkle the chopped parsley across the center of the ribs.

Braised Celery SERVES 4

Quartered celery bunches are braised on a bed of aromatic vegetables, then sauced and topped with buttered crumbs.

2 bunches celery hearts
4 slices bacon
1 medium onion, coarsely
   chopped
2 medium carrots, coarsely
   chopped
3 cups chicken broth
1 tablespoon all-purpose
   flour
3 tablespoons butter,
   softened
Salt and freshly ground
   white pepper
⅓ cup unseasoned bread
   crumbs

1. Trim the bottoms of the celery and remove any coarse outer ribs, but leave the bunches intact. Cut off the leafy ends so that each bunch measures 6 inches long. Cut each bunch lengthwise into quarters. Coarsely chop the celery trimmings and set aside.

2. Preheat the oven to 375°. In a Dutch oven or flameproof casserole, fry the bacon until crisp. Drain on absorbent paper and reserve for another use. Add the onion, carrots, and celery trimmings to the bacon fat and cook, stirring, until the onion is limp. Remove from the heat and arrange the celery quarters over the vegetables. Pour on the chicken broth and cover the pan. Bake for 25 to 30 minutes or until the celery is tender and the aromatic vegetables are soft. *(continued)*

3. Using a perforated spatula, transfer the celery to a shallow baking dish. Pour the cooking liquid and vegetables into the container of a blender or processor and whirl until smooth. Return it to the pan and place over high heat. Make a paste of the flour and 1 tablespoon of the butter. Bring the liquid to a boil and whisk in the flour mixture a little at a time. Season with salt and pepper and cook until slightly thickened. Pour over the celery.

4. Melt the remaining 2 tablespoons of butter in a small skillet and add the bread crumbs, tossing to coat evenly. Scatter the buttered crumbs over the celery. Slide the baking dish under the broiler and cook until the crumbs are nicely browned. Serve while bubbling hot.

Chayote (shy-OH-tay)

IT SEEMS THAT no other vegetable goes by so many different names — Australians call it chokos, inhabitants of the Caribbean Islands know it as christophene, and residents of Louisiana refer to it as mirliton, although in most other parts of the United States, this squash is labeled chayote.

Firm textured, chayote is extremely mild in flavor, and thus exceptionally versatile. Chayote appears in recipes of several divergent cuisines, including Mexican and Chinese. Frequently, its chief function is to provide textural contrast, because chayote retains its crisp character even when cooked. Peeled and simmered in a zesty sauce, slices of chayote readily absorb companion flavors.

TO SELECT:

There are several varieties of chayote. Consequently, you may find these squash to be pear shaped or rounded, furrowed or not, smooth skinned or slightly spiny. They may vary in color from white to pale yellow-green to dark green. Chayotes are available weighing as much as 2 pounds, but the smaller 6- to 8-ounce size will be more tender. Choose hard squash of uniform color, and avoid those with soft spots or bruises. Chayotes appear in the market from October to April.

TO STORE:	Like winter squash, uncut chayote can be kept in a cool, dark place for 3 to 4 weeks as long as the storage area is well ventilated. They may also be refrigerated, but because humidity hastens deterioration, use them within 1 to 2 weeks.
TO PREPARE:	Because the flesh of chayote is so bland, the best way to preserve its limited flavor is to boil, steam, or microwave the squash whole and unpeeled. When a skewer slides in easily, the chayote is cooked. You may then cool the squash by submerging it in cold water. When it is cool enough to handle, peel away the skin. Cut in half and remove the large elliptical seed. (You will usually find that a sharp knife easily cuts through the seed. In fact, the cooked seed, because it is edible and fairly soft, is sometimes mashed and used as a part of the filling in recipes for stuffed, baked mirliton.) Chayote may also be peeled raw and sliced or cut into chunks. This method is used in recipes in which the squash is expected to take on the flavor of other ingredients.

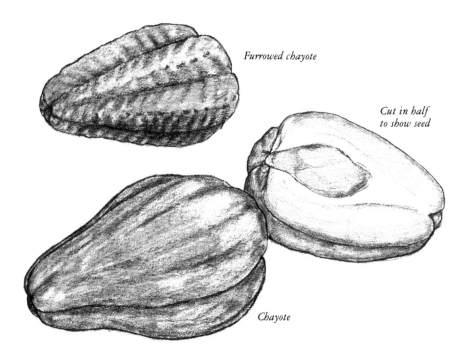

Furrowed chayote

*Cut in half
to show seed*

Chayote

Chayote Salad with Lime Vinaigrette

SERVES 4

Partially cooked slices of chayote are marinated in a lime dressing sparked with cilantro, then served atop crisp spinach leaves.

2 small chayotes (about 6 ounces each)
6 tablespoons olive oil
2 tablespoons lime juice
1 garlic clove, minced
½ teaspoon salt
½ teaspoon crushed red pepper
1 tablespoon chopped fresh cilantro
12 leaves raw spinach

1. Cut the chayotes in half lengthwise. Your knife will easily slice through the nutlike seed. Remove the seeds and any whitish membrane, then peel. Cut each chayote half into 6 long slices (as you would an avocado). Place the slices in a wide saucepan and add enough water to cover by 1 inch. Set over high heat and bring to a boil. Cook, uncovered, at a gentle bubble for 5 minutes. Drain in a colander set under cold running water and distribute over absorbent paper to drain.

2. Whisk together the oil, lime juice, garlic, salt, and red pepper. Stir in the cilantro. Place the chayote slices in a large bowl. Pour on the dressing and toss gently to coat. Cover the bowl and refrigerate for 4 to 6 hours or until thoroughly chilled.

3. Just before serving, arrange 3 spinach leaves on each of 4 salad plates, then arrange 6 slices of chayote on top of the spinach leaves. Whisk the dressing that remains in the bowl and pour it over the salads.

Sautéed Chayote with Parmesan Cheese

SERVES 4

Small chunks of cooked chayote are sautéed in butter and tossed with grated Parmesan cheese. Serve as a vegetable side dish with grilled veal chops.

3 small chayotes (about 6 ounces each)
4 tablespoons butter
Salt and freshly ground black pepper
⅓ cup freshly grated Parmesan cheese
1 tablespoon chopped fresh parsley

1. Drop the chayotes into a large pot of boiling, salted water and cook, uncovered, at a gentle bubble for 30 minutes or until tender when pierced. Lift out with a slotted spoon and submerge in cold water.

2. When the chayotes are cool enough to handle, cut them in half lengthwise and remove the peel. Remove the seeds and any whitish membrane. Cut each chayote half into small chunks.

3. Melt the butter in a large skillet and add the chayote, tossing to coat evenly. Season with salt and pepper. Sprinkle on the Parmesan cheese and parsley. Stir over medium heat until warmed through and serve at once.

Baked Stuffed Chayote

Chayote shells are stuffed with a flavorful ground-beef filling and baked until piping hot. Serve as a main course with a tossed green salad.

4 small chayotes (about 6 ounces each)
4 slices bacon, cut into ½-inch pieces
2 ribs celery, coarsely chopped
1 medium onion, coarsely chopped
1 green bell pepper, coarsely chopped
1 garlic clove, minced or pressed
1 pound ground beef
1 can (28 ounces) Italian tomatoes, undrained
1 teaspoon dried oregano
Salt and freshly ground black pepper
4 ounces Monterey Jack cheese, grated
1 large egg
½ cup unseasoned bread crumbs

1. Drop the chayotes into a large pot of boiling, salted water and cook, uncovered, at a gentle bubble for 30 minutes or until tender when pierced. Lift out with a slotted spoon and submerge in cold water.

2. When the chayotes are cool enough to handle, cut them in half lengthwise. Remove the seeds and any whitish membrane. Scoop out the chayote flesh, leaving the shells about ¼-inch thick. Coarsely chop the chayote flesh and set aside.

3. Fry the bacon until crisp. Transfer it to absorbent paper to drain. Add the celery, onion, green bell pepper, and garlic to the bacon fat, tossing to coat. Stir over medium heat until the onion is wilted. Add the ground beef and continue cooking until the beef is no longer pink. Stir in the tomatoes and chopped chayotes. Add the oregano, salt, and pepper. Cook over medium heat until all the liquid is evaporated and the mixture begins to stick to the bottom of the pan. Transfer to a large bowl and immediately stir in the bacon and two-thirds of the Monterey Jack cheese.

4. Preheat the oven to 350°. Generously butter a shallow baking dish. In a separate bowl, beat the egg and stir in the bread crumbs. Add the beef mixture and blend well. Spoon into the chayote shells. Distribute the remaining cheese over the tops and place in the prepared baking dish. Bake, uncovered, for 20 to 30 minutes or until the tops are nicely browned.

Chicory

IF YOU'VE EVER been confused about which vegetable is chicory and which vegetable is endive, you're not alone. (See also Belgian Endive.) Chicory, in most parts of the United States, is the name given to a loose-headed salad green with curly-edged leaves. Its appearance accounts for the fact that it is also referred to as curly endive. To complicate matters further, chicory is known in Europe as endive, and the vegetable we call Belgian endive is known there as Brussels chicory.

Ready to give up and eat spinach? The botanical title, *Cicorium endivia,* names a category of greens that consists of two different types — the curly, narrow-leafed chicory, and a broader-leafed green called escarole or Batavian endive. (Belgian endive belongs to a separate category known as *Cicorium intybus.*)

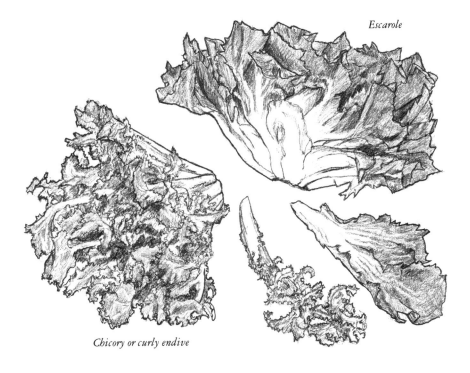

Escarole

Chicory or curly endive

Chicory forms a relatively flat head with open, loosely spreading leaves that allow you to see into the heart. The
interior leaves of chicory are white to yellowish green, and
they taste mildly bitter. The outer leaves are dark green,
intensely bitter, and frequently tough. Escarole also possesses a relatively flat head, but its broad leaves are more
tightly packed. The heart of escarole consists of yellowish
green leaves that are tender and mildly bitter tasting; the
outer leaves are dark green and more bitterly flavored. The
difference in taste between chicory and escarole is slight,
with escarole being the less bitter of the two. Although
both may be cooked, chicory is customarily reserved for
use in salads, and escarole is more frequently served sautéed or in soups. Chicory and escarole are both high in
vitamin A.

TO SELECT:

When purchasing either chicory or escarole, look for heads
with crisp, resilient leaves, and avoid those that feel soft or
wilted. Smaller heads tend to be more delicate and mildly
flavored. Some supermarkets have begun to label these
greens as endive chicory and endive escarole. This may be
some help, but keep in mind that the significant difference
in characteristics has to do with the width of the leaves —
those of chicory are narrow; those of escarole are broad.

TO STORE:

Place unwashed chicory or escarole inside a plastic bag and
secure it with a wire twist. Refrigerate and use within 3 to
5 days.

TO PREPARE:

Separate the leaves and discard any outer ones that may be
damaged or seem to have a tough consistency. Wash under
cool running water and pat dry. Tear into bite-size pieces and
add to other greens to make a salad. (Depending on the
degree of bitterness, you may want to vary the number of
leaves you use. The object is to create an interplay of flavors
by combining chicory or escarole with other more mildly
flavored greens.) Leaves of chicory and escarole can also be
sliced into shreds, or coarsely chopped, and sautéed in oil or
added to soups.

Escarole Soup

Picture the bright yellow yolk of a lightly poached egg haloed by its solidified white and bordered by the deep rich green of cooked escarole. This is a gorgeous soup.

1 head escarole
1 medium onion
4 cups chicken broth
1 bay leaf
Salt and freshly ground
    black pepper
4 large eggs
¼ cup freshly grated
    Parmesan cheese for
    garnish

1. Preheat the oven to 425°. Separate the leaves of escarole. Rinse them and shake off the excess water. Stack the leaves in bunches and cut into 1-inch-wide strips. Cut the onion in half lengthwise and slice into half-rings.

2. Combine the onion and chicken broth in a large saucepan. Add the bay leaf. Cover the pan and cook slowly until the onions are tender. Remove the bay leaf and season with salt and pepper. Stir in the escarole. Increase the heat and cook, uncovered, at a gentle bubble for 4 to 5 minutes or until the escarole is just limp.

3. Ladle a portion of the hot soup into an ovenproof soup dish. Push the escarole away from the center and drop an egg into the hot broth. Repeat with 3 other soup dishes and immediately place them in the oven. Cook for 5 to 8 minutes or until the eggs are set. Serve sprinkled with Parmesan cheese.

Chicory and Beet Salad

Chicory provides a sharp, slightly bitter counterpoint to the mild flavor of raw beets. Bacon bits add a unifying flavor.

¼ pound sliced bacon
1 head chicory
4 medium beets, peeled and
    cut into julienne strips
2 tablespoons red wine
    vinegar
1 teaspoon Dijon mustard
½ teaspoon Worcestershire
    sauce
5 tablespoons vegetable oil
Salt and freshly ground
    black pepper

1. Fry the bacon until crisp and drain on absorbent paper. Reserve 1 tablespoon of the bacon fat.

2. Remove any wilted outer leaves from the head of chicory, then tear the inner leaves into bite-size portions. Transfer to a salad bowl, add the beets, and combine.

3. Break the bacon into small bits and set aside. In a small bowl, whisk together the vinegar, mustard, and Worcestershire sauce. Whisk in the oil and the reserved bacon fat. Then pour the dressing on the salad. Add the bacon pieces and toss to combine. Sprinkle the chicory with salt and pepper to taste and serve immediately.

Chicory and Gruyère Salad

Delicate hearts of chicory and shredded Gruyère cheese are dressed with walnut oil and served atop warm garlic-flavored croutons.

2 garlic cloves, sliced
4 tablespoons olive oil
2 heads chicory
4 ounces Gruyère cheese, shredded
4 slices French bread, cut ½-inch thick
2 tablespoons red wine vinegar
½ teaspoon dry mustard
½ teaspoon salt
Pinch of cayenne
6 tablespoons walnut oil (or substitute olive oil)
¼ cup chopped fresh parsley

1. Combine the garlic and the olive oil in a small saucepan. Heat gently until the garlic turns golden. Do not allow it to brown. Remove from the heat and set aside.

2. Meanwhile, remove the dark green leaves from the chicory and reserve them for another use. Tear the white and yellowish green inner leaves into bite-size portions and place in a salad bowl. Add the Gruyère cheese and toss to combine.

3. Brush the garlic-flavored oil over both sides of the bread slices, then slide them under the broiler. Cook, turning once, until both sides are nicely browned.

4. In a small bowl, whisk together the vinegar, mustard, salt, and cayenne. Whisk in the walnut oil. Scatter the parsley over the chicory and pour on the dressing. Toss to coat evenly.

5. Place a warm slice of bread on each salad plate. Divide the chicory mixture among the 4 plates, arranging it over the bread. Serve immediately.

Sautéed Escarole and Garbanzo Beans

3 tablespoons olive oil
1 tablespoon butter
1 garlic clove, minced or pressed
1 head escarole, cut across into ½-inch-wide strips
1 teaspoon grated lemon zest
¼ cup chopped fresh parsley
Salt and freshly ground black pepper
1 cup canned garbanzo beans, drained
2 tablespoons lemon juice

This satisfying combination may be served hot as a vegetable side dish or chilled as an appetizer.

1. Heat the oil and butter in a large skillet until the butter is melted. Add the garlic and stir briefly over medium heat. Do not allow it to brown.

2. Immediately add the escarole to the skillet and continue stirring over medium heat until the escarole is wilted. Add the lemon zest and parsley. Season with salt and pepper, then mix in the garbanzo beans. Stir gently over medium heat until the beans are warmed through. Transfer to a serving bowl, sprinkle on the lemon juice, and serve immediately.

Chiffonade of Escarole and Red Cabbage   SERVES 4

Thin strips of bright green escarole and red cabbage create a stunning dish. Serve with roast pork or veal.

2 tablespoons vegetable oil
2 tablespoons butter
1 head red cabbage,
  shredded
1 cup water
2 teaspoons caraway seed
1 head escarole, sliced
  across into shreds
Salt and freshly ground
  black pepper

1. Heat the oil and butter in a large skillet until the butter is melted. Add the cabbage and toss to coat evenly. Cook, stirring, over medium heat for 1 minute. Pour on the water and reduce the heat. Stir in the caraway seed. Cover the pan and simmer for 10 to 12 minutes or until the cabbage is crisp-tender.

2. Add the escarole and stir to combine. Increase the heat and cook, stirring, until the escarole is limp and all the liquid is evaporated. Season with salt and pepper and transfer to a serving dish.

Collards

THESE DISTINCTIVE LEAVES are members of the cabbage family, a fact that immediately becomes clear as soon as you taste them. Collards are large, broad-leafed greens with a sturdy stem and central rib. They may be prepared according to any of the methods used for spinach, but the leaves are more coarse and possess a mild, cabbagy flavor. Collards are an excellent source of vitamins A and C and are available year round.

TO SELECT:

Collards are usually displayed loose in a tangled heap, although some produce managers tie them in bunches. Look for large, smooth, nearly round leaves with a resilient, but coarse, texture. Select collards that are fresh looking, and avoid any that are limp, yellowed, or riddled with holes.

TO STORE:

When you get collards home, pick them over and discard any leaves that are wilted or damaged. Without washing, transfer them to a plastic bag and secure with a wire twist. Refrigerate and use within 1 to 2 days.

TO PREPARE:

Fold the leaf in half lengthwise, so that the rib slightly protrudes, then pull the stem and rib away from the leaf.

The tough stem and center rib of each collard leaf needs to be removed for the most tender results. To do this easily, hold the leaf in one hand with the underside up, and bend the leaf in half lengthwise so that the rib slightly protrudes. Then, with the other hand, gently pull the stem and rib away from the leaf. Rinse the trimmed leaves under cool running water and place in a colander to drain.

Collards may be used raw if they are small and tender. In fact, they contribute a wonderful liveliness to tossed green salads. Larger leaves taste best when cooked. They may be blanched in an open pot of vigorously boiling water, or steamed in a covered pot with just the water that clings to their leaves after rinsing. The latter method, however, produces a stronger flavor and less vibrant color. Collards may also be coarsely chopped, then sautéed or stir-fried.

Southern-Style Collards

Collards cooked in a ham-flavored broth make a delicious meal when served with corn bread and barbecued spareribs.

¼ cup bacon fat
2 medium onions, sliced
4 cups water
½ pound smoked ham, cut into bite-size chunks
3 pounds collards, stems and center ribs removed
Salt and freshly ground black pepper
2 tablespoons cider vinegar

1. Melt the bacon fat in a large pot. Add the onions and toss to coat. Stir over medium heat until the onions are tender. Pour in the water. Add the ham and simmer, covered, for 30 minutes.

2. Bring the broth to a boil and add the collards, pushing them under the liquid as they wilt. Partially cover the pot and cook at a gentle bubble for about 1 hour or until tender.

3. Uncover the pot and cook, stirring, until almost all the liquid is evaporated. Season with salt and pepper and transfer to a serving dish. Sprinkle with vinegar and serve while hot.

Sautéed Collards with Bacon and Ziti

SERVES 4

Coarsely chopped collards and crisp bacon mingle with strips of red bell pepper and ziti to create an appealing luncheon dish or first course.

½ pound sliced bacon, cut into 1-inch lengths
2 pounds collards, stems and center ribs removed
1 medium onion, cut into 8 wedges and separated into layers
4 ribs celery, sliced
1 red bell pepper, cut into thin strips
1 cup water
⅓ cup red wine vinegar
½ teaspoon crushed red pepper
½ pound ziti, boiled and drained
Salt and freshly ground black pepper

1. Fry the bacon until crisp and drain on absorbent paper. Reserve 4 tablespoons of the bacon fat.

2. Chop the collards coarsely. Heat the bacon fat in a large skillet. Add the onion and celery and toss to coat evenly. Add the red bell pepper and cook, stirring, over medium heat until the onion is tender. Mix in the collards. Pour on the water and reduce the heat. Cover the pan and cook slowly for 10 to 12 minutes or until the collards are crisp-tender. Uncover the pan and increase the heat. Stir until almost all the liquid is evaporated.

3. Add the vinegar and red pepper. Stir in the hot, drained ziti and the bacon. Season with salt and pepper and transfer to a serving dish.

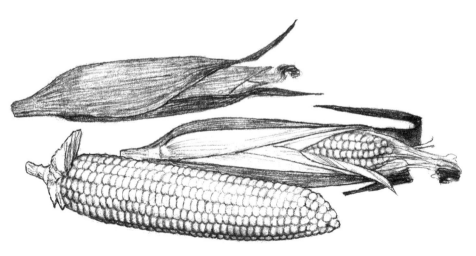

Corn

DURING THE YEARS that my family lived on a tobacco farm, we had access to a field of sweet corn that grew just beyond our driveway. I didn't consider myself lucky then, partly, I suppose, because I was the one who had to trudge out and pick the ears for the steaming pot. Now I would give anything to be able to cook corn brought in straight from the field.

Modern varieties of sweet corn have been specifically bred to store their carbohydrate content as sugar. However, as soon as an ear of corn is removed from the stalk, a process of conversion begins in which the sugar is rapidly transformed to starch. In fact, harvested corn loses one-half of its natural sugar in 24 hours. This explains why sweet-corn lovers are adamant about cooking corn on the cob within only a few hours of the time it was picked.

Sweet corn may be white, light yellow, deep yellow, or bicolored, having kernels of both yellow and white. It is available sporadically throughout the year in supermarkets, but unless it has been continuously and meticulously refrigerated, its flavor will be bland and starchy. The very best corn is that which is grown and sold locally, preferably at a farmer's stand that picks small batches several times a day to ensure freshness. Both white and yellow corn contain potassium and vitamins A and B, with yellow corn being somewhat higher in vitamin A.

TO SELECT:

Many produce stands still follow the practice of allowing you to peel back a bit of husk to inspect the kernels inside. But thoughtless and inconsiderate behavior on the part of customers is rapidly bringing this custom to an end. Lifting the husk away from an ear of corn exposes the kernels to the air and hastens deterioration. If you're fortunate enough to be able to select corn at a stand that lets you strip the ears, be honorable about it. Gently peel back a narrow piece of husk for only 2 to 3 inches. If you don't like what you see, replace the husk before returning the ear to the pile.

I think it's essential to see the kernels before purchasing corn, but there are other indications of quality you can rely on. The best way to judge freshness is by checking the stem end of the ear. It should look freshly broken or cut, and feel slightly damp. Dryness and a stale appearance indicate that the ear was picked some time ago. The silk tassel should be moist and golden where it emerges from the husk, and dark brown and dry at the tip. (The dryness is a sign that the corn is mature enough to be harvested.) Put the ear to your nose and smell the tassel where it meets the husk. It should have a fresh, vibrant, "corny" aroma. Good-quality corn will bear tightly folded husks of bright green; avoid any ears covered by loose, spongy husks.

The kernels of corn vary greatly in size, color, and shape among different varieties. There are pale white or light yellow ears with evenly spaced rows of glossy, rounded kernels that remind me of a string of pearls; and there are creamy white or deep yellow ears with crowded rows of rectangular kernels that are so tightly packed they appear to be squashed together. These characteristics are inherent in certain varieties, but they can also indicate maturity. Some people prefer young corn: It will be pale white or lightly colored, and exhibit evenly spaced rows of shiny, rounded kernels that contain a clear, watery liquid. Corn that is more mature will be creamy white or deep yellow in color, and exhibit tightly packed rows of rectangular kernels. (Overly mature ears frequently have rows so tightly packed they are crooked.) Mature kernels have a dull finish and give off an opaque, milky liquid when pricked. Whichever your preference, be sure to choose corn with firm, plump, fresh-looking kernels; shriveled kernels are a sign of age. Plan on an average serving of 2 ears per person.

TO STORE:

Because corn loses its sweetness so rapidly, it is crucial that it be refrigerated as much of the time as possible to impede the conversion of sugar to starch. Avoid, for example, purchasing corn and then driving around town to do other errands. Ideally, corn should be cooked on the same day it is picked. But if you are forced to keep it longer, immediately transfer the unhusked ears to a plastic bag and secure with a wire twist. You may refrigerate corn this way for 3 to 4 days, but you'll notice a significant loss in flavor.

TO PREPARE:

Corn may be cooked in the husk or out of the husk; on the cob or off the cob. To cook corn in the husk, gently peel the green leaves back, but do not detach them. Remove the tassel and silk strands. Rinse the corn under cool running water, brushing gently with a soft-bristled brush to dislodge any stubborn strands of silk. Bring the husks back up over the ear and tie with a string, if necessary, to hold them in place. Soak the entire ear in cold water for 10 minutes and then roast in the oven, barbecue on the grill, or microwave. (Unhusked corn on the cob may also be steamed.)

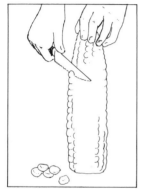

Stand the corncob on its stem end and, using a serrated knife, slice down the rows of kernels.

Corn may also be cooked stripped of its husks. Simply pull the leaves back to the stalk end and break them off. Pull away the tassel and silk strands. Rinse the corn and remove stray silks as described above. Then drop into rapidly boiling water or wrap the husked corn in aluminum foil and roast or barbecue.

To remove corn from the cob, stand a cooked or uncooked ear inside a pie pan on its stalk end. Then starting at the tip, slice down the rows of kernels with a serrated knife. The kernels will fall into the pie pan. Don't be concerned if a portion of the kernels remains on the cob. It's better to leave the base of the kernels behind than it is to risk cutting away any of the tough membranes on the surface of the cob. Raw corn cut from the cob may be steamed or cooked in a small amount of water and served with butter. Cooked kernels may be used in salads, flans, fritters, muffins, and a host of other delicious preparations. (Incidentally, for those times of the year when native corn is not available, don't be reluctant to try supermarket corn cut from the cob. It is often superior to frozen or canned for making chowder or baked goods.)

Fresh Corn Relish

8 ears corn, husks and silk
  removed
1 cup water
1 cup white vinegar
½ cup sugar
½ teaspoon salt
1 teaspoon celery seed
1 teaspoon mustard seed
1 teaspoon ground turmeric
½ teaspoon Tabasco sauce
1 green bell pepper,
  coarsely chopped
1 red bell pepper, coarsely
  chopped
4 green onions, green and
  white portion, thinly
  sliced
2 tablespoons chopped
  fresh cilantro

Lively with spices, this quick and easy relish is wonderful spooned atop grilled hamburgers.

1. Drop the corn into a large pot of boiling water. Partially cover the pot and cook at a gentle bubble for 3 minutes or until the kernels are crisp-tender. Remove from the pot and drain in a colander. When the corn is cool enough to handle, cut the kernels from the cobs.

2. Meanwhile, combine the water, vinegar, sugar, and salt in a large saucepan. Stir in the celery seed, mustard seed, turmeric, and Tabasco. Stir in the green and red bell peppers and onions. Bring to a gentle bubble and cook, uncovered, for 10 minutes.

3. Stir in the corn and cilantro and increase the heat. Cook, stirring, until almost all the liquid is evaporated. Transfer to a large bowl. Cover and refrigerate until thoroughly chilled.

Corn Chowder

¼ pound sliced bacon, cut
  into 1-inch lengths
1 medium onion, coarsely
  chopped
2 medium waxy potatoes,
  cut into cubes
1 tablespoon all-purpose
  flour
2 cups water
1½ cups uncooked corn
  kernels (4 or 5 ears)
4 cups milk
1 bay leaf
1 teaspoon salt
Freshly ground black
  pepper

Small squares of bacon contribute lusty flavor to this fresh corn soup — comforting fare for those first cold days of September.

1. Fry the bacon until crisp and drain on absorbent paper. Transfer 3 tablespoons of the fat to a large pan.

2. Add the onion and potatoes to the pan and stir over medium heat until the onion is tender. Sprinkle on the flour and continue to stir over medium heat until the mixture foams. Stir in the water and bring to a boil.

3. Add the corn and reduce the heat. Cover the pan and cook slowly for 5 to 8 minutes or until the corn is tender. Pour in the milk and add the bay leaf. Cover and cook until the potatoes are tender. Lift out the bay leaf. Season with salt and pepper, then stir in the bacon. Simmer until the bacon becomes limp and serve hot.

Corn and Red Pepper Salad

SERVES 4

4 ears corn, husks and silk removed
1 red bell pepper, cut into thin strips
2 ribs celery, thinly sliced
2 green onions, white and green portion, thinly sliced
1 tablespoon chopped fresh cilantro
⅓ cup vegetable oil
2 tablespoons white wine vinegar
½ teaspoon Dijon mustard
½ teaspoon salt
⅛ teaspoon sweet paprika
4 well-formed leaves of iceberg lettuce

Because iceberg lettuce heads so tightly, the inner leaves form deep, rounded cups that are just the thing for cradling this appealing corn salad.

1. Drop the corn into a large pot of boiling water. Partially cover the pot and cook at a gentle bubble for 3 minutes or until the kernels are crisp-tender. Remove from the pot and drain in a colander. When the corn is cool enough to handle, cut the kernels from the cobs.

2. Transfer the corn to a large mixing bowl. Add the red bell pepper, celery, and onions. Sprinkle on the cilantro and toss to combine.

3. In a small bowl, whisk together the oil, vinegar, mustard, salt, and paprika. Pour over the corn mixture and toss to coat. Cover the bowl and refrigerate for a couple of hours or until lightly chilled. Spoon into lettuce cups to serve.

Oven-Roasted Corn with Curry Butter

SERVES 4

Wrapping ears of corn in aluminum foil and baking them in the oven gives them a special flavor that nearly duplicates that of corn cooked over an open fire. But this method is neater and easier than grilling outdoors.

6 tablespoons butter, softened
1 teaspoon curry powder
4 ears corn, husks and silk removed
Salt and freshly ground black pepper

1. Preheat the oven to 400°. Blend the butter and curry powder together. Spread over the kernels of corn, then sprinkle each ear with salt and pepper.

2. Wrap each ear in aluminum foil and twist the ends to close tightly. Place directly on the oven rack and roast for 25 to 35 minutes. Serve immediately.

Corn Oysters

So named because of their resemblance to the familiar shell-fish, corn oysters are a classic variation of corn fritters.

2 cups uncooked corn
   kernels (4 large ears)
¼ cup all-purpose flour
½ teaspoon salt
Freshly ground black
   pepper
2 large eggs, separated
1 tablespoon water
Vegetable oil for frying

1. Place the corn kernels in a large mixing bowl. Sprinkle on the flour, salt, and pepper and toss to combine. In a separate bowl, whisk the egg yolks and water. Add to the corn and stir to blend well.

2. In another bowl, beat the egg whites until soft peaks form. Add to the corn mixture and fold in.

3. Heat ½ inch of oil in a large skillet. Drop in the batter by tablespoonfuls, allowing it to fall in oval, oyster-shaped mounds. Cook for 2 to 3 minutes, turning to brown both sides. Drain on absorbent paper and serve on a napkin-lined plate.

Corn Pudding

Finely chopped green chilies and grated Cheddar cheese give a contemporary twist to an old-time favorite. Bake in a casserole dish, in tomato shells, or in green bell peppers.

2 cups uncooked corn
   kernels (4 large ears)
½ cup grated Cheddar
   cheese
3 large eggs, plus 1 extra
   egg white
¼ cup butter, melted
½ cup light cream
1 teaspoon sugar
½ teaspoon salt
Pinch of cayenne
2 jalapeño peppers, seeded
   and finely chopped

1. Preheat the oven to 325°. Generously butter a 2-quart baking dish. Place the corn kernels and cheese in a large mixing bowl and toss to combine.

2. Separate the eggs and set the whites aside. Whisk together the egg yolks, melted butter, cream, sugar, salt, and cayenne. Stir in the jalapeño peppers. Pour over the corn and cheese and blend well.

3. Whisk the 4 egg whites until soft peaks form. Fold into the corn mixture. Transfer to the prepared baking dish and bake for 1 hour or until the surface is browned and the center is delicately set. Allow to cool for 10 minutes and serve.

Sautéed Corn with Basil

6 ears corn, husks and silk
   removed
2 tablespoons vegetable oil
2 tablespoons butter
1 red bell pepper, coarsely
   chopped
3 green onions, white and
   green portion, sliced
½ cup water
1 tablespoon chopped fresh
   basil
1 teaspoon sugar
½ teaspoon salt
Freshly ground black
   pepper

Flecked with bits of red bell pepper and fresh green basil, this beautiful dish captures the essence of summer.

1. Cut the corn from the cobs. Heat the oil and butter in a large skillet until the butter is melted. Add the corn and stir over medium heat for 1 minute. Add the red bell pepper and onions, and cook, stirring, for 1 minute more. Pour on the water and reduce the heat. Cover the pan and simmer until the corn is crisp-tender.

2. Sprinkle on the basil, sugar, salt, and pepper. Stir over high heat until all the liquid is evaporated. Serve immediately.

Corn Bread with Green Chili Peppers

1 cup all-purpose flour
1 cup yellow cornmeal
2 teaspoons baking powder
½ teaspoon baking soda
½ teaspoon salt
2 large eggs
¼ cup vegetable oil
½ cup sour cream
1 cup uncooked corn
   kernels (2 large ears)
4 green chili peppers, finely
   chopped
½ cup grated Monterey Jack
   cheese

Dotted with bits of green chili peppers, this lusty bread bursts with flavor. Cut into generous squares and serve warm with hearty bean soups or chile con carne.

1. Preheat the oven to 350°. Generously grease an 8-inch square pan. Combine the flour, cornmeal, baking powder, soda, and salt in a large mixing bowl. Whisk to blend thoroughly.

2. In a separate bowl, beat together the eggs, oil, and sour cream. Add to the dry ingredients and blend well. Stir in the corn, chili peppers, and cheese. Pour into the prepared pan and bake for 45 to 55 minutes or until a wooden pick inserted in the center comes out clean.

Fresh Corn Muffins

MAKES 1 DOZEN

Crunchy from the rough texture of cornmeal, these beautiful muffins are flecked with kernels of succulent fresh corn.

1 cup all-purpose flour
1 cup yellow cornmeal
¼ cup sugar
3 teaspoons baking powder
½ teaspoon salt
1 cup milk
1 large egg
¼ cup butter, melted
1 cup uncooked corn
   kernels (2 large ears)

1. Preheat the oven to 400°. Generously grease 12 muffin tins. Combine the flour, cornmeal, sugar, baking powder, and salt in a large mixing bowl. Whisk to blend thoroughly.

2. In a separate bowl, beat together the milk, egg, and melted butter. Add to the dry ingredients and blend well. Stir in the corn. Pour into the prepared muffin tins and bake for 20 to 25 minutes or until a wooden pick inserted in the center comes out clean.

Cucumbers

CUCUMBERS HAVE a cool, crisp, refreshing texture, so it's not surprising to see that they are frequently used raw in salads, relishes, and chilled soups. But there's more to cucumber cookery than that. When they are heated, cucumbers develop a mild, seductive flavor that is irresistible. Cucumbers can be sautéed, stir-fried, steamed, or stuffed and then baked. Available year round, the peak season for cucumbers occurs from June to September.

TO SELECT:

Three different types of cucumbers are commonly available at the produce stand: the 3- to 4-inch pickling cucumber, the 6- to 8-inch salad cucumber, and the foot-long European cucumber. Pickling cucumbers are pale green with light yellow streaks radiating from the stem end. Prominent, blunt spines dot their surface. Pickling cucumbers are sold for the purpose of making pickles, and consequently their exterior is left unwaxed. The standard salad cucumber is fatter and longer, and it bears a dark green skin, which is usually glossy from being heavily waxed. The European, or seedless, cucumber often measures up to 15 inches long,

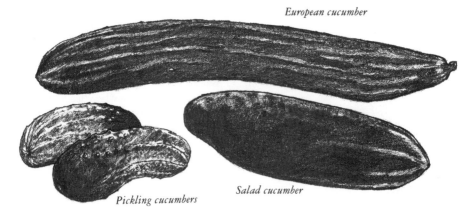

European cucumber

Salad cucumber

Pickling cucumbers

and it is quite slim. Lightly coated with wax, individual European cucumbers are wrapped in a tight plastic film.

When buying cucumbers of any kind, check for firmness, especially at the stem and blossom ends. Cucumbers are not as rugged as they might seem; deterioration occurs rapidly if they are stored at temperatures much above or below 45°, and soft spots are the first sign of quality loss. Avoid cucumbers that feel spongy, are light in weight for their size, or whose skin is shriveled or displays splotches of yellow.

Pickling cucumbers appear sporadically throughout the year in large supermarkets, but they are consistently available during the summer months at farmers' stands. Some cooks prefer to use them in place of salad cucumbers, because they have smaller seeds and their skin is left unwaxed. Salad cucumbers are still favored by many, however. They are of reliably good quality and reasonably priced. To obtain the best salad cucumbers, pick out the slenderest ones; fat cucumbers have large, woody seeds. European cucumbers, which are marketed as seedless, contain tiny pips not much bigger than a grain of salt. These are the glamorous stars. Thin, mildly flavored skin, and a subtle, almost sweet-tasting flesh combine to make them the most succulent choice. European cucumbers are expensive, but they taste so good that many consumers don't seem to mind. (These hot-house cucumbers, also referred to as English, are relatively "burpless" and therefore appealing to many people who suffer intestinal distress from eating regular cucumbers.)

TO STORE:

Cucumbers contain a high percentage of water and will dehydrate rapidly. This is the reason cucumbers are waxed before being shipped to market. (Pickling cucumbers aren't waxed because the coating would interfere with the pickling process.) The wax coating helps to maintain freshness by impeding moisture loss, but storage time is still relatively short because cucumbers are so finicky about temperature. When you get cucumbers home, wrap them individually in plastic wrap and place them in the vegetable drawer of the refrigerator. Do not store them near tomatoes, apples, or citrus fruit, all of which give off ethylene gas, and thus can cause cucumbers to decay. Use them within 2 to 3 days.

TO PREPARE:

To minimize the bitterness of pickling or salad cucumbers, remove the skin and trim both the stem and blossom ends. Scooping the seeds and seed membranes from the center also results in milder-tasting cucumbers. European cucumbers don't need such treatment; they may be served intact, skin and all.

Cucumbers may be peeled with a paring knife or swivel-blade peeler. To alleviate possible digestion problems, remove the darker green portion of the flesh directly under the skin. Continue peeling until you have a pale green cylinder of uniform color. Cooking cucumbers also makes them more easily digestible.

Cucumbers with Curried Cream Cheese

SERVES 8

Curry-flavored cream cheese makes an elegant stuffing for cucumber shells. Serve as an appetizer or as part of a picnic.

3 large cucumbers, peeled
1 large package (8 ounces) cream cheese, softened
3 tablespoons lemon juice
1 teaspoon curry powder
¼ teaspoon salt

1. Cut the cucumbers in half lengthwise and scoop out the seeds with a metal spoon or a butter curler. Trim off the ends and place the halves, cut side down, on absorbent paper.

2. In a large mixing bowl, combine the cream cheese and lemon juice and beat until smooth. Add the curry powder and salt. Pipe or spoon into the cucumber cavities and refrigerate until the cheese is firmly set. Cut each cucumber half into 2-inch lengths. Transfer to a glass plate or serve on crushed ice.

Dilled Cucumber Slices

SERVES 12

These crispy pickle slices are so simple to prepare you'll want to keep a steady supply on hand for nibbling.

4 large unwaxed
    cucumbers, unpeeled
1 medium onion, sliced and
    separated into rings
1 red bell pepper, cut into
    julienne strips
2 teaspoons salt
½ cup white wine vinegar
¾ cup sugar
1 tablespoon chopped fresh
    dill leaves

1. Thinly slice the cucumbers and place them in a large glass bowl. Add the onion and red bell pepper and toss to combine. Sprinkle on the salt and stir to coat evenly. Set aside and allow to stand at room temperature for 2 hours. Stir occasionally.

2. Combine the vinegar and sugar in a small bowl and stir until the sugar dissolves. Pour over the cucumber slices. Sprinkle on the dill leaves and stir to incorporate. Cover the bowl and refrigerate for 24 hours before serving. They will keep this way for 3 to 4 weeks.

Cucumber Bisque

SERVES 6

4 large cucumbers, peeled,
    seeded, and chopped
3 green onions, white and
    green portion, sliced
1 cup canned cannellini
    beans, drained
3 cups chicken broth
2 tablespoons chopped
    fresh chives
Salt and freshly ground
    white pepper
1 cup sour cream

An icy blend of cucumber and sour cream, this soup makes a refreshing starter for a summer luncheon.

1. In a large saucepan, combine the cucumbers, onions, beans, chicken broth, and 1 tablespoon of the chives. Cover the pan and cook at a gentle bubble for 20 minutes or until the cucumbers are tender.

2. Pour into the container of a blender or processor and whirl until smooth. Transfer to a large bowl. Blend in the salt, pepper, and sour cream. Cover the bowl. Refrigerate until thoroughly chilled. Serve cold, sprinkled with the remaining tablespoon of chives.

Cucumbers in Sour Cream

SERVES 4

2 large cucumbers, peeled and thinly sliced
1 large sweet onion, sliced and separated into rings
½ cup sour cream
½ cup mayonnaise, preferably homemade
2 tablespoons white vinegar
1 tablespoon sugar
Salt and freshly ground black pepper
1 tablespoon chopped fresh parsley

A cool, creamy cucumber-and-onion dish to serve on a hot summer night with grilled lamb.

1. Place the cucumbers and onion rings in a large bowl. Pour on enough cold water to cover by 1 inch. Drop in 6 ice cubes and refrigerate for 3 hours.

2. Drain the cucumbers and onion in a colander and return to the bowl. In a small bowl, blend together the sour cream, mayonnaise, and vinegar. Sprinkle the cucumbers and onion with the sugar. Season with salt and pepper. Add the parsley and toss to combine. Pour on the sour cream mixture and stir to coat. Refrigerate until thoroughly chilled.

Cucumber and Baby Shrimp Salad

SERVES 6

1 large cucumber, seeded and coarsely chopped
12 ounces tiny shrimp, cooked, peeled, and deveined
2 ribs celery, finely chopped
2 green onions, finely chopped
½ cup mayonnaise, preferably homemade
2 tablespoons medium or whipping cream
1 tablespoon lemon juice
1 tablespoon chopped fresh dill leaves
Salt and freshly ground black pepper
6 sprigs fresh dill for garnish

The complementary flavors of cucumber and shrimp are underscored by a sprinkling of fresh dill. Serve this chilled salad on lettuce leaves or as a filling for stuffed tomatoes.

1. Combine the cucumber, shrimp, celery, and onions in a large salad bowl.

2. Whisk together the mayonnaise, cream, and lemon juice. Pour over the cucumber mixture and stir to combine. Sprinkle on the dill leaves and season with salt and pepper. Cover and chill thoroughly. Serve garnished with sprigs of fresh dill.

Sautéed Cucumbers with Tarragon

SERVES 4

Narrow strips of mild, seedless cucumber are sautéed in butter, then polished with reduced cream. Serve with roast beef or veal.

2 European cucumbers, peeled
3 tablespoons butter
Salt and freshly ground white pepper
1 tablespoon chopped fresh tarragon
⅔ cup heavy cream

1. Cut the cucumbers in half lengthwise. Cut into 3-inch lengths, then into julienne strips.

2. Melt the butter in a large skillet. Add the cucumbers and stir over medium heat until limp. Season with salt and pepper. Add the tarragon and continue to stir over medium heat for 30 seconds. Pour on the cream and cook at a gentle bubble until the cream is reduced and slightly thickened. Serve immediately.

Baked Stuffed Cucumbers

SERVES 4

2 large cucumbers, peeled and cut in half lengthwise
3 tablespoons butter
2 green onions, white and green portion, thinly sliced
⅔ cup cooked rice
½ cup freshly grated Parmesan cheese
1 tablespoon chopped fresh basil
Salt and freshly ground black pepper
1 large egg yolk
2 tablespoons lemon juice
¼ cup grated Gruyère cheese

Cucumbers stuffed with lemon-flavored rice and Parmesan cheese are briefly baked to give the flesh a crisp-tender consistency. Serve them hot with grilled Italian sausage.

1. Preheat the oven to 375°. Generously butter a shallow baking dish. Remove the seeds from the cucumbers by scooping them out with a metal spoon or butter curler. Place the halves, cut side down, on absorbent paper.

2. Melt the butter in a small skillet and add the onions, stirring over medium heat until tender. Stir in the cooked rice, Parmesan cheese, basil, salt, and pepper. Cook until the cheese begins to melt. Remove from the heat.

3. Whisk together the egg yolk and lemon juice. Pour over the rice mixture and stir to blend well. Spoon into the cucumber cavities, then sprinkle the tops with Gruyère cheese. Transfer to the prepared baking dish and bake for 25 to 30 minutes or until the cucumbers are slightly softened and the tops are nicely browned.

D

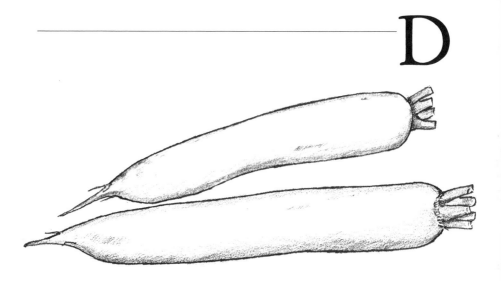

Daikon

THIS EXCEPTIONALLY long root vegetable is also known as Oriental radish. It possesses a mild, yet peppery, flavor, resembling that of the familiar red garden radish. Consequently, daikon is often served raw as part of a salad or as a refreshing accompaniment to enliven certain dishes, such as tempura.

TO SELECT:

The daikons found in American supermarkets are usually of the long, slender variety. This particular type measures approximately 1½ to 2 inches in width, and approximately 12 inches in length. Choose them as you would any root vegetable, picking out those that are firm, smooth, and unblemished. If the greens are still attached, their condition is a clue to the freshness of the daikon. One long daikon is sufficient to feed four people.

TO STORE:

You can successfully keep a whole, uncut daikon for 1 to 2 weeks by wrapping it loosely in plastic film and placing it in the refrigerator. Cut daikon does not store as well. Over a period of time, it becomes limp and develops an unpleasant flavor.

TO PREPARE: Rinse thoroughly under cool running water and scrape with a paring knife, or peel with a swivel-blade peeler. Pat dry and cut or slice according to your recipe. The texture of daikon is crisp and radishlike; the flesh should not be fibrous.

Daikon may be grated, shredded, or thinly sliced, and served raw, either with a dressing or alone. It may also be cut into chunks or julienne strips, and braised or stir-fried. Like potato, daikon has the ability to hold its shape and absorb flavors when simmered with other ingredients. In addition, it manages to retain its own characteristic zestiness, which makes daikon an excellent addition to soups and stews. It is also frequently pickled.

Pickled Daikon

SERVES 6

Pickled daikon makes a zesty appetizer or addition to a picnic basket.

1 large daikon, peeled and sliced
1 red bell pepper, diced
2 cups white vinegar
¾ cup water
2 cups sugar
1 teaspoon salt

1. Trim the daikon and cut into ¼-inch-thick rounds. Transfer to a bowl and mix with the red bell pepper.

2. In a saucepan, combine the vinegar, water, sugar, and salt. Bring the mixture to a boil and stir over high heat for 1 minute. Remove from the heat and pour over the vegetables. Stir to coat and refrigerate. When thoroughly cooled, cover the bowl with a sheet of waxed paper. Lay a sheet of aluminum foil over the waxed paper and secure tightly. Allow the vegetables to marinate for at least 24 hours before serving.

Daikon and Carrot Salad

SERVES 6

1 medium daikon, peeled
and shredded
4 medium carrots, peeled
and shredded
1 tablespoon chopped fresh
cilantro
2 tablespoons rice vinegar
2 tablespoons soy sauce
2 teaspoons Chinese
barbecue sauce
6 tablespoons vegetable oil
Salt and freshly ground
black pepper

Alive with zesty flavor, this vegetable combination goes well with cold smoked turkey or veal pâté.

1. In a large salad bowl, combine the daikon, carrots, and cilantro. Toss to mix thoroughly.

2. In a small bowl, whisk together the vinegar, soy sauce, and barbecue sauce. Blend in the oil. Pour the dressing over the daikon mixture and season with salt and pepper. Serve by heaping spoonfuls.

Stir-Fried Daikon

SERVES 4

The peppery flavor of daikon is complemented by the taste of a sweet-and-sour sauce. Serve with grilled chicken or shrimp.

2 tablespoons sugar
1 teaspoon cornstarch
3 tablespoons rice vinegar
3 tablespoons soy sauce
2 tablespoons ketchup
1 large daikon, peeled and
cut into 2-inch lengths
3 tablespoons vegetable oil
2 tablespoons water

1. In a small bowl, combine the sugar, cornstarch, vinegar, and soy sauce. Stir to dissolve the cornstarch and blend in the ketchup.

2. Cut the 2-inch lengths of daikon into julienne strips and set aside. Heat the oil in a wok or large skillet. Add the daikon and cook, stirring constantly, over high heat for 30 seconds. Sprinkle on the water by drops and continue stirring for 1 to 2 minutes or until the daikon begins to turn limp. Pour on the soy sauce mixture and stir until slightly thickened.

Dandelion Greens

THESE ARE the familiar spiky leaves that may grow wild in your lawn during the spring. There is also a cultivated variety, however, and it is less bitter and milder tasting. Eaten raw, dandelion greens possess an astringent tang. They are customarily torn into bite-size pieces and added to green salads as a flavor accent. Dandelion greens are also good when cut into fine slivers and scattered over a salad as you would fresh herbs. Cooked dandelion greens have a natural affinity for bacon and ham, and are delicious when simmered in a pork-flavored broth. Dandelion greens are exceptionally high in vitamin A and calcium. They are available all year, but are at their best in the spring.

TO SELECT:

Dandelion greens are usually sold in bunches attached at the root. The slim, sharply pointed leaves should be crisp and fresh looking. They should be bright green, but choose those of a pale tone; leaves that are deep green are older and more strongly flavored. Avoid dandelion greens that are wilted or yellow.

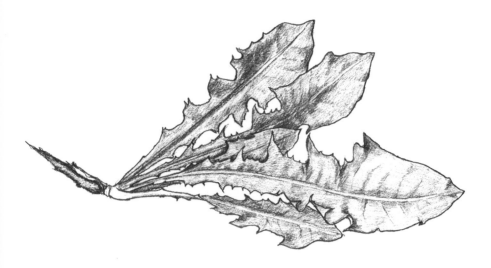

TO STORE: Without removing the root, place the unwashed greens in a plastic bag and secure with a wire twist. Refrigerate and use within 1 to 2 days.

TO PREPARE: Cut off the root and a small portion of the stem. Sort the leaves, discarding any that are limp or damaged. Plunge the greens into a basin of cool water and agitate them to dislodge the sand and dirt. Repeat if necessary in a fresh change of water. Trim off any large, tough stems. Stack the leaves on top of one another and cut into 1-inch lengths, or cook the greens whole. You may also slice the stacked leaves into shreds to scatter over salads and cooked egg dishes. Dandelion greens may be blanched lightly in water, simmered in a broth, sautéed in butter, or stir-fried in a little oil.

Dandelion Greens in Broth   SERVES 4

Coarsely chopped dandelion greens are simmered in a light pork broth until barely wilted. Fresh ginger, green onions, and slivers of cooked pork round out this delightful soup.

3 lean rib pork chops
2 pounds dandelion greens
5 cups water
½ cup soy sauce
½ cup rice vinegar
6 green onions, white and
  green portion, sliced
1 tablespoon minced fresh
  ginger

1. Broil the pork chops until nicely browned on both sides. Set aside until cool enough to handle.

2. Meanwhile, trim the dandelion greens and rinse thoroughly in a basin of cool water. Shake off the excess water. Stack the leaves in small bunches and chop coarsely.

3. Trim the fat from the pork chops and discard. Cut the meat away from the bone. Place the bones in a large saucepan. Add the water, soy sauce, vinegar, onions, and ginger. Bring to a boil, and cook, uncovered, at a gentle bubble.

4. Slice the pork into narrow strips and add to the simmering broth. Cook for 30 minutes, then lift out the bones. Add the greens to the broth and continue to simmer, uncovered, until barely wilted. Serve steaming hot.

Wilted Dandelion Greens Salad

SERVES 4

Dandelion greens are torn into bite-size pieces and wilted in hot bacon fat. Buttered, toasted bread crumbs contribute flavor and textural contrast.

1 pound dandelion greens
2 slices good-quality white bread
2 tablespoons butter, melted
3 tablespoons red wine vinegar
½ teaspoon sugar
½ teaspoon dry mustard
3 tablespoons vegetable oil
3 tablespoons bacon fat
1 garlic clove, minced or pressed

1. Trim the dandelion greens and rinse thoroughly in a basin of cool water. Shake off the excess water and scatter them over absorbent paper.

2. Break the slices of bread into bite-size pieces. Scatter them over the bottom of a shallow pan, slide under the broiler, and toast on all sides. When nicely browned, remove the bread and transfer to a blender or processor. Whirl to create bread crumbs. Toss with the melted butter to coat. Tear the dandelion greens into bite-size pieces and set aside.

3. In a small bowl, whisk together the vinegar, sugar, and mustard. Heat the oil and bacon fat in a large skillet until the bacon fat melts. Add the garlic and stir over medium heat for 30 seconds. Add the dandelion greens and continue stirring over medium heat until the greens are wilted. Pour on the vinegar mixture and toss to combine. Divide among 4 salad plates and scatter the buttered bread crumbs over the top.

Dandelion Greens Sautéed in Ginger Butter

SERVES 4

Freshly grated ginger highlights the zesty flavor of lightly cooked dandelion greens.

2 pounds dandelion greens
2 tablespoons vegetable oil
4 tablespoons butter
3 green onions, white and green portion, thinly sliced
1 tablespoon grated fresh ginger
Salt and freshly ground black pepper

1. Trim the dandelion greens and rinse thoroughly in a basin of cool water. Shake off the excess water. Stack the leaves in small bunches, then cut into 1-inch lengths.

2. Heat the oil and butter in a large skillet until the butter is melted. Add the onions and ginger and stir over medium heat until the onions are limp. Add the dandelion greens and continue stirring over medium heat until they wilt. Season with salt and pepper and transfer to a serving dish.

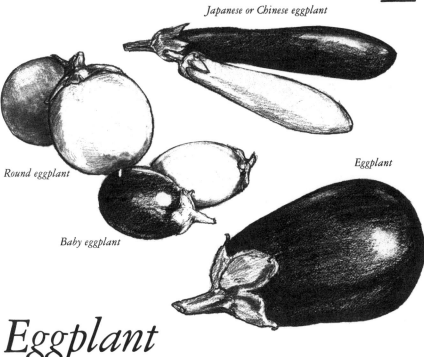

Japanese or Chinese eggplant

Round eggplant

Eggplant

Baby eggplant

Eggplant

IF THERE WERE a prize for versatility, eggplant would win hands down. It can be baked, broiled, grilled, steamed, or stir-fried; in fact, eggplant is served in every conceivable manner except raw. Mild tasting with absorbent flesh, this vegetable literally soaks in companion flavors, and because of its texture, it is often used as a substitute for meat and pasta. Eggplant is available year round, but is at its best during August and September.

TO SELECT:

Eggplant comes in a variety of different shapes and sizes: there are the long, slender purple or white cylinders referred to as Japanese or Chinese eggplant; round eggplant colored white or deep yellow; baby purple eggplant the size of a small egg; slightly larger teardrop-shaped eggplant commonly referred to as Italian; and the standard 6- to 8-inch purple eggplant shaped like a large pear. All are similar in taste and texture and can be used interchangeably, except in those cases in which color or size is a significant factor.

The most common eggplant available is the standard purple variety. Purchase only those that have taut, satiny skin and a firm, green stem cap. Reject any with wrinkled skin, blemishes, or soft spots. Size is not a reliable indicator of quality because large eggplants can turn out to have just as good a texture as small ones; however, overripe eggplants (which are invariably large) will have tough skin, overly developed seeds, and bitter juices. So your safest bet is to choose small eggplants unless you need a bigger size for stuffing or creating large slices.

To test for texture, press gently on the flesh with your thumb. It should give slightly, but feel resilient. A soft, spongy consistency is a sign of long storage or age, both of which result in the presence of bitter juices. Plan on 1½ pounds to feed 4 people.

TO STORE:

Eggplant is one of the more perishable vegetables. If it isn't kept under perfect conditions, it will quickly develop spongy flesh and tough skin. For that reason, it's best to use eggplant within 1 day. When you get it home, place the unwrapped eggplant in the refrigerator without washing. Leave the stem cap intact until just before using.

TO PREPARE:

Contemporary farming methods have just about eliminated the bitterness in eggplant that cooks used to extract by salting. If you have purchased freshly picked, tender-skinned eggplant, you can now skip this technique in most recipes. The exceptions would be in preparing eggplant for frying or for dishes in which excess moisture might upset the balance of the ingredients.

While it's true that eggplant treated with salt absorbs much less oil during frying, if you're restricting salt intake, you can handle this situation in other ways. For example, you can broil eggplant instead. Or use a nonstick skillet, which enables you to fry unsalted eggplant using little or no oil. Also, eggplant that is protected by a batter or an egg and bread crumb coating, will not absorb excess oil, so salting in this case is unnecessary. In recipes in which excess moisture would be a problem, you can sweat the liquid out by using a microwave oven. Place the sliced eggplant in a glass casserole and cover the dish. Microwave on high power for 4 to 6 minutes or until beads of moisture appear on the flesh.

Remove and allow to stand, covered, for 2 minutes. Then, gently pressing on the eggplant, drain off the liquid.

Whether to peel eggplant or not is very much a matter of personal preference. But keep in mind that overripeness and long storage tend to produce tough skin, and large eggplants many times have skin that refuses to soften during cooking, so peeling is generally a good idea. Rinse eggplant under cold running water and pat dry. Using a swivel-blade peeler, peel away from you in broad, firm strokes. If you see a green tinge under the purple skin, that's a sign of freshness, and it need not be removed.

When you cut into an eggplant, notice the color and size of the seeds. Dark, well-developed seeds indicate a more mature, and possibly overripe, eggplant; pale, tiny seeds indicate a less mature eggplant.

Sprinkle salt on the flesh or submerge it in a salt-and-water brine, if you desire. In either case, rinse the eggplant thoroughly to avoid excessive saltiness in the final dish. Plan to complete the recipe immediately, because the flesh of eggplant darkens when exposed to the air.

Eggplant Caviar

SERVES 8 TO 10

2 medium eggplants, unpeeled
2 garlic cloves, pressed
¼ cup unflavored yogurt
2 tablespoons lemon juice
2 tablespoons chopped fresh mint
½ teaspoon salt
Freshly ground black pepper

A whole, unpeeled eggplant can be baked in the oven and then mashed with garlic and fresh mint to create this delightful spread. Serve with whole wheat or sesame crackers.

1. Preheat the oven to 400°. Place the eggplants in a shallow roasting pan and bake for 30 to 40 minutes or until tender when pierced. Transfer to a platter to cool.

2. When cool enough to handle, cut the eggplants in half and scoop out the flesh. Mash with a fork and blend in the garlic. Stir in the yogurt, lemon juice, mint, salt, and pepper. Transfer to a serving bowl and refrigerate. Serve lightly chilled or at room temperature.

Broiled Eggplant Slices

SERVES 4

Here is a quick and easy way to prepare eggplant. The best part is that this technique involves very little oil. Consequently, it produces a light result that is also low in calories. Eggplant slices prepared according to step #1 may be substituted in other recipes that call for slices that have been breaded and fried.

1 medium eggplant, peeled
    or unpeeled
2 to 4 tablespoons olive oil
Salt and freshly ground
    black pepper
2 large tomatoes, peeled
    and sliced
1 tablespoon chopped fresh
    basil
4 ounces mozzarella cheese,
    grated

1. Slice the eggplant into ½-inch-thick rounds. Generously brush both sides of each slice with oil. Place on a flat baking sheet and sprinkle with salt and pepper. Slide under the broiler and cook for 8 to 10 minutes, turning once, until the eggplant is tender and lightly browned.

2. Top each slice of eggplant with a tomato slice and sprinkle with fresh basil. Scatter the mozzarella cheese over the tomato and return to the broiler to melt the cheese. Serve immediately.

Stir-Fried Eggplant

SERVES 4 TO 6

1 medium eggplant, peeled
    and sliced into ½-inch-
    thick rounds
2 tablespoons rice vinegar
1 teaspoon cornstarch
2 tablespoons soy sauce
1 teaspoon sugar
½ teaspoon sesame seed
    oil (dark)
Several drops of Tabasco
    sauce
2 tablespoons vegetable oil
1 tablespoon minced fresh
    ginger
½ cup chicken broth

Freshly chopped ginger and a sauce of rice vinegar and sesame seed oil give eggplant strips an Oriental flavor. Serve warm as a vegetable side dish or chilled as an appetizer.

1. Cut the rounds of eggplant into ½-inch strips. In a small bowl, combine the vinegar and cornstarch and stir to dissolve. Blend in the soy sauce, sugar, sesame seed oil, and Tabasco. Set aside.

2. Heat the vegetable oil in a wok or large skillet. Add the eggplant and stir over high heat for 30 seconds. Add the ginger and chicken broth and reduce the heat. Cover the pan and simmer for 3 to 5 minutes or until the eggplant is partially tender. Pour on the soy sauce mixture and stir briefly over high heat. When the sauce is slightly thickened, transfer the eggplant to a bowl. Serve immediately or cover the bowl and refrigerate until lightly chilled.

Grilled Eggplant

SERVES 4

Grilled eggplant halves are an attractive and tasty companion for grilled lamb chops or veal sausage.

2 small eggplants, unpeeled
½ cup olive oil
Salt and freshly ground
  black pepper
1 tablespoon chopped fresh
  thyme

1. Cut the eggplants in half lengthwise. Then make a series of shallow gashes, 1 inch apart, diagonally across the surface of each half. Make another series of gashes in the opposite direction, creating a diamond-shaped grid.

2. Brush the surface of the flesh with oil and sprinkle with salt and pepper. Scatter the thyme over the surface and then, using your fingertips, press some of the thyme down into the gashes. Place eggplants flesh side down, on a grill and cook for 3 to 5 minutes or until lightly browned. Brush the skin sides with oil and turn the eggplants over. Continue grilling until the flesh is tender but not mushy.

Eggplant Française with Lemon

SERVES 4

A delicate egg batter gives slices of fried eggplant a light, crisp coating. Eggplant Française makes an excellent accompaniment for grilled chicken or roast lamb.

1 cup all-purpose flour
1½ teaspoons salt
Generous amount of freshly
  ground black pepper
2 medium eggplants, peeled
  and sliced into ¼-inch-
  thick rounds
2 large eggs
2 teaspoons cold water
Vegetable oil for frying
1½ lemons for garnish

1. In a deep pie plate, combine the flour, salt, and pepper. Stir with a fork to blend thoroughly. Coat the eggplant slices with the seasoned flour. Place on a baking sheet in a single layer.

2. In a small bowl, whisk together the eggs and water and set aside. Pour the oil into a large skillet to the depth of ½ inch. Heat until the surface ripples. Using 2 forks, dip the flour-coated slices of eggplant into the beaten eggs. Lower into the hot oil and cook over medium heat until nicely browned. Turn once to cook both sides. Transfer to absorbent paper to drain, then arrange on a serving plate. Sprinkle with the juice of ½ lemon. Cut the remaining lemon into wedges and use to garnish the plate.

French-Fried Eggplant

SERVES 4

Eggplant, cut into narrow strips, may be cooked in deep fat and then served as you would french-fried potatoes.

2 medium eggplants, peeled
3 large eggs
3 teaspoons cold water
Salt and freshly ground
  black pepper
Unseasoned bread crumbs
Vegetable oil for deep-
  frying
Coarse salt

1. Cut the eggplants lengthwise into ½-inch-thick slices. Cut the slices into ½-inch-wide strips, then cut the strips into 3½-inch lengths. Place in a large bowl and add enough cold water to cover by 1 inch. Allow to stand for 30 minutes. Drain in a colander and distribute over absorbent paper. Pat dry.

2. In a wide mixing bowl, whisk together the eggs, water, salt, and pepper. Dip the strips of eggplant into the beaten eggs, then coat with bread crumbs. Place on a baking sheet and allow to stand for 30 minutes.

3. Heat the oil in a deep-fat fryer. When it reaches 375°, add the eggplant in small batches. Cook until lightly browned and drain on absorbent paper. Sprinkle with coarse salt and serve on a napkin-lined plate.

Ratatouille

SERVES 8

The classic vegetable mélange known as Ratatouille is at its best when cooked for a relatively short period of time. The object is to preserve the flavor and character of each individual ingredient so that the final dish offers several different taste sensations.

⅓ cup olive oil
1 large onion, coarsely
  chopped
2 garlic cloves, minced
2 medium eggplants, peeled
  or unpeeled, cut into
  1-inch cubes
2 green bell peppers, cut
  into 1-inch cubes
3 small zucchini, cut into
  1-inch cubes
1 bay leaf
1 teaspoon dried thyme
Salt and freshly ground
  black pepper
3 tablespoons dry white
  wine
6 medium tomatoes, peeled,
  seeded, and cut into
  1-inch chunks
12 black oil-cured olives
12 green olives (unstuffed)
½ cup chopped fresh
  parsley

1. Heat the oil in a Dutch oven. Add the onion and garlic and toss to coat. Stir over medium heat until the onion is tender. Add the eggplant and continue to stir over medium heat until the eggplant begins to soften.

2. Preheat the oven to 350°. Mix in the green bell peppers, zucchini, bay leaf, thyme, salt, and pepper. Sprinkle on the wine. Stir in the tomatoes, black olives, green olives, and parsley. Bring the mixture to a gentle bubble. Reduce the heat and cover the pan. Simmer for 10 minutes. Uncover the pan and remove the bay leaf. Place in the oven and bake for 30 minutes or until the eggplant is tender when pierced.

Eggplant Pudding with Fresh Tomato Coulis

Eggplant is so often prepared in combination with other vegetables that its singular flavor is seldom appreciated. Here, eggplant is puréed and blended with eggs and cream to create a subtly flavored pudding. Surrounded by a fresh tomato purée, Eggplant Pudding makes a lovely luncheon dish or first course.

1 medium eggplant, peeled and cut into chunks
4 tablespoons butter
3 large eggs
½ cup medium or whipping cream
½ teaspoon salt
Pinch of cayenne
6 medium tomatoes, peeled, seeded, and chopped
½ teaspoon sugar
2 teaspoons chopped fresh thyme
Salt and freshly ground black pepper

1. Place the chunks of eggplant in a colander. Sprinkle generously with salt, turning the chunks to sprinkle all sides. Allow to stand for 1 hour. Set the colander under cool running water and rinse the eggplant thoroughly, lifting the chunks with your hands. Drain well.

2. Melt 2 tablespoons of the butter in a large skillet. Add the eggplant and stir over medium heat until all the moisture is evaporated and the eggplant is tender but not mushy. Transfer to the container of a blender or processor and whirl until smooth.

3. Preheat the oven to 350°. Generously butter 6 timbale molds or individual soufflé dishes. In a large bowl, whisk together the eggs, cream, salt, and cayenne. Stir in the puréed eggplant. Pour into the prepared molds and place in a shallow roasting pan. Add hot water to the depth of 1 inch. Cover the pan with aluminum foil. Bake for 25 to 30 minutes or until the blade of a knife inserted in the center of each pudding comes out clean.

4. Meanwhile, place the tomatoes in a saucepan. Add the sugar and stir over high heat until the tomatoes are soft. Transfer to the container of a blender or processor and whirl briefly to purée, but do not overliquefy. Return to the saucepan and stir in the thyme, salt, and pepper. Place over low heat to keep warm.

5. When the puddings are cooked, remove them from the hot water and allow them to stand for 10 minutes. Run a knife around the perimeter of each pudding and unmold onto individual plates. Spoon some of the tomato purée around each pudding and serve at once.

Eggplant and Ricotta Casserole

Slices of broiled eggplant are layered with ricotta cheese and a fresh tomato sauce to create a hearty end-of-the-summer casserole.

3 medium eggplants, peeled and sliced into ¼-inch-thick rounds
Olive oil
3 tablespoons vegetable oil
1 medium onion, coarsely chopped
2 medium carrots, grated
1 garlic clove, minced or pressed
1 pound ground lamb or beef
6 medium tomatoes, peeled, seeded, and chopped
1 tablespoon chopped fresh basil
1 teaspoon dried oregano
½ teaspoon salt
Freshly ground black pepper
1 pound ricotta cheese
6 ounces feta cheese, crumbled
¾ cup freshly grated Parmesan cheese

1. Generously brush both sides of the eggplant slices with olive oil. Place on a baking sheet and broil until lightly browned on both sides. Transfer to a large plate and set aside.

2. Heat the vegetable oil in a large skillet. Add the onion, carrots, and garlic and stir over medium heat until the onion is tender. Stir in the ground meat and cook until no longer pink. Add the tomatoes, basil, and oregano and bring to a gentle bubble. Reduce the heat and cover the pan. Simmer for 10 minutes. Season with salt and pepper and increase the heat. Cook, uncovered, at a gentle bubble for 30 minutes or until thickened.

3. Preheat the oven to 350°. Generously butter a shallow, rectangular baking dish. Spoon in enough tomato sauce to cover the bottom of the pan. Layer on half of the eggplant slices. Spoon the ricotta cheese over the eggplant and scatter on half the feta cheese and half the Parmesan cheese. Ladle half of the remaining tomato sauce over the cheese. Layer on the remaining eggplant slices and then sprinkle with the remaining feta cheese and Parmesan cheese. Ladle the remaining tomato sauce over the cheese and cover the dish with aluminum foil. Bake for 30 minutes. Uncover the dish and bake for 15 to 20 minutes or until the sauce is bubbling.

Eggplant and White Bean Casserole

A stick of cinnamon flavors this engaging combination of eggplant and white cannellini beans. Serve as a vegetable side dish with grilled hamburgers or lamb patties.

3 tablespoons olive oil
1 medium onion, coarsely chopped
1 garlic clove, minced
6 tomatoes, peeled, seeded, and chopped
2 tablespoons red wine vinegar
1 teaspoon sugar
½ teaspoon salt
Freshly ground black pepper
1 cinnamon stick
1 medium eggplant, peeled and sliced into ½-inch-thick rounds
1½ cups canned cannellini beans, drained
1 tablespoon chopped fresh basil
1 tablespoon chopped fresh parsley
2 tablespoons butter
¼ cup unseasoned bread crumbs

1. Preheat the oven to 350°. Generously butter a 2-quart casserole. Heat the oil in a large skillet. Add the onion and garlic and toss to coat. Stir over medium heat until the onion is tender. Stir in the tomatoes, then add the vinegar, sugar, salt, and pepper. Submerge the cinnamon stick in the mixture. Bring to a gentle bubble and cook, uncovered, for 30 minutes.

2. Meanwhile, cut the rounds of eggplant into ½-inch-wide sticks, then cut the sticks into ½-inch cubes. Transfer to the prepared casserole dish. Add the beans and stir to combine. Cover and bake for 30 minutes.

3. Remove the cinnamon stick from the sauce and force the sauce through a food mill. Take the eggplant from the oven and stir in the tomato sauce. Blend in the basil and parsley.

4. Melt the butter in a small saucepan. Add the bread crumbs and toss to coat. Scatter the buttered crumbs over the eggplant mixture and return to the oven. Bake, uncovered, for 30 minutes.

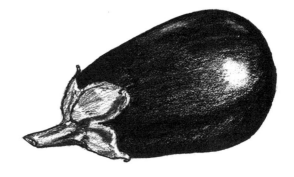

Spaghetti with Eggplant

6 tablespoons olive oil

1 medium eggplant, peeled and cut into ½-inch cubes

1 green bell pepper, cut into 2-inch-long strips

1 medium onion, coarsely chopped

1 garlic clove, minced or pressed

3 pounds tomatoes, peeled, seeded, and chopped

½ cup dry white wine

12 black oil-cured olives, pitted and sliced

6 flat anchovy fillets, finely chopped

1 tablespoon capers, drained

1 tablespoon chopped fresh basil

1 tablespoon chopped fresh parsley

Salt and freshly ground black pepper

¾ pound spaghetti, boiled and drained

Freshly grated Parmesan cheese

Small chunks of eggplant and fresh tomatoes combine to form a hearty, full-flavored sauce for boiled spaghetti.

1. Heat the oil in a large skillet. Add the eggplant, green bell pepper, onion, and garlic. Toss to coat with oil and stir over medium heat until the eggplant begins to soften. Add the tomatoes and wine and bring to a boil. Reduce the heat and simmer, covered, for 20 minutes.

2. Stir in the olives, anchovies, capers, basil, and parsley. Season with salt and pepper. Increase the heat and cook, uncovered, for 10 to 15 minutes or until the mixture is reduced to a thickened consistency. Add the hot, drained spaghetti and toss to combine. Serve with Parmesan cheese.

F

Fennel

WHEN IT COMES to confusion, this vegetable takes first prize. Fennel bears the same name as a seed used for seasoning Mediterranean-style dishes. In addition, its flavor is likened to that of anise, another aromatic seed. And to make matters worse, fennel is frequently marketed as anise, to which it is only remotely related.

Sweet fennel, also called Florence fennel and finocchio, is botanically known as *Foeniculum vulgare dulce*. It is a particularly gorgeous plant with green feathery leaf stalks and a plump white bulb. All parts of the plant are edible, although the green stalks are usually too woody to use for anything other than soups. The tender white bulb is the most sought-after component, and it is served both raw and cooked in a variety of ways. The feathery greens, which resemble sprigs of fresh dill, are frequently used as an herb. And that may be the basis for some of the confusion between sweet fennel and fennel seed, which comes from an entirely different variety of the *Foeniculum* family. Sweet fennel is commonly available during the fall and winter months. It is high in vitamin A and is an excellent source of potassium and calcium.

TO SELECT:

Fennel is usually sold loose and unwrapped. Probably as a space-saving consideration, fennel is also trimmed of most of its greenery. (When fennel is harvested it can have leaf stalks of 2- to 2½-feet long.)

A head of fennel is a large white bulb with overlapping layers that looks like swollen celery. Each white layer terminates in a leafy stalk of varying lengths, and because the stalks in the center of the bulb are shorter, they will still have their feathery, dill-like leaves attached. Select fennel bulbs with a firm white base and fresh-looking leaves. The outer layers of the bulb should not be discolored or cracked. Avoid fennel that feels spongy or looks shriveled. Check the base of the bulb where the root was once attached, and push on it gently. It should not feel soft. One head of fennel serves 2 people.

TO STORE:

Cover fennel loosely with plastic wrap, and place in the vegetable drawer of your refrigerator. It will stay fresh for 3 to 4 days.

TO PREPARE:

Rinse the fennel under cool running water and pat dry. Remove and discard any outer layers that are discolored or bruised. Using a paring knife, cut away the green stalks at the point where the pale green coloration blends into white. The outer layers of white often have strings that need to be removed. A quick and easy approach is to insert the knife

Insert the knife behind the stalk and slice almost all the way through. Tug toward you to complete the break, then pull away the strings.

behind the stalk and slice almost all the way through. A gentle tug toward you will complete the break and pull away the strings at the same time. A swivel-blade peeler may also be used to remove the strings. Trim the root end, then slice the bulb according to your recipe. Reserve the stalks for slicing and adding to soup, and pick off the feathery leaves to use as an herb or garnish.

Sweet fennel may be thinly sliced and served raw. Its crunchy texture makes it a welcome addition to salads and crudité trays. Thinly sliced fennel may also be stir-fried or sautéed in butter. When halved or quartered, fennel bulbs may be braised or baked. Fennel is also delicious blanched, and then grilled or broiled.

Fennel and Tomato Soup SERVES 6

Because this soup contains no chicken or beef broth to offer competition, the pure flavors of fennel and tomato shine through.

2 heads fennel
2 tablespoons olive oil
2 tablespoons butter
1 medium-size mealy
  potato, cut into ½-inch
  cubes
1 medium onion, coarsely
  chopped
4 cups water
2½ pounds tomatoes,
  peeled, seeded, and
  chopped
1 teaspoon dried thyme
½ teaspoon salt
Generous pinch of cayenne
½ cup heavy cream

1. Trim the fennel, reserving the feathery leaves. Cut across the heads, slicing the fennel into ¼-inch-thick rounds. Separate the rounds into strips. Pick out 6 attractive fennel leaves and set them aside for a garnish. Tear the rest into small pieces.

2. Heat the oil and butter in a large saucepan until the butter is melted. Add the fennel, potato, and onion and toss to coat evenly. Stir over medium heat until the onion is tender. Pour in the water. Add the fennel leaves, tomatoes, thyme, salt, and cayenne. Bring to a gentle bubble. Cover and cook for 30 minutes or until the potato is soft.

3. Transfer to the container of a blender or processor and whirl until smooth. Return to the saucepan. Stir in the cream and heat until warmed through. Serve hot garnished with the 6 reserved sprigs of fennel leaves.

Fennel and Orange Salad

Strips of fennel and slices of orange are dressed with a citrusy mustard sauce.

2 heads fennel
2 tablespoons lemon juice
4 large oranges
1 teaspoon Dijon mustard
¼ teaspoon salt
Pinch of cayenne
6 tablespoons olive oil
12 pitted ripe black olives,
   coarsely chopped
1 bunch watercress or
   mâche

1. Rinse and trim the fennel, and then separate into layers as you would ribs of celery. Remove the strings from the outer layers if necessary. Slice each layer lengthwise into 2-inch julienne strips. Transfer to a mixing bowl. Add enough cold water to cover by 1 inch. Stir in 1 tablespoon of the lemon juice.

2. Peel 3 of the oranges. Slice them across and set aside.

3. In a small bowl, whisk together the remaining tablespoon of lemon juice, the juice of the remaining orange, and the mustard. Blend in the salt and cayenne, then whisk in the oil.

4. Arrange 3 or 4 slices of orange on each of 6 salad plates. Drain the fennel strips and scatter them over a clean kitchen towel. Pat dry and arrange the fennel over the orange slices. Scatter the olives over the fennel strips and place a few sprigs of watercress or mâche to one side. Pour on the dressing and chill briefly to serve.

Baked Fennel

SERVES 4

Fennel halves, slowly baked in wine, receive a final flourish of Parmesan cheese and buttered bread crumbs.

4 tablespoons butter
2 heads fennel
½ cup dry white wine
⅓ cup unseasoned bread
   crumbs
2 tablespoons freshly grated
   Parmesan cheese
Salt and freshly ground
   black pepper

1. Preheat the oven to 375°. Melt 3 tablespoons of the butter in a shallow casserole dish. Trim the fennel, then cut each head in half lengthwise. Arrange, cut side down, in the melted butter. Pour in the wine and cover the dish. Bake for 25 to 30 minutes or until tender when pierced.

2. Melt the remaining tablespoon of butter in a small skillet and add the bread crumbs, tossing to coat. Stir in the Parmesan cheese. Turn the fennel over so that the cut side is up. Season with salt and pepper, then sprinkle on the buttered bread crumbs. Return to the oven and bake about 10 minutes or until the crumbs are lightly browned. Transfer to a serving dish and spoon on the pan juices.

Fennel and Red Pepper Sauté

SERVES 4

Feathery fennel leaves accent this stunning combination of white fennel slices and roasted red pepper strips.

2 heads fennel
1 tablespoon fresh fennel
  leaves
3 tablespoons butter
1 shallot, minced
¼ cup water
1 red bell pepper, roasted
  (see p. 254) and cut into
  thin strips
Salt and freshly ground
  black pepper
½ cup heavy cream

1. Trim the fennel, reserving the feathery leaves. Cut across the heads, slicing the fennel into ¼-inch-thick rounds. Separate the rounds into strips. Tear the fennel leaves into small pieces and measure out 1 tablespoon. Set aside.

2. Melt the butter in a large skillet. Add the fennel strips and shallot and toss to coat evenly. Stir over high heat for 30 seconds. Pour on the water and reduce the heat. Cover the pan and simmer for 8 to 10 minutes or until the fennel is crisp-tender. Increase the heat and cook, stirring, until almost all the liquid is evaporated.

3. Stir in the red bell pepper and cook until warmed through. Season with salt and pepper, then transfer to a serving dish. Pour the cream into the skillet and add the fennel leaves. Bring to a boil and cook, stirring, until the cream is reduced by half. Pour over the fennel and red bell pepper to serve.

Broiled Fennel with Mustard Vinaigrette

SERVES 4

The aniselike flavor of fennel makes it a perfect partner for poached salmon or broiled swordfish.

2 heads fennel
1 tablespoon fennel leaves
2 tablespoons lemon juice
1 teaspoon Dijon mustard
½ teaspoon salt
Pinch of cayenne
6 tablespoons olive oil
1 shallot, minced

1. Trim the fennel, reserving the feathery leaves. Coarsely chop the leaves and measure out 1 tablespoon. Set aside. Cut the heads in half lengthwise and drop into a large pot of boiling, salted water. Cook, uncovered, at a gentle bubble for 20 to 25 minutes or until tender when pierced. Remove with a slotted spoon and drain on absorbent paper. Pat dry.

2. Meanwhile, whisk together the lemon juice, mustard, salt, and cayenne. Whisk in the oil, then stir in the shallot and fennel leaves. Brush over the surface of the fennel and arrange the halves, cut side up, in a shallow broiling pan. Slide under the broiler and cook, basting frequently, for 10 to 12 minutes or until the surface looks slightly golden and bubbly. Serve hot or at room temperature, spooning on any remaining vinaigrette.

Fiddleheads

IN THE FIRST fresh weeks of early spring when the dogwood blooms, woodland ferns begin to poke their tightly closed heads through the moist, cool soil. One variety in particular, namely the ostrich fern, is prized for its furled shoots known as fiddleheads. These unopened, immature ferns possess a distinctive woodsy flavor that might best be described as a combination of asparagus and green snap beans.

TO SELECT:

The fiddlehead season is very short, lasting only about 1 week in any given location. As the warm weather moves north, the fiddlehead season moves with it, providing a total harvest of about 4 weeks. Although in limited supply, fiddleheads are available in large supermarkets and specialty food shops.

Look for tightly curled shoots whose coiled shape reminds you of the carved scroll at the head of a violin. Fiddleheads are usually sold loose and are displayed swimming in an unsightly container of water. But don't let that deter you. Reach in and pick out the smallest fiddleheads you can find. In some cases, the stem will be covered with a thin papery sheath. This can be interpreted as a sign of freshness, because after the shoots sit in the water for a while the papery covering falls off and floats around in the display

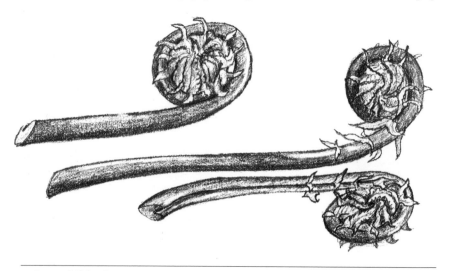

container. Good-quality fiddleheads are colored a characteristic fern green. They should feel firm and smooth to the touch; avoid any fiddleheads that are darkened, mushy, or covered with an excessive amount of brown fuzz. One pound is ample for 6 servings.

TO STORE: Fiddleheads are exceptionally perishable, and therefore are best when prepared on the day of purchase. If necessary, however, they may be placed in a tightly sealed plastic bag and refrigerated for 1 or 2 days.

TO PREPARE: Trim some of the stem, leaving a short, graceful portion attached. Submerge in a basin of cold water and agitate to loosen any papery membrane that is present. Pick off and discard any brownish leaf sprouts.

Fiddleheads may be steamed or blanched until crisp-tender. They may be served cold with a vinaigrette dressing, or sautéed in butter and presented warm with lemon juice or hollandaise sauce.

Fiddleheads Mimosa
SERVES 6

Fiddleheads are steamed until crisp-tender and then tossed with a garlic vinaigrette. When chilled, the fiddleheads are garnished with sieved egg yolks and served on shredded romaine.

1 pound fiddleheads
2 tablespoons lemon juice
½ teaspoon dry mustard
½ teaspoon salt
Pinch of cayenne
6 tablespoons olive oil
1 garlic clove, minced or pressed
1 tablespoon chopped fresh chives
1 head romaine, shredded
2 hard-boiled eggs

1. Trim the fiddleheads and arrange them in a steam basket. Place over boiling water and steam for 10 to 15 minutes or until crisp-tender. Drain in a colander set under cold running water. Shake gently to remove as much water as possible. Transfer to a large mixing bowl.

2. In a small bowl, whisk together the lemon juice, mustard, salt, and cayenne. Whisk in the oil. Then stir in the garlic and chives. Pour over the fiddleheads, tossing to coat evenly. Cover the bowl and refrigerate until thoroughly chilled.

3. Just before serving, divide the shredded romaine among 6 salad plates. Spoon on the chilled fiddleheads in an attractive pattern. Separate the hard-boiled egg yolks from the egg whites and reserve the whites for another use. Force the egg yolks through a sieve and then sprinkle over the fiddleheads. Serve immediately.

Fiddleheads with Avgolemono Sauce

SERVES 4 TO 6

Chicken broth, lemon juice, and egg yolks create a silken sauce with zesty flavor — a piquant partner for fiddleheads.

1 pound fiddleheads
3 large egg yolks
2 tablespoons lemon juice
⅔ cup chicken broth
Salt and freshly ground
  pepper

1. Trim the fiddleheads and drop them into a large pot of boiling, salted water. Cook, uncovered, at a gentle bubble for 5 to 8 minutes or until crisp-tender. Drain in a colander set under cold running water. Shake gently to remove as much water as possible.

2. Whisk together the egg yolks and lemon juice until thick and pale yellow. Whisk in the chicken broth. Then pour the mixture into a small saucepan and place over medium-low heat. Cook, stirring, until the mixture thickens slightly.

3. Transfer the cooked fiddleheads to a serving dish. Sprinkle them with salt and pepper. Pour on the lemon sauce and serve immediately.

Sautéed Fiddleheads with Bacon and Cheese

SERVES 4 TO 6

Bacon and Parmesan cheese punctuate the earthy flavor of fresh green fiddleheads.

1 pound fiddleheads
¼ pound sliced bacon, cut
  into 1-inch lengths
4 tablespoons butter
Salt and freshly ground
  black pepper
¼ cup freshly grated
  Parmesan cheese
Juice of half a lemon

1. Trim the fiddleheads and drop them into a large pot of boiling, salted water. Cook, uncovered, at a gentle bubble for 5 to 8 minutes or until crisp-tender. Drain in a colander set under cold running water. Shake gently to remove as much water as possible.

2. Fry the bacon in a large skillet. When it is crisp, drain on absorbent paper and set aside. Reserve the fat for another use.

3. Melt the butter in the same skillet and add the fiddleheads. Toss to coat evenly and stir over medium heat for 1 minute or until warmed through. Season with salt and pepper. Stir in the Parmesan cheese and add the bacon. Cook until the cheese begins to melt, then transfer to a serving dish. Squeeze on the lemon juice and serve immediately.

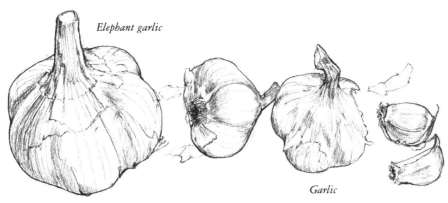

Elephant garlic

Garlic

Garlic

G ARLIC HAS a reputation for being strongly flavored and odoriferous. And it is true that garlic flesh contains the same sulfur compounds responsible for the pungency of onions. However, few cooks realize that they can control the assertiveness of garlic by the way they prepare it.

Recent research has discovered that what might be referred to as "garlic oils" do not exist in whole, undisturbed garlic flesh. Rather, they are produced when the cells of the flesh are crushed. Even slicing garlic, which gently crushes the layers of flesh, will start the enzymatic reaction that creates garlic oils. This explains why whole garlic cloves, either simmered or roasted, possess a mild, sweet, almost nutty flavor, while at the other extreme, a paste of salt and crushed raw garlic has an overpowering flavor. It also sheds light on the mincing versus pressing controversy. Many discerning cooks favor mincing garlic as opposed to pressing it, claiming that garlic forced through a press has a bitter taste. Now it is clear why — by pressing garlic, you thoroughly crush the flesh and produce an overabundance of garlic oil.

TO SELECT:

Garlic is available year round and is sold loose, or packed in small boxes of two. The entire bulb is referred to as "a head of garlic," and the individual segments of the bulb are called "cloves." Bulbs of garlic come in two basic sizes — the familiar 1½- to 2-inch head and a newer variety called elephant garlic, which can measure up to 4 inches across and have cloves weighing 1 ounce apiece.

When you select garlic, pick it up in your hand and feel the entire surface of the bulb. Look for a firm head that is stout and feels heavy for its size. Pass up any heads that have shriveled cloves or green sprouts. The parchmentlike outer skin may be white, yellowish white, or white streaked with purple.

TO STORE:

Under favorable conditions, garlic may be stored for 2 to 3 months. The key is to provide adequate air circulation and avoid dampness. With that in mind, place garlic bulbs in a wire or mesh basket, wicker bowl, or an unglazed pottery crock with holes in it. (The unglazed surface will absorb any moisture that is present and the holes allow air to circulate inside the container.) Store in a cool, dry, well-ventilated spot away from any light source. Do not refrigerate garlic because the moisture that accumulates inside a refrigerator causes garlic to decay.

TO PREPARE:

For the mildest possible garlic flavor, simmer or sauté garlic cloves whole and unpeeled. A slightly stronger flavor may be obtained by removing the skins before cooking. From this point, keep in mind that the degree to which you crush the cells of the flesh will determine how strong a flavor you obtain. Slicing a peeled clove, for example, will give you the next level of assertiveness. Next comes mincing, then pressing, and finally puréeing the garlic to obtain the strongest flavor of all.

To peel a garlic clove, slice off the hard end and strip away the skin.

To peel a single clove of garlic, slice off the hard end where it was once attached to the bulb. Strip away the brittle skin. (Most cookbooks suggest pressing on the side of the clove with the flat blade of a knife until the skin cracks open, but I prefer my method because it is just as fast and it doesn't crush the clove.) If you have a number of garlic cloves to peel, blanch them in boiling water for a few seconds. The skins will slip right off. To temper the flavor of garlic, cook unpeeled cloves in boiling water for 3 to 5 minutes or until tender when pierced with a knife. Garlic cloves pretreated this way are so mild they may be sliced and added to salads or pizza.

A unique and delicious way to prepare garlic is to roast the entire unpeeled bulb. Bake alongside a roast, or place in a baking dish and drizzle lightly with oil. Roast at 350° for 1 hour or until tender when pierced.

Garlic may be minced or chopped ahead of time and submerged in oil. Stored in a glass jar in the refrigerator, the mixture will keep for up to 3 weeks. This eliminates the task of mincing or chopping garlic every time you need it, and the oil is delicious spread on bread or used as a component of salad dressing.

Roast Garlic

SERVES 6

To eat Roast Garlic, pull a clove away from the head with your fingers. Squeeze gently at one end and the flesh will slide out of its parchment skin. Offer Roast Garlic, spread on crusty bread, as an appetizer or an accompaniment for a hearty soup.

6 large heads garlic
½ cup olive oil

1. Preheat the oven to 350°. Generously butter a small baking dish.

2. Using the tip of a paring knife, lift away the outermost layer of parchment surrounding each head. The individual cloves should be visible, but still covered with their own wrapping of parchment. Trim the root end just enough so that the heads will sit straight. Place in the baking dish and drizzle on the oil.

3. Bake for 1 to 1½ hours, basting frequently with the oil in the baking dish. The garlic is done when the flesh feels tender when pierced. Serve while warm but cool enough to handle.

Drizzle the unpeeled garlic bulbs with oil before baking. When tender, pull a clove from the bulb and gently squeeze one end to remove the flesh from its skin.

Bruschetta

Slices of grilled garlic toast may be served as an appetizer or paired with slices of fresh tomato and fresh mozzarella and offered for lunch. Since the flavor of the olive oil is such an important element of this preparation, use good-quality extra-virgin olive oil.

½ cup extra-virgin olive oil
6 cloves garlic, peeled and cut in half crosswise
4 slices Italian bread, cut 1 inch thick from a large round loaf
Salt and freshly ground black pepper

1. In a small saucepan, combine the oil and garlic and set over low heat. Cook slowly until the garlic is tender and golden. Do not allow it to brown. The object is to warm the oil gently and heat the garlic to encourage it to release its flavor.

2. Arrange the slices of bread on a hot grill and cook until both sides are toasted. Transfer to a serving plate.

3. Remove the garlic from the oil with a slotted spoon and discard. Generously brush the surface of each slice of toast with warm olive oil. Sprinkle with salt and pepper and serve immediately.

Cream of Roast Garlic Soup

Whole heads of garlic are roasted in the oven and then peeled and puréed to create a rich, velvety soup with an enticing flavor.

4 large heads garlic
3 tablespoons butter
2 tablespoons all-purpose flour
6 cups chicken broth
½ teaspoon salt
Freshly ground white pepper
1 teaspoon dried thyme
½ cup medium or whipping cream
Toasted croutons for garnish
Paprika for garnish

1. Remove any excess outer parchment from the garlic heads and place them in a lightly greased shallow pan. Roast in a 350° oven for 1 to 1½ hours or until the cloves are tender when pierced. Set aside until cool enough to handle. Separate the cooled cloves and peel them.

2. Melt the butter in a large saucepan. Blend in the flour and stir over medium heat until the mixture foams. Stir in the chicken broth and bring to a boil. Stir in the salt, pepper, and thyme. Add the peeled garlic cloves and reduce the heat. Simmer, uncovered, for 10 minutes.

3. Transfer to the container of a blender or processor and whirl until smooth. Return to the saucepan and blend in the cream. Place over medium heat and warm gently, but do not allow the soup to boil. Ladle into soup bowls and garnish generously with croutons and paprika.

Garlic and Tomato Salad

SERVES 4

Blanching unpeeled cloves of garlic gives them a sweet, nutlike flavor that is mild and unexpectedly refined.

2 heads garlic
2 tablespoons white wine
  vinegar
½ teaspoon dry mustard
½ teaspoon salt
Freshly ground black
  pepper
6 tablespoons olive oil
1 tablespoon chopped fresh
  basil
Leaves of Boston lettuce
4 medium tomatoes, peeled
  and sliced

1. Separate the garlic into cloves and then drop them into a large pot of boiling, salted water. Cook, uncovered, at a gentle bubble for 3 to 5 minutes or until tender when pierced. Drain in a colander and set aside to cool.

2. Meanwhile, whisk together the vinegar, mustard, salt, and pepper. Whisk in the oil and stir in the basil.

3. When cool enough to handle, pinch an end of each garlic clove to force the flesh to slide out of its parchment skin. Place the cooked garlic in a small bowl and pour on the prepared dressing. Toss to coat, then refrigerate until thoroughly chilled.

4. Just before serving, line 4 salad plates with lettuce leaves. Arrange the tomato slices over the lettuce. Scatter the garlic over the tomatoes in an attractive manner, then whisk the dressing that remains in the bowl and pour some over each salad.

Grape Leaves

IN RECENT YEARS, a number of small wine producers have established vineyards in different parts of the country, and as a side benefit, fresh grape leaves are increasingly available. These delightful greens are used in the various cuisines of the Middle East to provide a moist wrapping for savory fillings of rice, meat, or fish.

TO SELECT:

The best time of year for fresh grape leaves is in May or June, depending on your location. They should be picked when they have reached full size, but are still young and tender. Look for fresh, resilient leaves that are finely veined; choose thin leaves rather than thick ones, and pass up those with more prominent veins. Medium-size leaves measure about 5 to 5½ inches across, and are a good choice for

appetizers; large leaves measure 6 to 7 inches across, and are the ones to use for main-course servings. Grape leaves are most commonly sold in specialty food shops and ethnic markets catering to Middle Eastern cuisines.

TO STORE: Unwashed grape leaves may be placed in an airtight plastic bag and refrigerated for 2 to 3 days. They may also be frozen for longer storage by packing them in plastic containers. To freeze, remove the stem at the base of each leaf, and stack the leaves together in groups of 25 or 30. Place the leaves in a plastic container that is wide enough to hold the leaves flat. Separate each group of leaves with 2 squares of waxed paper to facilitate removing them at a later time.

TO PREPARE: Rinse fresh grape leaves under cool running water. Trim the stems at the base of the leaves. Stack the leaves in groups of 20 or 25 and set aside. Bring a shallow pan of salted water to a gentle boil. Then, using wooden or plastic tongs (so as not to damage the leaves), take up a stack of leaves and submerge it in the hot water. Because the leaves were rinsed, their damp surfaces should hold the stack together, but you may keep the tongs positioned gently on the leaves if they appear to be floating apart. Blanch the leaves for approximately 1 minute or until they are limp. Test by lifting the stack from the water. The leaves should droop gracefully, but still retain some firmness of texture. Stacks of frozen grape leaves should be blanched without defrosting.

Blanched grape leaves may be wrapped around cheese or a flavorful filling of rice, meat, or fish. They are then baked and served hot, cold, or at room temperature.

Grape Leaves Stuffed with Goat Cheese   SERVES 6

When grilled, these grape-leaf bundles develop a crispy exterior, which provides a brittle contrast to the smooth melted cheese inside. Serve as a light meal with grilled bread and fresh tomato slices, or offer as an appetizer.

24 large grape leaves
1 tablespoon chopped fresh thyme
1 tablespoon chopped fresh basil
12 ounces soft, unripened goat cheese, such as Montrachet
1 red bell pepper, cut into 24 short, thin strips
Olive oil
Salt and freshly ground black pepper

1. Prepare the grape leaves as described earlier (see TO PREPARE). Drain on absorbent paper and pat dry. Preheat the oven to 375°. Generously coat a shallow baking pan with oil. In a small bowl, combine the thyme and basil and toss to mix.

2. Take up a grape leaf and lay it in front of you underside up. Place a tablespoon of goat cheese at the stem end. Sprinkle with the herb mixture and lay on a strip of red bell pepper. Fold the sides over and roll into a tight bundle. Transfer to the prepared pan seam side down. Repeat with the remaining leaves, arranging them in the baking dish with some space between bundles.

3. Generously brush the surface of the leaves with olive oil, then sprinkle with salt and pepper. Bake, uncovered, for 15 minutes. Transfer to a hot grill and cook, turning frequently, until all sides of the leaves are crisp. (Or finish under the broiler to crisp the outsides of the leaves.)

Place a tablespoon of goat cheese at the stem end, fold over the sides, then roll the leaf into a tight bundle.

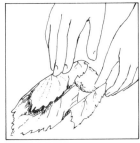

Grape Leaves Stuffed with Rice

Grape leaves wrapped around an aromatic filling of rice, raisins, and pine nuts may be served hot as an accompaniment to roast lamb or offered cold as an appetizer.

32 large grape leaves
3 tablespoons olive oil
3 tablespoons butter
2 medium onions, coarsely chopped
⅓ cup raisins
½ cup chopped fresh parsley
1 tablespoon chopped fresh mint
1 tablespoon chopped fresh basil
¼ teaspoon ground cinnamon
½ teaspoon salt
Generous pinch of cayenne
1½ cups cooked rice
¼ cup pine nuts, toasted
3 tablespoons lemon juice

1. Prepare the grape leaves as described earlier (see TO PREPARE). Drain on absorbent paper and pat dry. Set aside.

2. In a large skillet, heat the oil and butter until the butter melts. Add the onions, tossing to coat. Stir over medium heat until the onions are tender. Add the raisins, parsley, mint, basil, cinnamon, salt, and cayenne. Stir over medium heat for 1 minute. Mix in the rice and pine nuts and remove from the heat.

3. Select 24 of the most well-formed leaves and reserve the rest. Take up a leaf and lay it in front of you underside up. Place a tablespoon of filling at the stem end. Fold the sides over and roll into a tight bundle. Repeat with the remaining leaves.

4. To cook, line a large skillet or Dutch oven with the reserved leaves. Sprinkle on 2 tablespoons of the lemon juice, then arrange the bundles over the leaves seam side down. Make 2 layers if necessary. Add enough water to cover the leaves. Cover the pan and simmer for 30 minutes. Transfer with a slotted spoon to a serving dish and sprinkle with the remaining tablespoon of lemon juice. Serve hot or refrigerate until chilled.

Horseradish Root

A S ANY HORSERADISH lover will tell you, in order to get the most vibrant, zesty flavor, you must grate your own fresh horseradish root. This brownish white root can be found sporadically in large supermarkets, but it is in especially ample supply during the spring.

TO SELECT: A horseradish root is customarily about 8 inches long and 1½ to 2 inches in diameter. One end is usually slender and rounded; the opposite end is fatter and gnarled. Choose a root that is firm and has no soft spots; pass up any that are shriveled or have begun to sprout.

TO STORE: Place the unwashed root in the refrigerator without wrapping. Use as soon as possible, at least within 5 days.

TO PREPARE: With a stiff brush, scrub the horseradish root under cool running water. Peel with a paring knife and cut out any dark spots. Slice into 2-inch pieces, then cut into matchsticks or shave off thin slivers with a swivel-blade peeler. Horseradish root may also be grated, but the oils that are released will irritate your eyes, so you might want to use a food processor for this task. Cut the peeled horseradish root into small cubes and place in the container of a processor. Pulse briefly to attain a grated texture. For a smoother consistency, like the commercially produced horseradish that comes in a jar, combine the cubed root with vinegar and whirl in a blender or processor until the desired consistency is reached. (Be sure to avert your eyes when you lift the cover of the container because the fumes are quite strong.) Grated or puréed horseradish adds interest to cold sauces and is frequently often blended into sour cream, mayonnaise, mustard, and ketchup. Horseradish root is customarily served raw, because its characteristic zing is lost if heat is applied.

Creamy Horseradish

MAKES 3 CUPS

1 horseradish root, peeled and cubed
1 pound small turnips, peeled and thinly sliced
1 teaspoon salt
Freshly ground white pepper
1 teaspoon sugar
1 cup white vinegar

Freshly grated horseradish is a versatile condiment to have on hand. Use as is, or combine it with ketchup to create your own seafood-cocktail sauce.

1. Place the horseradish in the container of a processor. Add the turnips, salt, pepper, and sugar. Turn the processor on and slowly pour the vinegar through the feed tube. Whirl until almost puréed.

2. Transfer to a glass jar with a screw-top lid and refrigerate. It will keep for up to 6 weeks.

Horseradish Mousse

Serve slim wedges of this zippy mousse as an accompaniment to roast beef. Or unmold onto an attractive plate and surround with wheat crackers as an appetizer.

2 cups ricotta cheese
1 medium onion, coarsely chopped
½ cup grated horseradish root (or use Creamy Horseradish)
⅓ cup medium or whipping cream
2 tablespoons lemon juice
½ teaspoon salt
Freshly ground white pepper
2 tablespoons cold water
1 package unflavored gelatin

1. In the container of a blender or processor, combine the ricotta cheese and the onion and whirl until smooth. Add the horseradish, cream, lemon juice, salt, and pepper. Whirl to combine. Pour the mixture into a large mixing bowl.

2. Pour the water into a glass measuring cup. Sprinkle on the gelatin and allow it to soften. Set the cup in a saucepan containing a small amount of boiling water and stir until the gelatin is dissolved. Add the dissolved gelatin to the horseradish mixture and blend thoroughly. Pour into a round mold or a shallow round baking dish. Cover with plastic wrap and refrigerate until firm. Dip the mold briefly in warm water to loosen. Unmold and cut into slim wedges or serve whole.

Horseradish Spread with Belgian Endive

½ cup sour cream
2 tablespoons grated horseradish root (or use Creamy Horseradish)
1 tablespoon lemon juice
¼ teaspoon salt
Generous pinch of cayenne
1 cup heavy cream
2 heads Belgian endive, separated into spears

Spoon this light, creamy spread into spears of Belgian endive to serve as an appetizer or salad.

1. Combine the sour cream, horseradish, lemon juice, salt, and cayenne in a small bowl and mix until well blended. In another bowl, whisk the cream until soft peaks form. Fold into the sour cream mixture and chill.

2. To serve, spoon the mixture into the lower third of each endive spear and arrange the filled leaves in a spoke-like fashion on a large glass serving plate. Set a small container of spread in the center for dipping if you wish.

J

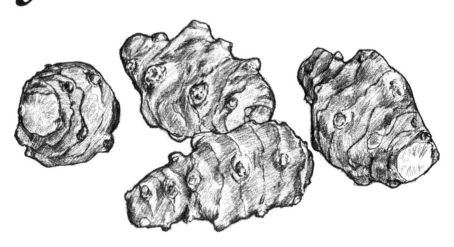

Jerusalem Artichokes

ONE OF THE MOST interesting things about this root vegetable is its misleading name. For not only is it *not* from Jerusalem, it is not even an artichoke. Instead, it is a member of the sunflower family, which explains why it was first referred to as a girasol, a term given to plants whose flowers turn to face the sun. In all probability, "girasol" was mispronounced as "Jerusalem," and that, plus the artichokelike flavor of its root, resulted in Jerusalem artichoke becoming its commonly accepted name. But farmers and marketing experts have sensed that the consumer is confused, so they have initiated a campaign to label Jerusalem artichokes as sunchokes or sun roots.

TO SELECT:

Jerusalem artichokes are a tuberous root vegetable whose gnarled shape brings to mind oversize fresh ginger. Usually light brown in color, they may also be tinged with purple, green, or yellow. Select the smoothest ones you can find because the knobby protuberances result in waste. (Farmers are attempting to breed out the knobbiness, so at times you may see varieties that are much smoother than others.) Jerusalem artichokes of good quality will be firm, clean, and unblemished; avoid any that have soft spots or broken skin. Jerusalem artichokes are available year round, with the peak season occurring from October to April. They are exceptionally high in iron and are a good source of vitamin C. Plan on purchasing 1½ pounds to serve 4 people.

TO STORE: Unwrapped Jerusalem artichokes may be successfully stored in a cool, dry, well-ventilated place away from any light source. They may also be loosely wrapped and kept in the vegetable drawer of your refrigerator. Depending on their condition on the day of purchase, Jerusalem artichokes may retain their quality for 1 to 3 weeks.

TO PREPARE: Jerusalem artichokes have white flesh with a refreshing, crunchy consistency similar to that of jicama (see Jicama). Their flavor is sweet, mild, and nutty, and I think more accurately described as similar to that of water chestnuts than of artichokes. They may be served raw as a crudité or a salad component, but because the flesh darkens upon exposure to the air, uncooked Jerusalem artichokes must be coated with dressing immediately or submerged in acidulated water. Cooked Jerusalem artichokes may be served hot or chilled.

As with potatoes, the skins of Jerusalem artichokes are edible and delicious. Consequently, they may be baked, fried, steamed, or boiled, and served in their jackets. Jerusalem artichokes may also be peeled. First, rinse the outer surfaces thoroughly under cool running water. Brush the crevices well with a vegetable brush. Then slice away any small knobs and remove the skin with a swivel-blade peeler. Grate or shred the flesh to use raw, or cook them whole. However, when boiling, steaming, or microwaving Jerusalem artichokes, it's easier to cook them first and then remove the peel.

The important thing to keep in mind when cooking Jerusalem artichokes is that even though they resemble potatoes, they cook faster and do not achieve the same kind of starchy consistency. In fact, they have a quirk — Jerusalem artichokes will turn mushy in the blink of an eye. So monitor their cooking closely, testing for tenderness often, and remove them from the heat as soon as a metal skewer slides into the flesh easily.

Jerusalem Artichoke Soup

6 cups chicken broth
1 pound Jerusalem
    artichokes, peeled and
    quartered
1 medium-size mealy
    potato, peeled and
    quartered
6 thin slices baked ham,
    coarsely chopped
2 tablespoons lime juice
⅛ teaspoon ground cumin
12 ounces fresh spinach
Salt and freshly ground
    white pepper
½ cup medium or whipping
    cream

Thin strips of lightly cooked spinach add a vibrant note to this smooth, rich soup.

1. In a large saucepan, combine the chicken broth, Jerusalem artichokes, potato, and ham. Cover and cook at a gentle bubble for 20 minutes or until the vegetables are tender.

2. Transfer to the container of a blender or processor and whirl until smooth. Return to the saucepan and blend in the lime juice and cumin.

3. Rinse the spinach and remove the tough stems. Stack the leaves in small bunches and cut across into thin shreds. Add to the soup. Season with salt and pepper and stir in the cream. Place over medium heat and warm gently, but do not boil. When the spinach is wilted, ladle into soup bowls and serve hot.

Jerusalem Artichoke and Bacon Salad

Thin slices of uncooked Jerusalem artichoke combine with crisp bacon and romaine to create an appealing salad.

2 tablespoons lemon juice
½ teaspoon Dijon mustard
½ teaspoon dried tarragon
¼ teaspoon salt
Pinch of cayenne
6 tablespoons olive oil
1½ pounds Jerusalem
    artichokes
1 shallot, minced
¼ pound sliced bacon
1 head romaine

1. In a small bowl, whisk together the lemon juice, mustard, tarragon, salt, and cayenne. Whisk in the oil and set aside.

2. Peel the Jerusalem artichokes and cut them in half lengthwise. Slice each half lengthwise as thinly as possible. Transfer to a mixing bowl. Scatter the minced shallot over the Jerusalem artichokes and pour on the prepared dressing. Toss to coat all the slices. Cover the bowl and refrigerate for 1 hour.

3. Fry the bacon until crisp and drain on absorbent paper. Rinse the romaine and tear into bite-size pieces. Place in a large salad bowl. Add the Jerusalem artichoke slices and toss to combine. (Drizzle on any remaining dressing, if desired.) Crumble the bacon and distribute over the salad. Serve immediately.

Jerusalem Artichoke Purée

Puréed Jerusalem artichokes make an excellent substitute for mashed potatoes. Serve them piping hot with roast or grilled meats.

1½ pounds Jerusalem
    artichokes, unpeeled
2 tablespoons medium or
    whipping cream
4 tablespoons butter, cut
    into small pieces
Salt and freshly ground
    black pepper
Freshly grated nutmeg

1. Boil or steam the Jerusalem artichokes until tender when pierced. Drain in a colander and set aside.

2. When cool enough to handle, peel the Jerusalem artichokes and force them through a sieve or food mill, allowing them to fall into a large saucepan. Beat in the cream and place over medium heat. Add the butter and stir continuously until it is melted. Season with salt and pepper, then transfer to a serving dish. Sprinkle with nutmeg and serve while hot.

Jerusalem Artichokes Sautéed in Butter

SERVES 4

Unpeeled slices of Jerusalem artichokes are tossed with butter and lemon and accented with fresh chives.

1½ pounds Jerusalem
    artichokes, unpeeled
6 tablespoons butter
1 tablespoon lemon juice
3 tablespoons water
3 tablespoons freshly grated
    Parmesan cheese
Salt and freshly ground
    black pepper
1 tablespoon chopped fresh
    chives

1. Drop the Jerusalem artichokes into a large pot of boiling, salted water and cook, uncovered, for 10 to 15 minutes or until crisp-tender. Drain in a colander and set aside.

2. When cool enough to handle, slice the unpeeled Jerusalem artichokes into ¼-inch-thick rounds. Melt the butter in a large skillet. Stir in the lemon juice and water and add the slices of Jerusalem artichokes. Toss to coat evenly and reduce the heat. Cover the pan and cook slowly for 10 to 12 minutes or until tender when pierced.

3. Increase the heat and sprinkle on the Parmesan cheese. Season with salt and pepper and add the chives. Stir over medium heat until the cheese begins to melt. Serve immediately.

Jicama (HEE-ka-mah)

T HIS BROWN-SKINNED ROOT vegetable, popular in Mexican cookery and the cuisine of the American Southwest, possesses a surprisingly crisp, juicy texture and a mildly sweet flavor closely resembling that of water chestnuts. Usually served raw, which best shows off its refreshing character, jicama may also be boiled, steamed, or fried like Irish potato. When cooked briefly, such as in a stir-fry dish, jicama retains its crispness just like water chestnuts do. Consequently, jicama can be sliced like water chestnuts and used in their place.

TO SELECT:

Looking remarkably like turnips, these squat globes have a tough, scruffy, brown skin, and they are sometimes furrowed on each side. Jicamas are available from November to June. Choose those that are firm and free of blemishes, and avoid any with wrinkled skin or that feel soft and spongy to the touch. Although jicamas may weigh up to 6 pounds, those closer to 1 pound, which will feed 3 to 4 people, are the easiest to manage. Larger jicamas tend to be woody.

TO STORE:

An uncut jicama may be stored at room temperature for 1 to 2 weeks; however, if it is to be served raw, it's imperative that jicama first be thoroughly chilled in order to highlight its icy crispness. Cut jicama should be covered with plastic wrap and refrigerated. It will keep this way for 4 or 5 days.

TO PREPARE:

The outer skin of jicama is quite tough, but you can strip it off easily with a paring knife or by pulling it away with your fingers. If a fibrous undercoating remains, remove it with a swivel-blade peeler. Jicama does not brown when exposed to the air, so it can be sliced or shredded ahead of time without the use of acidulated water. Submerge prepared jicama in cold water and refrigerate until needed to retain crispness and prevent drying.

Pickled Jicama

SERVES 8

2 cups water
1 cup white vinegar
½ cup vegetable oil
1 teaspoon salt
6 garlic cloves, peeled and
  cut in half
1 teaspoon black
  peppercorns
1 teaspoon mustard seed
3 bay leaves, broken in half
½ teaspoon dried thyme
½ teaspoon dried oregano
¼ teaspoon dried marjoram
2 medium jicamas, peeled
  and cut into ¼-inch-thick
  strips
4 ribs celery, sliced
1 large onion, sliced and
  separated into rings
1 red bell pepper, cut into
  ½-inch squares
4 jalapeño chili peppers,
  seeded and cut into ¼-
  inch-thick rounds

Offer this lively combination of jicama, onion, and red bell pepper as an appetizer or as an accompaniment to a hearty casserole.

1. In a large nonreactive saucepan, combine the water, vinegar, oil, and salt. Place over high heat and bring to a boil. Stir in the garlic, peppercorns, mustard seed, bay leaves, thyme, oregano, and marjoram.

2. Add the jicamas, celery, onion, and red bell pepper and reduce the heat. Simmer, uncovered, for 10 minutes. Mix in the chili peppers and simmer for 5 minutes. Transfer to a glass bowl. Cover and refrigerate for 1 or 2 days to absorb the full flavor of the marinade. Serve chilled.

Jicama Salad with Lime Mayonnaise

SERVES 6

The vibrant flavors of lime and fresh cilantro underscore the juxtaposition of jicama and tart green apples.

2 medium jicamas
2 tart green apples, such as
  Granny Smith
Juice of 3 limes
Salt and freshly ground
  black pepper
1 tablespoon chopped fresh
  cilantro
½ cup mayonnaise,
  preferably homemade
½ teaspoon sugar

1. Peel the jicamas and the apples and cut them into julienne strips. Combine the strips in a mixing bowl and sprinkle with the juice of 2 limes. Toss to coat and refrigerate until chilled.

2. When chilled, season the mixture with salt and pepper. Add the cilantro and toss gently. Transfer to an attractive serving plate. In a small bowl, blend together the mayonnaise, sugar, and the juice of the remaining lime. Mix thoroughly and pour over the jicamas and apples. Serve immediately.

Jicama and Shrimp Salad

SERVES 4

2 medium jicamas, peeled
  and shredded
6 tomatillos, sliced
1 shallot, minced
1 tablespoon chopped fresh
  cilantro
1 pound shrimp, cooked,
  peeled, and deveined
Salt and freshly ground
  black pepper
6 tablespoons olive oil
2 tablespoons white wine
  vinegar
1 teaspoon sugar
1 green chili, such as
  Serrano, finely chopped

Shredded jicama is tossed with cooked shrimp and sliced tomatillos to form a winning combination of textures and tastes.

1. Combine the jicamas, tomatillos, shallot, and cilantro in a large mixing bowl. Add the shrimp and toss to mix. Season with salt and pepper.

2. In a small bowl, whisk together the oil, vinegar, and sugar. Stir in the chopped chili and pour over the jicama mixture. Cover the bowl and refrigerate until thoroughly chilled. Serve with fresh tomato slices.

Stir-Fried Jicama and Celery with Red Bell Pepper SERVES 4

2 tablespoons water
1 tablespoon soy sauce
1 tablespoon rice vinegar
1 teaspoon sugar
3 tablespoons vegetable oil
2 medium jicamas, peeled
  and cut into julienne
  strips
1 tablespoon minced fresh
  ginger
6 celery ribs, sliced on the
  diagonal
1 red bell pepper, cut into
  ½-inch squares
1 tablespoon chopped fresh
  cilantro

Strips of jicama and slices of celery retain their crisp crunchiness when cooked briefly in an Oriental sauce. Serve as a vegetable side dish with roast pork or broiled pork chops.

1. In a small bowl, combine the water, soy sauce, vinegar, and sugar. Blend well and set aside.

2. Heat the oil in a wok or large skillet. Add the jicama and ginger and toss to coat evenly. Cook, stirring over high heat, for 30 seconds. Add the celery and red bell pepper. Stir over high heat for 30 seconds more.

3. Pour on the soy sauce mixture and reduce the heat. Stir over medium heat until most of the liquid is evaporated, then mix in the cilantro. Serve immediately.

K

Kale

K ALE IS EASILY identified by the bluish grey tint to its leaves. Sturdy and tightly curled, these greens are more mildly flavored than most. Kale has a rather coarse texture, so it holds up during cooking to a greater extent than spinach and some of the other more delicate greens.

One of the interesting characteristics of kale is its ability to withstand severe frost and even snow cover. Consequently, good-quality kale is available all year, with the exception of the hot summer months. Kale is an excellent source of calcium, potassium, and vitamins A and C.

TO SELECT:

Look for resilient, bouncy leaves with lacy edges. If possible, pick out the smallest leaves because they will be more tender and delicately flavored; avoid any that are limp or yellow. Tiny kale greens may be sautéed lightly or served raw in a salad, but they are not commonly available. Most of the kale sold in supermarkets needs to be cooked, so plan on purchasing 1 to 1½ pounds for 4 servings, depending on the size of the center rib, which is discarded.

TO STORE:	Like all greens, kale contains a high percentage of water. As this water is given off during respiration, the leaves become limp and wilted. Successful storage, then, depends on keeping moisture loss to a minimum. After snapping off any exceptionally large stems, transfer the unwashed kale to a plastic bag and secure with a wire twist. Refrigerate and use within 1 to 2 days.
TO PREPARE:	For the most tender results, remove the stem and center rib of each leaf by folding it in half so that the underside of the rib protrudes, and then gently pull the rib away from the leaf. Wash the trimmed leaves in a basin of cold water. Be especially careful to inspect the curly edges for any insects that may be lingering there. Transfer the clean leaves to a colander to drain.

Kale may be prepared whole, chopped coarsely, or cut into thin strips. It may be cooked in salted water at a rolling boil or sautéed in butter. Coarsely chopped, kale is delicious when stir-fried; julienne strips make a wonderful addition to clear broths and hearty bean soups.

Kale with Crushed Peanuts   SERVES 4

Leaves of kale are boiled until crisp-tender and then finished with bacon fat and crushed peanuts.

1½ pounds kale
½ cup unsalted peanuts
3 tablespoons bacon fat
Salt and freshly ground
   black pepper

1. Prepare the kale as described earlier (see TO PREPARE), then submerge it in a large pot of boiling, salted water. Cook, uncovered, at a gentle bubble for 5 minutes or until the leaves are crisp-tender. Drain in a colander set under cold running water. Shake gently to remove as much water as possible. Chop the kale coarsely and set aside.

2. Scatter the peanuts between 2 sheets of waxed paper and crush them with a rolling pin.

3. Melt the bacon fat in a large skillet. Add the chopped kale and toss to coat evenly. Stir over medium heat for 2 minutes or until glossy. Season with salt and pepper and sprinkle on the peanuts. Continue stirring over medium heat until warmed through, then serve at once.

Stir-Fried Kale with Ham

SERVES 4

3 tablespoons vegetable oil
½ pound baked ham, cut
   into julienne strips
1½ pounds kale, cut into
   ½-inch shreds
2 green onions, white and
   green portions, sliced
3 tablespoons water
3 tablespoons butter, cut
   into small pieces
2 tablespoons coarsely
   chopped unsalted
   cashews

Strips of kale are stir-fried with ham and green onions. Serve in place of a salad course or with scrambled eggs as a late-night supper.

1. Heat the oil in a large skillet or wok. Add the ham and stir over high heat for 30 seconds. Using a slotted spoon, transfer the ham to a platter or bowl.

2. Add the kale to the hot pan and stir over high heat until wilted. Add the onions and water and continue to stir for 30 seconds. Reduce the heat and cover the pan. Simmer for 5 minutes or until the kale is crisp-tender. Return the ham to the pan. Add the butter and cashews and stir over medium heat until the butter is melted. Transfer immediately to a serving dish.

Portuguese Kale Soup

SERVES 8

1 pound kale
3 tablespoons vegetable oil
3 tablespoons butter
2 medium onions, coarsely
   chopped
2 medium carrots, coarsely
   chopped
2 ribs celery, coarsely
   chopped
2 medium potatoes, coarsely
   chopped
2 garlic cloves, minced or
   pressed
6 cups beef broth
3 cups water
½ pound chorizo, thinly
   sliced
1 cup canned kidney beans,
   drained
2 teaspoons dried oregano
1 teaspoon dried basil
Salt and freshly ground
   black pepper
1 small green cabbage,
   shredded

Fresh kale and chorizo, a Portuguese sausage, contribute inimitable flavor to this hearty soup.

1. Prepare the kale as described earlier (see TO PREPARE) and tear the leaves into bite-size pieces. Set aside.

2. Heat the oil and butter in a large pot until the butter is melted. Add the onions, carrots, celery, potatoes, and garlic and toss to coat evenly. Cover the pan and cook slowly until the onions are tender.

3. Pour in the beef broth and water. Add the chorizo, kidney beans, oregano, basil, salt, and pepper. Cover and cook slowly for 30 minutes. Stir in the kale and cabbage and cook, uncovered, at a gentle bubble for 30 to 45 minutes or until the cabbage is tender. Ladle into warmed bowls and serve steaming hot.

Kohlrabi (cole-RAH-bee)

KOHLRABI IS a distinctive looking vegetable whose main edible portion is variously referred to as a root, a bulb, or a stem. This confusion probably arises from the fact that kohlrabi looks like it should be a root vegetable, or at the very least, a bulb. In fact, it is neither. Kohlrabi is a swollen part of the stem that forms just above ground. The firm, fleshy sphere may be greenish white or purple, and it has several slender leaf stalks emerging from its surface.

TO SELECT:

Kohlrabi is a form of cabbage with a delicate turnip flavor, and the most important consideration when making a purchase is its size. Choose small kohlrabies that measure 1½ to 2 inches in diameter. Anything larger than that will be pithy and strongly flavored.

Produce managers usually prepare kohlrabi for display by cropping the leaf stalks. You'll see them piled in a heap with 2- or 3-inch stalk remnants sticking out like heavy whiskers. Select only those that are small and firm with smooth, uncracked skin. If the greens are attached, they should be perky and fresh-looking. Kohlrabi is available all year; plan to purchase 1 or 2 per person.

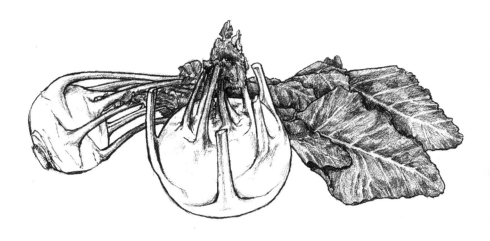

TO STORE: If you have purchased kohlrabi with the leaves attached, remove the leaves and stalks and store them in a separate airtight bag. Refrigerate and use within 3 to 4 days as you would any greens. Transfer the stems, without washing them, to another plastic bag. Secure it with a wire twist and refrigerate. Kohlrabi stems will keep for 7 to 10 days.

TO PREPARE: Rinse the kohlrabies and trim off any emerging leaf stalks with a paring knife. For maximum flavor, boil, steam, or microwave them without peeling. Cook until tender, then allow the kohlrabies to cool slightly. Remove the skins, cut the flesh into slices, sticks, or cubes. Combine with a sauce and bake, or sauté briefly in melted butter seasoned with freshly chopped herbs. Cooked kohlrabi may also be mashed or puréed.

Kohlrabi is frequently served raw. In this case, the skin should be removed with a paring knife or swivel-blade peeler. The flesh may then be grated or shredded and used as a component of a salad. Narrow strips of uncooked kohlrabi may be included as part of a crudité tray.

To prepare kohlrabi leaves, gently fold each leaf in half so that the center stalk protrudes, and pull the stalk from the leaf. The stalks are tough, so it is best to discard them, but the leaves possess a cabbagelike flavor, and are quite delightful when blanched lightly and tossed with butter and nutmeg.

Sautéed Kohlrabi

SERVES 4

Matchsticks of crisp-tender kohlrabi are lightly sautéed in butter. Chopped fresh chervil provides a lively accent.

4 small kohlrabies
3 tablespoons olive oil
3 tablespoons butter
1 tablespoon chopped fresh
   chervil
Salt and freshly ground
   white pepper

1. Peel the kohlrabies and then slice them into ¼-inch-thick rounds. Cut each round into ¼-inch-wide strips. Drop into a large pot of boiling, salted water and cook, uncovered, for 10 to 12 minutes or until crisp-tender. Drain in a colander.

2. Heat the oil and butter in a large skillet until the butter is melted. Add the kohlrabi strips and toss to coat. Sprinkle on the chervil and season with salt and pepper. Stir over medium heat until warmed through. Transfer to a serving dish and serve immediately.

Kohlrabi Purée

Kohlrabi Purée is softened with butter and cream, then seasoned with freshly grated nutmeg.

4 small kohlrabies, unpeeled
4 tablespoons butter, cut into small chunks
¼ cup heavy cream
Salt and freshly ground white pepper
Freshly grated nutmeg

1. Place the kohlrabi in a steam basket set over boiling water and cook for 30 to 40 minutes or until tender when pierced. Transfer to a colander and allow to cool.

2. When cool enough to handle, peel the kohlrabies and cut them into chunks. Force through a food mill or purée in a food processor.

3. Transfer to a wide saucepan and beat in the butter. When the butter is melted, blend in the cream, salt, and pepper. Stir over medium heat until the cream and butter are absorbed. Transfer to a serving bowl and sprinkle the surface with nutmeg.

Kohlrabi Au Gratin

Cooked kohlrabi is sliced and then blanketed with a cream cheese sauce punctuated with dill. Baked until brown, this casserole makes a wonderful accompaniment for roast turkey.

4 small kohlrabies, unpeeled
½ cup medium or whipping cream
1 large package (8 ounces) cream cheese
2 tablespoons lemon juice
1 tablespoon chopped fresh dill leaves
Salt and freshly ground white pepper
Paprika
2 ounces Gruyère cheese, grated

1. Drop the kohlrabies into a large pot of boiling, salted water and cook at a gentle bubble until tender when pierced. Drain in a colander. When cool enough to handle, peel the kohlrabies and slice into ¼-inch-thick rounds.

2. Preheat the oven to 375°. Generously butter a shallow baking dish. In a small saucepan, combine the cream, cream cheese, lemon juice, dill, salt, and pepper. Heat gently until the cream cheese melts. Whisk to blend and smooth out.

3. Arrange the kohlrabi slices in the prepared baking dish in overlapping rows. Pour on the sauce. Sprinkle the surface with paprika and then scatter the grated Gruyère cheese over the top. Bake for 20 minutes or until the surface is nicely browned.

Kohlrabi and Bacon Tart

SERVES 6

4 tablespoons butter
4 small kohlrabies, peeled
　　and shredded
Salt and freshly ground
　　white pepper
¼ cup water
¼ pound sliced bacon
1 large sweet onion, coarsely
　　chopped
1 teaspoon sugar
3 large eggs
1 cup medium or whipping
　　cream
6 ounces Gruyère cheese,
　　grated
9-inch pastry shell, partially
　　baked (recipe follows)
2 tablespoons freshly grated
　　Parmesan cheese

Serve warm wedges of this custardlike tart for brunch or offer cold as picnic fare.

1. Melt the butter in a large skillet. Add the kohlrabies and toss to coat. Season with salt and pepper. Add the water and stir over medium heat until the kohlrabies are limp and the liquid is evaporated. Remove from the heat.

2. Fry the bacon until crisp and transfer to absorbent paper. Pour off all but 2 tablespoons of the fat from the pan. Add the onion and toss to coat. Sprinkle on the sugar and stir over medium heat until the onion is golden. Mix in the kohlrabies.

3. Preheat the oven to 350°. Break the cooked bacon into bite-size pieces and set aside. In a large mixing bowl, beat the eggs and cream. Stir in the kohlrabi mixture, bacon, and Gruyère cheese. Pour the mixture into the prepared pastry shell and bake for 25 minutes or until the surface is partially set. Sprinkle the tart with Parmesan cheese and continue baking for 5 to 10 minutes or until a knife inserted in the center comes out clean.

Pastry Shell

1 cup all-purpose flour
½ teaspoon baking powder
½ teaspoon salt
4 tablespoons butter
2 tablespoons solid
　　shortening
3 to 4 tablespoons cold
　　water

1. To prepare the pastry shell, combine the flour, baking powder, and salt in a large mixing bowl. Whisk to blend thoroughly and add the butter and shortening. Cut in with a knife or pastry blender until the lumps of fat are reduced to the size of tiny peas.

2. Gradually sprinkle in the water, tossing the mixture constantly. When the mixture begins to hold together, gather it into a ball and roll it around the inside of the bowl to pick up any stray particles. Enclose in plastic wrap and refrigerate for 20 minutes.

3. Preheat the oven to 425°. Roll out the dough and transfer to a 9-inch tart pan or quiche dish. Prick the bottom and sides with a fork and line the pastry with aluminum foil. Pour in 1 pound of dried beans or distribute pie weights over the foil. Bake for 8 minutes. Remove the weights and foil and set the pastry shell aside. Do not prick a second time.

L

Leeks

J UDGING FROM the physical characteristics of leeks, it is quite apparent that they are a member of the onion family. But there the resemblance ends. The unique flavor of leeks, so subtle and intriguing, sets them apart from all the other, more assertive members of the group.

Leeks are available all year; however, they are at their best from the fall through the end of winter. They may be used as an aromatic, contributing their refined, seductive flavor to complex dishes, or they may be prepared and served on their own. Leeks contain calcium, potassium, and vitamin C, and they are a good source of dietary fiber.

TO SELECT:

Most supermarkets today are selling leeks untrimmed and unwrapped, which is good, because cutting off the hairy root ends or the tops of the dark green leaves hastens deterioration, and wrapping leeks airtight in plastic film causes them to rot. Purchase only those leeks that have a clean white base, and firm, fresh leaves; avoid any that look bedraggled.

Leeks are considered mature enough to harvest when they grow to ½-inch in diameter. Unfortunately, they seldom reach the market at this young stage. If you do happen upon leeks that are this slim, you've found a prize. Tie them in a bundle, steam them whole, then serve them cold with a vinaigrette dressing.

The more common size for leeks is 1½ to 2½ inches in diameter. Choose the narrowest ones with straight sides; root ends that have begun to curve into bulbs are a sign that the leeks may be overly mature. During the early spring, it's a good idea to check the center of the greens for a seed stalk. Part the wide, flat leaves in the middle and look for a hard yellowish green stalk. Pass up any leeks that have this, because a seed stalk indicates that the interior of the leek contains a tough, woody core. Plan on 2 medium leeks per person when serving them as a vegetable side dish.

TO STORE:

Leeks possess a wonderful aroma that will fill your car as you drive home from the store. You wouldn't want the same thing to happen inside your refrigerator, however, so wrap the leeks loosely with plastic film to contain the smell. If you have room, refrigerate the leeks without trimming them to prolong freshness. They will keep, stored in the vegetable drawer, for 1 week.

TO PREPARE:

During the cultivation process, leek plants are repeatedly banked with soil so that the white portion will grow to a sizeable length and remain pure white in color. If the soil is distributed around the plant with care, the interior layers of the leek will be relatively free of dirt. On the other hand, when soil is piled above the point where the leaves divide, you'll find large quantities of sand lodged amongst the layers of the leek. This explains why it is necessary to thoroughly rinse leeks before using them.

Begin to prepare leeks by cutting off the hairy root ends and the base of the white root. Then, remove any coarse or damaged outer leaves and discard them. Using scissors or a knife, cut off the dark green portion of the leaves, leaving a segment of lighter green about 2 inches long. Reserve the darker leaves for another use, if desired. Cut the leek in half lengthwise and rinse under cool running water, separating the layers to expose hidden sand. Drain on absorbent paper, then slice according to your recipe.

After trimming both ends of the leek, make a cut all the way through both the green and white portions, leaving a central segment uncut. Rinse under running water to remove all dirt and sand.

To prepare leeks for cooking whole, make a 2-inch lengthwise cut in the green portion, slicing all the way through. Then make a similar cut in the white portion, leaving a center segment intact to hold the leek together during cooking. (Many cookbooks suggest cutting down the entire length of the leek and leaving the very end of the white portion intact, but I find that many times that's just where the sand or dirt is lurking.) Rinse the leek under cool running water, separating the layers to flush out any hidden particles of sand.

Whole leeks may be braised, steamed, grilled, or boiled gently. They should be cooked only until they are tender, but still offer some resistance when pierced in the center with a paring knife. Overcooked leeks become mushy and develop a slimy consistency. Leeks may also be sliced and stir-fried, or cooked gently in butter. They are delicious eaten hot or at room temperature. Leeks may be served raw (thin slices or baby leeks are best for this), or cooked and served chilled. The green leaves of leeks are frequently added to stock or broth, and they may also be cooked briefly and used as a wrapper for a filling of vegetable or seafood mousse.

Leek Pâté with Lemon Sauce

This beautiful pâté is created by alternating white and pale green layers of tender braised leek. When slices of the pâté are turned on their sides, the final effect is truly stunning.

12 medium leeks, white and
 light green portion, cut in
 half lengthwise and
 rinsed
1 teaspoon dried thyme
3 cups chicken broth
3 tablespoons butter
1 shallot, minced
⅓ cup dry white wine
3 tablespoons lemon juice
½ teaspoon dried tarragon
¼ teaspoon salt
Pinch of cayenne
½ cup heavy cream
Watercress or arugula sprigs
 for garnish

1. Preheat the oven to 325°. Generously butter a large rectangular baking dish. Arrange the leeks in the baking dish in a single layer. (Placing 2 halves together to form a whole leek saves space in the baking dish.) Sprinkle on the thyme and add enough chicken broth to come halfway up the leeks. Cover with aluminum foil and bake for 30 to 40 minutes or until tender when pierced. Baste occasionally with the pan juices.

2. Transfer the leeks to a plate to cool. (Save the broth and use for soup at a later time.) Generously coat a loaf pan with oil and line the pan with plastic wrap, allowing it to hang over the sides of the pan. Separate the leeks into layers. Then, lay the leeks in the pan in such a way as to alternate portions of green and white and create an attractive color pattern. Press down firmly as you form the layers. Cut the leeks, if necessary, to fit the pan so that the result is a smooth loaf.

3. Bring the plastic wrap up over the leek pâté to cover the surface. Fit a second loaf pan inside to weigh the pâté down, then fill the second pan with dried beans or pie weights. Refrigerate for 24 hours or until firm and thoroughly chilled. Occasionally, pour off any liquid that may be exuded.

4. Thirty minutes before serving, melt 1 tablespoon of the butter in a small saucepan. Add the shallot and stir

Place the braised leeks in a loaf pan, alternating the arrangement of the green and white portions. When sliced, the pâté will then exhibit an attractive color pattern.

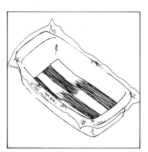

over medium heat until wilted. Stir in the wine, lemon juice, tarragon, salt, and cayenne. Cook until the liquid is almost evaporated. Add the cream and bring to a boil. Cook for 30 seconds and remove from the heat. Swirl in the remaining 2 tablespoons of butter and pour through a sieve. Allow to cool slightly.

5. By carefully lifting the plastic wrap, transfer the pâté to a flat surface. Cut gently into slices and place the slices flat on their side. Spoon some lemon sauce across each slice and serve garnished with watercress or sprigs of arugula.

Leek and Cheese Soup

SERVES 6

6 medium leeks, white and light green portion, cut in half lengthwise and rinsed
2 tablespoons vegetable oil
4 tablespoons butter
4 medium-size mealy potatoes, peeled and cut into cubes
6 cups chicken broth
¼ teaspoon freshly grated nutmeg
Salt and freshly ground black pepper
½ cup medium or whipping cream
12 ounces Gouda cheese, shredded

Shredded cheese tops this hearty, wintertime soup. Serve piping hot with pumpernickel bread.

1. Thinly slice the leeks. Heat the oil and butter in a large saucepan until the butter melts. Add the leeks and toss to coat evenly. Cover the pan and cook over low heat for 20 minutes or until the leeks are tender.

2. Meanwhile, combine the potatoes and broth in another saucepan and cook until the potatoes are tender. Transfer to the container of a blender or processor and whirl until smooth. Pour into the cooked leeks. Stir in the nutmeg, salt, and pepper. Blend in the cream and heat gently, but do not allow the soup to boil. Divide among 6 soup bowls and then scatter a generous amount of Gouda cheese over the steaming soup.

Steamed Leek Salad

Leeks, steamed until crisp-tender, are dressed with an anchovy vinaigrette.

6 medium leeks
6 tablespoons olive oil
2 tablespoons red wine
  vinegar
Pinch of cayenne
1 shallot, minced
6 flat anchovy fillets,
  minced
1 tablespoon capers,
  drained

1. Prepare the leeks as described earlier (see TO PRE-PARE), cutting them in half and trimming them so that they measure 6 inches in length. Reserve the trimmings for another use. Arrange the leeks, cut side up, in a steam basket and set over boiling water. Cook for 12 to 15 minutes or until limp but still somewhat crisp.

2. Meanwhile, whisk together the oil, vinegar, and cayenne. Stir in the shallot and anchovies. Set aside.

3. Transfer the leeks to 4 salad plates. Arrange them, cut side down, placing 3 halves on each plate. Spoon the dressing over the warm leeks and scatter on the capers. Serve warm or at room temperature.

Leek and Cannellini Bean Purée

Aromatic leeks and white cannellini beans are puréed and then topped with freshly grated Asiago cheese to create a robust accompaniment for roast game.

2 tablespoons olive oil
4 tablespoons butter
4 medium leeks, white and
  light green portion, cut in
  half, rinsed, and sliced
1 teaspoon dried thyme
½ teaspoon salt
Freshly ground black
  pepper
¼ cup water
1 cup canned cannellini
  beans, drained
Freshly grated Asiago
  cheese (or substitute
  Parmesan)

1. Heat the oil and butter in a large skillet until the butter is melted. Add the leeks, tossing to coat. Sprinkle on the thyme, salt, and pepper. Cover the pan and cook over low heat for 10 to 12 minutes or until the leeks are tender.

2. Preheat the oven to 350°. Generously butter an ovenproof serving dish. Add the water and the beans to the leeks and increase the heat. Stir constantly until all the liquid is evaporated and the mixture begins to stick to the bottom of the pan. Transfer to the container of a blender or processor and whirl until smooth.

3. Pour into the prepared dish and sprinkle with the Asiago or Parmesan cheese. Bake for 5 to 8 minutes or until the cheese is melted and the purée is piping hot. Serve immediately.

Stir-Fried Leeks and Romaine

¼ cup water
2 tablespoons soy sauce
2 tablespoons rice vinegar
3 tablespoons vegetable oil
4 medium leeks, white and light green portion, cut in half, rinsed, and sliced
1 medium head romaine, shredded
1 teaspoon crushed red pepper

Slices of leek are stir-fried with shredded romaine to achieve a crisp-tender consistency. Serve with grilled tenderloin of pork or grilled chicken.

1. In a small bowl, combine the water, soy sauce, and vinegar. Set aside. Heat the oil in a wok or large skillet. Add the leeks, tossing to coat evenly. Stir over high heat for 30 seconds. Add the romaine and toss to combine.

2. Pour on the soy sauce mixture and reduce the heat. Sprinkle on the red pepper. Continue stirring over medium heat until all the liquid is evaporated. Serve at once.

Grilled Leeks with Mustard-Lemon Sauce

Halves of partially cooked leek are coated with olive oil and grilled and served with a mustard-lemon dressing.

6 medium leeks
Olive oil
2 tablespoons lemon juice
1 teaspoon Dijon mustard
6 tablespoons butter
½ teaspoon salt
Freshly ground black pepper
1 tablespoon chopped fresh chives

1. Prepare the leeks as described earlier (see TO PRE-PARE), cutting them in half and trimming them so that they measure 6 inches in length. Reserve the trimmings for another use. Arrange the leeks, cut side up, in a steam basket and set over boiling water. Cook for 12 to 15 minutes or until limp but still somewhat crisp. Brush the surface of the leeks with oil and place on a hot grill, cut side down.

2. Meanwhile, whisk the lemon juice and mustard together in a small saucepan. Add the butter, salt, pepper, and chives. Heat slowly until the butter is melted. Remove from the heat.

3. Turn the leeks once to grill both sides. Transfer to a serving plate, cut side up. Whisk the warm dressing and pour over the leeks to serve.

Lemongrass

LEMONGRASS, which grows in slender bunches from a bulbous root, closely resembles a green onion in appearance. Its sweet lemony taste contributes unique flavor tones to dishes of the Oriental cuisines.

TO SELECT:

Look for pale green or greyish green shoots 18 to 24 inches long with a white bulb and a generous portion of white stem. Like green onions, lemongrass should be perky and fresh looking with no signs of wilt. Lemongrass is commonly sold in specialty food shops and Oriental grocery stores.

TO STORE:

Lemongrass may be wrapped loosely in plastic film and kept in the vegetable drawer of your refrigerator for about 5 to 7 days.

TO PREPARE:

Rinse the lemongrass under cool running water, rubbing the bulb vigorously to dislodge any sand or dirt. Remove the outer leaves if they seem limp. Trim off the base of the bulb and slice the lemongrass according to the directions in your recipe. The customary technique in Asian cookery is to thinly slice the white portion of the stem, and then bruise the slices with a mortar and pestle or the handle of a cleaver to release the maximum amount of flavor.

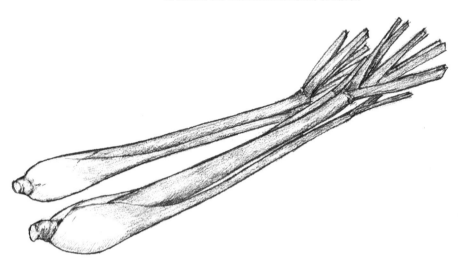

Lemongrass may be sliced across like a green onion and added to soups, or used as an ingredient in stir-fry dishes. It is also appearing more frequently as a salad component, and the uncooked greens are being served as an accompaniment or garnish.

Rice Noodle Soup with Lemongrass SERVES 6

4 stalks lemongrass
6 cups chicken broth
3 green onions, white and green portion, sliced diagonally
⅓ cup soy sauce
1½ teaspoons finely chopped fresh ginger
½ cup chopped fresh cilantro
6 ounces rice noodles
Thin slices of peeled cucumber for garnish

Chicken broth infused with lemongrass is the basis for this sassy rice noodle soup.

1. Cut the stalks of lemongrass to a length of 5 inches and reserve the tops for another use. (You may chop them finely and scatter over a tossed green salad.) Slice the stalks thinly and place in a mortar. Bruise gently with a pestle to release the flavor.

2. In a large saucepan, combine the chicken broth, lemongrass, and onions. Bring to a gentle bubble and stir in the soy sauce, ginger, and cilantro. Simmer, uncovered, for 30 minutes. Add the noodles and stir to separate. Cook for about 2 minutes or just until the noodles become tender. Serve hot garnished with slices of cucumber.

Stir-Fried Sole with Lemongrass SERVES 4

4 stalks lemongrass
⅓ cup dry white wine
2 tablespoons rice vinegar
1 teaspoon crushed red pepper
¼ teaspoon salt
3 tablespoons vegetable oil
3 green onions, white and green portion, thinly sliced
1 pound fillet of sole, cut into 1-inch pieces

Lemongrass imparts a lemony flavor to stir-fried sole. Serve with rice and Bean Sprouts and Romaine Salad (p. 36).

1. Cut the stalks of lemongrass to a length of 5 inches and reserve the tops for another use. (You may chop them finely and scatter over a tossed green salad.) Slice the stalks thinly and place in a mortar. Bruise gently with a pestle to release the flavor.

2. In a small bowl, combine the wine, vinegar, red pepper, and salt.

3. Heat the oil in a wok or large skillet. Add the onions and lemongrass and stir for 30 seconds over high heat. Add the fish a few pieces at a time. Stir constantly, but gently, so as not to break the fish apart. Pour on the wine mixture and bring to a boil. Stir gently for 30 seconds and transfer immediately to a serving dish.

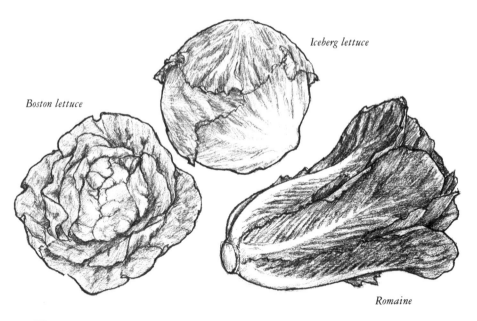

Boston lettuce

Iceberg lettuce

Romaine

Lettuce

IF, LIKE ME, you remember when only one kind of lettuce was sold, you also must be excited by the diverse assortment available today. What a wonderful treat it is to see bin after bin overflowing with lush greenery. Loosely headed varieties with light green, buttery soft leaves compete for attention beside crinkly heads of ruby-tipped leaves and crisp bunches of dark green spears. The choice is overwhelming.

Basically, lettuce can be divided into two main categories — head lettuce and leaf lettuce. Head lettuce, which furls its leaves like cabbage, includes the tightly packed iceberg and the loosely headed Boston, Bibb, and hydroponic varieties. Leaf lettuces are those that do not form a head. Generally available types are red leaf, also called ruby lettuce, green leaf, known as salad bowl, and romaine, which is also referred to as cos lettuce. Oakleaf and mâche, which is variously called lamb's lettuce and corn salad, are also leaf lettuces. All types of lettuce are available year round, but a seasonal decline in supply occurs during midwinter.

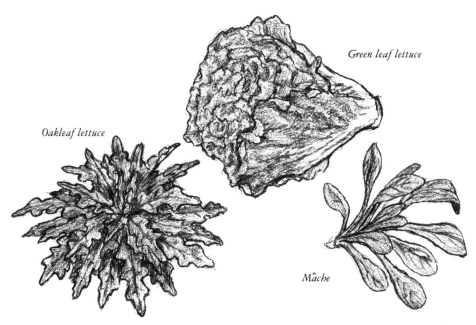

Green leaf lettuce

Oakleaf lettuce

Mâche

TO SELECT:

Almost all kinds of lettuce, except iceberg, are displayed loose and unwrapped. Hydroponic lettuce comes in a cellophane cone with the root cluster still attached.

When purchasing head lettuce, look for firm, resilient leaves that show no signs of rust. Iceberg heads should feel heavy for their size, although excessively heavy heads tend to be so tightly packed that the leaves refuse to separate neatly. Boston, Bibb, and hydroponic heads have delicate, loosely furled leaves, and consequently feel lighter in weight. Leaf lettuce should be crisp and fresh looking; avoid any that is wilted or spotted with brown. The stem end should feel firm to the touch, but don't be surprised if it is discolored because scarring occurs when the head is harvested.

TO STORE:

Iceberg lettuce is noted for its durability and long storage life. Tightly wrapped as a guard against moisture loss, iceberg will keep in your refrigerator for 6 to 7 days. Other kinds of lettuce are considerably more delicate and will not retain their quality for as long. After breaking off any blemished outer leaves, transfer the unwashed lettuce to a plastic bag and secure tightly with a wire twist. If an excessive amount of moisture accumulates inside the bag (produce managers spray lettuce with cold water to keep it looking fresh), turn the bag inside out and replace the head, or change the bag entirely. Too much moisture will cause lettuce to decay. Refrigerated inside a plastic bag, most lettuce will keep for 3 to 4 days.

TO PREPARE: Break off the number of leaves you need from the head and wash each one under cold running water. Pay particular attention to crinkly leaves because sand and insects are apt to lurk within the folds. Distribute the clean leaves over an absorbent kitchen towel and pat dry. Tear the leaves into bite-size pieces, if you wish, then gently roll up the towel. Place it in the refrigerator for 1 to 2 hours, but no longer. Torn lettuce exposed to the air develops brown edges.

Iceberg lettuce, which is frequently sliced rather than torn, is so tightly packed that the interior leaves seldom need rinsing. Simply pull off any blemished or wilted outer leaves and break the head apart, or shred with a sharp knife.

Lettuce is most commonly served as a salad component, but it may also be braised, sautéed, or made into soup. Leaves of lettuce are sometimes used as a wrapping to provide flavorful moisture for fish, or to form a protective cocoon inside which fresh peas may be steamed.

Cream of Lettuce Soup   SERVES 6

2 heads iceberg lettuce, shredded
4 ribs celery, coarsely chopped
2 green onions, white and green portion, coarsely chopped
3 cups chicken broth
Salt and freshly ground white pepper
2 tablespoons lemon juice
1 cup heavy cream
Chopped fresh parsley for garnish

Iceberg lettuce creates a delicate, yet surprisingly flavorful soup. It may be served either hot or cold.

1. In a wide saucepan, combine the lettuce, celery, onions, and chicken broth. Simmer, uncovered, for 30 minutes or until the vegetables are tender. Add the salt, pepper, and lemon juice.

2. Transfer to the container of a blender or processor and whirl until smooth. Blend in the cream. Return to the saucepan and heat gently, but do not allow the soup to boil. Serve garnished with chopped fresh parsley.

Red and Green Leaf Salad

SERVES 6

1 medium head red leaf
lettuce
1 medium head green leaf
lettuce
8 tablespoons olive oil
4 thin slices prosciutto,
coarsely chopped
½ cup chopped walnuts
2 tablespoons red wine
vinegar
Salt and freshly ground
black pepper
1 tablespoon chopped fresh
basil

*Bits of sautéed prosciutto and walnuts enliven this gorgeous
combination of red and green leaves.*

1. Rinse the lettuce and dry thoroughly. Meanwhile,
heat 2 tablespoons of the oil in a small skillet. Add the
prosciutto and walnuts and stir over medium heat until the
nuts are lightly browned. Set aside.

2. Whisk together the remaining 6 tablespoons of
oil, the vinegar, salt, and pepper. Add the mixture from
the skillet and stir to blend.

3. Tear the lettuce into bite-size pieces and place in a
large salad bowl. Pour on the dressing and toss to mix.
Sprinkle the basil over the salad and serve immediately.

Wilted Romaine with Cashews

SERVES 4

*Dark green spears of wilted romaine glisten when coated
with warm garlic-flavored oil. Coarsely chopped cashews,
scattered over the leaves, provide a nubbly contrast.*

⅓ cup olive oil
2 garlic cloves, sliced
2 tablespoons soy sauce
½ teaspoon sesame seed oil
(dark)
Several drops of Tabasco
sauce
2 large heads romaine
1 tablespoon chopped fresh
cilantro
¼ cup coarsely chopped
unsalted cashews

1. In a small saucepan, combine the olive oil and
garlic and cook over low heat until the garlic turns golden.
Do not allow it to brown. Remove the garlic with a slotted
spoon, then whisk in the soy sauce, sesame seed oil, and
Tabasco sauce. Continue whisking until warmed through.
Cover and keep warm.

2. Separate the romaine leaves, reserving the light
yellowish inner leaves for another use. Submerge the green
leaves in a large pot of boiling, salted water and cook,
uncovered, for 30 seconds or until wilted. Drain and
immediately immerse in ice water. When cool enough to
handle, lift out the leaves and spread them on absorbent
paper. Blot to dry. Divide among 4 salad plates, arranging
the leaves so that the root ends are at one side of the plate.
Scatter the cilantro and cashews over the leaves, then whisk
the warm dressing and pour it over the romaine. Serve
immediately.

Romaine in Cream

SERVES 4

For an interesting change of pace, offer this warm romaine in place of a salad course.

2 heads romaine
2 tablespoons vegetable oil
2 tablespoons butter
1 shallot, coarsely chopped
1 cup medium or whipping
  cream
1 tablespoon chopped fresh
  chives
Salt and freshly ground
  white pepper to taste
4 lemon wedges

1. Separate the leaves of romaine and rinse them. Drain on absorbent paper and pat dry. Stack 5 or 6 leaves at a time and slice across into ½-inch-wide strips.

2. In a large skillet, heat the oil and butter until the butter melts. Add the shallot and stir over medium heat until tender.

3. Add the romaine and cook, stirring over medium heat, until limp. Pour on the cream and allow the mixture to bubble gently until almost all the cream is absorbed. Sprinkle on the chives and season with salt and pepper. Divide among 4 salad plates and serve with wedges of lemon.

Sautéed Romaine with Green Onions

SERVES 4

Narrow strips of romaine and sliced green onions are sautéed in butter, with bacon fat added for more intense flavor.

1 large head romaine
3 tablespoons butter
1 tablespoon bacon fat
½ teaspoon sugar
6 green onions, white and
  green portion, sliced
⅓ cup water
Salt and freshly ground
  white pepper to taste
⅓ cup heavy cream

1. Separate the leaves of romaine and rinse them. Drain on absorbent paper and pat dry. Stack 5 or 6 leaves at a time and slice across into ½-inch-wide strips. Slice the strips in the opposite direction to chop them coarsely.

2. Melt the butter and bacon fat in a large skillet. Add the romaine and toss to coat evenly. Sprinkle on the sugar and stir over medium heat until the romaine is beginning to turn limp. Scatter the onions over the romaine, pour on the water, and continue stirring until the onions are soft and all the liquid is evaporated. Season with salt and pepper, then blend in the cream. Cook, stirring, until it is absorbed. Serve immediately.

Braised Lettuce Amandine

SERVES 4

Halved heads of Boston lettuce are braised in wine and chicken broth, then served with a scattering of almonds.

2 heads Boston lettuce
2 tablespoons vegetable oil
2 tablespoons butter
1 large mealy potato,
    coarsely chopped
1 medium onion, coarsely
    chopped
Salt and freshly ground
    black pepper
½ teaspoon dried thyme
½ teaspoon dried tarragon
½ cup dry white wine
½ cup chicken broth
¼ cup heavy cream
½ cup toasted almonds,
    coarsely chopped

1. Remove any wilted outer leaves from the heads of lettuce and drop the heads into a large pot of boiling, salted water. Cook, uncovered, at a gentle bubble for 2 to 3 minutes or until the lettuce is wilted. Immediately remove the lettuce and submerge in cold water. When cool enough to handle, lift out the lettuce and shake it gently to remove as much water as possible. Cut off the stem ends and slice each head in half lengthwise.

2. Preheat the oven to 350° and generously butter a glass baking dish. Heat the oil and butter in a large skillet until the butter is melted. Add the potato and onion and stir over medium heat until the onion is tender. Sprinkle with salt and pepper and stir in the thyme and tarragon.

3. Scatter the potato and onion over the bottom of the glass baking dish, and lay the lettuce, cut side down, on top of the them. Bring the wine and chicken broth to a boil in a small saucepan and pour over the lettuce. Cover the baking dish with aluminum foil and bake for 30 minutes or until the lettuce is tender when pierced.

4. Transfer the lettuce to a serving plate. Pour the remaining contents of the baking dish into a blender or processor and whirl until smooth. Blend in the cream and transfer to a pan. Heat until bubbling, then pour over the lettuce. Sprinkle on the toasted almonds and serve.

Stir-Fried Romaine and Rice

SERVES 4

A tasty companion for grilled chicken or pork.

1 medium head romaine
½ cup chicken broth
2 tablespoons soy sauce
2 tablespoons rice vinegar
3 tablespoons vegetable oil
1 garlic clove, minced
1½ teaspoons finely
    chopped fresh ginger
½ cup raw rice, cooked

1. Separate the leaves of romaine and rinse them. Drain on absorbent paper and pat dry. Stack 5 or 6 leaves at a time and slice across to shred.

2. In a small bowl, combine the chicken broth, soy sauce, and vinegar.

3. Heat the oil in a wok or large skillet. Add the garlic and ginger and stir to coat evenly. Add the romaine and continue stirring until the romaine is wilted. Add the rice and mix in thoroughly. Pour on the sauce and stir until the liquid is heated. Serve immediately.

Lettuce Leaves Stuffed with Ham Mousse

SERVES 4

Obtaining ham already baked from the deli reduces the time needed to prepare the filling, and consequently makes it possible to create these elegant lettuce bundles in less than 30 minutes.

1 cup heavy cream
1 large egg
1 shallot, sliced
2 teaspoons dried tarragon
2 tablespoons lemon juice
1 pound sliced baked ham
2 to 3 heads Boston lettuce
½ cup chicken broth
¼ cup dry white wine
Salt and freshly ground
   black pepper
4 tablespoons butter

1. In the container of a blender or processor, combine ½ cup of the cream, the egg, shallot, and 1 teaspoon of the tarragon. Blend briefly, then add 1 tablespoon of the lemon juice. Tear the ham into small pieces and add to the container. Whirl until smooth. The mixture should be quite stiff and hold its shape on a spoon. Add the remaining ½ cup cream as needed to form the proper consistency. Set the filling aside.

2. Preheat the oven to 375°. Generously butter a shallow baking dish. Remove 16 of the dark green outer leaves from the heads of lettuce and reserve the rest for another use. Submerge the leaves in a large pot of boiling, salted water. Cook, uncovered, for 30 seconds or until limp. Drain and immediately immerse in ice water. When cool enough to handle, lift out the leaves and spread them on absorbent paper. Pat dry.

3. Place a generous spoonful of stuffing at the base of each leaf. Fold the sides of the leaf over and roll up. Arrange in the prepared baking dish, allowing some space between bundles. Pour in the chicken broth and wine, then sprinkle the bundles with salt and pepper. Cover the dish with aluminum foil and bake for 30 minutes.

4. Meanwhile, combine the butter, the remaining tablespoon lemon juice, and the remaining teaspoon tarragon in a small saucepan. Heat until the butter is melted and pour over the cooked bundles to serve.

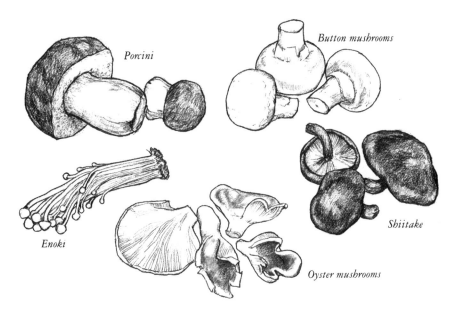

Porcini

Button mushrooms

Enoki

Shiitake

Oyster mushrooms

Mushrooms

I REMEMBER, not that many years ago, feeling quite adventurous as I purchased and prepared fresh mushrooms. At that time, the only kind occasionally available at the market were the white, cultivated button mushrooms, and only the most sophisticated cooks knew what to do with them.

All that has changed. Cultivated mushrooms are widely available throughout the year, and even beginning cooks feel comfortable preparing them. Now it's wild mushrooms that are causing culinary excitement. Several different varieties are beginning to appear in large supermarkets and specialty food shops. And many of them are still relatively unfamiliar, but I'm guessing that in a very short time, wild mushrooms will attain the same degree of popularity as their cultivated cousin.

The first step in purchasing fresh mushrooms is knowing what the various types look like. Fortunately, their physical characteristics are so distinct that telling the different kinds apart is easier than it might seem.

Button Mushrooms: These are the familiar white mushrooms with domed caps that are usually closed so tightly you can not see the gills. Button mushrooms come in several varieties and may be colored beige or ivory. The surface of the cap is smooth or lightly scaled, and the stems, which are straight, may vary from fat to slender.

Shiitake (shee-TAH-keh): Originally from Japan, these wild mushrooms, like many of the other wild varieties, are being grown commercially in the United States under conditions that duplicate their natural habitat. Shiitakes are medium-size mushrooms with a wide, shallow cap and a slender stem. The surface of the cap is brownish purple, and the gills are cream colored. Shiitakes are also marketed as golden oak, black forest, or winter mushrooms.

Porcini: These Italian mushrooms are known as cepes in the cuisine of France and as steinpilz in the cookery of Germany. Porcini come in all sizes, from quite small to 5 or 6 inches in diameter. They have bark-brown caps and the underpart more nearly resembles a sponge than it does gills. The stem is unusually plump and swells at the base.

Morels: Tall, pointed caps with a convoluted, honey-combed surface immediately set these mushrooms apart. Morels may be beige, yellow, or blackish brown. The stems are short, and the conical caps are hollow.

Chanterelles: These orange-yellow mushrooms have deep, trumpet-shaped caps that look as though they've been turned inside out. Deep gills, like folds of fabric, extend almost all the way down the stem. Chanterelles come in an assortment of sizes. They are referred to as girolles in the cuisine of France.

Enoki (eh-NO-kee): Also called enokitake, these Japanese mushrooms are sold in clusters of slim, ivory-colored stalks, resembling long white nails with rounded heads. They are exceptionally thin and delicate.

Oyster Mushrooms: The stems of these mushrooms are eccentric; that is to say, they grow at one side of the cap rather than in the center. Consequently, oyster mushrooms resemble scallop shells. Greyish ivory on the top, the flat, fan-shaped caps exhibit deep, cream-colored gills.

Morel

Chanterelle

Cultivated button mushrooms are sold either loose or packaged in plastic-covered containers. Most wild mushrooms are sold in plastic pouches or cardboard boxes covered with plastic film; only occasionally are they sold loose. Both types should be free of all signs of moisture. Beads of condensation on the inside of the package or wet spots on the surface of the mushrooms indicate poor quality. Button mushrooms should feel fairly firm to the touch; wild mushrooms will feel less firm, but should not be spongy. Generally speaking, smaller mushrooms will be more tender and flavorful when cooked.

TO STORE:

All types of mushrooms are extremely absorbent, and will soak up any moisture that is available. Moisture causes mushrooms to decay rapidly, however, so the single most important aspect of storing mushrooms is to keep them free of moisture.

As soon as you get them home, remove mushrooms from their packaging. Handle them as little as possible, and do not wash them. Transfer the mushrooms to a brown paper bag, or wrap them in cheesecloth or a clean kitchen towel. The object is to allow air to circulate, and to provide a slightly absorbent surface that will take in whatever moisture is given off by the mushrooms during respiration. A cloth-lined straw basket or an unglazed ceramic crock also works well.

Mushrooms may be refrigerated this way for as long as 5 to 7 days, with cultivated button mushrooms being somewhat sturdier. If the mushrooms begin to dry out, use them immediately. Dryness precludes their being served raw, but they may still be used in cooked preparations. In fact, mushrooms that are a bit dry tend to have a stronger flavor.

TO PREPARE:

When preparing mushrooms, keep in mind their absorbent character. Button mushrooms, especially those that are prepackaged, often arrive in pristine condition. Wipe them gently with a damp cloth and trim the ends of the stem. Wild mushrooms, and button mushrooms sold loose, are usually a little scruffier looking, and may need to be lightly brushed with a soft-bristled mushroom brush. If you feel the need to rinse them, do so quickly by holding each individual mushroom under cool running water from the tap. Never allow mushrooms to sit in water. They will become mushy and waterlogged.

Button mushrooms are relatively bland, but they are endlessly versatile, and they can be subjected to somewhat harsher treatment than wild mushrooms. Button mushrooms may be served raw or cooked in a number of ways, including high-heat methods such as broiling and prolonged sautéing.

Wild mushrooms are more assertively flavored and are seldom served uncooked, with the notable exception of enoki mushrooms, which are mild in flavor and served raw as a matter of course. Wild mushrooms may be cooked in most of the same ways as button mushrooms; however, they should not be subjected to high heat or cooked until brown, because they will toughen and develop an unpleasant flavor.

Chinese Stuffed Mushrooms   SERVES 12

An Oriental version of an ever-popular appetizer. In this recipe, mushroom caps are filled with a shrimp and pork stuffing and then braised in a flavorful liquid.

48 medium button mushrooms
3 tablespoons vegetable oil
½ pound ground pork
½ pound raw shrimp, peeled, deveined, and finely chopped
6 green onions, white and green portion, sliced separately
1 tablespoon finely chopped fresh ginger
3 tablespoons soy sauce
3 tablespoons Madeira
3 tablespoons butter
2 tablespoons oyster sauce
Several drops of Tabasco sauce
¾ cup chicken broth
1 tablespoon cornstarch

1. Rinse the mushrooms and pat dry. Remove the stems and set the caps aside. Chop the stems coarsely. Heat the oil in a skillet and add the pork. Stir over medium heat until no longer pink. Add the shrimp, the chopped mushroom stems, and the white portion of the onions. Continue stirring until the onions are tender. Blend in the ginger, soy sauce, and Madeira. Remove from the heat and set aside.

2. Melt the butter in a large skillet. Add the mushroom caps and toss to coat. Reduce the heat to low, cover the pan, and cook for 10 minutes, turning once. Remove the caps from the skillet with a slotted spoon and fill with the stuffing, pressing down lightly.

3. To the butter and juices in the skillet, add the oyster sauce, Tabasco, and ½ cup of the chicken broth. Stir to blend and return the mushrooms to the pan. Cover and cook over low heat for 20 minutes, basting frequently. Transfer the mushrooms to a serving dish. Dissolve the cornstarch in the remaining ¼ cup chicken broth and stir into the sauce in the skillet. Add the green portion of the onions and increase the heat. Cook until the sauce is thickened. Pour over the mushrooms to serve.

Mushroom Caviar

SERVES 10

2 tablespoons olive oil
2 tablespoons butter
1 medium onion, finely
    chopped
1 pound button
    mushrooms, finely
    chopped
2 tablespoons lemon juice
2 tablespoons Cognac
½ teaspoon dried thyme
Salt and freshly ground
    black pepper
2 tablespoons sour cream

Finely chopped mushrooms sautéed in butter and olive oil make an appealing appetizer spread. Offer with thin triangles of toast or wheat crackers.

1. Heat the oil and butter in a skillet until the butter melts. Add the onion, tossing to coat evenly. Cover the pan and cook slowly until the onion is tender.

2. Add the mushrooms and stir over medium heat until the mushrooms begin to release their juices. Sprinkle on the lemon juice, Cognac, thyme, salt, and pepper. Increase the heat. Continue stirring until all the liquid has evaporated and the mushrooms are darkened, but not browned. Remove from the heat and transfer to a mixing bowl. Stir in the sour cream. Cover the bowl and refrigerate. Serve lightly chilled or at room temperature.

Pickled Mushrooms

SERVES 8

1 pound button
    mushrooms, whole
¾ cup white wine
½ cup white wine vinegar
1 teaspoon sugar
½ teaspoon salt
2 garlic cloves, cut in half
2 bay leaves
1 teaspoon fennel seed
1 teaspoon dried oregano
1 teaspoon dried rosemary
12 peppercorns
½ cup olive oil

This welcome appetizer of mushrooms marinated in a flavorful broth should be made several days in advance.

1. Rinse the mushrooms and cut off the ends of the stems, leaving most of the stems in place.

2. In a nonreactive saucepan, combine the wine, vinegar, sugar, and salt. Add the garlic, bay leaves, fennel seed, oregano, rosemary, and peppercorns. Boil, uncovered, for 5 minutes. Blend in the oil, then pour into a large bowl. Add the mushrooms and toss to coat. Allow to stand for 4 hours, stirring occasionally, and refrigerate. Allow the mushrooms to marinate in the refrigerator for 5 to 6 days, then serve chilled or at room temperature.

Mushroom Salad

4 tablespoons red wine
  vinegar
1 teaspoon Dijon mustard
1 teaspoon A-1 Steak Sauce
½ teaspoon salt
Freshly ground black
  pepper
½ teaspoon dried oregano
½ teaspoon dried thyme
½ cup olive oil
1 pound button
  mushrooms, sliced
Arugula (or substitute
  spinach leaves) for
  garnish

Steak sauce adds an element of mystery to this salad, and tangy sprigs of arugula provide a jaunty contrast.

1. In a large mixing bowl, whisk together the vinegar, mustard, steak sauce, salt, and pepper. Blend in the oregano and thyme and allow to stand for 30 minutes.

2. Whisk in the oil. Then add the mushrooms and toss to coat evenly. Divide among 4 glass salad plates and garnish with sprigs of arugula.

Mushroom and Fennel Salad

SERVES 6

1 garlic clove
½ teaspoon salt
3 tablespoons lemon juice
Freshly ground black
  pepper
6 tablespoons olive oil
2 tablespoons chopped
  fresh parsley
1 tablespoon chopped fresh
  thyme
12 ounces button
  mushrooms, sliced
1 red bell pepper, seeded
  and cut into julienne
  strips
1 head fennel

Julienne strips of red bell pepper and fennel are combined with raw sliced mushrooms, then tossed with a lemony, garlic dressing.

1. In a ceramic mixing bowl, crush the garlic and the salt with a pestle to form a paste. Whisk in the lemon juice, pepper, and oil. Blend in the parsley and thyme. Add the mushrooms and red bell pepper, then toss to coat evenly.

2. Rinse and trim the fennel. Separate it into layers as you would ribs of celery. Remove the strings from the outer layers if necessary. Slice each layer lengthwise into julienne strips. Add to the mushroom mixture and toss to combine. Divide among 6 salad plates and serve immediately.

Gratin of Three Wild Mushrooms

SERVES 4

Wild mushrooms baked in wine and cream may be prepared in small individual gratin dishes and served as a first course. They may also be baked in a large casserole and offered as an accompaniment to grilled steak.

6 ounces fresh porcini
6 ounces fresh chanterelles
6 ounces fresh oyster
  mushrooms
4 tablespoons butter
4 tablespoons dry white
  wine
4 teaspoons lemon juice
2 shallots, finely chopped
Salt and freshly ground
  black pepper
½ cup heavy cream

1. Preheat the oven to 350°. Cut the mushrooms into ¼-inch-thick slices and place them in a bowl. Toss to mix and set aside.

2. Place 1 tablespoon of butter in each of 4 gratin dishes. Add 1 tablespoon of wine and 1 teaspoon of lemon juice to each dish. Place the dishes in the oven and heat until the butter melts.

3. Remove from the oven and divide the shallots among the dishes, scattering them over the bottom. Place one-quarter of the mushroom slices in each dish. Sprinkle with salt and pepper and cover the dishes with aluminum foil. Bake for 10 minutes. Uncover and pour on the cream, dividing it among the dishes. Continue baking, uncovered, for 15 to 20 minutes or until the mixture is bubbling and the mushrooms are tender.

Mushrooms Stuffed with Lobster

SERVES 4

An elegant, yet easy-to-prepare first course.

2 tablespoons butter
8 large button mushrooms
  (2 to 2½ inches in
  diameter), stems removed
1 large egg
2 tablespoons lemon juice
¼ cup mayonnaise,
  preferably homemade
1 tablespoon chopped fresh
  dill
8 ounces lobster meat,
  coarsely chopped
1 rib celery, finely chopped
4 tablespoons unseasoned
  bread crumbs
Salt and freshly ground
  black pepper

1. Melt the butter in a small skillet. Add the mushroom caps, tossing to coat them with butter. Cover the pan and cook over low heat for 5 minutes. Turn the mushrooms once, cover the pan, and cook for an additional 5 minutes.

2. Meanwhile, whisk the egg and lemon juice until slightly thickened. Whisk in the mayonnaise and blend in the dill. Add the lobster, celery, 2 tablespoons of the bread crumbs, salt, and pepper and stir to combine.

3. Preheat the oven to 375° and lightly butter a shallow baking dish. Transfer the mushrooms to the prepared dish. Increase the heat under the skillet and cook until the liquid is almost evaporated. Add the remaining 2 tablespoons of bread crumbs and toss to coat.

4. Spoon the lobster filling into the mushroom caps and sprinkle the tops with the coated bread crumbs. Bake for 12 to 15 minutes or until the mushrooms are completely tender when pierced.

Wild Mushroom Pizza SERVES 4

14-inch pizza crust (recipe follows)
Olive oil
6 ounces Gouda cheese
Salt and freshly ground black pepper
3 green onions, white and green portion, thinly sliced diagonally
4 ounces fresh porcini, sliced
4 ounces fresh chanterelles, sliced
4 ounces fresh shiitake, sliced

Melted Gouda cheese and slivers of green onion provide a flavorful backdrop for this light, crispy pizza of fresh wild mushrooms.

1. Prepare the pizza crust according to the directions that follow.

2. Preheat the oven and baking stone to 500°. Generously apply the oil over the surface of the pizza dough with your fingertips.

3. Scatter the cheese over the dough and sprinkle with salt and pepper. Distribute the onions over the cheese. Combine the mushroom slices in a bowl and toss to mix. Scatter over the onions and cheese. Transfer to the preheated baking stone and bake for 5 minutes. Remove the foil from the bottom of the pizza crust and continue baking for 7 to 12 minutes or until the crust is lightly browned. Transfer to a cutting board and slice into 12 wedges.

Pizza Crust

1 cup warm water
1 package dry yeast
Small pinch plus ½ teaspoon sugar
2 to 2½ cups bread flour (preferably bromated)
½ teaspoon salt

1. To prepare the pizza dough, combine the water, yeast, and pinch of sugar. Stir to dissolve the yeast and sugar and then set aside. In a separate bowl, combine 2 cups of the flour, salt, and the remaining ½ teaspoon of sugar. Whisk to blend thoroughly.

2. Pour two-thirds of the flour mixture into the dissolved yeast. Beat vigorously with a wooden spoon until the dough pulls away from the bowl in ropy strands. The mixture will be very wet.

3. Dump out all but 2 tablespoons of the remaining flour mixture onto a work surface and spread it out in a circle. Empty the dough onto the flour and sprinkle the remaining 2 tablespoons over the dough. Using a pastry scraper, lift and fold the dough over on itself. Press down to work the flour in. Repeat the process of folding and pressing with the pastry scraper until the flour is entirely absorbed. Shape the dough into a ball (actually it will be more like a flabby mass), lightly dust with flour, and place in a greased bowl. Cover with plastic wrap and secure with an elastic band to keep the dough moist. Set in a draft-free place to rise (about 1½ hours).

4. When the dough is double in size, turn out onto a floured work surface. Pat down into a flat circle, dusting

any moist spots with flour. Press the circle as flat as you can, working out any air bubbles you see. Fold the dough in half, dust with flour, and press into a flat semicircle. Fold into quarters, dust with flour, and press flat. Tucking the corners underneath, form the dough into a ball. Dust with flour and return to the bowl. Cover with plastic wrap and secure with an elastic band. Allow the dough to rise until doubled (about 1 hour).

5. Twenty minutes before you plan to assemble the pizza, place a baking stone on a rack in the oven. Preheat the oven and the baking stone to 500°. Cover a large pastry board with 18-inch extra-heavy aluminum foil. Grease the foil generously with solid shortening. Turn the dough out onto a lightly floured surface and flatten into a large circle by pressing down with your hands. Fold in half and then into quarters and transfer to the greased foil. Unfold the dough and shape into a 14-inch circle, forming a rim around the outside edge.

6. (Pick up here with step 3 in Wild Mushroom Pizza, after generously applying the olive oil over the surface of the dough with your fingertips.)

Stir-Fried Mushrooms and Chinese Noodles   SERVES 4

Sliced mushrooms are cooked briefly in a small amount of oil, coated with a sesame-flavored sauce, and tossed with Chinese noodles.

⅓ cup soy sauce
⅓ cup rice vinegar
½ cup chicken broth
½ teaspoon sesame seed oil (dark)
2 teaspoons cornstarch
2 tablespoons cold water
½ pound Chinese noodles, boiled and drained
3 tablespoons vegetable oil
1 pound button mushrooms, sliced
3 green onions, white and green portion, sliced
1 red bell pepper, cut into julienne strips

1. Combine the soy sauce and vinegar in a measuring cup. Stir to blend and pour half into a small bowl. To the bowl, add the chicken broth and sesame seed oil. Dissolve the cornstarch in the water and stir in. Set aside.

2. Place the drained noodles in a large bowl and pour on the soy sauce mixture remaining in the measuring cup. Toss to coat evenly.

3. Heat the vegetable oil in a wok or large skillet. Add the mushrooms, tossing to coat evenly. Stir over high heat for 10 seconds. Add the onions and red bell pepper and continue to stir over high heat for 30 seconds. Pour on the chicken broth mixture and bring to a boil. Add the noodles and reduce the heat to medium. Toss the mixture to combine and cook until the noodles are warmed through. Serve immediately.

Grilled Mushrooms

Precooking mushrooms in the microwave oven or on the stove top softens them slightly so they can be skewered easily.

16 to 20 medium button
  mushrooms
½ cup butter, melted
Salt and freshly ground
  black pepper

1. Rinse the mushrooms if necessary and trim the stems. Place the mushrooms in a glass casserole dish for the microwave or in a wide saucepan for the stove top. To microwave, add 1 tablespoon water and cover the dish. Cook at high power for 2½ to 3 minutes. To cook on the stove top, add ¼ cup water and bring to a boil. Stir over high heat for 30 seconds. Cover the pan and remove from the heat. Allow to stand 15 minutes. The mushrooms should be firm but pliable.

2. Slide the mushrooms onto metal skewers or bamboo skewers that have been soaked in water for 1 hour. Brush the mushrooms with melted butter and place on a hot grill. Continue to baste occasionally with melted butter, grilling the mushrooms until they are slightly charred. Season with salt and pepper and serve immediately.

Veal Scallops with Enoki Mushroom Sauce

Enoki mushrooms are cooked briefly in a mustard-spiked cream sauce and then served over sautéed veal scallops.

6 veal scallops
Salt and freshly ground
  black pepper
All-purpose flour for
  dredging
3 tablespoons vegetable oil
3 tablespoons butter
1 shallot, finely chopped
½ cup beef broth
½ cup dry white wine
1 tablespoon lemon juice
1 teaspoon Dijon mustard
½ cup heavy cream
4 ounces enoki mushrooms

1. Sprinkle the veal with salt and pepper, and dredge with flour. Set aside. Heat the oil and butter in a large skillet until the butter melts. Add the shallot and stir over medium heat until tender. Remove the shallot with a slotted spoon and transfer to a plate.

2. Add the veal scallops to the pan and cook over medium-high heat until nicely browned on both sides. Transfer to a plate.

3. Pour the beef broth, wine, and lemon juice into the pan and cook briskly until reduced by half. Remove from the heat and blend in the mustard and cream. Add the mushrooms and return to the heat. Bring to a boil. Then add the veal and the shallot, spooning the sauce and the mushrooms over the meat. When the veal is warmed through, transfer to a serving plate and pour on the sauce.

Mustard Greens

THERE ARE TWO common varieties of mustard greens — those with smooth, flat leaves, and those with curly-edged leaves. The leaves of both types are a light yellowish green. They are narrow and rounded, and approximately the same length as dandelion greens. Notorious for its sharp, bitter taste, this vegetable is probably the most strongly flavored of all the leafy greens. Mustard greens are available all year, but they are at their best in the spring. They are an excellent source of vitamins A and C.

TO SELECT:

Choose the smallest, lightest-colored leaves available. They are the youngest ones, and therefore will be the most tender and mildly flavored. Take only those that are firm and resilient, passing up any that are limp or wilted.

TO STORE:

Place the unwashed mustard greens in a plastic bag and secure it with a wire twist. Refrigerate and use within 1 to 2 days.

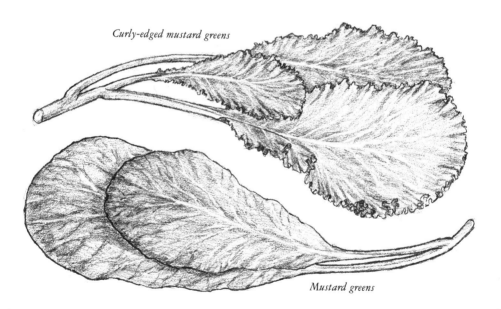

Curly-edged mustard greens

Mustard greens

TO PREPARE:

The stems and tough center ribs should be removed from the leaves. To do this easily, hold the leaf in one hand with the underside up, and bend the leaf in half so that the rib slightly protrudes. Then, with the other hand, gently pull the stem and rib away from the leaf. Rinse the trimmed leaves under cool running water and drain in a colander.

Mustard greens are exceptionally bitter, so all but the tiniest leaves should be cooked in water or broth to temper their flavor. And because the leaves are somewhat coarse, cooking to the tender stage takes longer than for spinach or other more delicate greens. Ham broth, pork broth, or chicken broth may all be used as a cooking medium, and they produce an interesting, full-flavored result. Tiny mustard greens may be cut into julienne strips and scattered over meat or vegetable salads.

Mustard Greens Soup

1 pound mustard greens
6 cups water
2 medium onions, coarsely
   chopped
2 medium carrots, coarsely
   chopped
2 ribs celery, coarsely
   chopped
1 garlic clove, minced
1 bay leaf
¼ cup soy sauce
2 tablespoons rice vinegar
1 tablespoon finely chopped
   fresh ginger
Salt and freshly ground
   black pepper to taste
½ cup orzo (or substitute
   rice)

Finely chopped fresh ginger contributes vibrant flavor to this sensational soup.

1. Rinse the mustard greens and submerge them in a large pot of boiling, salted water. Cook, uncovered, for 2 minutes or until limp. Drain in a colander set under cold running water. Squeeze out the excess water with your hands, then chop the greens coarsely. Set aside.

2. In a large saucepan, combine the water, onions, carrots, celery, and garlic. Add the bay leaf and bring to a boil. Cover and cook at a gentle bubble for 30 minutes or until the vegetables are tender. Lift out the bay leaf. Transfer the mixture to the container of a blender or processor and whirl until smooth.

3. Return the puréed mixture to the heat and stir in the soy sauce, vinegar, and ginger. Add salt and pepper to taste. Stir in the chopped mustard greens and add the orzo. Cook, uncovered, until the orzo is tender.

Mustard Greens Salad with Mustard Vinaigrette

SERVES 4

12 ounces small mustard
  greens
6 tablespoons olive oil
2 tablespoons honey
2 tablespoons white wine
  vinegar
1 teaspoon Dijon mustard
½ teaspoon salt
Freshly ground black
  pepper
1 tablespoon chopped fresh
  chives

Zesty mustard greens are wilted by a warm dressing, sweet with honey.

1. Rinse the mustard greens and remove the stems and center ribs if they seem tough. Drain on absorbent paper and pat dry.

2. In a large skillet, combine the oil, honey, vinegar, mustard, salt, and pepper. Whisking continuously, heat until the honey melts. Add the mustard greens and sprinkle on the chives. Toss until slightly wilted and transfer to 4 salad plates. Serve warm.

Mustard Greens with Balsamic Vinegar

SERVES 4

The specific process used to create Balsamic vinegar results in a sweet, mellow flavor that is only faintly acidic. Consequently, it is the perfect foil for bitter mustard greens.

1 pound mustard greens
4 tablespoons butter
6 tablespoons Balsamic
  vinegar
Salt and freshly ground
  black pepper to taste
½ cup finely chopped
  pecans

1. Prepare the mustard greens as described earlier (see TO PREPARE). Then submerge them in a large pot of boiling, salted water and cook, uncovered, until tender. Drain in a colander set under cold running water. Squeeze out the excess water with your hands and chop the greens coarsely. Set aside.

2. Melt the butter in a wide saucepan, stir in the vinegar, and add the mustard greens. Toss to coat the greens and stir over medium heat until warmed through. Season with salt and pepper and stir in the pecans. Transfer to a warmed serving dish.

N

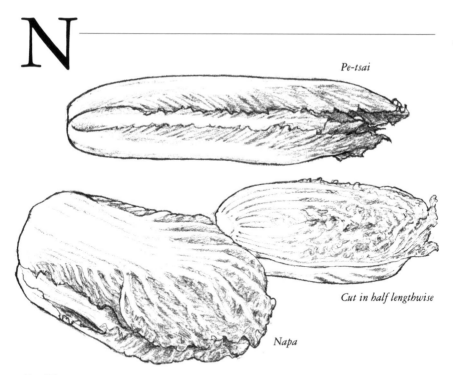

Pe-tsai

Cut in half lengthwise

Napa

Napa

THE TWO TYPES of cabbage most often called for in Chinese recipes are napa and bok choy. (See also Bok Choy.) Napa, which is also known as Chinese cabbage and celery cabbage, has a distinctive appearance and shouldn't be mistaken for bok choy, even though both are loosely referred to as Chinese cabbage.

Napa is possibly called celery cabbage because of its mild flavor, which more closely resembles that of celery than cabbage. Measuring about 8 inches in length, this Chinese cabbage is a stout, tightly packed head of overlapping leaves. (A longer, more slender version is known as pe-tsai.) Napa leaves are pale yellowish green with delicate, crinkly edges; the white center ribs are broad and flat with faintly raised ridges. It is available all year, but is at its best when harvested during the winter months.

TO SELECT:	A fine head of napa will feel plump, heavy, and compact. The leaves should be crisp and fresh looking, and have white, unblemished ribs. Avoid napa that is wilted or spotted with brown.
TO STORE:	Like bok choy, napa keeps well when tightly wrapped in plastic film. The unwashed head may also be placed in a plastic bag secured with a wire twist. Refrigerate and use within 3 to 4 days.
TO PREPARE:	Because the leaves of napa are so closely packed, washing the interior of the head is seldom necessary. Trim off the end of the head and rinse the outside leaves. Pat dry and slice or shred according to the recipe.

The tender tips of napa may be served raw as a salad by tearing the leaves into pieces or making thin slices across the leaves to create a chiffonade. Napa may also be cut in half lengthwise (which makes handling easier), then sliced across into 2-inch pieces for stir-frying or for adding to soup.

Napa Salad

SERVES 4

1 medium head napa
4 green onions, white and
    green portion, sliced
1 teaspoon celery seed
¾ cup unflavored yogurt
3 tablespoons rice vinegar
2 tablespoons soy sauce
1 tablespoon minced fresh
    ginger
1 garlic clove, pressed
½ teaspoon salt
Several drops of Tabasco
    sauce

In China, vegetables are seldom eaten raw. Consequently, salads with an Oriental flair are the invention of Western cooks.

1. Shred the napa by slicing across the head with a serrated knife. Place in a large bowl. Add the onions and celery seed. Toss to combine.
2. In a small bowl, whisk together the yogurt, vinegar, soy sauce, ginger, garlic, salt, and Tabasco. Pour over the cabbage and mix thoroughly. Refrigerate until lightly chilled.

Shred napa with a serrated knife, cutting the head crosswise into thin slices.

Napa with Linguine

1 tablespoon dried shrimp
2½ cups chicken broth
12 dried Chinese
  mushrooms, such as
  shiitake
4 tablespoons soy sauce
4 tablespoons rice vinegar
1 tablespoon cornstarch
1 teaspoon sugar
3 tablespoons vegetable oil
6 green onions, white and
  green portion, sliced
1 large head napa, cut
  across into thin shreds
1 tablespoon minced fresh
  ginger
½ pound linguine, boiled
  and drained

One of the flavor components of this dish is dried shrimp, a staple ingredient of the Chinese cuisine. These tiny shrimp, which have been shelled, salted, and then dried, are sold in small plastic packets in food stores catering to Oriental cookery.

1. In a wide saucepan, combine the dried shrimp and chicken broth. Bring to a boil and reduce the heat. Simmer, uncovered, for 30 minutes.

2. Place the mushrooms in a small bowl and cover with warm water. Allow to stand for 30 minutes. Lift out the mushrooms with a slotted spoon and cut into thin slivers. Add to the chicken broth.

3. In a small bowl, combine the soy sauce, vinegar, and cornstarch. Stir to dissolve the cornstarch and blend in the sugar.

4. Heat the oil in a wok or large skillet. Add the onions and stir over high heat for 30 seconds. Add the napa and ginger and continue stirring until the napa is crisp-tender. Pour in the chicken broth, then add the soy sauce mixture. Stir until slightly thickened. Add the drained linguine and toss to combine. Serve immediately.

Stir-Fried Napa and Chinese Noodles

1 medium head napa
½ cup chicken broth
3 tablespoons soy sauce
3 tablespoons rice vinegar
1 garlic clove, minced
1 tablespoon minced fresh
  ginger
Several drops of Tabasco
  sauce
3 tablespoons vegetable oil
4 green onions, white and
  green portion, sliced
6 ounces Chinese noodles,
  boiled and drained

This savory mélange of stir-fried napa and Chinese noodles goes especially well with roast pork.

1. Cut the napa into ½-inch-wide strips by slicing across the head with a serrated knife. In a small bowl, combine the chicken broth, soy sauce, vinegar, garlic, ginger, and Tabasco.

2. Heat the oil in a wok or large skillet. Add the napa and stir over high heat until limp. Add the onions and continue stirring for 30 seconds. Pour on the chicken broth mixture and cook, stirring, until most of the liquid is evaporated.

3. Add the drained noodles and stir continuously until the noodles are warmed through and all the liquid is evaporated. Serve immediately.

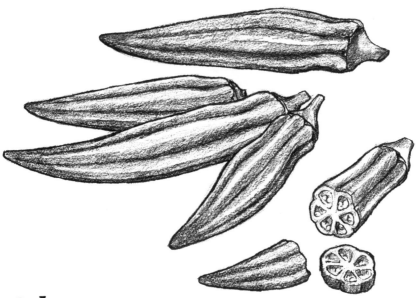

Okra

THIS VEGETABLE has a distinctive feature for which it is both praised and panned — when cut, the flesh exudes a milky liquid with a slippery, slimy consistency. Cooks who favor okra rely on its mucilaginous attributes to thicken soups and stews, and to create the silken, gel-like smoothness for which gumbo is renowned. Those not quite convinced of okra's qualities tend to avoid preparing it, which is unfortunate because okra has a lovely companionable flavor that goes exceptionally well with tomatoes, garlic, and ham. Okra is available sporadically all year, with the peak supply occurring during late summer and early fall.

TO SELECT: Okra is the seed pod of a flowering plant. Look for slim, bright green pods about 3 to 4 inches long. The pointed, tapering spears will have a ridged surface, usually covered by a fine, sticky fuzz. (There is also a smooth, fuzzless variety, but it is not as commonly sold.) Okra is highly perishable and does not ship well, so it is important to select only the choicest ones. Good-quality okra is plump and flexible and feels as though it would snap in half like a fresh green bean. The smallest ones are the most tender; large okra are apt to be stringy or woody. Prolonged exposure to the air causes okra to darken, so while a few rust spots are acceptable, don't purchase any that have blackened skin. Plan on one pound for 3 to 4 servings.

TO STORE: Because okra is extremely fragile, the best approach is to serve it on the day of purchase. If you must store it for a longer period of time, refrigerate the unwashed okra in a paper bag or wrapped in absorbent paper. The idea is to keep it free of moisture, which would hasten deterioration.

TO PREPARE: Rinse okra under cool running water, removing the fuzz with a vegetable brush or the blade of a paring knife. Trim off the stem end and cap, being especially careful not to puncture the pod if you plan to use the okra whole. Cutting into the pod allows the milky liquid to run out, which impairs the quality of dishes in which the okra is served in one piece.

Whole spears of okra are frequently batter coated and then deep-fried, or rolled in cornmeal and then sautéed. Whole okra may also be boiled, steamed, or microwaved, but these methods seem to accentuate this vegetable's gluey texture. The best techniques, it seems to me, are the ones in which okra is sliced and then cooked in combination with other ingredients.

An interesting aspect to okra cookery is that acids, such as lemon juice and vinegar, react with the milky liquid in such a way as to temper its slippery nature. Consequently, recipes for sautéed okra often call for lemon juice, and a classic technique for preparing okra involves soaking it overnight in a mixture of lemon juice and water. This also explains why pickled okra does not display an objectionable consistency.

Pickled Okra

1 pound okra
3 green chili peppers, cut
  lengthwise into thin
  strips
4 garlic cloves, sliced
1½ cups white vinegar
½ cup water
1 tablespoon chopped fresh
  dill leaves
1 teaspoon salt
12 peppercorns

Green chili peppers and garlic flavor the pickling broth in which okra pods marinate. Serve pickled okra as a condiment with fried chicken or roast turkey.

1. Rinse the okra and pat dry. Place in a large glass mixing bowl. Add the peppers and garlic and toss to combine.

2. In a small saucepan, combine the vinegar, water, dill, salt, and peppercorns. Bring to a boil, then pour over the okra. Cover the dish and refrigerate. Allow the okra to marinate for 3 to 4 days, stirring occasionally to promote even absorption.

Fried Okra

Small okra pods are dipped into beaten egg, coated with cornmeal, and then cooked in shallow oil. A squirt of fresh lemon juice accentuates their flavor.

1 pound small okra
1 cup yellow cornmeal
1 teaspoon salt
2 large eggs
Vegetable oil
4 lemon wedges

1. Rinse the okra and pat dry. Combine the cornmeal and salt in a pie dish and whisk to blend thoroughly.

2. In a small bowl, whisk the eggs with 1 tablespoon of vegetable oil. Dip the okra into the beaten eggs and then roll in the cornmeal.

3. Pour vegetable oil into a large skillet to the depth of ½ inch. Add the okra in small batches and fry until crisp. Drain on absorbent paper and serve with lemon wedges.

Stewed Okra, Tomatoes, and Corn

SERVES 6

4 slices bacon
1 pound okra
4 ears corn
1 medium onion, coarsely
  chopped
1 green bell pepper, cut into
  ½-inch squares
1 teaspoon sugar
Salt and freshly ground
  black pepper
4 large tomatoes, peeled,
  seeded, and cut into
  chunks
Several drops of Tabasco
  sauce

This colorful mélange makes a superb side dish for fried fish.

1. Fry the bacon until crisp. Drain on absorbent paper, reserving the bacon fat. When the bacon is cool enough to handle, break it up into small pieces and set aside.

2. Rinse the okra and pat dry. Slice into ¼-inch-thick rounds. Cut the corn from the cobs.

3. Heat the bacon fat. Add the onion and green bell pepper, tossing to coat. Stir in the okra and corn and cook over medium heat until the onion is limp.

4. Sprinkle on the sugar, salt, and pepper. Add the tomatoes and Tabasco and cover the pan. Simmer for 30 minutes. Stir in the bacon pieces and serve.

Sliced Okra and Shrimp

SERVES 4

1 pound okra
3 tablespoons vegetable oil
3 tablespoons butter
1 medium onion, coarsely
  chopped
1 green bell pepper, seeded
  and coarsely chopped
4 large tomatoes, peeled,
  seeded, and chopped
½ cup dry white wine
2 tablespoons lemon juice
1 tablespoon chopped fresh
  cilantro
Salt and freshly ground
  black pepper
1 pound shrimp, peeled and
  deveined

Okra, tomatoes, and shrimp are remarkably compatible. Here they are simmered in wine and sparked with fresh cilantro. Serve over rice.

1. Rinse the okra and pat dry. Cut into ¼-inch-thick rounds. Heat the oil and butter in a large skillet until the butter is melted. Add the onion and green bell pepper and toss to coat evenly. Stir in the okra and cook over medium heat until the onion is limp.

2. Add the tomatoes, wine, lemon juice, cilantro, salt, and pepper. Simmer, stirring occasionally, until the tomatoes begin to disintegrate. Add the shrimp and continue cooking for 3 minutes or until the shrimp turns opaque. Spoon over hot rice to serve.

Onions

W HEN IT COMES to cooking with onions, there are two major concerns — the degree to which they are pungent or mild, and how to peel and chop them without tears.

The significant characteristic of onions is that they possess large amounts of volatile sulfur compounds. A high proportion of these sulfur compounds results in flesh that is harsh and pungent. Onion varieties that are lower in sulfur compounds are considered mild or sweet.

Prolonged cooking will mollify the flavor of all onions, so it's important to use assertively flavored onions, such as the all-purpose white or yellow globe, for dishes that are simmered slowly. Mild, sweet onions, such as the white Bermuda, or the yellow-skinned Vidalia, are the ones to use when serving onions raw. (Incidentally, it's interesting to note that the newly popular Vidalia, Walla Walla, and Maui onions, which are often so mild you can

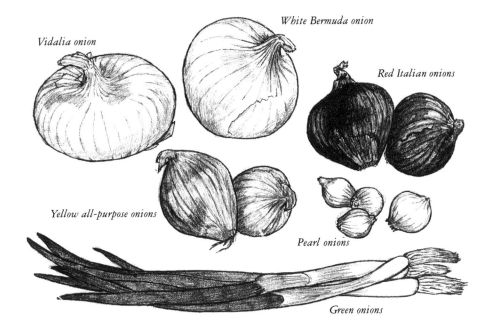

White Bermuda onion

Vidalia onion

Red Italian onions

Yellow all-purpose onions

Pearl onions

Green onions

eat them out of hand, are grown in low-sulfur soil — a condition that produces exceptionally sweet onions.)

The proportion of sulfur compounds contained in an onion also determines how irritating its fumes will be to your eyes. When the flesh of an onion is exposed to the air and the sulfur compounds are released, they interact with the moisture in your eyes to form sulfuric acid, a compound that causes a burning and stinging sensation. The speed at which the compounds are released can be slowed, however, by subjecting an onion to cool temperatures. Therefore, it's a good idea to refrigerate onions that you plan to slice or chop later in the day so you can perform the task without tears. (If you forget to refrigerate onions in preparation for slicing or chopping, place them in the freezer for 30 minutes to cool them down.)

Most types of onions are available year round, with the sweet onions at their peak in late spring and early summer. Onions contain vitamins A and C and folic acid.

TO SELECT:

Shopping for onions is tricky business because produce managers too often fail to label the different types with any kind of useful information. Assertively flavored onions are easy to find. They're the yellow-skinned, round ones that come in a 1-pound or 3-pound net bag. After that, things get more complicated. Moderately mild onions, which can be used for cooking or served raw, may have white, yellow, or red skins, and are referred to as Bermuda, Spanish, or Italian onions. Larger than the all-purpose yellow globes, these onions are usually flattened in shape. The sweetest, mildest onions are the very large, yellow-skinned Vidalia, Walla Walla, or Maui varieties. (Actually they are all the same Granex-type variety; their names connote the locations in which they thrive and grow sweet.) These onions are quite flat and generally wider than they are high. If you purchase what you believe to be sweet onions and are disappointed with the flavor, blame the climate and soil. Sweet onions are finicky and will grow successfully only under the right combination of conditions.

Other types of onions available include the tiny pearl or button onions, and green onions, also called spring onions or scallions. Pearl onions come with white, yellow, or red skins. They are customarily cooked whole and served as a vegetable side dish, or pickled. Green onions, which are harvested before the root curves out into a bulb, have white, moist-skinned roots and bright green leaves. The white portion may be served raw, or sliced and then cooked; the green portion, which is stronger in flavor, may be added to salads or soups, or cooked in a stir-fry preparation.

When choosing dry-skinned onions, look for those that are firm and dry. Check the neck of the onions where the leaves once emerged; pass up any that have soft, spongy areas or signs of decay. Good-quality onions will have brittle, parchmentlike skin, free of green spots or blemishes. Avoid those with sprouts, with woody centers in the neck, or with a musty odor. Green onions should have clean white roots with hairy root ends and fresh-looking greens; refuse green onions that are limp.

TO STORE:

Keep dry-skinned onions in a dark, dry, well-ventilated place at 40° to 50°. Onions may be refrigerated for short periods of time, but the moisture that accumulates inside a refrigerator causes decay. Onions that contain low levels of sulfur spoil more rapidly, so plan to use sweet onions within 1 month. Moderately sweet onions keep for longer periods of time, and pungent onions may be stored for 2 to 3 months. Green onions are highly perishable and should be refrigerated, unwashed, inside a plastic bag. They will keep this way for 4 to 5 days.

TO PREPARE:

Dry-skinned onions may be peeled and cut, or cooked whole in their skins. Green onions should be rinsed, trimmed of their hairy root ends, and sliced if desired. The entire green leaf is edible and may be sliced or finely chopped, and used as you would chives; however, the flavor gets progressively stronger toward the end of the leaf, so use your own judgment concerning how much of it to include.

Because the sulfur compounds in onions are soluble in water, they dissipate during cooking. Consequently, the longer you cook onions, the milder they will be. Also, you can speed the process of attenuation by cooking them uncovered.

It is not advisable to slice or chop raw onions ahead of time because prolonged exposure to the moisture in the air causes them to develop an acrid flavor and odor. I don't recommend chopping them in the food processor either, because the action of the blade bruises and tears the flesh, which results in the release of an excessive amount of pungent sulfur compounds.

Caramelized Onion Spread

SERVES 8

Onions cooked slowly until golden brown are puréed with cream cheese to form a delightful appetizer spread. Offer with crisp rye or pumpernickel crackers.

4 tablespoons vegetable oil
4 tablespoons butter
2 pounds large sweet onions, sliced and separated into rings
2 teaspoons sugar
½ teaspoon salt
Pinch of cayenne
1 large package (8 ounces) cream cheese, softened

1. Heat the oil and butter in a Dutch oven until the butter melts. Add the onions and toss to coat. Cover the pan and cook over the lowest possible heat for 20 minutes.

2. Sprinkle the onions with sugar, salt, and cayenne. Increase the heat to medium-low and cook, stirring, until the onions are golden brown.

3. Pour into the container of a blender or processor and add the cream cheese. Whirl until smooth. Transfer to a small bowl and refrigerate. Serve lightly chilled.

Pickled Pearl Onions

SERVES 6

The spicy, fruity flavor of Gewürztraminer wine is essential to this refreshing appetizer.

3 cups Gewürztraminer wine
½ cup sugar
1 teaspoon dried thyme
5 bay leaves
12 peppercorns
1½ pounds pearl onions, peeled

1. In a nonreactive saucepan, combine the wine, sugar, thyme, bay leaves, and peppercorns. Bring to a boil and add the onions. Cover the pan and simmer for 20 minutes or until the onions are tender when pierced.

2. Remove the onions and bay leaves with a slotted spoon and place them in a glass bowl. Increase the heat and boil the liquid until it is reduced to a slightly syrupy consistency. Pour over the onions and toss to coat. Cover and refrigerate until chilled. Just before serving, lift out the bay leaves and discard.

Sweet and Sour Pearl Onions

SERVES 6

Tiny pearl onions shimmer in a sweet-and-sour glaze. Serve cold as an appetizer or warm as a condiment.

¼ cup bacon fat
2 tablespoons butter
1½ pounds pearl onions, peeled
⅓ cup white wine vinegar
⅓ cup sherry
Salt to taste
2 tablespoons light brown sugar

1. In a wide saucepan, heat the bacon fat and butter until melted. Add the onions and toss to coat. Pour in the vinegar and sherry. Cover the pan and cook slowly for 30 minutes or until the onions are tender when pierced.

2. Sprinkle on the salt and brown sugar. Increase the heat and cook, stirring constantly, until most of the liquid is evaporated and the onions are glazed. Transfer to a serving dish.

Green Onion Bows with Peanut Sauce

SERVES 6

24 green onions
½ cup smooth peanut butter
½ cup water
2 tablespoons molasses
2 tablespoons soy sauce
1 garlic clove, pressed
Several drops of Tabasco sauce

After blanching them briefly, green onions can be tied into bow knots.

Tiny green onions, blanched until limp and then tied into loose bows, are served with a peanut dipping sauce.

1. Rinse the onions, trim the root ends, and cut off some of the green portion so that the onions measure 10 inches long. Drop them into a large pot of boiling, salted water and cook, uncovered, for 30 seconds or until the green portion is limp. Lift out and immediately submerge in cold water. When cool enough to handle, drain the onions and lay them on absorbent paper.

2. Pull the tough outer layer from each onion and discard. Tie the onions into loose bow knots, as shown in the illustration. Arrange on a serving plate and cover with plastic wrap. Chill until serving time.

3. In a saucepan, combine the peanut butter, water, molasses, soy sauce, garlic, and Tabasco. Heat gently until the mixture attains a thick dipping consistency. Transfer to a small bowl and serve warm or at room temperature, accompanied by the chilled onion bows.

Red Onion Marmalade

SERVES 6

Not a true marmalade in terms of a spread for breakfast toast, but a flavorful relish to serve with roast or grilled meats, or with rounds of French bread as an appetizer.

3 large red onions, sliced
  and separated into rings
¼ cup olive oil
1 tablespoon sugar
½ cup raspberry vinegar (or
  substitute red wine
  vinegar)

1. Place the onions in a large mixing bowl and cover with cold water. Allow them to stand for 1 hour. Drain the onions and scatter them over absorbent paper. Blot dry.

2. Combine the oil and sugar in a wide saucepan and add the onions. Cover and cook slowly for 20 minutes or until tender. Stir in the vinegar and increase the heat. Cook, stirring, until the liquid evaporates and the onions begin to break apart. Transfer to a serving dish and offer while warm or at room temperature.

Green Onion Bisque

SERVES 6

Generous dollops of whipped cream dissolve into a delicate froth when spooned atop this hot green onion soup.

3 tablespoons vegetable oil
3 tablespoons butter
3 medium leeks, white and
  green portion, cut in half
  lengthwise, then thinly
  sliced
2 tablespoons all-purpose
  flour
6 cups chicken broth
24 green onions, white and
  green portion, thinly
  sliced
1 tablespoon chopped fresh
  chives
1 teaspoon dried thyme
Salt and freshly ground
  white pepper
1 teaspoon grated lemon
  zest
2 tablespoons lemon juice
1 cup heavy cream, whipped

1. Heat the oil and butter in a large saucepan until the butter is melted. Add the leeks and toss to coat. Cover the pan and cook over low heat for 20 minutes. Sprinkle on the flour and stir over medium heat until the mixture foams. Pour in the chicken broth and bring to a boil.

2. Add the onions, chives, and thyme. Reduce the heat and simmer, uncovered, for 20 minutes or until the onions are tender. Season with salt and pepper to taste. Remove from the heat and stir in the lemon zest and lemon juice. Ladle into bowls and spoon a generous dollop of whipped cream in the center. Serve immediately.

Onion Soup Gratinée

4 tablespoons vegetable oil
4 tablespoons butter
4 large sweet onions, thinly
  sliced and separated into
  rings
1 garlic clove, minced
1 tablespoon sugar
6 cups beef broth
3 tablespoons Cognac
⅛ teaspoon ground allspice
1 bay leaf
2 one-inch strips orange zest
Salt and freshly ground
  black pepper
6 rounds French bread,
  toasted
3 tablespoons freshly grated
  Parmesan cheese
½ cup grated Gruyère or
  Muenster cheese

Traditionally served in individual ceramic pots, this soup may also be presented in a large, wide casserole dish. The idea is to provide ample surface area for what many people consider an essential part of the soup — toasted rounds of French bread liberally sprinkled with melted cheese.

1. Heat the oil and butter in a Dutch oven until the butter is melted. Add the onions and garlic and toss to coat. Cover the pan and cook over the lowest possible heat for 20 minutes. Sprinkle on the sugar and increase the heat. Cook, stirring gently, until the onions are golden.

2. Pour in the beef broth. Add the Cognac, allspice, bay leaf, and orange zest. Cover the pan and simmer for 30 minutes to allow the flavors to meld. Lift out the bay leaf and orange zest and season with salt and pepper.

3. Ladle into ovenproof serving dishes. Top with the toasted bread rounds. Sprinkle on the Parmesan cheese and then scatter the Gruyère or Muenster cheese over the bread. Slide under the broiler and heat until the cheese is melted and lightly browned.

Deep-Fried Onion Shreds

Unlike batter-coated onion rings, these crisp shreds are light and delicate. Sprinkle with salt and serve as you would popcorn, or tuck into a pita sandwich.

3 large sweet onions, thinly
  sliced and separated into
  rings
½ cup all-purpose flour
Vegetable oil for deep-
  frying
Salt to taste

1. Place the onion rings in a large mixing bowl. Sprinkle on the flour and toss to distribute evenly. (Don't expect the flour to adhere. The reason for using it is to blot up excess moisture.)

2. Heat the oil to 350°. Take up the onion rings by generous handfuls and drop them into the oil. Fry until crisp and then drain on absorbent paper. Salt to taste and serve in a napkin-lined basket.

Grilled Onions

Thick slices of sweet onion, cooked over coals until lightly charred, are sensational atop hamburgers, steak, or grilled lamb.

2 large sweet onions
⅓ cup olive oil
Juice of half a lemon
1 garlic clove, pressed
1 teaspoon dried rosemary,
    crushed with a mortar
    and pestle
Salt and freshly ground
    black pepper

1. Slice the onions across into ½-inch-thick rounds. Place on a baking sheet and set aside.

2. In a small bowl, whisk together the oil, lemon juice, garlic, and rosemary. Brush over both sides of the onion slices. Sprinkle with salt and pepper, then place the onions on a hot grill. Cook for 8 to 10 minutes or until lightly charred, basting occasionally and turning once. (The rings may tend to separate, but with adroit turning, they will, for the most part, stay together.)

Oven-Roasted Onions

Onions, roasted in their skins, develop a mild, intriguing flavor. To serve, slice off the top, or stem end, of each onion and place one on each dinner plate as you would a baked potato. Top with butter and season with salt and pepper.

6 large sweet onions
1 garlic clove, pressed
1½ teaspoons dried oregano
½ teaspoon salt
6 tablespoons butter,
    softened

1. Preheat the oven to 350°. Rinse the onions under cool running water, but do not peel. Pat dry. Combine the garlic, oregano, and salt in a mortar. Crush with a pestle, then work in the butter to form a smooth paste.

2. Rub the paste over the outer surface of each onion and place in a shallow baking dish. Bake, uncovered, for 1½ to 2 hours or until tender when pierced.

Just before serving, slice off the top (stem end) of each onion.

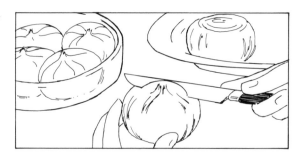

Braised Stuffed Onions

6 large sweet onions
3 tablespoons vegetable oil
1 garlic clove, minced
½ pound ground beef
½ pound ground pork
4 medium tomatoes, peeled, seeded, and chopped
3 green chili peppers, finely chopped
¼ cup raisins
2 tablespoons tomato paste
2 tablespoons red wine vinegar
¼ teaspoon ground cinnamon
⅛ teaspoon ground cloves
Salt and freshly ground black pepper
12 pimiento-stuffed green olives, coarsely chopped
1 tablespoon chopped fresh cilantro
3 tablespoons freshly grated Parmesan cheese
1 cup beef broth

Onions, stuffed with a savory filling of beef and pork, are braised in beef broth until tender. Serve as a luncheon or light supper.

1. Without peeling, drop the onions into a large pot of boiling, salted water. Cook, uncovered, for 20 minutes. Drain in a colander set under cold running water. When cool enough to handle, remove the outer skin and slice off the top and bottom of each onion. Gently push out the centers, leaving a shell consisting of 2 or 3 layers. Place the shells in a generously buttered baking dish. Chop enough of the centers to measure ½ cup and set aside.

2. Combine the oil, garlic, and chopped onions in a large skillet and cook slowly until tender. Add the beef and pork and cook, stirring, until no longer pink. Blend in the tomatoes, chili peppers, and raisins. Add the tomato paste, vinegar, cinnamon, cloves, salt, and pepper and stir to blend. Simmer, uncovered, for 20 minutes or until almost all the liquid is evaporated.

3. Preheat the oven to 350°. Remove the meat mixture from the heat and stir in the olives and cilantro. Spoon the stuffing into the onion cavities and mound it attractively. Sprinkle the tops with Parmesan cheese. Pour the beef broth into the baking dish. Cover with aluminum foil and bake for 45 to 55 minutes or until the onions are tender when pierced.

Onion Tart

This savory tart is wonderfully aromatic when served warm. It also makes a delightful addition to a picnic basket.

1½ pounds yellow all-purpose onions, thinly sliced
3 tablespoons olive oil
3 tablespoons butter
Salt and freshly ground black pepper
9-inch partially baked tart shell
1 large tomato, peeled and cut into ¼-inch-thick slices
1 tablespoon chopped fresh basil
6 ripe black olives, pitted

1. Select 12 of the largest onion slices and set them aside. Separate the remaining slices into rings.

2. Heat the oil and butter in a large skillet until the butter is melted. Add the onion rings and toss to coat. Sprinkle with salt and pepper. Cover the pan and reduce the heat. Simmer for 20 minutes or until golden. Lift out with a slotted spoon and reserve the oil.

3. Preheat the oven to 425°. Distribute the cooked onions over the prepared tart shell. Then arrange the reserved onion slices around the perimeter of the tart in an overlapping fashion. Place the tomato slices in the center of the tart, overlapping them also. Brush the entire surface with the reserved oil and sprinkle on the chopped basil. Cut the olives in half and place one half on each large onion slice. Bake for 30 to 40 minutes or until the top layer of onions has begun to brown. Serve in generous wedges.

P

Parsnips

IT HAS BEEN SAID that given time, all things in life come full circle. And the parsnip is certainly a case in point.

Before the latter part of the eighteenth century, parsnips were eagerly consumed in many parts of the world. Then their popularity diminished and during the centuries that followed, parsnips were almost totally ignored. Today, however, with the emphasis placed on fresh vegetables by proponents of the new American cuisine, parsnips are making a startling comeback.

It is a welcome return. Parsnips are a versatile vegetable with a suprisingly sweet, delectable flavor. Similar in texture to carrots, parsnips may be served alone or in combination with other vegetables. They are a good source of potassium and vitamin C.

TO SELECT:

Parsnips are long tapering roots, resembling carrots in appearance, except that parsnips are a pale yellowish white. Look for those that have a smooth outer skin and are well formed. Good-quality parsnips are of medium size (about the width of a stout carrot) and feel firm to the touch. Avoid any that are limp or shriveled.

There is a fascinating aspect to the quality of parsnips. Much like potatoes, they are high in starch. And also, as with potatoes, the starch is converted to sugar by exposure to cold temperatures. For parsnips, however, this is considered a desirable change, which is not so with potatoes.

The starch-to-sugar conversion caused by cold temperatures is the reason why the sweetest and very best parsnips are those harvested after a long, harsh cold spell. In fact, many cooks prefer parsnips that have remained in the ground through the winter and are dug in early spring, because at that point their sugar content is at its peak.

If at all possible, purchase parsnips at a farmer's stand where you will most likely find the vegetable covered with dirt. Don't be put off by their appearance. The dirt clinging to the roots is an indication that they are freshly dug or that they have been stored in cold, damp soil, which is almost as beneficial. Parsnips are also sold in plastic bags, but they seldom compare in taste with those that have been stored in soil. Plan on 1 pound of parsnips to feed 4 people.

TO STORE:

When you get parsnips home, trim off the greens if they are present, and without washing, transfer the parsnips to a plastic bag. Secure with a wire twist and refrigerate. Parsnips lose their sweetness when stored for too long, so plan to use them within 5 days.

TO PREPARE:

Parsnips may be cooked by any of the methods used for carrots and flavored by the same spices and sweeteners customarily added to sweet potatoes.

Scrub parsnips under cool running water with a stiff brush to dislodge any sand and dirt. Then peel with a swivel-blade peeler and cut into whatever shape your recipe requires. (Parsnips may also be cooked without peeling, then submerged in cold water. When they are cool enough to handle, scrape gently to remove their skins.) If the center core seems woody, which is often a characteristic of large parsnips, you should remove it by quartering the parsnip, then cutting the core from each portion. Cooked parsnips may be mashed or puréed. They may also be finished by glazing them in butter or stir-frying them with a sweetened sauce.

Parsnips are not usually cooked whole because the slim tapered ends cook much faster than the wider tops. They may, however, be cut into segments, then steamed or placed around a roast to bake in its flavorful juices. That way, it's possible to retrieve those segments that become tender ahead of the others. Another approach, which is suggested by some new cuisine recipes, is to shape parsnip segments into nuggets of the same size so they will cook evenly and look attractive on the plate.

Keep in mind that it is easier to cut up a cooked, rather than a raw, parsnip. Therefore, you may find it expedient to divide the parsnips into large segments, then steam, boil, or microwave them until tender. These segments can be easily diced, sliced, or cut into julienne strips.

Like carrots, parsnips may also be eaten raw. They are delicious when grated and served, either alone or in combination with other vegetables, as a wintertime slaw.

Parsnip and Apple Soup
SERVES 6

2 tablespoons vegetable oil
2 tablespoons butter
2 medium onions, coarsely chopped
1 tablespoon brown sugar
6 cups chicken broth
1 pound parsnips, peeled and sliced
2 large mealy potatoes
2 tart apples, such as Granny Smith, peeled and cored
1 tablespoon lemon juice
¼ teaspoon ground cinnamon
⅛ teaspoon ground mace
3 tablespoons apple brandy
½ cup heavy cream
Salt and freshly ground white pepper
Freshly grated nutmeg

Tart grated apple contributes a pleasing flavor and texture to this creamy parsnip soup.

1. Heat the oil and butter in a large saucepan until the butter is melted. Add the onions and toss to coat. Sprinkle on the brown sugar. Cover the pan and cook over low heat until the onions are golden.

2. Pour in the chicken broth. Add the parsnips and potatoes. Cover the pan and simmer for 30 minutes or until tender. Meanwhile, grate the apples and place them in a bowl. Sprinkle on the lemon juice and toss to coat. Set aside.

3. Pour the parsnip mixture into the container of a blender or processor and whirl until smooth. Return to the saucepan. Stir in the apples, cinnamon, mace, and brandy. Cook for 20 minutes or until the apples release their flavor. Remove from the heat and gradually blend in the cream. Season with salt and pepper. Return to low heat and warm gently. Do not allow the soup to boil. Ladle into soup bowls and garnish with a dusting of freshly grated nutmeg.

Parsnip Slaw

3 tablespoons orange juice
2 tablespoons dark rum
2 teaspoons sugar
6 tablespoons vegetable oil
1 tablespoon finely chopped
  fresh ginger
1 pound parsnips, shredded
Salt and freshly ground
  white pepper
1 cup sour cream

Shredded raw parsnips are marinated in an orange-and-rum flavored dressing, then blended with sour cream.

1. In a large mixing bowl, combine the orange juice, rum, and sugar. Whisk in the oil, then blend in the ginger.

2. Add the parsnips to the liquid and toss to coat. Sprinkle with salt and pepper and cover the bowl. Place in the refrigerator. Allow to marinate for 2 hours, stirring occasionally, and then blend in the sour cream. Transfer to a salad bowl and serve lightly chilled.

Glazed Parsnips

Butter-braised nuggets of parsnip are veiled with a citrusy glaze.

1 pound parsnips
6 tablespoons butter
1 cup water
Salt and freshly ground
  black pepper
Freshly grated nutmeg
⅓ cup orange marmalade
Juice of 1 lemon

1. Peel the parsnips and cut into 1-inch lengths. Using a paring knife or swivel-blade peeler, round the edges of each piece to form nuggets of approximately the same shape.

2. Melt 4 tablespoons of the butter in a large skillet. Add the parsnips and toss to coat. Pour in the water and cover the pan. Simmer for 20 to 30 minutes or until tender when pierced.

3. Sprinkle with salt, pepper, and nutmeg. Add the remaining 2 tablespoons of butter, the marmalade, and lemon juice. Increase the heat and stir constantly until the liquid evaporates and a syrupy glaze is left. Toss to coat all the nuggets evenly and transfer to a vegetable dish.

Parsnip Cakes

SERVES 4

Parsnip cakes may be served with almost any meat, but they are particularly delicious with roast goose.

1 pound parsnips, peeled and cut into 1½-inch lengths
1 small onion, peeled but uncut
3 tablespoons butter, melted
1 large egg, beaten
¼ cup all-purpose flour
½ teaspoon baking powder
½ teaspoon salt
Bacon fat for frying

1. Drop the parsnips and onion into a large pot of boiling, salted water and cook for 20 to 30 minutes or until tender. Drain in a sieve, then transfer to a blender or processor. Pour in the melted butter and whirl until smooth.

2. Transfer the mixture to a bowl and blend in the egg. Sprinkle on the flour, baking powder, and salt, then beat until smooth.

3. Drop by generous tablespoonfuls onto a hot griddle that has been brushed with bacon fat. With the back of a spoon, shape into ½-inch-thick patties and fry until golden on both sides. Serve on a napkin-lined platter.

Puréed Parsnips with Sherry

SERVES 4

1 pound parsnips, peeled and cut into 1½-inch lengths
6 tablespoons butter, cut into chunks
4 tablespoons heavy cream
2 tablespoons sherry
½ teaspoon salt
Pinch of cayenne
Freshly grated nutmeg
½ cup coarsely chopped pecans

Try puréed parsnips in place of mashed turnips at your next Thanksgiving Day dinner.

1. Boil or steam the parsnips until tender. Drain in a colander, then force through a food mill or sieve, allowing the puréed parsnips to fall into a large bowl.

2. Preheat the oven to 350° and generously butter a casserole dish. Add the butter to the hot parsnips and beat until thoroughly melted. Blend in the cream, sherry, salt, and cayenne. Pour into the prepared dish. Sprinkle with nutmeg and scatter the pecans over the surface. Bake for 20 minutes and serve at once.

Parsnip Pie

2 large eggs, separated
⅔ cup medium or whipping
  cream
1½ cups mashed, cooked
  parsnips (1 pound)
½ cup brown sugar
2 tablespoons lemon juice
1 teaspoon grated lemon
  zest
½ teaspoon freshly grated
  nutmeg
¼ teaspoon salt
⅓ cup granulated sugar
9-inch partially baked pie
  shell

Puréed parsnips, lightened with whipped egg whites, create a moist, delicate pie filling. Serve with nutmeg-flavored whipped cream if you like.

1. Preheat the oven to 375°. In a large mixing bowl, whisk the egg yolks and cream until frothy. Stir in the parsnips, brown sugar, lemon juice, lemon zest, nutmeg, and salt.

2. In a separate bowl, beat the egg whites until soft peaks form, then gradually beat in the granulated sugar. Add to the parsnip mixture and fold in. Pour into the prepared pie shell and bake for 45 to 55 minutes or until firm. Serve warm or at room temperature.

Pea Pods

STRICTLY SPEAKING, all pea pods are edible. In fact, it has long been customary for some cooks to shell peas and then reserve the pods for turning into purées and soups. The recent popularity of Chinese cooking, however, has sparked great interest in those varieties grown specifically for the delectability of their pods. These particular types, known as Snow Peas, Sugar Peas, Chinese Pea Pods, and Sugar Snaps, possess a thinner-walled, nonwaxy pod, and are therefore more tender and delicate than the pods of regular garden peas.

Edible pea pods are of two distinct forms — those with flat pods and those with plump pods. The flat pea pods are the ones most closely associated with Chinese cookery. Snow Peas, Sugar Peas, and Chinese Pea Pods are all names for the same flat edible pod. Sugar Snaps have a plump pod with more well-developed peas inside. They

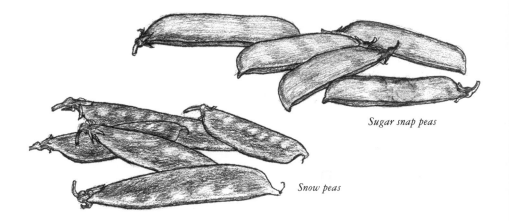

Sugar snap peas

Snow peas

are a cross between flat pea pods and regular garden peas, and they may be prepared according to the methods for either type.

TO SELECT:

Flat pea pods are sweet, tender, and crunchy. Available all year, they stir-fry well and are tender enough to eat raw. Sugar Snaps are available from late spring through the summer. Their plump pods are somewhat less tender and generally need to be blanched before serving raw. They do, however, stir-fry successfully, and when stuffed, make an excellent appetizer.

Whichever type of pea pod you choose, look for firm, crisp pods; avoid any that are limp or shriveled. The walls of flat pea pods are so delicate that it is not unusual for the tiny peas inside to create prominent bulges. This does not necessarily indicate over-maturity. The walls of plump pea pods, however, should be smooth. The smallest pods of either type are the sweetest and most tender. Six to 8 ounces of pea pods are sufficient for 4 people when served as an appetizer, salad, or component of a stir-fry; purchase slightly more to serve them as a vegetable side dish.

TO STORE:

Pea pods are perishable, but not nearly so much as garden peas. Transfer them, without washing, to a plastic bag and secure with a wire twist. Pea pods may be refrigerated this way for 3 to 4 days. If you wish to restore their crispness, soak pea pods in ice water for several hours. Drain and pat dry before using.

TO PREPARE:

Most pea pods need to have their strings removed, although newer varieties, like the Sugar Daddy, have been bred to be stringless. The only way to determine whether or not it is necessary to string the pods is to bite into one. If stringing is needed, break off the stem end and pull the string down the pod. Turn the pod in your hand and break off the tail, pulling the string down the other side of the pod. Some pea pods benefit from being blanched. Again, tasting is the only sure test. If the pod seems a bit tough, submerge the lot in boiling water for 1 minute. Drain immediately and hold under cold running water to stop the cooking process. Pat dry and use in a salad or serve chilled with a dipping sauce. To stuff pea pods, slit them open along one seam with the tip of a paring knife. (Whether you choose the straight seam or the curved seam is a matter of personal choice. Just be sure you're consistent, because each creates a different effect.) When stir-frying pea pods, take care not to overcook them. They should retain their juicy crispness.

Pea Pods Stuffed with Crabmeat

SERVES 12

48 pea pods
12 ounces snow crabmeat
½ green bell pepper, seeded
  and finely chopped
2 tablespoons crushed
  pineapple, drained
2 slices baked ham, finely
  chopped
⅓ cup mayonnaise,
  preferably homemade
Salt and freshly ground
  black pepper

Pea pods stuffed with chilled crabmeat make a refreshingly elegant appetizer.

1. String and blanch the pea pods if necessary. Slit them open along one seam with a paring knife and set aside.

2. Flake the crabmeat into a small bowl. Add the green pepper, pineapple, ham, and mayonnaise and stir to blend. Season with salt and pepper. Spoon the filling into the opened pea pods. Stand them, seam side down, in a shallow, rectangular serving dish, packing them tightly. Cover the dish and refrigerate until thoroughly chilled.

For a uniform appearance and attractive presentation, be sure to open all the pea pods along the same seam side.

Pea Pods with Mint Sauce

Sugar Snap pea pods are a plump, round variety of edible pods. They are delicious when lightly blanched and served chilled with a light green mint-flavored dipping sauce.

48 Sugar Snap pea pods
1 cup sour cream
¼ cup mayonnaise,
   preferably homemade
1 teaspoon sugar
½ teaspoon salt
1 tablespoon chopped fresh
   mint
Mint leaves for garnish

1. String the pea pods and drop them into a large pot of boiling, salted water. Boil for exactly 1 minute, then drain in a colander set under cold running water. Transfer to a clean kitchen towel and pat dry. Refrigerate until serving time.

2. In the container of a blender or processor, combine the sour cream, mayonnaise, sugar, salt, and mint. Whirl until smooth, then pour into a small glass dish. Cover the dish and refrigerate until cool.

3. Arrange the chilled pea pods on a large serving plate or over a bed of crushed ice. Garnish with fresh mint leaves and serve with the mint dipping sauce on the side.

Pea Pod Soup

Pea pods simmered in chicken broth and then puréed create a velvety soup with a lively fresh-pea flavor.

3 tablespoons vegetable oil
3 tablespoons butter
1 pound pea pods
6 green onions, white and
   green portion, sliced
6 cups chicken broth
1 tablespoon chopped fresh
   chives
2 tablespoons lemon juice
½ cup heavy cream
Salt and freshly ground
   pepper to taste
Sour cream for garnish
Chopped fresh chives for
   garnish

1. Heat the oil and butter in a wide saucepan until the butter is melted. Add the pea pods and cook, stirring, over high heat for 30 seconds or until the pea pods are glossy and bright green. Stir in the onions. Cover the pan and reduce the heat. Cook slowly for 10 minutes.

2. Pour in the chicken broth and add the chives. Cook, uncovered, and at a gentle bubble for 30 minutes or until the pea pods are very tender. Transfer to the container of a blender or processor and whirl until smooth. Pour through a sieve back into the saucepan.

3. Blend in the lemon juice, then stir in the cream. Season with salt and pepper and heat gently, but do not allow the soup to boil. Ladle into soup bowls and garnish with dollops of sour cream and a sprinkling of chopped fresh chives.

Pea Pod Salad with Shrimp

SERVES 4

Chilled pea pods and shrimp combine to create a memorable summer salad. Serve for luncheon or a light supper.

8 ounces pea pods
1 cup water
½ cup dry white wine
4 tablespoons vegetable oil
2 bay leaves
½ teaspoon fennel seed
½ teaspoon mustard seed
12 black peppercorns
24 medium shrimp, raw,
  peeled, and deveined
1 small red onion, sliced
  and separated into rings
Salt to taste
2 tablespoons lemon juice
Boston lettuce
Alfalfa sprouts

1. String and blanch the pea pods if necessary. Refrigerate until serving time.

2. In a nonreactive saucepan, combine the water, wine, oil, bay leaves, fennel seed, mustard seed, and peppercorns. Cover the pan and simmer for 20 minutes. Increase the heat, bringing the mixture to a boil, and drop in the shrimp. Immediately cover the pan and remove it from the heat. Allow to stand for 10 minutes, then lift out the shrimp with a slotted spoon. Place in a bowl and refrigerate until chilled.

3. Return the saucepan to high heat and reduce the liquid to ½ cup. Pour through a sieve and refrigerate until chilled.

4. Just before serving, combine the pea pods and shrimp in a large salad bowl. Add the onion rings and toss to combine. Season with salt. Whisk the lemon juice into the reduced liquid and pour over the salad. Toss to coat and spoon onto 4 glass salad plates lined with leaves of Boston lettuce. Scatter alfalfa sprouts over the top.

Stir-Fried Pea Pods with Water Chestnuts

SERVES 4

This vegetable side dish is an excellent partner for grilled shrimp.

8 ounces pea pods
½ cup chicken broth
2 tablespoons soy sauce
2 tablespoons rice vinegar
½ teaspoon sesame seed oil
  (dark)
3 tablespoons vegetable oil
½ cup sliced water
  chestnuts

1. String the pea pods if necessary and set aside. In a small bowl, combine the chicken broth, soy sauce, vinegar, and sesame seed oil. Whisk to blend.

2. Heat the vegetable oil in a wok or large skillet. Add the pea pods and toss to coat evenly. Cook, stirring over high heat, for 30 seconds. Pour on the chicken broth mixture and continue stirring over high heat until most of the liquid is evaporated. Add the water chestnuts and stir briefly to warm through. Serve immediately.

Peas

W HEN YOU WALK down the produce aisle of a modern supermarket and see the variety of fresh vegetables spilling out of their bins, it probably doesn't occur to you to think in terms of scarcity. But the unpleasant fact is that good-quality fresh peas are seldom available in supermarkets. I'm sure this is due to all sorts of complex economic factors, such as the cost of shipping an item that is 50 percent waste, and the lucrative advantages of selling to huge freezing or canning plants. Nevertheless, it's a shame that this delicious vegetable has become so scarce in its fresh, natural state.

TO SELECT:

During the cool months of spring and early summer, fresh peas will appear occasionally in supermarkets, specialty food shops, and at farmers' stands. Look for plump, smooth, bright green pods with fresh stem ends; avoid any pods that are shriveled or have bulges caused by large peas. Peas that are too big are overly mature and will taste mealy. The most reliable sign of freshness is the condition of the pod. Check by pressing your thumb against the seam of the pod where it curves into the tail, over the last pea in the row. A plump, crisp pod will pop right open. Of course, the ultimate test is how they taste; good-quality fresh peas have an unparalleled sweetness and grassy flavor. Purchase 2 pounds of unshelled peas to serve 4 people.

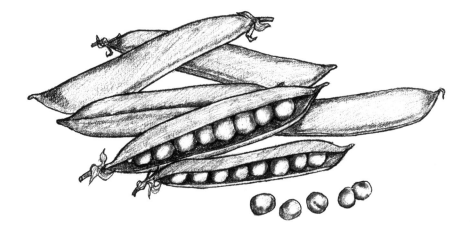

TO STORE:

Part of the problem with merchandising fresh peas, and I suspect, some of the reason why supermarkets shy away from handling them, is the astonishing rate at which their natural sugar converts to starch. In order to ensure the quality of peas, it is necessary to keep them under constant refrigeration. And even then, the result is often more starchy than sweet.

If you're lucky enough to find fresh peas, plan to serve them the same day. Peas are even more finicky than corn, and the same warnings hold true — you may refrigerate peas in a tightly sealed plastic bag for 1 or 2 days, but you'll notice a marked decrease in flavor.

TO PREPARE:

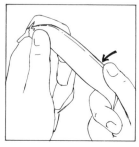

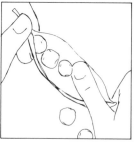

To pop open a pea pod, press gently on the tail end. Then run your thumb down the inside of the pod to dislodge the peas.

If the pods are plump, it's easy to shell peas by popping the pod open. Place your thumb over the seam where the pod curves into its tail, over the last pea in the row. Press gently to pop the pod open, then run your thumb down the inside of the pod to dislodge the peas. Pods that are not quite plump don't open as readily. Tackle them by breaking off the stem end and pulling the string down the pod. Press gently on the seam to open the pod and run your finger down the inside to dislodge the peas.

Fresh peas should be cooked as briefly as possible. They may be boiled in a large amount of water or in barely enough water to cover the bottom of the pan. Steaming and microwaving peas is also an excellent way to prepare them, but my favorite method is butter braising. Toss the peas in a generous amount of melted butter over high heat for 1 minute or until they are glossy and intensely green. Then add a small amount of water, reduce the heat to low, and cover the pan. Cook for 3 to 5 minutes or until the peas are crisp-tender.

Many cooks suggest adding sugar to fresh peas (and it does wonders for frozen peas, too). Purists carp about adding sugar to anything, but consider this — you're only replacing the natural sugar that has been lost through conversion to starch.

Minted Peas

2 pounds peas, shelled
1 medium cucumber,
    peeled, seeded, and diced
2 tablespoons butter
½ cup water
3 tablespoons chopped
    fresh mint
1 tablespoon chopped fresh
    chives
2 tablespoons lime juice
Salt and freshly ground
    black pepper
Boston lettuce

Lime juice and fresh mint give a refreshing dash to a salad of chilled fresh peas.

1. Combine the peas, cucumber, butter, and water in a saucepan. Cover and cook at a gentle bubble for 8 minutes or until the peas are crisp-tender. Drain in a sieve and transfer to a large bowl.

2. While the peas are still hot, stir in the mint and chives. Cover with plastic wrap and refrigerate. Just before serving, blend in the lime juice and season with salt and pepper. Spoon onto chilled lettuce leaves to serve.

Risi e Bisi

A classic Italian combination of spring peas and rice, Risi e Bisi is a blend of simple, fresh flavors. Serve as a first course or as an accompaniment to roast chicken or lamb.

3 cups chicken broth
2 pounds peas, shelled
4 tablespoons butter
1 medium onion, coarsely
    chopped
2 ribs celery, coarsely
    chopped
¾ cup rice, preferably
    short-grained Arborio
½ cup dry white wine
⅓ cup freshly grated
    Parmesan cheese
Salt and freshly ground
    black pepper

1. Bring the chicken broth to a boil in a saucepan. Add the peas and cook at a gentle bubble for 10 minutes or until tender. Remove the peas with a slotted spoon and transfer to a bowl, reserving the broth.

2. Meanwhile, melt the butter in a wide saucepan. Add the onion and celery and toss to coat. Stir over medium heat until the onion is tender. Add the rice, stirring to coat each kernel. Ladle about 1 cup of reserved broth into the rice and regulate the heat so that the mixture bubbles gently. Stir in the wine and continue cooking until all the liquid is evaporated. Add more broth and continue cooking until the rice is tender and a creamy consistency develops. (This may take 25 to 30 minutes, and you may not need to add all the chicken broth.) Stir in the peas and Parmesan cheese. Season with salt and pepper and serve immediately.

Peas Steamed in Lettuce

SERVES 4

The moisture released by the shredded lettuce gently steams sweet, young peas.

1 small head iceberg
  lettuce, shredded
2 pounds peas, shelled
1 teaspoon sugar (optional)
2 sprigs fresh savory
2 tablespoons water
4 tablespoons butter
Salt and freshly ground
  black pepper

1. Scatter half of the shredded lettuce over the bottom of a wide saucepan. Distribute the peas over the lettuce. Sprinkle on the sugar if you wish. Lay the savory sprigs atop the peas, then scatter on the remaining shredded lettuce.

2. Drizzle the water over the top layer of the lettuce and cover the pan tightly. Place over high heat for 30 seconds or until you hear sputtering sounds inside the pan. Immediately reduce the heat to low and cook gently for 30 minutes. Do not uncover the pan during that time.

3. At the end of 30 minutes, the peas should be tender. Part the lettuce and remove the savory. Add the butter, salt, and pepper and toss until the butter is melted. Transfer to a serving bowl and lay one of the savory sprigs in the center as a garnish.

Green Peas in Cream

SERVES 4

Reduced cream sparked with fresh chervil combines with fresh green peas in this traditional dish.

2 tablespoons sugar
2 pounds peas, shelled
1 cup heavy cream
1 tablespoon chopped fresh
  chervil
2 tablespoons butter
Salt and freshly ground
  black pepper

1. Bring a large pot of water to a boil. Stir in the sugar. Pour in the peas and cook, uncovered, at a gentle bubble for 10 to 12 minutes or until tender.

2. Meanwhile, combine the cream and chervil in a large saucepan and cook slowly until the cream is reduced to ½ cup. Drain the peas and add to the cream. Stir in the butter and season with salt and pepper.

Pasta Shells with Peas and Prosciutto

SERVES 4

6 tablespoons butter
6 green onions, white and
  green portion, sliced
8 leaves Boston lettuce, cut
  across into shreds
2 pounds peas, shelled
½ cup chicken broth
¼ pound thinly sliced
  prosciutto, cut into
  julienne strips
1 tablespoon chopped fresh
  basil
Salt and freshly ground
  black pepper
½ cup freshly grated
  Parmesan cheese
1 cup sour cream
1 tablespoon lemon juice
½ pound small pasta shells,
  boiled and drained

Fresh peas are butter-steamed with lettuce and green onions, then tossed with prosciutto and pasta shells. Serve cold as a salad or luncheon dish.

1. Melt the butter in a large skillet. Add the onions, shredded lettuce, and peas, tossing to coat. Cover the pan and cook over low heat for 15 to 20 minutes or until the peas are crisp-tender.

2. Pour on the chicken broth. Add the prosciutto, basil, salt, and pepper. Stir over high heat until most of the liquid is evaporated. Blend in the Parmesan cheese and remove the pan from the heat.

3. Stir in the sour cream and lemon juice. Add the drained pasta shells and toss to combine. Cover and refrigerate until thoroughly chilled.

Peppers: Hot

HOT PEPPERS, which are also referred to as chilies, are members of the same family as sweet peppers. Their distinguishing feature, however, is the presence of an oily acid called capsaicin, which is located in the seeds and membranous tissue, and determines their potency. The hotness of peppers depends not only on the variety, but also on the growing conditions. In areas where the summer is long, hot, and dry, the harvested peppers will be hotter than those grown in cooler regions that receive more rain.

Like their sweet cousins, all types of hot peppers are green at the immature stage. As they ripen, their color changes to yellow or red. Color, therefore, is not a reliable guide to how hot a particular pepper will be, but rather an indication of its maturity. In fact, in some cases, the sweetness that red peppers acquire as they mature counterbalances the effects of the hot oils, resulting in a mellow flavor that is perceived as less than hot.

Generally speaking, red chilies are sold dried because that is the form required by most recipes. The hot peppers available fresh in supermarkets are usually of the green and yellow varieties, so those are the ones discussed here. (It is interesting to note that many of the hot peppers used fresh during their green phase are also used in the dried form when they have been allowed to mature and turn red. Consequently, the same pepper is often called by two different names according to whether it is fresh or dried. For example, the green poblano becomes the dried red ancho, and the fresh green jalapeño is known as a chipotle when it ripens and is dried.)

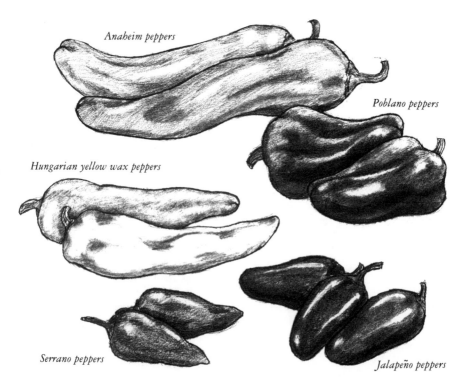

Anaheim peppers

Poblano peppers

Hungarian yellow wax peppers

Serrano peppers

Jalapeño peppers

TO SELECT:

Purchasing fresh hot peppers can be a confusing experience. Each variety goes by several different names, and these change from one region to another. And to make matters worse, many produce managers simply label them all "hot peppers." So it is to your advantage to know how to recognize the various types by their appearance.

When shopping for hot peppers, keep in mind this rule of thumb: the smaller the pepper, the hotter the taste. Select only those that have smooth, glossy skin; avoid any with soft spots or signs of decay. Shriveled skin is a sign of prolonged storage.

There are over 200 varieties of hot peppers, but most of them are only available in regional markets or local ethnic food stores. The following types are the ones more widely available in supermarkets:

Serrano (seh-RAH-no): This is one of the smallest and hottest of the chilies. Bright, glossy green serranos are plump but narrow, and usually measure no more than 2 to 2½ inches long.

Jalapeño (hala-PAIN-nyoh): Somewhat larger than serranos, although similar in shape, these peppers are a darker green. Jalapeños are also plump and taper to a rounded point. They measure about 3½ inches long and 1½ inches wide at the stem end. They are hot, but not as hot as the serranos.

Poblano (poe-BLAH-no): These dark green chilies are larger than jalapeños and are milder than both jalapeños and serranos. Poblano chilies look like small, deflated bell peppers.

Anaheim (ANNA-hyme): These long, slim, light green chilies are similar in appearance to those peppers often sold as Italian frying peppers. They are 6 to 7 inches long and about 2 inches wide at the stem end. Anaheims vary from mild to medium hot depending on their growing conditions.

Hungarian Yellow Wax: This pepper ranges from 5 to 7 inches long and measures about 2 inches wide at the stem end. It closely resembles the sweet yellow banana pepper and is moderately hot. The various yellow chilies look very much alike, so it is often difficult to gauge their potency at the produce stand. Two other kinds are the guero (GWEAR-oh), which is pale yellow and remarkably hot, and the banana chili, which is mild.

TO STORE:

Fresh chilies keep best if they are exposed to the air, so wrap them loosely in absorbent paper or leave them unwrapped. Without washing, place the chilies in the vegetable drawer of the refrigerator and use within 5 to 7 days.

TO PREPARE:

Slit open the hot pepper lengthwise. Holding it under a gentle stream from the tap, lift out the membranes and seeds. (Wear rubber gloves when handling hot peppers if your skin is sensitive.)

The main concern when preparing hot peppers is removing the seeds and oil-bearing membranes. Since the capsaicin contained within them can burn delicate tissue, it is important to remember not to touch your face while working with chilies. Cooks with sensitive skin even wear rubber gloves to prevent incurring a rash on their hands.

Rinse the whole peppers and pat them dry. Slit a pepper open, and holding it under a gentle stream from the tap, lift out the membranes and rinse away the seeds. Then slice or chop the chilies according to your recipe.

An alternative approach is to roast the peppers under the broiler, just as you would sweet peppers, until the skin is charred. Then transfer them to a bowl, cover with a clean kitchen towel, and allow them to cool. The skins will easily come away with a paring knife. Slit a pepper and carefully scrape out the seeds and membranes.

After you've worked with hot peppers a few times, you'll begin to notice that you can judge how hot the peppers are by smelling them once they are cut. (Don't inhale too energetically, just sniff gently.) Peppers that are more potent than you desire can be soaked in water, or a mixture of water and vinegar, to lessen their strength. Just keep in mind that most of the wallop is in the seeds and membranes. Recipes that direct you to include them will produce much hotter results.

Fresh green chilies are occasionally used raw in sauces or relishes, but they are most commonly cooked in some manner. They may be pickled, roasted, grilled, sautéed, stuffed and baked, simmered in a sauce, or included as a component of complex dishes.

Chili Con Queso

Chili Con Queso, which translates to "chili peppers with cheese," might best be described as a cheese fondue. In this recipe, Monterey Jack cheese is melted slowly with finely chopped green chilies. Serve as an appetizer with tortilla chips.

3 tablespoons butter
1 garlic clove, pressed
3 green chilies, seeded and cut into thin, 1-inch-long strips
1 tablespoon all-purpose flour
½ teaspoon salt
1 cup light cream
1 pound Monterey Jack cheese, grated

1. Melt the butter in a large saucepan. Add the garlic and chilies and toss to coat. Stir over medium heat for 30 seconds. Sprinkle on the flour and salt and stir over medium heat until the mixture foams. Remove from the heat and stir in the cream. Return to medium heat and cook, stirring, until the mixture is slightly thickened.

2. Gradually add the Monterey Jack cheese, stirring it in until melted. Transfer the mixture to a fondue pot and place over an alcohol burner to keep warm. If the mixture thickens as it stands, stir in a small amount of cream.

Chilies Stuffed with Cream Cheese and Walnuts

Large green chilies are stuffed with a cream cheese and walnut purée sparked with cinnamon and cilantro. Serve warm as an appetizer or first course.

8 large green chilies, such as Poblano or Anaheim
1 large package (8 ounces) cream cheese, softened
¾ cup coarsely chopped walnuts
2 tablespoons white wine vinegar
½ teaspoon salt
¼ teaspoon ground cinnamon
½ cup golden raisins
1 tablespoon chopped fresh cilantro

1. Roast the chilies by sliding them under the broiler and cooking them until the skin is blistered and charred on all sides. Transfer the chilies to a bowl and cover with a clean kitchen towel. When cool enough to handle, lift off the skin with a paring knife. Cut each pepper down one side and scoop out the seeds and membrane. Set aside on absorbent paper.

2. In the container of a blender or processor, combine the cream cheese, walnuts, and vinegar. Process until the walnuts are very fine and the mixture has a grainy consistency. Transfer to a large mixing bowl. (The mixture should be firm but spreadable. If it seems too stiff, blend in a small amount of cream.) Stir in the salt, cinnamon, raisins, and cilantro.

3. Preheat the oven to 350°. Generously butter a shallow baking dish. Spoon the filling into the chili pepper cavities and press closed. Arrange, seam side down, in the baking dish. Cover with aluminum foil and bake for 12 to 15 minutes or until heated through. Transfer to 4 small plates and serve immediately.

Cold Pasta Salad with Chilies

SERVES 4

½ cup olive oil
6 green onions, green and white portion, thinly sliced
1 red bell pepper, coarsely chopped
2 garlic cloves, minced
3 green chilies, coarsely chopped
Salt and freshly ground black pepper
½ pound spaghetti, boiled and drained
¼ cup crumbled feta cheese
1 tablespoon chopped fresh basil
1 tablespoon chopped fresh parsley

Zesty green chilies enliven this cold pasta salad made with spaghetti.

1. Heat the oil in a large skillet. Add the onions, red bell pepper, garlic, and chilies. Stir over medium heat until the onions are tender. Season with salt and pepper and remove from the heat.

2. Add the drained spaghetti to the sauce and toss to coat each strand with oil. Sprinkle on the feta, basil, and parsley. Toss to combine. Transfer to a large bowl and refrigerate. When thoroughly chilled, serve the pasta salad with sliced tomatoes.

Green Chili Custard

SERVES 6

3 tablespoons butter
1 medium onion, coarsely chopped
1 garlic clove, minced or pressed
4 chili peppers, seeded and coarsely chopped
8 large eggs
¾ cup light cream
½ teaspoon salt
1 tablespoon chopped fresh cilantro
12 ounces Monterey Jack cheese

Fresh chili peppers and cilantro lend lively flavor to this cheese and egg custard. Serve with grilled steak or barbecued chicken.

1. Preheat the oven to 350°. Generously butter a shallow casserole dish. Melt the butter in a small skillet. Add the onion, garlic, and chili peppers and toss to coat. Stir over medium heat until the onion is tender.

2. In a large mixing bowl, whisk the eggs and cream until well blended. Add the onion mixture, salt, and cilantro. Stir in the cheese and transfer to the prepared baking dish. Bake, uncovered, for 30 minutes or until the surface is nicely browned and the custard is set.

Chilies Rellenos

Large green chilies are roasted and stuffed with a cheese-and-tomato filling. The stuffed peppers are then batter coated and fried.

8 large green chilies, such as
    Poblano or Anaheim,
    stems attached
½ pound Monterey Jack
    cheese, grated
2 green onions, white
    portion only, thinly sliced
2 medium tomatoes, peeled,
    seeded, and chopped
4 large eggs, separated
¼ teaspoon salt
½ teaspoon baking powder
¼ cup all-purpose flour
Vegetable oil for frying

1. Roast the chilies by sliding them under the broiler and cooking them until the skin is blistered and charred on all sides. Transfer the chilies to a bowl and cover with a clean kitchen towel. When cool enough to handle, lift off the skin with a paring knife. Cut each pepper down one side, leaving the stem attached. Scoop out the seeds and membrane, then set the chilies aside on absorbent paper.

2. In a large mixing bowl, combine the cheese, onions, and tomatoes. Toss to combine and spoon into the chili pepper cavities. Press the cut edges in slightly. Transfer to a plate and cover with plastic wrap. Refrigerate for 1 hour.

3. In a small bowl, whisk the egg yolks until they are slightly thickened. Whisk in the salt and baking powder, then whisk in the flour. In a separate bowl, beat the egg whites, until soft peaks form. Fold them into the egg yolk mixture.

4. Heat 1 inch of oil in a large skillet. Dip the chilies into the egg batter and fry in hot oil. Turn the chilies once, cooking them until lightly browned. Transfer to absorbent paper to drain. Serve immediately.

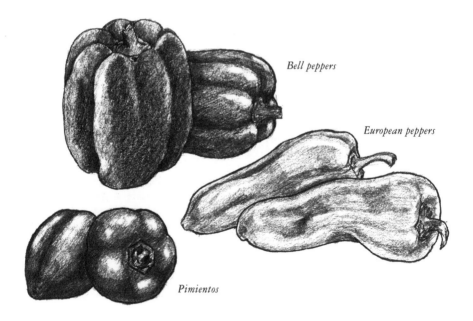

Bell peppers

European peppers

Pimientos

Peppers: Sweet

BASICALLY, SWEET PEPPERS come in two styles: those with a squat, boxy shape are commonly called bell peppers, and those with a slim, elongated form are referred to as European peppers. The true pimiento, which is smaller than the bell pepper, possesses a cone-shaped frame, and falls between the two categories.

Bell Peppers: These are available in a wide range of colors and nuances of flavor. The popular green bell pepper is harvested at an immature stage. Its flavor is relatively brash and acidic and is sometimes described as "grassy." When left to ripen fully, this same pepper takes on a brilliant red hue and develops a sweet, mellow, nonacidic flavor.

In addition to the familiar green and red sweet bell peppers, there are two newcomers with skins of yellow and of purplish brown. Yellow bell peppers represent the mature stage of a special variety that starts out green; those with a purplish brown skin are the immature phase of a separate variety that ripens to green, then finally becomes red. Yellow bell peppers are the sweetest, least acidic of all. The purplish brown ones, often described as being black or chocolate-skinned, are light green inside and taste almost as harsh as ordinary green bell peppers.

European Peppers: These slim, tapered sweet peppers also come in green and yellow tones. Probably most familiar are the narrow, light green Italian peppers, also called frying peppers. The yellow elongated peppers are referred to as Hungarian wax peppers or sweet banana peppers. (There is also a hot variety of long yellow peppers that looks identical. They are sold as Hungarian yellow wax hot peppers.) European peppers possess thinner flesh than bell peppers and have an intense sweet-pepper taste.

Pimientos: Similar in flavor to red bell peppers, these are slightly smaller and are tapered at the bottom like a fat cone. But their sweet, thick walls are meatier than the flesh of red bells.

TO SELECT: All kinds of sweet peppers are available year round; however, the red bell variety tends to be more abundant and reasonably priced in the fall, and the yellow and purplish brown varieties appear more sporadically. All sweet peppers should have smooth, taut, glossy skin. Pass up any that are flabby or that have a pitted, shriveled surface. Peppers of good quality will feel firm and heavy for their size. They will be well shaped and intensely colored. Sweet peppers are an excellent source of vitamins A and C, with red peppers being particularly high in vitamin A.

TO STORE: Place whole, unwashed peppers in a plastic bag, secure with a wire twist, and refrigerate. They will keep for 2 to 5 days. Because the mature bell varieties — those with red or yellow skin — are more perishable than the immature green and purplish brown ones, plan to use them within 2 to 3 days.

TO PREPARE: Sweet peppers of all types may be served raw or cooked, although the long European types are customarily fried or roasted. When serving cooked peppers, you may remove the skins if you wish; raw peppers are served without peeling. Whole peppers may be broiled, grilled, or sautéed, and then steamed inside a paper bag in order to loosen their skin for ease of peeling.

To serve peppers raw, rinse under cool running water and pat dry. Slice in half and cut away the stem and center core. Remove the seeds and ribs of tissue. Stray seeds may be rinsed out if necessary. Cut the pepper into strips or chunks according to your recipe. To prepare whole raw peppers for stuffing and baking, insert the blade of a serrated grapefruit knife into the top of the pepper and cut around the stem cap. Pull out the stem and central seed core with your fingers, then gently scrape out the ribs of tissue with a spoon. Rinse out the insides of the peppers and invert on absorbent paper to drain.

Roasted Peppers

SERVES 6

Red, green, and yellow bell peppers may all be broiled or grilled in the same manner. Commonly described as "roasted," peppers prepared this way acquire a characteristic depth of flavor. Roasted peppers may be dressed with oil and vinegar, as they are in this recipe, and served as an appetizer or layered on a sandwich. They may also be used without dressing as a component in numerous recipes.

6 red, green, or yellow bell peppers
Salt and freshly ground black pepper
6 tablespoons olive oil
2 tablespoons red wine vinegar
1 teaspoon dried oregano
1 large garlic clove, cut into 3 pieces
6 slices fresh mozzarella cheese (optional)

1. Rinse the peppers and blot dry. Place on a charcoal or gas grill or directly on an oven rack set as close to the broiler unit as possible. (Place a shallow drip pan on a rack underneath to catch the juices.) Grill or broil the peppers until the skin blisters and small areas become charred. Turn the peppers with tongs to cook all sides, including the tops and bottoms.

2. Transfer the cooked peppers to a large bowl and cover with a clean kitchen towel. When the peppers are cool enough to handle, peel away the skin and cut the peppers in half. Remove the seeds and membranes. Tear or cut the flesh into 1½ inch-wide strips and place in a bowl. Sprinkle with salt and pepper to taste.

3. Whisk together the oil, vinegar, and oregano. Drop in the garlic and pour the dressing over the peppers. Stir to combine. Cover the bowl and refrigerate at least 24 hours. Remove the garlic and serve the peppers on glass salad plates with a slice of fresh mozzarella cheese, if desired.

Red Pepper Mousse

A purée of roasted red bell peppers and cream cheese, lightened with whipped cream, makes a delightful dipping sauce for spears of Belgian endive.

6 red bell peppers
1 large package (8 ounces)
   cream cheese, softened
½ teaspoon salt
¼ teaspoon sweet paprika
1 cup heavy cream, whipped
6 small heads Belgian
   endive, separated into
   leaves

1. Roast the peppers by sliding them under the broiler and cooking them until the skin is blistered and charred on all sides. Transfer to a bowl and cover with a clean kitchen towel. When the peppers are cool enough to handle, lift off the skin with a paring knife. Remove the seeds and membranes and tear the peppers into strips.

2. In the container of a blender or processor, combine the roasted peppers, cream cheese, salt, and paprika. Whirl until smooth and pour into a large bowl. Cover with aluminum foil and refrigerate for 3 hours or until chilled and lightly set.

3. Just before serving, fold in the whipped cream and transfer to a large glass bowl. Arrange the spears of Belgian endive around the perimeter of the bowl, standing them upright in the red pepper mousse.

Red Bell Peppers Stuffed with Goat Cheese

4 red bell peppers
6 ounces soft, unripened
   goat cheese, such as
   Montrachet
1 small package (3 ounces)
   cream cheese, softened
2 tablespoons medium or
   whipping cream
2 large egg yolks
2 teaspoons chopped fresh
   thyme
Salt and freshly ground
   black pepper
Olive oil

Wide strips of sweet red pepper hold a warm, lightly puffed goat-cheese filling spiked with fresh thyme. Offer as an appetizer to eat out of hand or combine with lightly dressed salad greens and serve as a salad course.

1. Cut the sweet peppers lengthwise into quarters, and remove the seeds and membranes. Rinse under cool running water and pat dry.

2. In the container of a blender or processor, combine the goat cheese, cream cheese, cream, and egg yolks. Whirl until smooth and transfer to a small bowl. Blend in the thyme, salt, and pepper.

3. Preheat the oven to 450°. Lightly oil a baking sheet. Brush both sides of the pepper strips with olive oil. Spoon the cheese onto the pepper strips and transfer to the baking sheet. Bake for 12 to 15 minutes or until the filling is puffed and beautifully browned.

Green Bell Pepper Soup

SERVES 6

3 tablespoons butter
1 medium onion, coarsely
    chopped
1 garlic clove, minced
4 large green bell peppers,
    coarsely chopped
4 cups chicken broth
1 cup cannellini beans,
    drained
1 bay leaf, broken in half
½ cup chopped fresh
    parsley
1 tablespoon chopped fresh
    oregano
Salt and freshly ground
    black pepper
½ cup medium or whipping
    cream
2 tablespoons lemon juice
Lemon zest strips for
    garnish

This chilled soup, made from green bell peppers, is most attractive when served in glass punch cups.

1. Melt the butter in a large saucepan. Add the onion, garlic, and green bell peppers and toss to coat. Stir over medium heat until the onion is tender. Pour in the chicken broth. Add the beans, bay leaf, parsley, and oregano. Cover the pan and cook at a gentle bubble for 20 minutes or until the peppers are soft.

2. Lift out the bay leaf and transfer the mixture to the container of a blender or processor. Whirl until smooth. Pour into a large bowl. Season with salt and pepper and blend in the cream. Cover the bowl and refrigerate until thoroughly chilled. Just before serving, stir in the lemon juice and garnish with thin strips of lemon zest.

Grilled Pepper Salad

SERVES 4

1 green bell pepper
1 yellow bell pepper
1 red bell pepper
3 tablespoons vegetable oil
1 large sweet onion, cut into
    ½-inch-thick slices
4 tablespoons olive oil
2 tablespoons red wine
    vinegar
1 garlic clove, minced or
    pressed
4 mushrooms, sliced
Salt and freshly ground
    black pepper
1 tablespoon chopped fresh
    basil

Multicolored strips of grilled sweet pepper are combined with rings of grilled onion and raw mushroom slices. Lightly dressed with oil and vinegar, this salad is served warm.

1. Cut the 3 bell peppers into quarters. Remove the seeds and membranes and rinse under cool running water. Pat dry and brush all sides with vegetable oil. Place the peppers on a hot grill. Brush the onion slices with vegetable oil and transfer to the grill. Cook the peppers and onion, turning the peppers often but the onion only once.

2. Meanwhile, combine the olive oil, vinegar, and garlic in a small bowl. When the peppers and onions are tender and lightly charred, remove them from the grill. Cut each piece of pepper lengthwise into 3 narrow strips and place in a salad bowl. Add the onion slices and mushrooms. Sprinkle with salt and pepper and scatter the basil over the top. Whisk the dressing to blend and pour it over the mixture. Toss gently to coat and serve while warm.

Tian of Peppers and Squash

SERVES 8

½ cup olive oil
3 medium yellow squash, unpeeled
3 medium zucchini, unpeeled
2 small red onions
2 large yellow bell peppers
2 large green bell peppers
2 large red bell peppers
Salt and freshly ground black pepper
1 tablespoon chopped fresh basil
1 tablespoon chopped fresh thyme

A tian is a baked vegetable dish from the cuisine of southern France. Many times, in preparing a tian, the vegetables are layered sideways so their colors create a beautiful mosaic.

1. Preheat the oven to 375°. Generously brush the surface of a 9x13-inch baking dish with some of the oil.

2. Prepare the vegetables by slicing the squashes and onions into ¼-inch-thick rounds. Then cut the rounds in half. Cut all the bell peppers in half lengthwise and remove the seeds and membranes. Slice lengthwise into 1½-inch-wide strips.

3. Beginning with the yellow squash, stand 4 or 5 pieces on their cut side at one end of the dish to form a yellow row. Next, add a row of red onions, then green peppers, laying the pepper strips lengthwise so they will be about the same height as the squash. Continue to layer the vegetables into the dish using any combination of squash and peppers you like. The object is to alternate the colors of yellow, red, and green.

3. Generously brush the surface of the vegetables with oil, then sprinkle with salt and pepper. Scatter the basil and thyme over the top and cover with aluminum foil. Bake for 30 minutes. Uncover the vegetables and continue to bake for 20 to 30 minutes or until the squash and peppers are tender. Brush occasionally with oil to keep the surface from drying out.

Slice the bell peppers lengthwise into 1½-inch-wide strips and the squashes and onions into ¼-inch-thick rounds; then cut the rounds in half. Arrange the vegetables, cut sides down, in a single layer, forming alternating rows of color.

Hungarian Wax Peppers and Pork

Chunks of lean pork and sweet yellow peppers are simmered in a paprika-laced broth. If you cannot find sweet yellow Hungarian wax peppers, you may substitute Italian frying peppers.

2 tablespoons vegetable oil
1 tablespoon bacon fat
2 medium onions, coarsely chopped
1½ pounds boneless pork, cut into ½-inch cubes
½ cup dry white wine
9 sweet yellow Hungarian wax peppers
3 medium tomatoes, peeled, seeded, and chopped
1½ tablespoons sweet Hungarian paprika
Salt and freshly ground black pepper

1. Heat the oil and bacon fat in a large skillet. Add the onions and toss to coat. Stir over medium heat until the onions are tender. Add the pork and continue stirring until the surface of the meat is no longer pink. Pour in the wine. Cover the pan and reduce the heat. Simmer for 20 minutes. (Add water if necessary to prevent sticking.)

2. Meanwhile, cut the Hungarian wax peppers in half lengthwise and remove the seeds and membranes. Rinse under cool running water and pat dry. Slice the peppers lengthwise into ½-inch-wide strips and set aside. Spoon off 2 tablespoons of fat from the simmering pork and transfer it to another skillet. Re-cover the pork and continue to simmer.

3. Heat the fat in the second skillet and add the peppers. Toss to coat and stir over medium heat until the peppers are limp. Mix in the tomatoes, paprika, salt, and pepper. Stir over medium heat until the tomatoes soften.

4. Add the pepper mixture to the pork and continue to simmer, covered, until the peppers are soft and the pork is very tender. Serve piping hot with rice or crusty bread.

Green Peppers Stuffed with Veal

SERVES 6

Flecks of grated lemon zest accent a filling of ground veal and rice.

6 large green bell peppers
3 tablespoons vegetable oil
2 tablespoons butter
1 medium onion, coarsely
  chopped
1 garlic clove, minced or
  pressed
1 pound ground veal
1 large egg, beaten
1 cup cooked rice
½ cup grated fontina cheese
¼ cup freshly grated
  Parmesan cheese
¼ cup slivered almonds,
  toasted
3 tablespoons chopped
  fresh parsley
1 tablespoon lemon juice
1½ teaspoons grated lemon
  zest
⅛ teaspoon ground allspice
½ teaspoon salt
Freshly ground black
  pepper

1. Preheat the oven to 350° and lightly oil a baking dish. Rinse the green bell peppers and drop them into a large pot of boiling, salted water. Cook, uncovered, for exactly 2 minutes. Lift the peppers out with a slotted spoon and immediately submerge in cold water. When they are cool enough to handle, slice off the stem end of each pepper and remove the seeds and membranes. Rinse the insides with cold water if necessary to remove all the seeds. Stand the peppers cut side down, on absorbent paper to drain.

2. Heat the oil and butter in a large skillet until the butter is melted. Add the onion and garlic and toss to coat. Stir over medium heat until the onion is tender. Add the veal and continue stirring until the meat is no longer pink. Transfer to a large bowl and blend in the beaten egg. Mix in the rice, fontina cheese, Parmesan cheese, almonds, and parsley. Add the lemon juice, lemon zest, allspice, salt, and pepper.

3. Spoon the filling into the pepper cavities, mounding it slightly. Arrange in the prepared baking dish so that the peppers stand close together. Bake, uncovered, for 30 to 40 minutes or until the peppers are tender.

Chicken with Red and Yellow Peppers

SERVES 4

3 tablespoons vegetable oil
1½ pounds boneless
chicken breast, cut into
bite-size pieces
1 red bell pepper, seeded
and cut into strips
1 yellow bell pepper, seeded
and cut into strips
1 large sweet onion, cut into
16 narrow wedges
⅔ cup dry vermouth
1 garlic clove, minced
1½ teaspoons grated lemon
zest
2 tablespoons chopped
fresh parsley
Salt and freshly ground
black pepper

The sweetness of red and yellow peppers is piqued by the tartness of lemon zest. Serve with small steamed potatoes.

1. Heat the oil in a wok or large skillet. Add the chicken pieces and stir over high heat until the chicken is lightly browned.

2. Add the red and yellow bell peppers and onion and continue to stir for 30 seconds. Pour in the vermouth. Reduce the heat and cover the pan. Cook slowly for 5 to 8 minutes or until the vegetables are crisp-tender.

3. In a small bowl, combine the garlic, lemon zest, and parsley. Toss to mix and sprinkle over the chicken. Season with salt and pepper. Increase the heat and stir until almost all the liquid is evaporated. Serve immediately.

Spinach Fettuccine with Red Pepper Sauce

SERVES 4

Roasted sweet red peppers are puréed to form a sensational sauce for green pasta.

6 large red bell peppers
3 tablespoons olive oil
2 tablespoons butter
1 medium onion, coarsely
chopped
1 garlic clove, minced or
pressed
1½ cups chicken broth
Salt and freshly ground
black pepper
2 tablespoons chopped
fresh basil
½ cup heavy cream
1 pound spinach fettuccine,
boiled and drained

1. Roast the red bell peppers by sliding them under the broiler and cooking them until the skin is blistered and charred on all sides. Transfer to a bowl and cover with a clean kitchen towel. When the peppers are cool enough to handle, lift off the skin with a paring knife. Remove the seeds and membranes. Coarsely chop the roasted peppers and set aside.

2. Heat the oil and butter in a large saucepan until the butter is melted. Add the onion and garlic and toss to coat. Stir over medium heat until the onion is tender. Add the roasted peppers and chicken broth and reduce the heat. Simmer, uncovered, for 20 minutes.

3. Transfer to the container of a blender or processor and whirl until smooth. Return to the saucepan and place over medium heat. Season with salt and pepper. Stir in the basil and cream. Heat gently to warm through, but do not allow the sauce to boil. Spoon over the drained fettuccine to serve.

Italian Peppers and Sausage

Italian frying peppers and hot sausage are a traditional ethnic treat. They may be served as a main dish or as a filling for hero sandwiches. Squares of fried polenta make a particularly apt accompaniment.

9 long Italian frying peppers
3 tablespoons olive oil
1 large onion, sliced
2 garlic cloves, minced or pressed
8 medium tomatoes, peeled, seeded, and cut into chunks
2 cups water
6 hot Italian sausages
1½ teaspoons sugar
Salt and freshly ground black pepper
1 tablespoon chopped fresh basil
1 tablespoon chopped fresh oregano

1. Roast the Italian peppers by sliding them under the broiler and cooking until the skin is blistered and charred on all sides. Transfer to a bowl and cover with a clean kitchen towel. When the peppers are cool enough to handle, lift off the skin with a paring knife. Remove the seeds and membranes and slice the peppers lengthwise into quarters. Set aside.

2. Combine the oil, onion, and garlic in a large skillet. Stir over medium heat until the onion is tender. Add the tomatoes and water and bring to a gentle bubble. Prick the sausages in several places and arrange in the simmering liquid. Cook, uncovered, for 10 minutes or until the sausages are no longer pink. Increase the heat and cook until half of the liquid is evaporated.

2. Reduce the heat and sprinkle on the sugar. Season with salt and pepper. Add the strips of Italian pepper. Stir in the basil and oregano. Simmer for 5 minutes. Serve spooned over hot, crusty bread as an open-faced sandwich or with squares of fried polenta on the side.

Plantains

PLANTAINS, WHICH ARE also called cooking bananas, are remarkably similar to their cousin, the dessert banana. Both family members mature more successfully after they have been picked. Therefore, they are both harvested green and allowed to ripen at room temperature. The significant difference is that plantains are frequently eaten at the green stage, but dessert bananas are never used until they turn yellow.

Left to ripen, plantains will eventually turn yellow, then develop numerous black spots. This indicates that

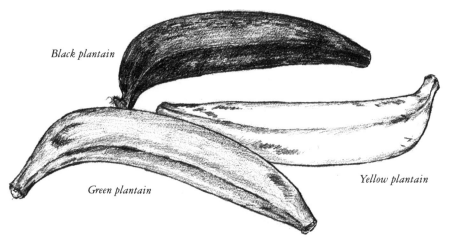

Black plantain

Green plantain

Yellow plantain

they are partially mature. The skin of a fully mature plantain is completely black. Plantains may be used at all three stages of maturity. When green and immature, they possess a firm, starchy texture. As plantains ripen, the flesh becomes softer and acquires a sweet taste that might be compared with that of acorn squash with light banana overtones.

TO SELECT:

Plantains are available sporadically throughout the year at large supermarkets and ethnic food stores catering to Caribbean, Latin American, or Mexican cuisines. They are usually presented for sale like bananas — unwrapped and in bunches. Pick out firm, unblemished green plantains. (If you prefer them ripe, it is advisable to buy plantains green and ripen them at home where they won't get bruised from excessive handling.)

Expect plantains to look like large green bananas with relatively thick skin. Select those that have a substantial stem attached because the absence of a stem causes rapid deterioration and halts ripening. Plan on 3 plantains to feed 4 people.

TO STORE:

Like bananas, green and yellow plantains do best when stored at room temperature. Depending on the stage of immaturity at the time of purchase, it may take 7 to 12 days for a green plantain to develop black skin. Once plantains are fully ripe, they may be wrapped loosely in plastic film and refrigerated for 2 to 3 days. Plantains that are less mature should not be refrigerated.

TO PREPARE:

Cut off the stem end of the plantains and peel as you would a banana. However, green plantains often resist peeling, and you may find it necessary to use a paring knife to remove the skin. Lift off the stringy fibers that run the length of the plantain, then slice or cut the flesh according to the directions in your recipe.

Plantains are customarily cooked to bring out their full flavor and to develop their starchy consistency. They may be boiled, broiled, or grilled, pan-fried as fritters, or deep-fried as chips. Plantains are also frequently simmered in soups and stews or roasted in their skins.

Roasted Plantains

SERVES 4

Plantains may be roasted in their skins at any stage of maturity. When cooked, young green plantains have a starchy consistency and a potatolike taste; more mature plantains, with yellow or black skin, have a creamier texture and a squashlike taste.

4 small plantains, with
  green, yellow, or black
  skin
Salt and freshly ground
  black pepper
4 tablespoons butter,
  melted

1. Preheat the oven to 350°. Lightly butter a shallow baking dish. Cut off both ends of each plantain and discard. Slit the peel lengthwise and place the plantains in the prepared pan. Cover with aluminum foil and bake for 25 to 30 minutes or until the plantains are tender when pierced.

2. Pull the peel apart to expose some of the flesh. Sprinkle on the salt and pepper and drizzle on the melted butter. Serve as an accompaniment to roast pork or grilled lamb.

Trim the ends from the plantain and slit the peel lengthwise. After baking, pull apart the peel to expose the flesh.

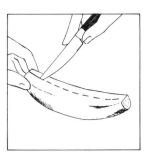

Plantain Chips

I first tasted plantain chips at a large hotel in Puerto Rico, where they are served like potato chips — with everything.

2 to 3 plantains, with green
   skin
Vegetable oil for deep-
   frying
Coarse salt

1. Cut about 1 inch of the tapering ends from each plantain and discard. Cut the plantains in half crosswise. To facilitate peeling, make 4 lengthwise slits through the green skin. Lift the skin at one corner with the tip of a paring knife and pull it away from the flesh. Slice the peeled plantains into very thin rounds.

2. Heat the vegetable oil in a deep-fat fryer to 375°. Fry a handful of plantain slices at a time. Turn them to brown both sides and drain on absorbent paper. Sprinkle with coarse salt and serve warm or at room temperature.

Plantain Soufflé

When you unmold this soufflé from its baking dish, slices of plantain form an attractive pattern across the surface. Serve as a vegetable side dish with grilled meat or fish.

2 large plantains, with
   yellow or black skin
4 tablespoons butter
1 tablespoon sugar
½ teaspoon ground
   cinnamon
8 ounces Monterey Jack
   cheese, shredded
Unseasoned bread crumbs
3 large eggs, separated

1. Cut about 1 inch of the tapering ends from each plantain and discard. Cut the plantain in half crosswise. To facilitate peeling, make 4 lengthwise slits through the skin. Lift the skin at one corner with the tip of a paring knife and pull it away from the flesh. Slice the peeled plantain into ¼-inch-thick rounds.

2. Melt the butter in a large skillet and add the plantains. Toss to coat evenly and stir over medium heat until lightly browned. Drain on absorbent paper.

3. In a small bowl, whisk the sugar and cinnamon to blend thoroughly. Stir in the cheese. Set aside. Preheat the oven to 350°. Generously butter a 1-quart bowl-like baking dish and coat with bread crumbs. Arrange slices of plantain over the bottom and sides of the dish.

4. Whisk the egg yolks until slightly thickened. In a separate bowl, beat the egg whites until soft peaks form. Stir the cheese mixture into the egg yolks, then fold in the whipped egg whites. Pour half the mixture into the prepared baking dish. Arrange a layer of plantain slices over the egg mixture. Pour on the remaining batter. Bake,

uncovered, for 30 to 35 minutes or until the center is set. Remove from the oven and allow to stand for 10 minutes. Run a knife around the perimeter of the dish. Invert and turn out onto a serving platter. Serve immediately.

Plantain Crisps

Frying slices of plantain twice is a technique borrowed from the cuisines of Africa and Latin America. Although green- or yellow-skinned plantains may be used, black-skinned plantains will produce crisps with a sweet, squashlike flavor. Serve with roast or grilled meat.

3 plantains, with green, yellow, or black skin
1 teaspoon salt
Vegetable oil for deep-frying
Coarse salt

1. Cut about 1 inch of the tapering ends from each plantain and discard. Cut the plantains in half crosswise. To facilitate peeling, make 4 lengthwise slits through the skin. Lift the skin at one corner with the tip of a paring knife and pull it away from the flesh.

2. Slice the peeled plantain into ¾-inch-thick rounds. Place the plantains in a large bowl and add enough cold water to cover by 1 inch. Stir in the salt and allow to stand for 30 minutes.

3. Lift out the plantains with a slotted spoon and drain on absorbent paper. Pat the plantains dry. Heat the vegetable oil to 325°. Fry 10 to 12 rounds at a time. Turn them frequently until they become pale golden. Do not allow them to brown. Lift the rounds out with a slotted spoon and drain on absorbent paper.

4. Pressing down gently with a mallet or metal spatula, flatten the plantains to ⅜-inch thickness. Increase the heat of the oil to 375°. Return the plantains to the hot oil and fry until crisp and lightly brown. Transfer to absorbent paper to drain. Sprinkle with coarse salt and serve hot.

After trimming the ends from the plantain, cut it in half crosswise. Make 4 slits down the length of each half. With the tip of the knife, lift a corner of the skin and peel it away from the flesh.

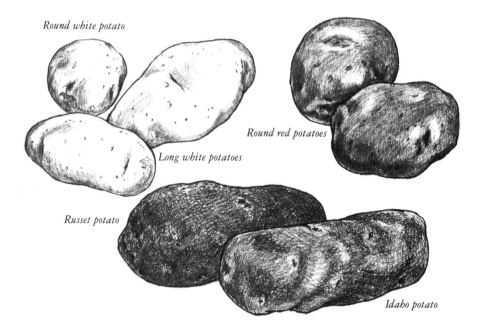

Round white potato

Round red potatoes

Long white potatoes

Russet potato

Idaho potato

Potatoes

A T THE PRODUCE COUNTER, potatoes are labeled in a number of ways. They may be named for
the state in which they were grown, such as California,
Idaho, or Maine potatoes; they may be classified according
to their shape or color, for example, round reds or long
whites; they may also be defined according to the time of
harvest, such as new potatoes, young potatoes, or fall
potatoes. But these classifications can be more distracting
than helpful, because from a culinary standpoint, the most
important consideration is the texture of a potato's flesh.

When it is cooked, potato flesh develops either a
firm, waxy texture or a starchy, mealy consistency. Those
varieties that have a waxy texture are best used for boiling
or steaming whole and for preparing potato salad, because
their firm flesh holds its shape and offers some resistance to
the teeth. Varieties that cook up with a fluffy, mealy
texture are an excellent choice for baking, mashing, or
frying. (Also available are white, round, thick-skinned

potatoes that are marketed as "all-purpose." They are frequently sold in 10-pound bags at a relatively low price. The problem is that they are neither starchy nor waxy, but something in between. The only thing they are really good for is making potato chips.)

TO SELECT:

When you purchase potatoes, keep in mind how they will be used. Mealy potatoes contain a high percentage of starch cells, which swell when heated to create a dry, fluffy consistency. Waxy potatoes contain less starch and more moisture. When heated, their flesh retains a certain degree of firmness; it never develops the fluffy consistency of mealy potatoes.

Generally speaking, you can judge the two types of potatoes by the appearance of their skin. Waxy potatoes, often called new potatoes, have smooth, glossy skin that is thin and delicate. In fact, the skin of waxy potatoes can, in many instances, be rubbed off. Waxy potatoes may be long and white, round and white, or round and red. Mealy potatoes, often called Idahoes and russets, have thicker skin that lacks sheen. Mealy potatoes are long and white, and the surface of their skin possesses a webbed texture. (It is quite pronounced on Russet Centennials, but less obvious on Idaho and Washington potatoes.)

It is usually more expensive to select individual potatoes than it is to buy a prepackaged sack, but the cost may even out in the long run. A package of potatoes invariably contains one or two that must be discarded, plus potatoes of several different sizes. If you choose only those potatoes you want, you can be certain of the overall quality and can select potatoes of uniform size. Look for firm potatoes with shallow eyes. (Digging out eyes results in a considerable loss of flesh.) Avoid any potatoes that are spongy or that have cuts in the skin. Potatoes of good quality smell like freshly turned earth; a musty odor is a sign of deterioration.

Most types of potatoes are now available year round in supermarkets, but because starchy potatoes keep better, they are more likely to be of better quality than any waxy variety you might buy during the winter months. Plan on purchasing 6 ounces of potato per serving.

TO STORE:

Potatoes are much more fragile than you might think. They bruise easily, so handle them gently. At home, transfer the potatoes, without washing, to a cool, dry, well-ventilated area away from any light source. Sunlight or artificial light causes green spots to appear, which indicates the presence of solanine, a toxin that can cause mild intestinal discomfort.

The ideal storage temperature for potatoes is between 40° and 50° because the carbohydrates contained in potatoes have an interesting trait — at temperatures that are too high or too low, potato starch transforms itself into natural sugar, and vice versa. If you store potatoes above 50°, any natural sweetness will disappear in 2 to 3 weeks as the sugar converts to starch. Conversely, potatoes held in the refrigerator lose their starchy character and become overly sweet. The sugar content of potatoes not only affects their flavor, but also causes a change in the way they brown during cooking. For example, if the sugar content is too high, french fries are apt to burn before they cook through; if the sugar content is too low, the desirable amount of browning won't take place.

TO PREPARE: If you've ever looked closely at a thin slice of potato, you've probably noticed that the center of the slice is a different color and density than the outer portion. This is because the center of a potato contains significantly more moisture and less carbohydrates than the outer flesh. Then too, most of the nutrients are concentrated in the outer layers, especially that portion directly under the skin. Consequently, to preserve the maximum amount of nutritional elements, the best way to cook potatoes is in their skins.

When peeling is absolutely essential, remove as thin a layer as possible by applying light strokes of a swivel-blade peeler. Keep in mind that by removing the outer flesh, you're also removing nutrients and starch. This is especially significant when you're dealing with potatoes that have deep eyes or bruises. Discarding too much of the outer layer alters the consistency and reduces the nutritional value.

Rinsing sliced potato or submerging it in water to retard discoloration also causes a decrease in the amount of nutrients and carbohydrates. Consequently, holding potatoes in cool water for any length of time is not a nutritionally sound practice, because important elements are leached out. Rinsing exposed potato flesh washes away surface starch that may or may not be helpful from a culinary point of view. When you're making french fries, for instance, pesky surface starch can cause potato slices to stick together and hamper successful frying. On the other hand, surface starch can be a help in certain dishes, like nests made from shoe-

string potatoes, where the starch actually glues the pieces of potato to one another.

The key to successful potato cookery is matching the right consistency of potato flesh to the method of preparation. Starchy, mealy potatoes cook up dry and fluffy, and therefore produce the best mashed, baked, and deep-fried potatoes. On the other hand, the flesh of mealy potatoes tends to crumble, so they are a poor choice for dishes in which you expect slices or cubes of potato to remain intact. Waxy potatoes are the best ones to use in salads and casseroles for just this reason. Waxy potatoes are also good steamed or boiled and served whole. However, waxy potatoes don't mash well. In fact, they develop an unpleasant gluey consistency and turn grey if they are puréed. The high moisture content of waxy potatoes also makes them poor candidates for deep-frying or for using as baked potatoes.

Stuffed Potato Skins

SERVES 8

These crispy potato shells filled with melted, savory cheese are exceptionally popular. Offer as an appetizer or pair with a salad and serve for lunch.

8 large well-formed mealy
   potatoes
¼ cup vegetable oil
¼ cup butter
Coarse salt and freshly
   ground black pepper
¾ cup grated Kasseri cheese
¾ cup grated Muenster
   cheese

1. Preheat the oven to 375°. Scrub the potatoes under cool running water and prick each one in several places with a metal skewer. Bake for 45 minutes to 1 hour or until the potatoes are soft when squeezed.

2. Immediately cut each potato into quarters lengthwise. Scoop out most of the flesh, leaving about ⅛ inch of potato shell. Reserve the flesh for another use.

3. In a saucepan, heat the oil and butter until the butter is melted. Brush over both surfaces of the potato skins and place on a baking sheet. Sprinkle generously with salt and pepper. Bake at 500° for 10 to 12 minutes or until crisp.

4. In a large mixing bowl, combine the Kasseri and Muenster cheeses with a fork. Distribute the cheese over the potato skins and return to the oven. Bake for 3 minutes or until the cheese is melted. Serve immediately.

Red Potato Salad

SERVES 6

10 small red-skinned waxy
potatoes, unpeeled
2 tablespoons butter
12 medium mushrooms,
sliced
3 tablespoons lemon juice
1 tablespoon Pommery
whole-grain mustard
½ teaspoon salt
Pinch of cayenne
¾ cup olive oil
1 cup canned cannellini
beans, drained
1 red onion, sliced and
separated into rings
12 black oil-cured olives,
pitted and quartered
1 tablespoon chopped fresh
thyme
1 tablespoon chopped fresh
parsley

*White cannellini beans provide a colorful counterpoint to the
red-skinned potatoes and red onions.*

1. Drop the potatoes into a large pot of boiling,
salted water and cook, uncovered, at a gentle bubble until
tender when pierced. Meanwhile, melt the butter in a
skillet. Add the mushrooms and toss to coat. Stir over
medium heat until they are tender. Set aside to cool.

2. In a small bowl, whisk together the lemon juice,
mustard, salt, and cayenne. Whisk in the oil.

3. Drain the cooked potatoes in a colander and immediately cut them in half. Transfer to a large bowl and
pour on the dressing. Toss to be certain that all surfaces of
the potatoes are coated. Mix in the beans, onion, olives,
mushrooms, thyme, and parsley. Cover the bowl and allow
the salad to stand at room temperature for 1 hour before
serving or chill for 3 hours and serve cold.

Hot Potato Salad with Indian Spices

SERVES 6

6 tablespoons vegetable oil
1 medium onion, coarsely
chopped
1 garlic clove, minced
1 teaspoon fennel seed
1 teaspoon cumin seed
1 teaspoon mustard seed
1 teaspoon ground turmeric
6 large waxy potatoes,
boiled and cut into cubes
½ teaspoon salt
Generous pinch of cayenne
2 tablespoons lemon juice
1 tablespoon chopped fresh
parsley
1 tablespoon chopped fresh
cilantro

*Turmeric colors this dramatic potato salad golden, while
other spices lend an intense flavor characteristic of the cuisine of India. Serve this unusual hot salad with cold roast
chicken or lamb steaks from the grill.*

1. Heat the oil in a large skillet. Add the onion and
garlic and toss to coat. Stir over medium heat until the
onion is tender. Add the fennel seed, cumin seed, mustard
seed, and turmeric. Continue stirring over medium heat
for 2 to 3 minutes or until the aroma of the spices becomes
strong.

2. Stir in the potatoes and cook until heated through.
Season with salt and cayenne. Sprinkle on the lemon juice,
parsley, and cilantro. Transfer to a serving dish and offer
while hot.

Baked Potato Purée

Mounded high in a serving dish and topped with a square of melting butter, this potato purée looks like any other bowl of mashed potatoes. But wait until you taste them. Baking potatoes in their skins and puréeing the flesh results in an unparalleled depth of flavor. For a slightly assertive taste, substitute sour cream for the sweet cream in this recipe.

6 medium-size mealy
   potatoes
8 tablespoons butter, cut
   into 8 equal portions
½ cup medium or whipping
   cream, or sour cream
Salt and freshly ground
   black pepper
Freshly grated nutmeg

1. Preheat the oven to 375°. Generously butter an ovenproof serving dish. Scrub the potatoes under cool running water and prick each one in several places with a metal skewer. Bake for 45 minutes to 1 hour or until the potatoes are soft when squeezed.

2. Immediately cut each potato in half lengthwise and scoop out the flesh, allowing it to fall into a coarse sieve placed over a bowl. Using a wooden pestle, force the hot potato through the sieve. Beat in 6 tablespoons of the butter with a wooden spoon. Gradually add the cream, beating to blend thoroughly. Season with salt and pepper. Transfer to the prepared baking dish. Sprinkle the top with nutmeg and bake for 10 to 15 minutes to heat through. Make a depression in the center and place the remaining 2 tablespoons butter there to melt. Serve immediately.

Roasted Potatoes with Fresh Thyme

Here is an excellent way to prepare crispy, flavorful potatoes for a large crowd. Of course, the amounts may easily be reduced to serve fewer people.

½ cup vegetable oil
½ cup butter
24 small red-skinned waxy
   potatoes, rinsed and cut
   in half
2 tablespoons chopped
   fresh thyme
Salt and freshly ground
   black pepper

1. Preheat the oven to 375°. Place half the oil and half the butter into each of two 9x13-inch glass baking dishes. Slide the dishes into the oven and heat until the butter is melted. Stir to combine the oil and butter.

2. Place the potatoes, skin side down, in the baking dishes. Brush the surfaces of the potatoes with the oil and butter. Bake, uncovered, for 15 minutes. Turn the potatoes, brush with oil and butter, and bake for another 15 minutes. Turn the potatoes a third time and sprinkle them with thyme, salt, and pepper. Continue to roast for 10 to 15 minutes or until tender and nicely browned.

Persian Potatoes and Mint

Mint provides an unexpected flavor element in this recipe from the cuisine of the Middle East. Serve with grilled lamb.

8 medium-size mealy
   potatoes, peeled
8 tablespoons butter
Salt and freshly ground
   black pepper
2 medium onions, coarsely
   chopped
1 garlic clove, minced
¼ teaspoon ground
   turmeric
½ cup medium or whipping
   cream
1 tablespoon chopped fresh
   mint
Mint sprigs for garnish

1. Drop the potatoes into a large pot of boiling, salted water and cook, uncovered, at a gentle bubble until tender when pierced. Drain in a colander and immediately return to the pot. Break the potatoes up with a fork and stir over medium heat until they begin to stick to the bottom of the pot. Remove from the heat. Add 4 tablespoons of the butter and beat into the potatoes. Season with salt and pepper.

2. In a large skillet, melt the remaining 4 tablespoons of butter. Add the onions and garlic and toss to coat. Stir over medium heat until the onions are tender. Add the turmeric and continue stirring over medium heat for 30 seconds. Pour in the cream and add the mint. Heat until warmed through, but do not allow the cream to boil.

3. Gradually add the onion mixture to the potatoes, beating until smooth. Stir over medium heat to warm through and serve garnished with sprigs of mint.

Potato Pudding

SERVES 8 TO 10

A cheesy potato casserole with a custardlike consistency.

4 tablespoons butter
2 medium onions, finely
   chopped
4 cups shredded mealy
   potato (about 2 pounds)
¼ cup all-purpose flour
½ teaspoon salt
Freshly ground white
   pepper
½ pound Gruyère cheese,
   grated
3 large eggs
1 cup half-and-half

1. Preheat the oven to 350°. Generously butter a 7x11-inch glass baking dish. Melt the butter in a large skillet. Add the onions and toss to coat. Stir over medium heat until the onions are tender. Mix in the shredded potatoes. Sprinkle on the flour, salt, and pepper. Stir over medium heat for 1 minute.

2. Remove from the heat and distribute the cheese over the potato mixture. Blend well. In a small bowl, whisk the eggs with the half-and-half and combine with the potato mixture. Transfer to the prepared baking dish and bake for 25 to 30 minutes or until the top is nicely browned. Allow to cool for 10 minutes and cut into squares to serve.

Grilled Potato Planks

Thick slices of parboiled or microwaved potato are brushed with a flavorful sauce and grilled.

4 large well-formed mealy
  potatoes
6 tablespoons olive oil
2 tablespoons lemon juice
1 teaspoon dried basil
½ teaspoon dried oregano
½ teaspoon dried rosemary,
  crushed with a mortar
  and pestle
½ teaspoon salt
Freshly ground black
  pepper

1. Scrub the potatoes under cool running water. To parboil, drop them into a large pot of boiling, salted water and cook, uncovered, at a gentle bubble for 10 to 15 minutes or until partially tender. To microwave, place the potatoes around the outside rim of a plate and cover with waxed paper. Cook on high power for 5 to 8 minutes or until partially tender.

2. In a small bowl, combine the oil, lemon juice, basil, oregano, and rosemary. Add the salt and pepper and whisk to blend thoroughly.

3. Allow the potatoes to cool slightly. Cut them lengthwise into ¼-inch-thick slices. Set aside the rounded outside slices for another use. Brush both sides of the flat slices with the oil mixture and place on a hot grill. Frequently brush on the remaining oil mixture and turn the potato slices to cook them evenly. Grill for 5 to 8 minutes or until tender and lightly charred.

Potato and Cheese Frittata

Cheddar cheese adds an assertive flavor to this potato omelet. Serve as a quick, late-night supper.

4 tablespoons butter
1 medium onion, grated
4 large mealy potatoes,
  shredded
Salt and freshly ground
  black pepper
4 large eggs
1 cup half-and-half
6 ounces Cheddar cheese,
  grated

1. Melt the butter in a 10-inch skillet. Add the onion and potatoes and stir to combine. Sprinkle with salt and pepper. Cover the pan and cook over low heat until the potatoes begin to stick together and the bottom is lightly browned.

2. Preheat the oven to 375°. In a large mixing bowl, whisk together the eggs and half-and-half. Stir in the Cheddar cheese. Pour over the potatoes and cover the pan. Continue cooking over low heat for 3 to 5 minutes or until partially set. Transfer to the oven and bake, uncovered, for 15 to 18 minutes or until the surface is puffed and golden brown. Serve immediately.

Potato Tart

Unseasoned bread crumbs
4 medium-size mealy
  potatoes
4 tablespoons butter
¼ cup medium or whipping
  cream
2 large eggs
1 cup ricotta cheese
¾ cup freshly grated
  Parmesan cheese
1 tablespoon chopped fresh
  chives
Pinch of freshly grated
  nutmeg
Salt and freshly ground
  black pepper

This crustless tart is cut into wedges and served either hot or at room temperature. Take it on a picnic along with cold barbecued chicken or a ham loaf.

1. Preheat the oven to 375°. Generously butter a tart pan or quiche dish and coat with bread crumbs. Scrub the potatoes under cool running water and prick each one in several places with a metal skewer. Bake for 45 minutes to 1 hour or until the potatoes are soft when squeezed.

2. Immediately cut each potato in half lengthwise, scoop out the flesh, and force it through a coarse sieve or ricer. Add the butter and cream and beat until smooth.

3. In a large mixing bowl, whisk the eggs and blend in the ricotta cheese. Add the Parmesan cheese, chives, nutmeg, salt, and pepper. Stir in the potato mixture. Blend thoroughly and pour into the prepared tart pan. Return to the oven and bake for 25 to 30 minutes or until the surface is puffed and lightly browned.

Potato Bread

This recipe makes a single loaf of the best white bread you've ever tasted.

1 cup milk
2 tablespoons butter or lard
1 tablespoon sugar
1 teaspoon salt
1 package dry yeast
¼ cup warm water
2 cups mashed or puréed
  potatoes (about 4
  medium-size mealy
  potatoes)
4 to 4½ cups all-purpose
  flour

1. In a small saucepan, combine the milk, butter, sugar, and salt. Place over medium heat and stir until the butter is melted. Transfer to a large mixing bowl.

2. Dissolve the yeast in the water and add to the milk mixture. Blend in the mashed potatoes and 1 cup of the flour. Beat until smooth.

3. Stir in enough of the remaining flour to form a stiff dough. Turn out onto a floured surface and knead until smooth and elastic, adding more flour if the dough seems too moist. Place in a bowl and cover with a clean kitchen towel. Allow the dough to rise until double in bulk.

4. Punch the dough down, then turn it out onto a floured surface. Shape into a loaf and place in a greased 9x5-inch loaf pan. Cover and allow to rise. When double in bulk, bake in a preheated 375° oven for 35 to 45 minutes or until the crust is nicely browned.

Raised Potato Doughnuts

It is a culinary legend that doughnuts made with puréed potato surpass any other kind of doughnut in lightness, taste, and texture.

3 medium-size mealy
   potatoes, peeled
5 to 6 cups all-purpose flour
2 large eggs
1¾ cups potato water
½ cup sugar
4 tablespoons butter
1 teaspoon salt
1 package dry yeast
1 teaspoon ground mace
¼ teaspoon freshly grated
   nutmeg
Lard or oil for deep-frying
Cinnamon sugar or
   confectioners' sugar glaze

1. Boil the potatoes until tender. Set aside the cooking liquid and force the potatoes through a sieve or food mill (do not use a food processor). Measure out 1½ cups potato purée.

2. In a large mixing bowl, combine the potato purée, 1 cup of the flour, and the eggs.

3. In a small saucepan, combine 1½ cups of the potato water, the sugar, butter, and salt. Stir over medium heat until the butter is melted. Add to the potato purée mixture and blend until smooth.

4. Dissolve the yeast in the remaining ¼ cup potato water. Add to the potato mixture. Blend in the mace and nutmeg, then beat thoroughly. Stir in enough of the remaining flour to form a stiff dough. Turn out onto a floured surface and knead until smooth and elastic. Transfer to a greased bowl and let rise until doubled in bulk (about 1½ hours).

5. Turn the dough out onto a floured surface and roll to ½-inch thickness. Cut the dough with a 2½-inch biscuit cutter and place the rounds on floured baking sheets. Cover and let rise until doubled in bulk. Fry in deep fat heated to 375° until golden brown on both sides. Drain on absorbent paper. Dust with cinnamon sugar or frost with a confectioners' sugar glaze.

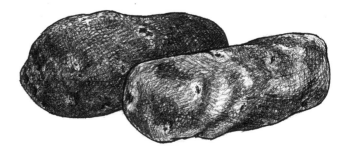

Pumpkins

THERE ARE PUMPKINS and then there are pumpkins. And if you're more interested in eating this vegetable than you are carving it into a jack-o'-lantern, it's wise to know the difference.

Because the major part of this fall crop is sold for decorative purposes, pumpkin farmers have developed varieties that grow tremendously large and have picture-pretty shapes with strong, durable walls. The problem is that they tend to be tough, stringy, and tasteless. Consequently, it's best to seek out a smaller, sweeter variety if you plan to cook with it. Pumpkins are an excellent source of vitamin A and potassium.

TO SELECT:

Eating pumpkins are frequently called sugar pumpkins, although I've also heard them referred to as cheese pumpkins (because their paler color resembles that of cheese). If the pumpkins on the stand are not labeled, look for one that's small (4 pounds or under), light golden orange, and

squat in shape. It should have a smooth, firm shell free of soft spots. Be sure to select one with a bit of stem still attached. To estimate yield, plan on obtaining approximately ¾ cup of purée per pound of whole pumpkin.

TO STORE: Like the other types of hard-shelled winter squash, pumpkins will keep for long periods of time in a cool (50° to 55°), dry, well-ventilated place. But humidity or extreme cold will hasten deterioration. Never refrigerate them or leave them outside in the cold. Plan to use pumpkins stored at room temperature within 2 to 3 weeks.

TO PREPARE: The easiest way to cook a whole pumpkin is to microwave or bake it in a conventional oven because once the flesh is soft, it is much easier to cut and peel and the seeds are easier to dislodge. Prick several holes around the top of the pumpkin with a metal skewer. These will act as steam vents. Place the pumpkin inside the microwave or directly on the rack of a conventional oven. Depending on size, microwave for approximately 20 minutes on high power; bake conventionally at 350° degrees for 45 minutes to 1 hour. Test for doneness by inserting a metal skewer. When it slides in easily, the flesh is cooked.

Pumpkin may also be prepared by cutting off the top, scooping out the seeds, and cutting it in half or into chunks. The pieces may be baked, steamed, or microwaved and then peeled, or peeled first and then cooked. Pumpkin may also be boiled, but this results in a considerable loss of flavor.

Cooked pumpkin may be puréed in a blender, processor, or food mill. However, the food mill gives the best results because it eliminates any stringy fibers. The processor and blender tend to produce a soupy consistency.

Drain puréed pumpkin thoroughly by allowing it to sit in a cheesecloth-lined sieve. If you plan to bake with it or use it as a filling ingredient, dry the pumpkin by pouring it into a saucepan and stirring it continuously over low heat until no more steam rises and it begins to stick to the bottom of the pan.

Pumpkin Fritters

SERVES 4 TO 6

Pile these tiny deep-fried fritters in a napkin-lined basket and serve as an appetizer or arrange them around a roast of beef as a vegetable accompaniment.

2 to 2½ cups all-purpose flour
1 teaspoon baking powder
½ teaspoon salt
1 cup pumpkin purée
⅓ cup milk
6 tablespoons butter, melted
1 large egg, beaten
Vegetable oil for deep-frying
Freshly grated nutmeg

1. In a large mixing bowl, combine 2 cups of the flour, the baking powder, and salt. Whisk to blend thoroughly. In a separate bowl, beat together the pumpkin, milk, butter, and egg. When well blended, add to the dry ingredients and mix. Add as much additional flour as needed to form a soft dough that rolls out easily.

2. Turn out onto a floured surface and roll to ½-inch thickness. Cut into small rounds (1 to 1½ inches) with a biscuit or canapé cutter. Heat the oil in a deep-fat fryer to 375° and add 10 to 12 fritters at a time. Fry until lightly browned on both sides and drain on absorbent paper. Sprinkle with nutmeg and serve hot.

Spiced Pumpkin Soup

SERVES 6

3 cups water
1 small pumpkin (about 2½ to 3 pounds), peeled, seeded, and cut into chunks
6 whole cloves
6 whole allspice
3 coriander seeds
2 cups medium or whipping cream
2 tablespoons butter
3 tablespoons dark rum
Salt and freshly ground black pepper
Toasted croutons for garnish

Laced with dark rum, this spicy soup is the perfect prelude to a fall holiday feast.

1. In a large saucepan, combine the water, pumpkin, cloves, allspice, and coriander seed. Cover and cook at a gentle bubble for 30 minutes or until the pumpkin is tender enough to mash against the side of the pan.

2. Put the mixture through a food mill. Then return it to the saucepan and stir in the cream. Add the butter, rum, salt, and pepper. Heat gently until warmed through. Ladle into soup bowls and garnish with toasted croutons.

Stuffed Pumpkin

1 medium pumpkin (about 4 pounds)
Salt and freshly ground black pepper
4 tablespoons vegetable oil
2 tablespoons butter
1 medium onion, coarsely chopped
1 garlic clove, minced or pressed
1½ pounds ground beef
Salt and freshly ground black pepper
½ teaspoon dried thyme
2 cups beef broth
½ cup red wine
2 tablespoons tomato paste
1 bay leaf
¼ cup raisins
¼ teaspoon ground allspice
1½ cups cooked rice
½ cup grated Cheddar cheese

This main-course dish makes a spectacular appearance at the table. Kids love it because it's so much fun, and adults love it because it tastes so good. When serving, make sure to scoop away a portion of the cooked pumpkin with each spoonful of stuffing.

1. Bake or microwave the pumpkin as described earlier (see TO PREPARE). When cool enough to handle, cut off the top and reserve it. Scoop out the seeds and membranes and discard. Sprinkle the flesh with salt and pepper.

2. Heat the oil and butter in a large skillet until the butter is melted. Add the onion and garlic and toss to coat. Stir over medium heat until the onion is tender. Add the ground beef and continue stirring until the meat is browned. Sprinkle on the salt, pepper, and thyme. Add the beef broth, wine, tomato paste, bay leaf, raisins, and allspice. Cook briskly until most of the liquid is evaporated. Remove the bay leaf.

3. Preheat the oven to 350°. Stir the cooked rice into the meat mixture. Then, spoon the stuffing into the pumpkin cavity and sprinkle with the grated cheese. Place the pumpkin on a flat baking sheet or an ovenproof platter and bake for 12 to 15 minutes to melt the cheese. Replace the top of the pumpkin and serve.

Puréed Pumpkin with Bourbon and Pecans

SERVES 6

A purée of fresh pumpkin with a fillip of bourbon to serve with roast turkey or goose.

1 small pumpkin (about 2½ to 3 pounds)
3 tablespoons bourbon
2 tablespoons light brown sugar
2 tablespoons honey
4 tablespoons butter, cut into chunks
Salt and freshly ground black pepper
Freshly grated nutmeg
½ cup coarsely chopped pecans

1. Bake or microwave the pumpkin as described earlier (see TO PREPARE). When cool enough to handle, remove the top and scoop out the seeds and membranes. Cut the pumpkin into quarters and spoon the soft flesh away from the rind.

2. Force the flesh through a food mill and transfer to a wide saucepan. Place over low heat and stir constantly until no more steam rises and the pumpkin begins to stick to the bottom of the pan. Immediately add the bourbon, brown sugar, honey, and butter. Continue stirring until the butter is melted and the honey is blended in. Remove from the heat and stir in the salt and pepper.

3. Preheat the oven to 350°. Generously butter a shallow casserole dish. Pour the pumpkin purée into the prepared dish and sprinkle the surface with nutmeg. Scatter the pecans over the top and bake for 12 to 15 minutes or until warmed through.

Pumpkin Cider Bread

MAKES 1 LOAF

Reducing cider intensifies the flavor it contributes to this fragrant quick bread.

2 cups apple cider
2 cups all-purpose flour
2 teaspoons baking powder
½ teaspoon baking soda
½ teaspoon salt
½ teaspoon ground cinnamon
¼ teaspoon freshly grated nutmeg
⅛ teaspoon ground cloves
2 large eggs
¼ cup vegetable oil
¾ cup light brown sugar
2 tablespoons orange zest
1 cup pumpkin purée
½ cup chopped walnuts

1. Preheat the oven to 375°. Generously grease a 9x5-inch loaf pan. Pour the cider into a nonreactive pan and bring to a boil. Cook, uncovered, until reduced to ½ cup.

2. Combine the flour, baking powder, soda, and salt in a large mixing bowl. Add the cinnamon, nutmeg, and cloves and then whisk to blend thoroughly.

3. In a separate bowl, beat together the eggs, oil, brown sugar, and orange zest. Stir in the pumpkin and the reduced cider. Add to the dry ingredients and blend well. Mix in the walnuts. Bake for 50 minutes to 1 hour or until a wooden pick inserted in the center comes out clean.

Pumpkin Hermits

MAKES 60 COOKIES

½ cup butter, softened
1 cup light brown sugar
1 large egg
2 cups pumpkin purée
2¾ cups all-purpose flour
1 teaspoon baking powder
½ teaspoon baking soda
½ teaspoon salt
1 teaspoon ground
  cinnamon
½ teaspoon freshly grated
  nutmeg
¼ teaspoon ground cloves
½ cup chopped walnuts
½ cup raisins

Hermits are chewy, old-fashioned cookies, and pumpkin purée makes them exceptionally moist and rich. You may serve them plain or frost them with a confectioners' sugar glaze.

1. Preheat the oven to 350°. Generously grease 2 or 3 cookie sheets. In a large mixing bowl, beat the butter until it is soft and fluffy. Gradually add the brown sugar and beat until well blended. Mix in the egg and pumpkin purée.

2. In a separate bowl, combine the flour, baking powder, soda, and salt. Add the cinnamon, nutmeg, and cloves and whisk to blend thoroughly. Gradually add to the butter mixture and blend well. Stir in the walnuts and raisins. Drop by generous teaspoonfuls onto a prepared cookie sheet, and bake for 12 to 15 minutes. Transfer to a rack to cool.

Pumpkin Spice Cake

MAKES 1 CAKE

Redolent of cinnamon, nutmeg, and cloves, this wonderful spice cake derives special richness from pumpkin purée. Serve plain or drizzled with Cream Cheese Glaze.

½ cup butter, softened
1¼ cups granulated sugar
2 large eggs
½ cup light brown sugar
1 cup pumpkin purée
1 teaspoon vanilla
3 cups all-purpose flour
2½ teaspoons baking
  powder
½ teaspoon baking soda
½ teaspoon salt
1 teaspoon ground
  cinnamon
½ teaspoon freshly grated
  nutmeg
¼ teaspoon ground cloves
½ cup milk
¼ cup orange juice
Cream Cheese Glaze

1. Preheat the oven to 350°. Generously grease a bundt pan. In a large mixing bowl, beat the butter until it is soft and fluffy. Gradually add the granulated sugar and beat until well blended. Beat in the eggs, one at a time. Blend in the brown sugar, pumpkin purée, and vanilla.

2. In a separate bowl, combine the flour, baking powder, soda, and salt. Add the cinnamon, nutmeg, and cloves and whisk to blend thoroughly. Gradually add to the butter mixture, alternating with the milk, then with the orange juice. Pour into the prepared bundt pan and bake for 45 to 55 minutes. Cool for 10 minutes on a rack. Turn out and serve warm or allow to cool and then drizzle on Cream Cheese Glaze.

3. To make Cream Cheese Glaze, combine 1 small package (3 ounces) softened cream cheese, 3 tablespoons confectioners' sugar, 1 tablespoon milk, and 1 teaspoon lemon extract in a small bowl. Beat until smooth and drizzle over Pumpkin Spice Cake.

Pumpkin Coffee Cake

Spicy pumpkin squares with a streusel-like topping. Serve with coffee-flavored whipped cream made by folding 1 teaspoon of finely crushed freeze-dried coffee into 1 cup heavy cream that has been whipped.

2 cups all-purpose flour
½ cup granulated sugar
1½ teaspoons baking
    powder
1 teaspoon salt
6 tablespoons butter
3 large eggs
⅓ cup milk
1¾ cups pumpkin purée
1 teaspoon cinnamon
½ teaspoon ground allspice
½ teaspoon ground ginger
½ cup light brown sugar
½ teaspoon freshly grated
    nutmeg

1. Preheat the oven to 350°. Generously grease a 9x13-inch glass baking dish. Combine the flour, granulated sugar, baking powder, and ½ teaspoon of the salt in a large mixing bowl. Whisk to blend thoroughly. Add the butter and cut in with a knife until the mixture is crumbly. Transfer half the mixture to another bowl and set aside.

2. In a separate bowl, beat together 1 of the eggs and the milk. Pour over one portion of the crumbly mixture and toss with a fork until moistened. Pat into the prepared baking dish to form a crust and bake for 10 minutes.

3. In another bowl, combine the pumpkin purée, the remaining 2 eggs, cinnamon, allspice, ginger, and the remaining ½ teaspoon salt. Add ¼ cup of the brown sugar and blend well. Pour the mixture over the cooked crust.

4. Stir the remaining ¼ cup brown sugar and the nutmeg into the reserved flour mixture and toss with a fork. Sprinkle over the pumpkin filling as you would a streusel topping. Bake for 30 to 40 minutes or until the filling is set. Cool completely to allow the filling to become firm. Cut into squares to serve.

Pumpkin Rum Custards

Dark rum contributes its mysterious flavor to these individual pumpkin custards.

1 cup light cream
1½ cups milk
½ cup light brown sugar
¼ cup dark rum
⅔ cup pumpkin purée
Pinch of salt
4 large eggs, beaten
Freshly grated nutmeg

1. In a small saucepan, combine the cream, 1 cup of the milk, the brown sugar, and rum. Heat until the sugar is completely dissolved. Remove from the heat and stir in the remaining ½ cup milk. Blend in the pumpkin purée and salt. Stir in the beaten eggs.

2. Preheat the oven to 325°. Generously butter 8 custard cups. Line a shallow roasting pan with a kitchen towel folded in half. Pour the pumpkin mixture into the prepared custard cups. Place the cups in the towel-lined

pan and pour in hot water to the depth of 1 inch. Bake for 25 to 30 minutes or until the blade of a knife inserted in the center of the custard comes out clean. Cool on a rack for 30 minutes, then refrigerate the custards until thoroughly chilled. Just before serving, run a knife around the perimeter of each custard cup and turn the custards out onto individual serving plates. Sprinkle the tops with freshly grated nutmeg.

Pumpkin Cheesecake

MAKES 1 CAKE

1¾ cups graham cracker crumbs
2 tablespoons granulated sugar
3 tablespoons butter, melted
2 large packages (8 ounces each) cream cheese, softened
¾ cup light brown sugar
2 large eggs
1¾ cups pumpkin purée
1 teaspoon ground cinnamon
½ teaspoon freshly grated nutmeg
¼ teaspoon ground cloves
¼ teaspoon ground ginger
Pinch of salt

Classic autumn spices enliven this smooth, creamy pumpkin-flavored cheesecake. Serve in place of the traditional pumpkin pie.

1. Preheat the oven to 350°. Generously butter a 9-inch springform pan. In a large mixing bowl, combine the graham cracker crumbs, granulated sugar, and melted butter. Toss with a fork until the crumbs begin to hold together. Then press them over the bottom and part way up the sides of the prepared pan. Bake for 10 minutes.

2. In a separate bowl, beat the cream cheese and brown sugar together until smooth. Add the eggs and blend well. Stir in the pumpkin purée, cinnamon, nutmeg, cloves, ginger, and salt. Pour into the prepared crust. Bake at 350° for 50 minutes to 1 hour or until the center barely jiggles. Cool on a rack for 30 minutes and remove the sides of the pan. Refrigerate until thoroughly chilled.

Pumpkin Gingersnap Ice Cream

SERVES 8

Pumpkin ice cream, rich with brown sugar, is studded with chunks of sassy gingersnaps.

2 cups medium or whipping cream
1 cup heavy cream
½ cup granulated sugar
1 cup pumpkin purée, chilled
4 tablespoons butter
½ cup light brown sugar
¼ teaspoon freshly grated nutmeg
12 gingersnaps, broken into small pieces

1. In the container of an ice cream machine, combine the medium cream, heavy cream, and granulated sugar. Stir to dissolve the sugar and blend in the pumpkin.

2. Combine the butter and brown sugar in a small saucepan and place over medium heat. Stir until the butter is melted. Then cook without stirring until the mixture reaches a syrupy consistency. Add to the cream mixture. Stir in the nutmeg and process according to the manufacturer's instructions.

3. Before placing the ice cream in the freezer to harden, stir in the crumbled gingersnaps.

Purslane

YOU CAN EASILY recognize purslane by its dainty sprigs of reddish stems and tiny oval leaves that are arranged in clusters like the petals of a flower. Purslane leaves have a tangy, faintly sour taste, and are delightful when coarsely chopped and used raw as you would a fresh herb. The fleshy leaves may also be cooked in soups and stews. It is interesting to note that purslane is exceptionally high in nutrients, specifically iron, calcium, and vitamins A and C.

TO SELECT:

Purslane is available sporadically throughout the year in large supermarkets and specialty food stores. Pick out lively looking sprigs with smooth, firm leaves; refuse any that are limp or slimy.

TO STORE:

Place unwashed purslane in a plastic bag, secure with a wire twist, and place in the refrigerator. Depending on its quality at the time of purchase, it will keep for 7 to 10 days.

TO PREPARE:

Rinse purslane under cool running water. Distribute over a double thickness of paper toweling to drain. Gently blot dry. Pick off the leaves and set aside the stems. Chop the leaves finely to scatter over a green salad or broiled fish; chop the leaves coarsely to add to soups and stews. The stems may be cut into lengths, simmered in acidulated water until crisp-tender, and then served cold with a vinaigrette dressing as part of a composed salad. The stems may also be included in your favorite recipe for mixed pickles.

Spring Green Salad

SERVES 6

A lively salad of spring greens, sprinkled with whole leaves of purslane and tossed with a light vinaigrette.

2 tablespoons lemon juice
½ teaspoon dry mustard
½ teaspoon salt
6 tablespoons olive oil
1 shallot, minced
Freshly ground black
   pepper
1 bunch purslane
1 bunch arugula
1 bunch watercress
4 ounces sorrel
4 ounces dandelion greens

1. In a small bowl, whisk together the lemon juice, mustard, and salt. Stir until the mustard is dissolved, then whisk in the oil. Add the shallot and pepper and stir to blend. Refrigerate while you prepare the greens.

2. Rinse the purslane and pat dry. Separate the leaves and stems, then set the leaves aside and reserve the stems for another use.

3. Rinse the arugula, watercress, sorrel, and dandelion greens and pat them dry. Tear into bite-size pieces and place in a salad bowl. Whisk the dressing briefly and pour it over the greens. Toss gently and sprinkle the purslane leaves over the salad. Serve immediately.

Purslane and Cucumbers

A cool, refreshing relish of purslane and chopped cucumber bound with yogurt. Serve as an appetizer to spoon onto triangles of toasted pita bread.

1 bunch purslane
2 tablespoons white wine
   vinegar
2 large cucumbers
½ teaspoon sugar
Salt and freshly ground
   black pepper
3 green onions, white
   portion only, finely
   chopped
1 garlic clove, pressed
1 tablespoon chopped fresh
   mint
3 tablespoons lemon juice
¾ cup unflavored yogurt
4 to 6 small pita rounds

1. Separate the leaves and stems of the purslane. Coarsely chop the leaves and set aside. Place the stems in a wide saucepan and add enough water to cover by 1 inch. Stir in the vinegar. Place over high heat and bring to a vigorous boil. Remove the pan from the heat and allow the purslane to stand for exactly 1 minute. Drain in a sieve held under cold running water. Distribute the purslane over absorbent paper to drain. Blot dry, and cut into ¼-inch lengths.

2. Cut the cucumbers in half lengthwise and remove the seeds. Chop coarsely and place in a mixing bowl. Sprinkle on the sugar, salt, and pepper. Add the purslane stems and leaves, the onions, garlic, and mint. Toss to combine and sprinkle on the lemon juice. Add the yogurt and stir to blend. Cover the bowl and refrigerate until thoroughly chilled. Just before serving, cut small pita rounds into eighths and separate the 2 layers. Toast under the broiler until crisp and transfer to a napkin-lined basket. Offer with the chilled spread.

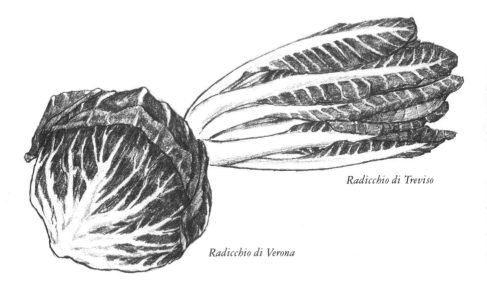

Radicchio di Treviso

Radicchio di Verona

Radicchio (rah-DEE-kee-o)

NOT TOO MANY YEARS AGO, the only way you could taste this elegant red chicory was to take a trip to northern Italy. But eventually, small shipments were flown to the United States to be served in exclusive restaurants. This sparked the American palate, and the popularity of radicchio soared. Now, although it is still relatively expensive, radicchio is grown here and is sold in large supermarkets almost all year.

There are two commonly available types of radicchio — radicchio di Verona and radicchio di Treviso. Don't let the Italian names discourage you, for the two kinds can be distinguished by their shape. The rounded radicchio di Verona resembles a small, loosely packed head of red cabbage; the loose, elongated leaves of radicchio di Treviso look like a head of romaine. Both types have deep purple-red, waxy leaves with a texture similar to that of Belgian endive. Radicchio is related to Belgian endive and possesses the same bittersweet flavor, but to a slightly more pronounced degree.

TO SELECT: The leaves of both types of radicchio should be soft yet crisp. They should have the same delicate smoothness as the leaves of Belgian endive or the interior leaves of a head of cabbage. Leaves that are dried around the edges are an indication of age. Avoid radicchio that is wilted or exhibits brown spots.

TO STORE: Radicchio keeps well for 3 or 4 days when refrigerated unwashed in an airtight plastic bag.

TO PREPARE: Separate the radicchio leaves and rinse each one under cool running water. Distribute over a soft kitchen towel and gently pat dry. The leaves may be left whole or torn into bite-size pieces, and then used in a salad. Although the center rib of the leaf looks like it should be discarded, it is actually quite tender and flavorful, so don't feel you must remove it. Radicchio may be cooked, but the brilliant red leaves lose their color when heated, and some cooks consider the resulting brown hue unappealing.

Radicchio and Fennel Salad

SERVES 4

Fennel provides a faintly sweet counterpoint to the bitter flavor of radicchio.

10 black oil-cured olives,
  pitted
6 tablespoons olive oil
2 tablespoons lemon juice
2 flat anchovies
¼ teaspoon salt
Generous pinch of cayenne
1 tablespoon chopped fresh
  oregano
1 medium head fennel
1 medium head radicchio

1. In the container of a blender or processor, combine 5 of the olives, the oil, lemon juice, anchovies, salt, and cayenne. Whirl until smooth and blend in the oregano.

2. Trim the fennel, cutting off the root and leaf stems to form a bulb. Slice the bulb lengthwise into 8 wedges, and then separate each wedge into layers.

3. Separate the radicchio leaves and rinse them. Drain on absorbent paper and pat dry. Divide among 4 salad plates, interspersing the radicchio leaves with fennel. Coarsely chop the remaining 5 olives and scatter them on top of each salad. Pour on the dressing and serve at once.

Radicchio and Goat Cheese Salad SERVES 4

Broiling the goat cheese atop a toasted crouton makes this popular salad more manageable to eat. Instead of sliding off the radicchio, the melted cheese remains on the crouton where it may be portioned out as you wish.

2 small heads radicchio
Juice of half a lemon
2 slices good-quality white
    bread
4 rounds goat cheese, cut
    from a log-shaped
    Montrachet
1 tablespoon chopped fresh
    thyme
Olive oil

1. Separate the radicchio leaves and rinse them. Drain on absorbent paper and pat dry. Divide among 4 salad plates and arrange in an attractive manner, leaving a space to one side of the plate. Sprinkle with lemon juice and place in the refrigerator.

2. Using a 2-inch biscuit cutter, cut 4 rounds from the bread slices. Toast or broil on both sides until lightly browned. Transfer to a shallow pan. Cut the rounds of goat cheese about ¾-inch thick and place a round of cheese atop each round of toasted bread. Sprinkle the tops of the cheese with thyme and press down gently. Pour enough oil over the cheese to coat the entire surface. Slide under the broiler and heat until the surface of the cheese looks golden and slightly bubbly. Set a crouton with its cheese to the side of each salad plate and serve at once.

Grilled Radicchio SERVES 4

Radicchio is the only leafy vegetable that can hold up to the heat of grilling. Although the bright red leaves will turn brown, grilling radicchio causes the tangy flavor to become more intense. Serve as an accompaniment to grilled chicken or fish.

½ cup olive oil
2 cloves garlic, sliced
2 tablespoons lemon juice
Salt and freshly ground
    black pepper
2 medium heads radicchio

1. In a small saucepan, combine the oil and garlic and cook over low heat until the garlic turns golden. Do not allow it to brown. Remove from the heat and pour through a sieve. Whisk in the lemon juice and salt and pepper.

2. Cut the radicchio in half lengthwise and brush the surface with the garlic-flavored oil. Place on a hot grill, cut side down. Cook for 3 to 5 minutes, turning once, until the radicchio is dull brown in color. Transfer to 4 salad plates and pour the remaining oil over the radicchio to serve.

Radishes

ONE OF THE MOST refreshing appetizers is a classic French offering of tiny red radishes, unsalted butter, coarse sea salt, and thinly sliced bread. The scarlet radishes, still attached to their bright, fuzzy greenery, are arranged on a plate with the butter and salt. Thin wedges of dark bread are presented on the side. According to custom, the correct approach is to butter the radish, rather than the bread, and then dip the buttered surface into the salt. The bread is eaten plain to counterbalance the vibrant flavors.

Other kinds of radishes, such as the elongated white icicle type and the round black radish, also possess a lively character. They are most commonly served raw and chilled to play up their crisp texture and peppery taste.

TO SELECT:

Radishes are available all year in one form or another. Small red spheres and short white fingers frequently come trimmed of their greens and packaged in plastic pouches, but they are only at their best when available in unwrapped

Black radishes

Red radishes

White icicle radishes

bunches with the stems and leaves intact. Prolonged storage inside a plastic bag tends to result in a loss of flavor and a woody consistency. Round black radishes, about the size of turnips, and long white radishes are most commonly available in the fall. They are usually displayed loose and unwrapped, but bereft of their stems and leaves.

Look for firm, plump radishes with unbroken skin. If the greens are attached, they should be perky and resilient; their freshness is a clue to the condition of the radishes. When no greens are present, check the stem end for signs of decay. Press gently on the spot where the stems were once attached and pass up any that feel soft. Radishes that yield to the pressure of your fingers will be woody or hollow. Depending on their size, plan on 3 or 4 radishes per serving.

TO STORE:

Remove the stems and leaves from red radishes and discard, or place them in a plastic bag and reserve for making soup. Transfer the radishes, without washing them, to a plastic bag and secure it with a wire twist. Refrigerate and use within 3 to 4 days. Long white radishes and black radishes, which usually come without greens, are more durable than red radishes. They may be loosely wrapped and refrigerated for 7 to 10 days, depending on their condition at the time of purchase.

TO PREPARE:

Rinse the radishes under cool running water, then trim the stem and taproot ends. If you like, you may accentuate their crispiness by submerging them in ice water for 3 to 4 hours.

Red and short white radishes have thin, tender skin, and therefore seldom need peeling, but black radishes and the longer white variety benefit from having their outer skins removed. All types of radishes may be served raw. They are customarily sliced, minced, grated, shredded, or cut into julienne strips. Raw radishes may be included in a salad or slaw, or they can stand on their own as a vegetable side dish. Radishes may also be cooked. They are frequently sautéed or used as part of a stir-fry.

Red Radish Canapés

SERVES 8

Delicate rounds of white bread are topped with whipped cream cheese and finely chopped red radishes. Serve as an appetizer or at tea.

1 bunch red radishes
1 small package (3 ounces)
    cream cheese, softened
2 tablespoons lemon juice
¼ teaspoon salt
8 slices thin white bread

1. Rinse the radishes and pat them dry. Using a processor or a butcher's knife, chop the radishes very fine.

2. In a small bowl, combine the cream cheese, lemon juice, and salt. Beat until light and fluffy.

3. Cut 1½- to 2-inch rounds from the bread with a biscuit or canapé cutter. Lightly spread each round with the whipped cream cheese. Generously sprinkle on the chopped radishes so that no cream cheese shows through. Press down gently to ensure that the radishes adhere. Arrange on a tray. Cover with plastic wrap and chill lightly.

Red Radish Soup

SERVES 6

Unpeeled red radishes are cooked and then puréed to create a surprisingly mellow soup with a delicate pink blush.

3 tablespoons butter
3 green onions, white
    portion only, sliced
6 cups chicken broth
2 bunches red radishes,
    rinsed, trimmed, and
    quartered
¼ cup long-grain rice
1 teaspoon finely chopped
    fresh ginger
1 tablespoon lemon juice
½ cup unflavored yogurt
Finely chopped fresh
    parsley for garnish

1. Melt the butter in a large saucepan. Add the onions and toss to coat evenly. Stir over medium heat until the onions are tender. Pour in the chicken broth. Add the radishes and rice. Cover the pan and cook at a gentle bubble for 20 minutes or until the radishes and rice are tender.

2. Pour into the container of a blender or processor and whirl until smooth. Return to the saucepan. Stir in the ginger and lemon juice and blend in the yogurt. Place over low heat and warm gently, but do not allow the soup to boil. Serve garnished with finely chopped parsley.

White Radish Salad

1 bunch white icicle
  radishes, rinsed and
  trimmed
2 carrots
1 small zucchini
Salt and freshly ground
  black pepper
2 tablespoons white wine
  vinegar
½ teaspoon dry mustard
1 teaspoon dried oregano
6 tablespoons olive oil
2 ounces Gorgonzola
  cheese, finely crumbled

Shredded white radishes, carrots, and zucchini combine to create a tasty and attractive slaw. Chill and serve with baked ham or corned beef.

1. By hand or with a food processor, shred the radishes, carrots, and zucchini. Place in a large mixing bowl and season with salt and pepper. Toss to combine.

2. In a small bowl, whisk together the vinegar and mustard until the mustard is dissolved. Stir in the oregano. Gradually whisk in the oil. Pour the dressing over the shredded vegetables and toss to coat. Cover the bowl and refrigerate for 2 to 3 hours or until lightly chilled. Just before serving, scatter the cheese over the salad and toss to incorporate.

Radishes in Cream

SERVES 4

Brilliant red radishes are lightly cooked in a white cream sauce. Serve this sophisticated dish with roast veal.

1 pound red radishes
½ teaspoon salt
3 tablespoons butter
1 tablespoon all-purpose
  flour
Generous pinch of cayenne
1 cup medium or whipping
  cream
1 tablespoon chopped fresh
  chervil
1 tablespoon lemon juice

1. Rinse and trim the radishes and place them in a wide saucepan. Add enough water to cover by 1 inch. Place over high heat and bring to a boil. Add the salt and reduce the heat. Cover the pan and simmer for 10 minutes or until the radishes are crisp-tender. Drain in a colander, but reserve ½ cup of the cooking liquid.

2. Melt the butter in a small saucepan. Add the flour and cayenne and stir over medium heat until the mixture foams. Remove from the heat and whisk in the cream. Return to the heat and blend in the reserved cooking liquid. Increase the heat and stir continuously until the sauce is thickened.

3. Blend in the chervil. Add the radishes and stir until heated through. Remove from the heat, stir in the lemon juice, and serve.

Stir-Fried Radishes with Green Onions SERVES 4

3 tablespoons vegetable oil
2 bunches red radishes, rinsed, trimmed, and thinly sliced
4 green onions, white and green portion, sliced
3 tablespoons water
Salt and freshly ground black pepper
2 tablespoons butter, cut into chunks

Thinly sliced radishes are combined with green onions and cooked lightly. Finished with melted butter, they make a delicious partner for grilled meat.

1. Heat the oil in a wok or large skillet. Add the radishes and toss to coat. Stir over high heat for 30 seconds. Add the onions and sprinkle on the water. Continue stirring over high heat until the water evaporates and the radishes are crisp-tender. Remove from the heat.

2. Season with salt and pepper, then add the butter. Toss until the butter is melted and serve immediately.

Rapini (rah-PEE-nee)

ALTHOUGH THIS leafy green vegetable is often labeled rapini at the supermarket produce counter, it is also known by several other names. It may appear in small specialty food shops as broccoletti, cima di rape, broccolirab, or rape. (This is an entirely different plant from the herb called rape that produces the seeds used for making rape oil. The herb, rape, belongs to the category *Brassica napus,* and has recently been deemed unhealthy.)

Rapini looks like a slender, single stalk of broccoli with thin branches bearing large, jagged leaves. Tiny buds on the broccolilike head open to reveal bright yellow flowers. Botanically speaking, rapini are the greens of a variety of turnip that does not form a tuberous root.

The flavor of rapini is assertively, but pleasantly, bitter. For this reason, some recipes suggest mixing rapini with spinach or other mildly flavored greens. The best approach, I think, is to meet power with power, and combine rapini with a generous portion of garlic. Rapini is available all year but may be difficult to find. Look in Italian grocery stores and in supermarkets that advertise they are having an "Italian festival."

TO SELECT:	Shop at a store that offers a loose display so you can feel how fresh the leaves are and pick out only the stalks you want. Rapini of good quality will have crisp, rough leaves and tightly closed, bright green bud heads. The appearance of yellow flowers indicates that the rapini is more mature, and consequently will be less tender and taste more bitter. Avoid rapini that is limp or spotted with brown. One pound will feed 4 people.
TO STORE:	Place the unwashed rapini in a plastic bag and secure with a wire twist. Refrigerate and use within 3 to 4 days.
TO PREPARE:	Rapini is customarily prepared one of two ways — it is boiled in salted water like beet greens and mustard greens, or it is sautéed in oil. Boiled rapini may be dressed simply with butter or vinegar and served hot, or tossed with a vinaigrette and served cold; sautéed rapini may also be served hot or cold.

Rapini with Fresh Ginger

Rapini sautéed with garlic and fresh ginger acquires an Oriental flavor. Serve with roast pork or grilled veal chops.

1½ pounds rapini
⅓ cup water
½ teaspoon sesame seed oil (dark)
3 tablespoons vegetable oil
1-inch piece fresh ginger, cut into thin strips
1 garlic clove, minced
1 tablespoon toasted sesame seed

1. Rinse the rapini and pat dry. Cut the heads, tender stems, and leaves from the center stalk. Cut large leaves in two and set aside. Cut the stalks into ½-inch lengths.

2. In a small bowl, combine the water and sesame seed oil and set aside. Heat the vegetable oil in a wok or large skillet. Add the ginger and garlic and stir briefly over high heat. Add the rapini stems, stalks, and heads and toss to coat. Pour in the water and oil mixture. Cover the pan and reduce the heat. Simmer for 3 to 4 minutes or until the stalks are crisp-tender. Add the rapini leaves. Increase the heat and stir continuously until all the liquid is evaporated. Transfer to a serving dish and sprinkle with sesame seed.

Rapini with Shrimp and Pasta

Bright green rapini and pink shrimp combine to create this beautiful warm pasta salad. Serve as a first course or for luncheon.

1 pound rapini
3 tablespoons vegetable oil
⅓ cup water
3 tablespoons olive oil
3 tablespoons butter
1 shallot, finely chopped
1 garlic clove, minced or pressed
⅓ cup dry white wine
2 tablespoons lemon juice
1 pound medium shrimp, peeled and deveined
½ pound rotelle, boiled and drained
Salt and freshly ground black pepper

1. Rinse the rapini and pat dry. Cut the heads, tender stems, and leaves from the center stalk. Cut large leaves in two and set aside. Cut the stalks into ½-inch lengths.

2. Heat the vegetable oil in a large skillet. Add the rapini stems, stalks, and heads and toss to coat. Pour in the water. Cover the pan and reduce the heat. Simmer for 3 to 4 minutes or until the stalks are crisp-tender. Add the rapini leaves and stir briefly until they are wilted. Transfer the contents to a plate.

3. Add the olive oil and butter to the skillet and heat until the butter is melted. Stir in the shallot and garlic and cook over medium heat until the shallot is tender. Add the wine and lemon juice and bring to a boil. Stir in the shrimp. Cook for 2 minutes or just until the shrimp curls and turns pink.

4. Add the drained rotelle and stir over medium heat to warm through. Season with salt and pepper. Add the rapini and stir briefly to heat, but do not overcook or the rapini will lose its vivid green color. Serve immediately.

Rhubarb

MANY FRUITS CROSS over the culinary line, establishing themselves in the vegetable domain. We think nothing, for example, of preparing and serving tomatoes, avocados, and eggplant as if they were vegetables. On the other hand, rhubarb is the only vegetable served almost exclusively as a fruit. Compotes, relishes, and chutneys made from rhubarb may be offered during the main course as an accompaniment to savory dishes, but the most popular way to use rhubarb is in desserts.

TO SELECT: Rhubarb is a sturdy leaf stalk measuring 12 to 18 inches long. The stalks may be pinkish red, bright red, or green mottled with red. Color is not a reliable indicator of quality, but generally speaking, pinkish red stalks tend to be younger and more tender. Bright red stalks and green stalks are usually older and therefore apt to be stringy. Rhubarb is sold both with and without its large green leaves. Since fresh-looking leaves are a clue to the freshness of the stalks, their presence is desirable when you're selecting rhubarb, but they are poisonous and should not be eaten.

The peak season for native rhubarb coincides with the asparagus and strawberry seasons. Although it continues to be available through the end of August, the stalks harvested later in the summer will not be as tender. Look for rhubarb stalks about the width of your thumb. They should feel firm and crisp; avoid rhubarb that is limp or that seems especially wide. Plan to purchase 1 pound for every 3 cups of raw, sliced rhubarb your recipe requires.

TO STORE: The quality of rhubarb decreases rapidly, so plan to use it as soon as possible. When you get rhubarb home, remove the leaves and discard them. Then wrap the stalks loosely in plastic wrap and place in the refrigerator. Use within 2 days.

TO PREPARE: Rinse the leafless stalks under cool running water and pat dry. Trim off the ends of each stalk and break it to determine its stringiness. If necessary, remove the strings by peeling the stalks as you would celery, then cut them into chunks or slices according to your recipe.

Rhubarb possesses a tart, acidic flavor, and is therefore usually sweetened with sugar, honey, or maple syrup. Rhubarb is customarily cooked until tender, either alone or in combination with other ingredients. It may be made into pies or cakes, or incorporated into chutneys or preserves.

Rhubarb and Spinach Salad   SERVES 4

Lightly cooked slices of rhubarb are spooned atop spinach leaves and veiled with a warm sweet-and-sour dressing.

4 stalks rhubarb, cut
   diagonally into thin slices
¼ cup sugar
2 tablespoons red wine
   vinegar
½ teaspoon salt
Freshly ground black
   pepper
16 to 20 spinach leaves
6 tablespoons vegetable oil

1. Place the rhubarb in a wide saucepan. Sprinkle on the sugar and add enough water to cover by 1 inch. Place over high heat and bring to a boil. Cook, uncovered, for exactly 2 minutes. Remove from the heat and pour through a large sieve into a bowl. Return the liquid to the pan. Stir in the vinegar, salt, and pepper and place over high heat. Cook, uncovered, until the mixture is reduced to ½ cup.

2. Meanwhile, divide the spinach among 4 salad plates. Arrange the rhubarb over the spinach. When the liquid is reduced, remove the pan from the heat and whisk in the oil. Pour over the salads and serve at once.

Rhubarb Conserve

Chinese five-spice powder lends a seductive flavor to this rhubarb and orange relish. Serve warm or at room temperature with roast pork or turkey.

3 oranges
1 pound rhubarb, cut into 1-inch lengths
3 cups sugar
½ teaspoon Chinese five-spice powder
½ cup raisins
½ cup coarsely chopped almonds

1. Squeeze the juice from the oranges and set aside. Remove the zest from the oranges with a swivel-blade peeler and cut into julienne strips.

2. In a wide saucepan, combine the orange juice, orange zest, rhubarb, sugar, five-spice powder, and raisins. Stir over medium heat until the sugar is dissolved. Reduce the heat and cook slowly for 30 to 45 minutes or until the mixture is thick. Stir in the almonds and cook for 2 minutes more. Remove from the heat and refrigerate or freeze in airtight plastic containers.

Rhubarb Bread

1 cup milk
2 teaspoons lemon juice
2 cups all-purpose flour
¾ cup light brown sugar
1 teaspoon baking powder
½ teaspoon baking soda
½ teaspoon salt
1 large egg
⅓ cup vegetable oil
½ teaspoon vanilla
½ pound rhubarb, diced (about 1 cup)
½ cup chopped pecans
2 tablespoons granulated sugar
½ teaspoon ground cinnamon

Cinnamon sugar sprinkled over the top of this loaf creates a tasty, colorful crust. Toasted rhubarb bread makes a wonderful teatime treat.

1. Preheat the oven to 375°. Generously grease a 9x5-inch loaf pan. In a small bowl, combine the milk and lemon juice. Set aside for 10 to 15 minutes or until the milk has soured or become slightly thickened.

2. Combine the flour, brown sugar, baking powder, soda, and salt in a large mixing bowl. Whisk to blend thoroughly. In a separate bowl, whisk together the soured milk, egg, oil, and vanilla. Add to the dry ingredients and blend well. Stir in the rhubarb and pecans. Pour into the prepared loaf pan.

3. Whisk together the granulated sugar and cinnamon. Sprinkle over the unbaked loaf. Place in the oven and bake for 50 minutes to 1 hour or until a wooden pick inserted in the center comes out clean.

Stewed Rhubarb with Spiced Whipped Cream SERVES 6

Rhubarb, gently cooked in a sugar syrup, is chilled and then served cold with generous dollops of spiced whipped cream.

½ cup water
2 cups sugar, plus 1 teaspoon
1½ pounds rhubarb, cut into 1-inch lengths
1 teaspoon vanilla
1 cup heavy cream
¼ teaspoon ground cinnamon
⅛ teaspoon ground cloves
Freshly grated nutmeg

1. In a large saucepan, combine the water and 2 cups of the sugar. Stir to partially dissolve the sugar and place over high heat. Bring to a boil. Reduce the heat and simmer, uncovered, for 5 minutes.

2. Add the rhubarb and continue to simmer for 10 to 15 minutes or until the rhubarb is tender and most of the liquid is evaporated. Stir in the vanilla and transfer to a bowl. Cover the bowl and refrigerate until thoroughly chilled.

3. Whip the cream until stiff. Blend in the remaining teaspoon sugar, the cinnamon, cloves, and nutmeg. Spoon the chilled rhubarb into stemmed goblets and top with the whipped cream.

Rhubarb and Strawberry Crisp SERVES 6

1½ pounds rhubarb, cut into ½-inch slices
1 pint strawberries, hulled and quartered
2 tablespoons quick-cooking tapioca
3 tablespoons light brown sugar
1¼ cups all-purpose flour
¾ cup granulated sugar
1 teaspoon ground cinnamon
1 teaspoon baking powder
¼ teaspoon salt
½ cup butter, melted

In this recipe, the familiar combination of rhubarb and fresh strawberries is baked under a light crumbly crust. Serve warm with slightly softened vanilla ice cream spooned over the top.

1. Preheat the oven to 350°. Generously butter an 8-inch square baking dish. In a large mixing bowl, combine the rhubarb and strawberries and toss to mix. Sprinkle on the tapioca, brown sugar, and ¼ cup of the flour. Stir gently and transfer to the prepared baking dish.

2. In a separate bowl, combine the remaining cup flour, the granulated sugar, cinnamon, baking powder, and salt. Whisk to blend thoroughly. Pour on the melted butter and toss with a fork to create a crumbly mixture. Scatter over the rhubarb and bake for 45 minutes to 1 hour or until the rhubarb is tender when pierced and the crust is lightly browned.

Rhubarb Upside-Down Cake

Rows of rosy rhubarb, glistening with reduced orange juice, make this upside-down cake particularly beautiful. For rave reviews, serve warm with sweetened whipped cream.

1½ pounds rhubarb, cut into 1-inch lengths
1 cup orange juice
1¾ cups sugar
1½ cups all-purpose flour
3 teaspoons baking powder
½ teaspoon salt
6 tablespoons butter, cut into small chunks
2 large eggs
⅓ cup milk
1 tablespoon grated orange zest

1. Preheat the oven to 350°. Generously butter a 9x13-inch baking dish. Arrange the rhubarb in the dish in a single layer. Pour on the orange juice and sprinkle with 1 cup of the sugar. Bake, uncovered, for 30 minutes and then set aside.

2. Generously butter a 9x5-inch loaf pan or narrow rectangular baking dish. Sprinkle ½ cup of the sugar over the bottom. Arrange the baked rhubarb in rows over the sugar, curved side down. Coarsely chop any that is left and distribute it over the 1-inch lengths.

3. Transfer the liquid from the baked rhubarb to a small saucepan. Place over medium heat and reduce to ½ cup. Set aside.

4. Combine the flour, the remaining ¼ cup sugar, the baking powder, and salt. Whisk to blend thoroughly. Cut in the butter until the mixture is crumbly. Whisk the eggs and milk together and stir in the orange zest. Add to the flour mixture. Toss to form a soft dough. Spoon over the rhubarb and smooth the surface. Bake for 30 to 40 minutes or until a wooden pick inserted into the center comes out clean. Cool on a rack for 10 minutes, then invert onto a serving plate. Spoon the reduced liquid over the warm cake. Serve warm, sliced into 1-inch-wide pieces, the width of the rhubarb rows.

Place the pieces of rhubarb, curved side down, in a loaf pan, arranging them in a single layer of rows.

Invert the cake onto a serving plate and spoon on any juices left in the baking pan.

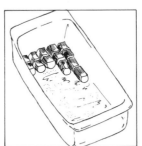
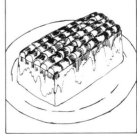

Rhubarb Sherbet

The fruity sweetness of Gewürztraminer wine enhances the tangy flavor of rhubarb in this cool, refreshing dessert. A few drops of red food coloring accentuate the pink blush customarily associated with rhubarb preparations.

1 pound rhubarb, cut into
  1-inch lengths
1 cup Gewürztraminer wine
½ cup light corn syrup
½ cup sugar
4 or 5 drops red food
  coloring
Fresh mint leaves for
  garnish

1. In a large saucepan, combine the rhubarb, wine, corn syrup, and sugar. Place over high heat and stir until the sugar dissolves. Cover the pan and reduce the heat. Simmer for 15 to 20 minutes or until the rhubarb is very tender.

2. Transfer to the container of a blender or processor and whirl until smooth. Blend in the food coloring, one drop at a time, until the mixture is a delicate pink.

3. Pour into the container of an ice cream machine and process according to the manufacturer's instructions. Freeze until firm and serve garnished with fresh mint leaves if you wish.

Rutabagas

THERE IS MUCH confusion concerning the differences between turnips and rutabagas (see Turnips). A considerable part of the problem, I suspect, has to do with the fact that rutabagas are also known as Swede turnips, because they originated in Scandinavia, and as yellow globe turnips.

Rutabagas are generally much larger than turnips, although the best ones are small, and they possess a darker, heavier skin. Whereas turnips are white with brilliant purple tops, rutabagas are yellowish orange with tops of dark purplish brown. The flavor of rutabagas is different, too. Rutabaga flesh tastes sweet and mild; turnips, while sweet, have a refreshing radishy element to their flavor.

One crucial similarity does exist, however. Like turnips, rutabagas must be purchased as close to harvest as possible in order to enjoy them at their best. Since rutabagas are harvested in the fall, preferably before the first frost, this is the time at which their flavor peaks. Rutabagas do store somewhat better than turnips, and you will see them on sale well into March, but a change in flavor and texture occurs. Rutabagas kept for any length of time develop a strong, assertive flavor and a woody, stringy consistency.

TO SELECT:

Rutabagas are usually sold loose and without their greens. The skin is heavily waxed to prevent dehydration. As in purchasing turnips, select the smallest rutabagas you can find, because the larger ones are invariably stringy and strong tasting. Look for those that feel heavy for their size, and pass up any that have nicks or gashes in the skin. Plan to purchase ½ pound per serving.

TO STORE:

Rutabagas may be kept for a short time in a cool, dark, well-ventilated storage area. They may also be refrigerated without any wrapping, but keep in mind that the sooner you use them, the better they will taste.

TO PREPARE:

Because the skin of a rutabaga is exceptionally thick and heavy, some cooks prefer to remove it with a sharp, sturdy knife. I use a swivel-blade peeler and apply it with firm, short strokes. Another method is to cut the rutabaga into wedges and then peel it.

Rutabagas may be baked, steamed, or microwaved whole. They are more commonly boiled, however, because the water serves to leach out some of the harshness that is often a concern. Fresh, good-quality rutabagas may be served raw, either grated in a salad or cut into sticks for a crudité. They are also delicious when deep-fried or sautéed in butter.

Rutabaga Soup

SERVES 6

Maple syrup lends a distinctive flavor to this rich creamy soup. Serve hot as a prelude to a winter dinner party.

4 tablespoons butter
1 medium onion, coarsely chopped
4 ribs celery, sliced
4 cups chicken broth
1 pound rutabaga, peeled and cut into chunks
½ cup heavy cream
¼ cup pure maple syrup
⅛ teaspoon ground cloves
Salt and freshly ground black pepper
Freshly grated nutmeg

1. Melt the butter in a wide saucepan. Add the onion and celery and toss to coat evenly. Cover the pan and cook over low heat for 20 minutes or until the vegetables are tender.

2. Pour in the chicken broth. Add the rutabaga and cover the pan. Simmer for 20 minutes or until the rutabaga is tender enough to mash against the side of the pan. Transfer to the container of a blender or processor and whirl until smooth. Return to the pan. Stir in the cream, maple syrup, cloves, salt, and pepper. Place over medium heat and warm gently, but do not boil. Serve hot, sprinkled with nutmeg.

Rutabaga and Potato Purée

SERVES 8

Sweetened with honey, this light, delicate purée is a perfect partner for roast turkey.

1½ pounds rutabaga, peeled and cut into chunks

1½ pounds mealy potatoes, peeled and cut into chunks

⅓ cup medium or whipping cream

4 tablespoons butter

3 tablespoons honey

1 tablespoon minced fresh ginger

Salt and freshly ground black pepper

1. Place the rutabaga in a steam basket and cook over boiling water for 15 minutes. Add the potatoes and continue steaming for an additional 15 to 20 minutes or until both vegetables are tender. Force through a food mill to purée and set aside.

2. In a wide saucepan, combine the cream, butter, and honey and heat until the butter is melted. Whisk to blend thoroughly. Stir in the ginger.

3. Gradually add the rutabaga and potato purée, beating with a wooden spoon over medium heat. When light and fluffy, season with salt and pepper and transfer to a serving dish.

Rutabaga and Apple Compote

SERVES 6

Chunks of rutabaga and apple are simmered together in a spicy broth. Serve as an accompaniment to roast pork or veal.

1 pound rutabaga, peeled and cut into ½-inch chunks

¾ cup sweet white wine, such as Gewürztraminer

¾ cup orange juice

3 tablespoons butter

2 tart apples, peeled, cored, and cut into ½-inch chunks

¾ cup sugar

6 whole cloves

½ teaspoon salt

2 cinnamon sticks, broken in half

½ cup raisins

1. In a wide saucepan, combine the rutabaga, wine, orange juice, and butter. Cover the pan and cook over medium heat for 10 to 12 minutes or until the rutabaga is partially tender.

2. Add the apples, sugar, cloves, salt, and cinnamon sticks. Continue cooking, uncovered, over medium heat. Stir occasionally. Cook until the rutabaga is tender. Add the raisins and increase the heat to high. Stir constantly until the liquid is reduced to a thick syrupy consistency. Remove the cinnamon sticks, spoon into a decorative bowl, and serve warm.

Rutabaga Pie

2 large eggs
1 cup medium or whipping cream
2 tablespoons honey
2 cups cooked, mashed rutabaga (about 1 pound)
½ cup light brown sugar
½ teaspoon ground ginger
¼ teaspoon freshly grated nutmeg
¼ teaspoon ground coriander
½ teaspoon salt
9-inch partially baked pie shell

Pale orange in color, this custard pie resembles pumpkin pie in appearance. Its flavor, however, is distinct.

1. Preheat the oven to 375°. In a large mixing bowl, whisk the eggs, cream, and honey until frothy. Stir in the rutabaga, brown sugar, ginger, nutmeg, coriander, and salt.

2. Pour into the prepared pie shell and bake for 45 to 55 minutes or until the blade of a knife inserted in the center comes out clean.

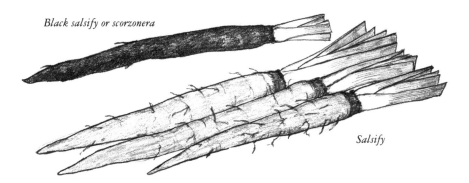

Black salsify or scorzonera

Salsify

Salsify

SALSIFY, A SLIM, cream-colored root vegetable, is also known as oyster plant, a linkage that seems tenuous at best. Through the years, salsify has been described as possessing an oysterlike flavor, but most contemporary cooks dispute that similarity. A more plausible reason for the implied comparison might be the shiny, slippery texture that salsify develops if it is overcooked. That, combined with its creamy white color, could understandably result in a connection between salsify and oysters.

TO SELECT:

Salsify is not widely available, but it is cultivated in the United States, and so it occasionally appears in specialty food shops, especially in large cities. Look for salsify in the late fall. It resembles a long, exceptionally thin carrot, except that it is oystery white. (A black-skinned variety, called scorzonera, is often sold as black salsify. Its flavor and texture are nearly identical to that of salsify, and the two may be used interchangeably.)

When purchasing salsify, use the same quality guidelines you would in selecting carrots. Pick out only those that are firm and unblemished; avoid any that feel limp or exhibit soft spots.

Wrap salsify loosely in plastic wrap and place it in the vegetable drawer of your refrigerator. Plan to use it within 2 to 3 days.

TO PREPARE:

Like carrots, salsify may be peeled before or after cooking. If peeled before it is cooked, salsify should be submerged immediately in acidulated water to keep its flesh white. In fact, the best approach is to fill a stainless-steel pot with cold water. Add the juice of 1 lemon, then cut the salsify over the pot, allowing the pieces to drop in. Set the pan on the stove and cook the salsify in the acidulated water.

Since cooking seems to bring out the flavor of salsify, I seldom recommend using it raw; however, some cooks do serve it as a salad component. The scallionlike greens, if you can get them, may be sliced thinly and used as a flavorful garnish.

Salsify may be cut into lengths and prepared like asparagus. It may also be sliced and sautéed, or added to meat pies. Boiled salsify is delightful when puréed for cream soup. Grated raw, like potatoes, salsify may be made into fritters or griddlecakes.

Salsify Bisque

SERVES 6

Rich with cream and velvety with egg yolk, this is indeed a special-occasion soup.

3 tablespoons butter
1 medium onion, coarsely
  chopped
4 cups chicken broth
1 tablespoon lemon juice
1 pound salsify, peeled and
  cut into 1-inch lengths
Salt to taste
Generous pinch of cayenne
2 large egg yolks
1 cup heavy cream
Freshly grated nutmeg for
  garnish

1. Melt the butter in a large saucepan. Add the onion and toss to coat evenly. Stir over medium heat until the onion is tender. Stir in the chicken broth, lemon juice, salsify, salt, and cayenne. Cover the pan and cook at a gentle bubble for 20 minutes or until the salsify is tender.

2. Transfer to the container of a blender or processor and whirl until smooth. In a large bowl, whisk together the egg yolks and cream, then gradually stir in the puréed mixture. Return to the saucepan and place over low heat. Stir until warmed through, but do not allow the soup to boil. Ladle into soup bowls and garnish with freshly grated nutmeg.

Salsify with Chive Butter

Fresh chives impart a complementary flavor to salsify sautéed in butter.

1½ pounds salsify, peeled
   and cut into 2-inch
   lengths
2 tablespoons lemon juice
6 tablespoons butter
Salt and freshly ground
   white pepper
2 tablespoons chopped
   fresh chives

1. Place the salsify in a nonreactive saucepan and immediately add enough cold water to cover by 1 inch. Stir in the lemon juice and bring to a boil. Reduce the heat and simmer, uncovered, for 20 minutes or until the salsify is tender when pierced. Do not allow the salsify to cook to the mushy stage.

2. Drain in a colander set under cold running water. Shake gently to remove as much water as possible.

3. Melt the butter in a large skillet. Add the salsify and toss to coat. Stir over medium heat until the salsify is lightly golden, but do not allow it to brown. Sprinkle on the salt, pepper, and chives. Continue stirring over medium heat for 30 seconds to allow the chives to release their flavor, then serve.

Salsify Cakes

SERVES 4 TO 6

Finely grated salsify is bound with a light batter and fried in vegetable oil. Serve with roast pheasant or veal.

3 large eggs
1 tablespoon cold water
3 tablespoons all-purpose
   flour
½ teaspoon salt
Pinch of cayenne
2 shallots, minced
1 pound salsify
Vegetable oil for frying

1. In a large mixing bowl, whisk together the eggs and water. Add the flour, salt, and cayenne and beat with a wooden spoon until smooth. Stir in the shallots.

2. Peel and finely grate the salsify, then immediately add it to the prepared batter. Stir to completely coat the salsify.

3. Heat a small amount of oil in a large skillet. Transfer the mixture to the hot oil by generous serving spoonfuls. Cook for 2 to 3 minutes, turning once to brown both sides. Serve on a napkin-lined plate.

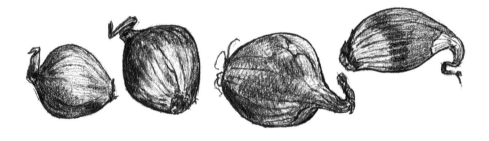

Shallots

A LTHOUGH SHALLOTS are technically a member of the onion family, you would never guess it by their demeanor. Shallots possess a mild, reticent taste, totally unlike the brash flavors of the other onions in the group. And because shallots contain a much lower proportion of volatile sulfur compounds, their aroma is delicate and their fumes are seldom irritating to the eyes.

TO SELECT:

In some parts of the country, it is customary to call scallions, or green onions, "shallots." But recipes that call for this special type of onion expect that you will use the true shallot. Look for small bulbs, sometimes consisting of two or three separate cloves attached at the root end, bearing a reddish brown, parchmentlike skin. This outer skin encloses each individual clove (unlike garlic, which has an outer skin that surrounds the entire bulb). When a recipe calls for one shallot, plan to use the entire bulb.

Select shallots that are firm and heavy for their size. They should be dry with no signs of decay; avoid any bulbs that are sending out green shoots. If you are presented with a choice of sizes, keep in mind that smaller shallots have a more delicate flavor. On the other hand, the larger ones are easier to peel.

TO STORE:

Like dry-skinned onions and garlic, shallots keep well if they are stored in a cool, dry place with plenty of air circulation. A hanging mesh bag, a wire basket, or a wicker bowl all provide an airy storage spot. Shallots that are properly stored will keep for up to 2 months, but prolonged storage causes sprouting. If green shoots do appear, you may still use the shallots. However, the green center core imparts a harsh, oniony flavor, so you may want to remove it. Simply cut the shallot in half and lift out the green portion in the middle.

TO PREPARE:

If the bulb consists of separate cloves, break them apart and slice off the hard root ends of each segment. Lift the peel away with a paring knife. Chop or mince finely according to the directions in your recipe.

Shallots may be used raw in salads and salad dressings; they may also be cooked gently in butter and used to flavor complex dishes and intricate sauces. It is important to sauté shallots carefully, however, because when browned they develop a bitter taste. An exceptionally elegant way to handle shallots consists of roasting or simmering them unpeeled. When they become tender, the mellow flesh may be mashed or puréed and blended into sauces or soups.

Because shallots are low in volatile sulfur compounds, they may be chopped or minced in the processor with reasonable success. Hand-chopping still produces better results, however, so I recommend it unless you have a tremendous quantity to prepare.

Pickled Shallots

SERVES 12

Peeled cloves are cooked briefly in a mild sweet-and-sour broth and then marinated for a week in the refrigerator. Serve as an appetizer with wooden picks, or use as a salad component or part of a relish tray.

1 pound shallots
1½ cups white wine vinegar
½ cup sugar
½ teaspoon salt
1 sprig fresh savory

1. Peel the shallots. Trim both ends and separate the cloves.

2. In a wide saucepan, combine the vinegar, sugar, and salt. Bring to a boil, stirring to dissolve the sugar. Add the shallots and stir to coat evenly. Cook briskly for exactly 1 minute and remove from the heat. Submerge the sprig of savory in the broth. Allow the mixture to stand until it cools to room temperature. Transfer to a glass bowl. Cover the bowl and refrigerate for at least 1 week. Shallots will keep this way for up to 2 months.

Roasted Shallots and New Potatoes

SERVES 4

Whole shallots roasted in olive oil are a soft, flavorful companion for crisp-skinned potatoes.

8 large shallots
8 to 12 small waxy potatoes, red or white skinned, unpeeled
½ cup olive oil
1 tablespoon lemon juice
1 tablespoon fresh rosemary leaves, unchopped
1 teaspoon coarse sea salt
Freshly ground black pepper

1. Preheat the oven to 400°. Remove the papery skin from the shallots. Carefully trim the root end, leaving the cloves attached. Place the shallots in a rectangular baking dish.

2. Rinse the potatoes. Pat them dry and cut them in half. Add to the baking dish. Pour on the oil and toss to coat evenly. Bake uncovered for 25 to 30 minutes, stirring occasionally. When the potatoes are almost tender, sprinkle on the lemon juice, rosemary, sea salt, and pepper. Bake 5 minutes more and serve.

Spaghetti with Shallots and Ham

SERVES 2

The delicate flavor and aroma of fresh shallots transform this quick-and-easy pasta dish into something very special.

¾ cup dry white wine
1 teaspoon dried oregano
½ teaspoon dried basil
½ cup olive oil
2 large shallots, coarsely chopped
4 slices smoked ham, cut into julienne strips
½ green bell pepper, cut into julienne strips
Salt and freshly ground black pepper
⅓ pound spaghetti, boiled and drained
3 fresh tomatoes, peeled, seeded, and chopped
2 teaspoons chopped fresh thyme
½ cup crumbled feta cheese

1. In a glass measuring cup, combine the wine, oregano, and basil. Set aside.

2. Heat the oil in a large skillet. Add the shallots and ham and stir over medium heat until the shallots are tender but not browned. Add the green bell pepper and cook briefly. The pepper should retain some of its crunch. Season with salt and pepper.

3. Pour on the wine mixture. Add the hot, drained spaghetti and toss to coat. Add the tomatoes and stir over medium heat. Sprinkle on the thyme and crumbled feta cheese. Cook only until the cheese begins to melt. Serve at once.

Shell Beans

LIKE PEAS, shell beans are grown for their mature seeds rather than for their pods, which is the case with snap beans. Their name presumably comes from the fact that the beans are taken out of the pod; that is to say, they are "shelled."

Numerous varieties of shell beans exist; however, most of them are sold dried. Navy beans, pinto beans, kidney beans, black beans, and garbanzos are among those that form the basis for popular regional and ethnic dishes, such as Boston baked beans, chili, black bean soup, and the garbanzo purée called hummus.

On the other hand, only three types of shell beans are commonly sold fresh. Lima beans (also called butter beans), fava beans (also called broad beans), and cranberry beans are available sporadically in large supermarkets and

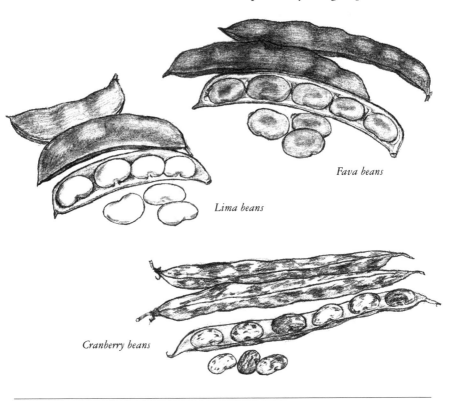

Fava beans

Lima beans

Cranberry beans

at farmers' stands. Lima beans are usually found during the months of July through September, fava beans are harvested in the spring, and cranberry beans appear from August through October.

TO SELECT: Limas and favas are flat, pale green, kidney-shaped beans in wide pods about the length of snap beans. Cranberry beans are red and white rounded ovals in cream-colored pods streaked with red.

Look for shell beans that have plump, fresh-looking pods with discernible bulges. The idea is to obtain beans of medium size — small enough to be tender, yet large enough to be flavorful. Pass up any pods that are limp, pitted with rust, or whose seed bulges are excessively fat. Because the pods of shell beans are thick walled and heavy, plan to purchase about 3 pounds to provide 4 servings.

TO STORE: Fresh shell beans are best when they are removed from the pod just before cooking. Therefore, transfer the pods, without washing them, to a plastic storage bag. Secure tightly with a wire twist, refrigerate, and use within 2 to 3 days.

TO PREPARE: If the pods seem dirty, place them in a colander and rinse with cool water. Shell the beans by breaking off the stem end of the pod and pulling the string down the length of the seam. Then place your thumb over the last bean in the row, where the pod curves into a tail, and press down. The pod should split, enabling you to insert your finger. (If the pods seem reluctant to cooperate, you can ease this task by running a swivel-blade peeler down the seam of the pod.) Open the pod with your finger and dislodge the beans, allowing them to fall into a colander. Rinse the shelled beans under cool running water and drain.

Shell beans may be boiled, braised, or steamed. The important point is to cook them until they are tender, but not mushy or waterlogged. Drain the cooked beans, then toss them with butter. They may also be combined with a sauce or mixed with other vegetables.

Fava beans and large limas often need to have their skins removed in order to be tender. The easiest method for accomplishing this is to boil the beans until tender, then drain them. Submerge the cooked beans in a large basin of cool water. Gently rub the beans. The skins will slip off and float to the surface. Fresh favas and limas resemble each other in appearance, although favas tend to be larger and more flavorful. They may be used interchangeably in most recipes.

It is important to note that in certain cuisines, tiny fresh fava beans are served raw. The custom consists of removing the beans from the pods and dipping them in a mixture of olive oil and salt. However, the furry lining of the fava pod contains a toxic substance that can cause severe illness, so this practice is best approached with caution. Fava pods should never be eaten raw or cooked.

Lima Bean Salad with Fresh Dill

SERVES 4

Chilled lima beans, tossed with minced shallots and chopped fresh dill leaves, create an exceptional salad.

3 pounds lima beans, shelled
3 sprigs fresh parsley
2 bay leaves
2 shallots, minced
2 tablespoons chopped fresh dill leaves
2 tablespoons lemon juice
1 teaspoon Dijon mustard
½ teaspoon salt
Pinch of cayenne
6 tablespoons olive oil
4 sprigs fresh dill for garnish

1. Place the beans in a large saucepan. Add enough cold water to cover by 1 inch and add the parsley and bay leaves. Bring to a gentle bubble and cook, uncovered, for 20 minutes or until the beans are tender. Remove the parsley and bay leaves and drain the beans in a colander set under cold running water. (If the skins are tough and shriveled, remove them as described earlier.) Transfer the cooked beans to a large bowl. Scatter the shallots and dill leaves over the beans and toss to combine.

2. In a separate bowl, whisk together the lemon juice and mustard. Blend in the salt and cayenne and whisk in the oil. Pour over the lima beans and toss to coat. Cover the bowl and refrigerate until lightly chilled. Spoon onto glass salad plates to serve. Garnish with sprigs of dill.

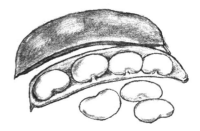

Mexican-Style Lima Beans

SERVES 4

3 pounds lima beans, shelled
2 tablespoons vegetable oil
2 tablespoons butter
1 medium onion, coarsely chopped
1 garlic clove, minced or pressed
2 medium tomatoes, peeled, seeded, and chopped
2 green jalapeño chilies, seeded and chopped
½ teaspoon salt
½ teaspoon ground cumin
Several drops of Tabasco sauce
1 large package (8 ounces) cream cheese

My favorite lima-bean recipe is this zesty dish consisting of lima beans, tomatoes, and jalapeño chili peppers smoothed with melted cream cheese. Serve with crispy fried chicken.

1. Boil or steam the beans until tender, and then, if necessary, remove the outer skins as described earlier (see TO PREPARE). Drain in a colander.

2. Heat the oil and butter in a large skillet until the butter is melted. Add the onion and garlic and toss to coat. Stir over medium heat until the onion is tender. Add the tomatoes, chili peppers, salt, cumin, and Tabasco. Continue stirring over medium heat for 8 to 10 minutes or until the chilies are tender and the tomatoes are soft.

3. Add the cream cheese and continue stirring until the cheese melts and forms a smooth sauce. Blend in the lima beans and heat gently until warmed through.

Baked Fresh Lima Beans with Pork Chops

SERVES 6

Fresh lima beans, simmered in apple juice laced with molasses and brown sugar, are baked with pork chops and apple slices.

3 tablespoons vegetable oil
6 rib pork chops, trimmed of excess fat
1 large onion, sliced and separated into rings
1 garlic clove, minced or pressed
1 cup apple juice
3 tablespoons molasses
3 tablespoons brown sugar
1 teaspoon dry mustard
½ teaspoon salt
Freshly ground black pepper
3 pounds lima beans, shelled
2 tart green apples, cored and sliced into rings

1. Preheat the oven to 350°. Generously butter a 9x13-inch baking dish. Heat the oil in a large skillet. Add the pork chops and cook over medium heat until browned on both sides. Transfer the pork chops to the prepared baking dish.

2. To the oil that remains in the skillet, add the onion and garlic and stir over medium heat until the onion is limp. Blend in the apple juice, molasses, brown sugar, mustard, salt, and pepper. Bring to a boil and add the lima beans. Cover the pan and reduce the heat. Simmer for 10 minutes.

3. Pour the mixture over the pork chops and cover the baking dish with aluminum foil. Bake for 30 minutes. Uncover the dish and arrange the apple slices over the lima beans. Continue baking, uncovered, for 20 to 30 minutes more or until the beans are tender and the pork is no longer pink when cut near the bone.

Fava Beans with Garlic and Sage

SERVES 4

Freshly chopped sage imparts its extraordinary flavor and aroma to this simply prepared dish of buttered fava beans. Serve with grilled veal chops.

3 pounds fava beans, shelled
3 tablespoons olive oil
3 tablespoons butter
2 garlic cloves, minced
1 tablespoon chopped fresh sage
Salt and freshly ground black pepper

1. Boil or steam the beans until tender and then remove the outer skins as described earlier (see TO PRE-PARE). Drain in a colander.

2. Heat the oil and butter in a large skillet until the butter is melted. Add the garlic and sage and stir over medium heat until the garlic is tender. Add the fava beans and stir to coat. Season with salt and pepper and transfer to a serving dish.

New England Succotash

SERVES 6 TO 8

A combination of cranberry beans and corn kernels, Succotash was one of the preparations using native ingredients that the Narragansett Indians taught to the first Plymouth settlers. Lima beans may be substituted and a small amount of cream may be added if you wish, but neither was a component of the original "recipe."

6 ears corn
3 pounds cranberry beans, shelled
¼ pound salt pork, cut into 4 pieces
2 teaspoons sugar
4 tablespoons butter
Salt and freshly ground pepper

1. Cut the kernels from the cobs and set aside. In a large saucepan, combine the beans and salt pork and add enough cold water to cover by 1 inch. Bring to a gentle bubble and cook, uncovered, for 15 to 20 minutes or until the beans are nearly tender.

2. Stir in the corn and add enough additional water to cover by 1 inch. Add the sugar and 2 tablespoons of the butter. Bring to a gentle bubble and cook, uncovered, for 5 minutes. Remove the salt pork and stir in the remaining 2 tablespoons butter until it is melted. Season with salt and pepper. Serve piping hot in individual bowls.

Sorrel

SORREL, WHICH HAS largely been ignored in the United States, is gaining new favor, probably as the result of current culinary trends that emphasize the use of fresh native ingredients. And sorrel certainly qualifies. Known also as chave, sour spinach, and sour grass, it grows wild throughout all the regions of North America. The cultivated varieties, however, are the ones sold at market.

Basically, there are two types of sorrel available — garden sorrel, which has long, narrow, spear-shaped leaves, and French sorrel, which has short, broad leaves. The distinctive features of sorrel are its sharp, lemony flavor and its ability to disintegrate into a purée. When sorrel leaves are sautéed briefly in butter, they practically melt into a smooth purée that can be enhanced with wine and cream to form a delightful sauce.

TO SELECT:

Sorrel is sold sporadically in large supermarkets and specialty food stores. The narrow-leafed garden sorrel possesses a stronger, more acidic flavor, and the French variety, with its broader leaves, has a milder lemony taste. Choose the smallest leaves with the lightest color, because the larger, darker leaves are more assertively flavored. Purchase only those leaves that are crisp and fresh looking; avoid any that are wilted or yellow.

TO STORE: Sorrel is extremely fragile and should be used on the day of purchase if possible, especially if you're planning to serve it raw in a salad. When absolutely necessary, you may place unwashed sorrel in a plastic bag and secure it with a wire twist. Refrigerate and use within 1 to 2 days.

TO PREPARE: Remove the tough stems and center rib of each sorrel leaf by folding the leaf in half so the underside of the rib protrudes slightly. Gently pull the stem and center rib away from the leaf. Submerge the trimmed leaves in a basin of cold water and agitate gently to rinse them. Transfer to a colander and allow to drain. Then scatter over a clean kitchen towel and blot dry.

Sorrel leaves may be torn into bite-size pieces and added to a salad, or stacked one upon the other and sliced into thin strips. These strips may be added to soups or sauces, or they may be chopped finely and used as an herb. Sorrel may also be coarsely chopped, then steamed or sautéed. However, because it is high in oxalic acid, sorrel should not be cooked in an aluminum pan.

Sorrel Cream Soup

SERVES 6

Because sorrel is so delicate, it needs only a brief simmering to release its enticing flavor.

1 pound sorrel
3 tablespoons butter
2 medium onions, coarsely
   chopped
¼ teaspoon cayenne
6 cups chicken broth
2 mealy potatoes, peeled
   and cubed
1 bay leaf
1 teaspoon dried chervil
1 cup medium or whipping
   cream
½ teaspoon salt

1. Rinse the sorrel and remove the tough stems. Stack the leaves and cut across into thin shreds. Set aside.

2. Melt the butter in a large saucepan. Add the onions and toss to coat evenly. Sprinkle on the cayenne and stir over medium heat until the onions are tender. Pour in the chicken broth. Add the potatoes, bay leaf, and chervil. Cover the pan and cook at a gentle bubble until the potatoes are tender.

3. Transfer to the container of a blender or processor and whirl until smooth. Return to the saucepan and blend in the cream. Stir in the sorrel and salt and place over low heat. Simmer gently for 5 minutes or until the sorrel is wilted. Ladle into soup bowls and serve hot, or cover and refrigerate until chilled and serve cold.

Wilted Sorrel Salad

SERVES 4

A creamy shallot dressing provides a smooth counterpoint to the sharp flavor of sorrel.

12 ounces sorrel
2 large hard-boiled eggs,
  coarsely chopped
4 tablespoons butter
2 shallots, minced
1 tablespoon all-purpose
  flour
1 cup hot water
1 teaspoon Dijon mustard
½ teaspoon salt
Pinch of cayenne

1. Rinse the sorrel and remove the tough stems. Tear into bite-size pieces and place in a salad bowl. Add the chopped eggs and toss to combine.

2. Melt the butter in a small saucepan. Add the shallots and toss to coat. Stir over medium heat until the shallots are tender. Sprinkle on the flour and continue stirring over medium heat until the mixture foams. Remove from the heat and whisk in the water. Return to medium heat and stir until the mixture bubbles and thickens. Blend in the mustard, salt, and cayenne.

3. Pour the hot dressing over the sorrel and toss immediately so that the leaves will wilt. Serve at once.

Smoked Pork Medallions with Mushrooms and Sorrel Sauce

SERVES 4

Like ham, smoked pork needs only brief cooking to warm it through. Here, pork medallions are sautéed and paired with sliced mushrooms and sorrel sauce.

4 smoked rib pork chops
12 ounces sorrel
5 tablespoons butter
8 ounces mushrooms, sliced
Salt and freshly ground
  black pepper
¾ cup dry white wine
2 shallots, minced
½ cup heavy cream
1 tablespoon lemon juice

1. Trim the fat and bone from each pork chop to create 4 medallions. Set aside. Rinse the sorrel and remove the tough stems. Stack the leaves and chop coarsely.

2. Melt 3 tablespoons of the butter in a large skillet. Add the mushrooms and stir over medium-high heat until tender. Season with salt and pepper and transfer to an ovenproof plate. Place in a 250° oven to keep warm. Add the remaining 2 tablespoons butter to the skillet and return to medium-high heat. When the butter is melted, add the pork medallions and cook for 2 minutes or until lightly browned on both sides. Transfer the medallions to a plate and set aside.

3. Pour the wine into the skillet, then add the shallots. Cook, stirring, until the shallots are tender and most of the wine is evaporated. Add the sorrel and continue

stirring for 2 to 3 minutes or until the sorrel has cooked down to a purée. Blend in the cream and stir until the sauce bubbles. Return the pork medallions to the pan and reduce the heat. Simmer for 2 minutes, turning the pork once. Divide the medallions among 4 plates and distribute the mushrooms over the top. Stir the lemon juice into the sorrel sauce and spoon it around the medallions. Serve immediately.

Spaghetti Squash

WHEN YOU CUT this squash in half and tug gently at the flesh inside with a fork, heaps of spaghettilike strands tumble forth. They possess a mild, nutty flavor, amazingly similar to that of pasta. Consequently, spaghetti squash is often served with a light tomato sauce or tossed with butter and freshly grated Parmesan cheese.

Like other varieties of winter squash (see Squash: Winter), spaghetti squash is an excellent source of vitamin A and potassium. A 2-pound squash will feed 4 people.

TO SELECT:

Spaghetti squash is a hard-shelled winter squash, so you will find it displayed with the acorn, butternut, and Hubbard squashes. Look for a pale-yellow oval somewhat resembling a football. The outer skin should be smooth and feel firm to the touch. Avoid spaghetti squash that feels spongy. If possible, choose one with a bit of stem attached.

TO STORE:

Place the unwashed spaghetti squash in a cool, dry, well-ventilated spot. Do not refrigerate. Spaghetti squash tends to be more perishable than the other hard-shelled squashes, so plan to use what you purchase within 2 to 3 weeks.

TO PREPARE:

Because of its unique structure, spaghetti squash is customarily cooked whole. Boiling, baking, or microwaving are all possibilities. Microwaving is the fastest and my favorite method, unless the conventional oven is on for something else. Baking a spaghetti squash takes almost twice as long as boiling one, but boiling requires a very large pot and lots of steaming water.

Whichever method you use, cook the squash until a metal skewer can be easily inserted in the flesh. Allow the squash to cool about 10 minutes or until you can handle it with a towel or potholders. Divide the squash in half by cutting it across its width. (Many recipes suggest slicing down the length of the squash, but I find cutting it width-wise produces longer strands.) Steady the squash with a kitchen towel, and scoop out the seeds and fibrous tissue. Then, holding the squash in one hand, invert it over a bowl or serving dish. Gently pull at the flesh with a fork. It will separate into strands as it falls from the shell.

Spaghetti Squash with Gingered Butter

SERVES 4

Cooked slowly in butter to release its essence, fresh ginger contributes delicate flavor to tender strands of spaghetti squash.

1 medium spaghetti squash
(about 2 pounds)
5 tablespoons butter
1 tablespoon honey
1 tablespoon minced fresh
ginger
Salt and freshly ground
black pepper
1 tablespoon chopped fresh
cilantro

1. Preheat the oven to 350°. Prick the upper portion of the squash shell in several places with a metal skewer to allow steam to escape. Set the squash directly on the oven rack, steam vents up. Bake for 45 minutes to 1 hour or until tender when pierced.

2. Meanwhile, combine the butter and honey in a small saucepan. Stir over low heat until the butter is melted and the honey is blended in. Add the ginger and cook slowly for 10 minutes.

3. When the squash is cool enough to handle, cut it in half across its width. Scoop out the seeds and fibrous tissue. Using a fork, pull the strands of squash from the cavity, allowing them to fall into a serving bowl. Sprinkle the squash with salt and pepper. Scatter on the cilantro. Pour the warm butter mixture over the squash and toss gently to coat the strands. Serve immediately.

Cut the baked spaghetti squash in half crosswise.

Scoop out and discard the seeds and fibrous tissue.

Using a fork, pull the strands of squash from the cavity.

Spaghetti Squash with Fresh Tomato Sauce   SERVES 4

Strands of spaghetti squash are liberally sprinkled with grated Parmesan cheese and dressed with a light, fresh tomato sauce.

1 medium spaghetti squash
    (about 2 pounds)
4 tablespoons olive oil
2 garlic cloves, peeled and
    cut in halves
6 medium tomatoes, peeled,
    seeded, and chopped
Salt and freshly ground
    black pepper
1 tablespoon chopped fresh
    basil
Freshly grated Parmesan
    cheese

1. Bake, boil, or microwave the spaghetti squash until tender when pierced. (To microwave, prick the shell of the squash in several places to allow steam to escape. Wrap the squash in a double layer of paper towels and cook on high power for 6 to 8 minutes. Turn the squash every 2 minutes to promote even cooking.)

2. Meanwhile, combine the oil and garlic in a large skillet. Stir over low heat until the garlic is golden. Do not allow it to brown. Remove the garlic with a slotted spoon and discard.

3. Blend in the tomatoes and increase the heat. Season with salt and pepper and stir over medium-high heat until the tomatoes soften. Mashing the tomatoes with the back of a fork, continue to cook them until a saucelike consistency is reached. Stir in the basil. Reduce the heat and simmer, uncovered, for 10 minutes.

4. When the squash is cool enough to handle, cut it in half across its width. Scoop out the seeds and fibrous tissue. Using a fork, pull the strands of squash from the cavity, allowing them to fall onto a large serving plate. Immediately sprinkle with Parmesan cheese and pour on the tomato sauce. Serve with additional Parmesan cheese if you wish.

Spaghetti Squash Moussaka

Cooked spaghetti squash layered with meat sauce and assertively flavored Kasseri cheese creates a hearty casserole.

1 large spaghetti squash
(about 3 pounds)
3 tablespoons vegetable oil
1 large onion, coarsely
chopped
1 pound ground beef
1 pound ground lamb
1 garlic clove, minced or
pressed
1 can (28 ounces) crushed
tomatoes
1½ teaspoons dried oregano
½ teaspoon dried basil
¼ teaspoon ground
cinnamon
⅛ teaspoon ground cloves
Salt and freshly ground
black pepper
12 ounces Kasseri cheese,
grated
6 ounces Parmesan cheese,
freshly grated

1. Preheat the oven to 350° and generously butter a 9x13-inch baking dish. Prick the upper portion of the squash shell in several places with a metal skewer to allow steam to escape. Set the squash directly on the oven rack, steam vents up. Bake for 45 minutes to 1 hour or until tender when pierced.

2. Meanwhile, heat the oil in a large skillet. Add the onion and toss to coat. Stir over medium heat until tender. Blend in the beef, lamb, and garlic and cook until the meat is no longer pink. Drain off the fat. Add the tomatoes, oregano, basil, cinnamon, cloves, salt, and pepper. Stir to mix. Simmer, uncovered, for 30 minutes.

3. When the squash is cool enough to handle, cut it in half across its width. Scoop out the seeds and fibrous tissue. Using a fork, pull the strands of squash from the cavity. Arrange half the squash in the bottom of the prepared baking dish. Spoon half the meat mixture over the squash. Sprinkle on half the grated Kasseri cheese and half the Parmesan cheese. Layer on the remaining squash, then add the rest of the meat mixture, spreading it evenly over the squash. Sprinkle the remaining cheeses over the top and bake, uncovered, for 30 minutes or until the top is lightly browned.

Spinach

SPINACH HAS BECOME so popular in recent years that it's hard to believe there was a time when people made jokes about it. Today, we eat spinach both cooked and raw. We enjoy it simply prepared or incorporated into custards and savory pies. Spinach is also used as a main ingredient in stuffings and fillings, soups and salads, and a variety of dishes bearing the sobriquet "à la Florentine." Fresh spinach is available year round; it is an excellent source of vitamins A and C and potassium. When trimmed and cooked, 1 pound of fresh spinach produces approximately 1 cup and amply serves 2 people.

TO SELECT:

Prepackaged fresh spinach is available all year, but there's a trick to successful selection. Carefully examine the clear plastic bag, turning it over and over in your hands. If the portion of the leaves that is visible looks bright green with no traces of dark green slime, and the bag doesn't contain any yellow leaves, you're on the right track. Choose a package that appears dry; excess moisture on the inside of the bag is a reliable indication that the leaves are beginning to rot. Squeeze the bag gently. You should get the sensation that the leaves are still springy; if you hear crunchy sounds, so much the better.

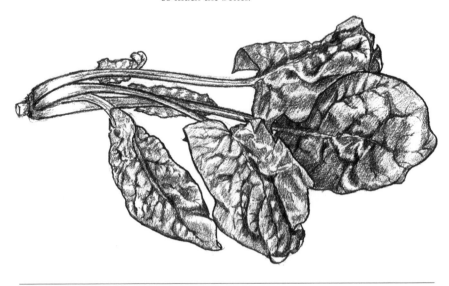

During the late spring and fall, you'll be able to find locally grown spinach displayed loose. This is spinach at its best. Depending on the variety, the surface of the leaves may be smooth or convoluted, but in either case, the smallest leaves are the most tender and delicately flavored. Avoid spinach with excessively large leaves because they come from overly mature plants, and they will have a tough consistency and bitter aftertaste. You will sometimes see loose spinach offered for sale with the root attached. This tends to be of excellent quality because the root helps preserve freshness, but it also increases the total weight of the spinach, particularly if the roots are kept in water. In such a case, it's important to adjust the amount you buy so you'll have enough once the roots and stems are removed.

TO STORE:

Fresh spinach has a high water content and is therefore extremely perishable. For that reason, it's important to use spinach the same day you buy it. If that's not possible, the best alternative is to blanch or steam the spinach, refresh it under cold water, and squeeze it dry, refrigerating it for later use. Cooked spinach reheats exceptionally well in a small amount of water or cream, so it is better to cook it ahead than to allow it to wilt.

If you must store uncooked spinach, pat the roots dry with absorbent paper and place it, unwashed, in a plastic bag. Secure with a wire twist, refrigerate, and use within 2 to 3 days. Prepackaged spinach should be opened as soon as you get it home. Pick it over and discard any leaves that show signs of decay. If it is damp, pat the spinach dry with absorbent paper and transfer, without rinsing, to a plastic bag. Secure with a wire twist and refrigerate for no more than 1 or 2 days. Keep in mind that native spinach is usually of a more delicate variety than the prepackaged kind. Bagged spinach tends to be more sturdy because it has been specifically grown to travel well and have as long a shelf life as possible.

TO PREPARE:

Fill the kitchen sink or a large basin with tepid water. Add the spinach and submerge it with your hands. Slosh the leaves up and down vigorously to dislodge any hidden sand and dirt. (Prepackaged spinach tends to be less sandy because it has been washed at the processing plant.) Lift it out by the handfuls and transfer to a colander. Repeat if necessary until all traces of sand and dirt are washed away. Trim off the root and remove the tough stem and center vein. To do this, hold the leaf in one hand with the underside up. Bend the leaf gently so that the center vein protrudes a bit. Then pull the stem away from the leaf using the other hand.

To preserve the maximum flavor and color of spinach, cook it briefly — that is, just to the point where the leaves wilt. It is important to use a stainless-steel or other nonreactive pan. If you use an aluminum pan, the oxalic acid that spinach contains will react with the metal during cooking to bring about an unpleasant change in taste. This interaction also causes spinach to lose its bright green color.

Spinach Soup

SERVES 6

4 tablespoons butter
6 green onions, white and green portion, sliced
6 cups chicken broth
1½ pounds spinach, rinsed and stemmed
2 mealy potatoes, peeled and cut into chunks
1 tablespoon chopped fresh savory
5 fresh sage leaves, finely chopped
½ teaspoon salt
Generous pinch of cayenne
½ cup heavy cream
1 tablespoon lemon juice

Redolent of savory and sage, this beautiful green soup may be served either hot or cold.

1. Melt the butter in a large saucepan. Add the onions and toss to coat. Stir over medium heat until tender. Add the chicken broth, spinach, potatoes, savory, sage, salt, and cayenne. Reduce the heat and cook, uncovered, for 20 to 25 minutes or until the potatoes are tender.

2. Transfer to the container of a blender or processor and whirl until smooth. Blend in the cream and return to the saucepan. Heat gently to warm through, but do not allow it to boil. Remove from the heat and stir in the lemon juice. Serve hot or refrigerate to serve chilled.

Wilted Spinach Salad with Fresh Horseradish Dressing

SERVES 4

1½ pounds spinach
4 tablespoons butter
1 tablespoon all-purpose
  flour
½ teaspoon salt
Pinch of cayenne
⅓ cup water
⅓ cup dry white wine
2 tablespoons lemon juice
2 tablespoons grated fresh
  horseradish (or Creamy
  Horseradish, p. 168)
½ teaspoon Worcestershire
  sauce
3 green onions, white and
  green portion, sliced

A warm horseradish dressing adds spark to fresh, bright green spinach leaves.

1. Rinse the spinach and remove the tough stems. Scatter over a clean kitchen towel and blot dry. Tear into bite-size pieces and transfer to a salad bowl.

2. Melt the butter in a small saucepan. Add the flour, salt, and cayenne. Stir over medium heat until the mixture foams. Remove from the heat and whisk in the water and wine. Return to medium heat and stir until the mixture bubbles and thickens. Blend in the lemon juice, horseradish, and Worcestershire.

3. Scatter the onions over the spinach and toss to combine. Pour on the hot dressing and toss immediately so that the leaves wilt. Serve at once.

Spinach Salad with Raspberry Dressing

SERVES 6

Raspberry vinegar contributes its unique fruity character to the sauce that dresses this crisp salad.

1½ pounds spinach
½ cup unflavored yogurt
2 tablespoons raspberry
  vinegar
¼ teaspoon salt
Pinch of cayenne
2 tablespoons chopped
  fresh parsley
2 shallots, minced

1. Rinse the spinach and remove the tough stems. Scatter over a clean kitchen towel and blot dry. Tear into bite-size pieces. Roll the spinach up in the towel and refrigerate.

2. In a small bowl, combine the yogurt, vinegar, salt, and cayenne. Whisk to blend.

3. Just before serving, divide the spinach among 6 glass salad plates. Scatter the parsley over the leaves and spoon on the dressing. Sprinkle the shallots over the dressing and serve at once.

Sautéed Spinach with Balsamic Butter

SERVES 4

Contrary to what you might expect, Balsamic vinegar has a sweet, almost fruity taste and none of the acidic characteristics usually associated with vinegars. It adds a surprising flavor to sautéed spinach.

1½ pounds spinach
3 tablespoons olive oil
3 tablespoons water
Salt and freshly ground
  black pepper
4 tablespoons Balsamic
  vinegar
2 tablespoons red wine
6 tablespoons cold butter,
  cut into 12 pieces

1. Rinse the spinach and remove the tough stems. Tear any large leaves in half and set aside.

2. Heat the oil in a large skillet or wok. Add the spinach and stir over high heat until wilted. Sprinkle on the water. Reduce the heat to low and cover the pan. Cook for 2 to 3 minutes or until the leaves are tender. Season with salt and pepper.

3. Meanwhile, combine the vinegar and wine in a small saucepan. Place over medium heat and cook until reduced by half. Remove from the heat and whisk in the butter, one piece at a time. Pour over the spinach to serve.

Stir-Fried Spinach and Red Onions

SERVES 4

2 tablespoons soy sauce
2 tablespoons rice vinegar
½ teaspoon sugar
½ teaspoon sesame seed
  oil (dark)
3 tablespoons vegetable oil
2 medium-size red onions,
  sliced and separated into
  rings
1½ pounds spinach, rinsed,
  stemmed, and torn into
  small pieces

Bright green spinach and red onion rings create an attractive vegetable side dish for roast chicken or pork.

1. In a small bowl, combine the soy sauce, vinegar, sugar, and sesame seed oil. Whisk to blend and set aside.

2. Heat the vegetable oil in a wok or large skillet. Add the onion rings and stir over high heat for 30 seconds. Add the spinach and continue stirring over high heat for 30 seconds more. Pour on the soy sauce mixture and reduce the heat. Stir continuously until the liquid is evaporated and the onions are crisp-tender. Serve immediately.

Sautéed Spinach with Pine Nuts

SERVES 2

Spinach, with water clinging to its leaves, is briefly cooked over high heat until limp. Pine nuts and golden raisins add flavor and textural contrast.

1 pound spinach
3 tablespoons olive oil
¼ cup pine nuts
¼ cup golden raisins
Salt and freshly ground
    black pepper
2 lemon wedges

1. Rinse the spinach and remove the tough stems. Tear any large leaves in half and place the spinach in a colander, but do not dry the leaves.

2. Heat the oil in a large skillet or wok. Add the spinach with the water that clings to its leaves. Stir continuously over high heat for 1 minute or until limp. Add the pine nuts and raisins and toss to combine. Season with salt and pepper. Serve with wedges of lemon.

Spinach Pesto

SERVES 4

Although pesto is traditionally composed mainly of fresh basil leaves, in this recipe, spinach leaves are the chief flavor component.

1½ pounds spinach
½ cup olive oil
6 tablespoons butter
½ cup freshly grated
    Parmesan cheese
4 flat anchovy fillets
1 garlic clove
¼ teaspoon salt
12 fresh basil leaves
½ cup unsalted cashews
1 pound fettuccine or
    similar pasta, boiled and
    drained

1. Rinse the spinach and remove the tough stems. Scatter over a clean kitchen towel and pat dry.

2. In the container of a blender or processor, combine the oil, butter, Parmesan cheese, anchovies, garlic, and salt. Whirl until smooth. Blend in the spinach and basil. Add the cashews and whirl briefly, creating a coarse, pebbly texture. Toss with the hot, drained pasta and serve.

Malfatti

SERVES 6 TO 8

These spinach and ricotta-cheese dumplings are wonderful when bathed simply in melted butter. They may also be served with tomato sauce.

2 pounds spinach
3 large eggs
2 cups ricotta cheese
1½ cups freshly grated
   Parmesan cheese
¼ cup unseasoned bread
   crumbs
¼ cup all-purpose flour
4 green onions, white and
   green portion, finely
   chopped
1 garlic clove, minced
12 fresh basil leaves, finely
   chopped
1 tablespoon chopped fresh
   parsley
½ teaspoon salt
Freshly ground black
   pepper
6 tablespoons butter,
   melted

1. Rinse the spinach and remove the tough stems. Submerge in a large pot of boiling, salted water and cook, uncovered, for 3 minutes or until tender. Drain in a colander set under cold running water. Take up by handfuls and squeeze dry. Chop coarsely and place in a small skillet. Stir over medium heat until the spinach begins to stick to the bottom of the pan. Transfer to a plate.

2. Beat the eggs in a large mixing bowl. Blend in the ricotta cheese, 1 cup of the Parmesan cheese, the bread crumbs, and flour. Add the spinach, onions, garlic, basil, parsley, salt, and pepper. Blend well. Cover the bowl and refrigerate for 3 hours or until firm.

3. Bring a large pot of water to a gentle bubble. Take up the spinach mixture by generous teaspoonfuls and roll into ovals between your hands. (Flour your hands, if necessary, to prevent sticking.) Drop 6 at a time into the hot water and cook until they rise to the surface. Remove with a slotted spoon and place on an ovenproof plate. Pour on the melted butter and sprinkle with the remaining ½ cup Parmesan cheese. Slide under the broiler for 2 minutes or until the cheese is melted and lightly browned.

Spinach Timbales

SERVES 6

1½ pounds spinach
4 tablespoons butter
1 medium onion, finely
   chopped
1½ cups medium or
   whipping cream
4 large eggs
½ teaspoon salt
Pinch of cayenne
¼ teaspoon freshly ground
   nutmeg
12 narrow strips canned
   pimiento, (or roasted red
   bell pepper) for garnish

Individual spinach custards topped with bright red pimiento strips add a festive touch arranged around a holiday roast.

1. Rinse the spinach and remove the tough stems. Submerge in a large pot of boiling, salted water and cook, uncovered, for 3 minutes or until tender. Drain in a colander set under cold running water. Take up by handfuls and squeeze dry. Chop coarsely and set aside.

2. Preheat the oven to 350°. Generously butter 6 timbale molds or individual soufflé dishes. Melt the butter in a large skillet. Add the onion and toss to coat. Stir over medium heat until tender. Add the spinach and toss to combine. Blend in ½ cup of the cream and stir over medium heat until the liquid is evaporated.

(continued)

3. In a large mixing bowl, combine the remaining 1 cup cream, the eggs, salt, cayenne, and nutmeg. Whisk to blend. Stir in the spinach, then pour into the prepared molds. Place in a shallow pan lined with a folded kitchen towel. Pour in enough hot water to come halfway up the sides of the molds. Cover the pan with aluminum foil. Bake for 25 to 30 minutes or until the blade of a knife inserted in the center comes out clean. Allow to stand for 10 minutes. Run a knife around the perimeter of each mold and turn out onto a serving plate. Garnish with 2 strips of pimiento placed across the top of each timbale in a crisscross fashion.

Spinach Tart

SERVES 6

1 pound spinach
1 large egg
1 pound ricotta cheese
⅓ cup all-purpose flour
½ cup freshly grated
    Parmesan cheese
4 tablespoons butter,
    melted
¼ teaspoon freshly grated
    nutmeg
½ teaspoon salt
9-inch tart shell, partially
    baked
3 ounces Gruyère cheese,
    grated

Serve warm wedges of this open-faced pie for luncheon or offer chilled as picnic fare.

1. Rinse the spinach and remove the tough stems. Submerge in a large pot of boiling, salted water and cook, uncovered, for 3 minutes or until tender. Drain in a colander set under cold running water. Take up by handfuls and squeeze dry. Chop coarsely and set aside.

2. Preheat the oven to 350°. Beat the egg in a large mixing bowl and add the ricotta cheese. Stir in the spinach, flour, Parmesan cheese, butter, nutmeg, and salt. Pour into the prepared tart shell and bake for 30 minutes. Scatter the Gruyère cheese over the surface and continue baking for 10 to 12 minutes or until the blade of a knife inserted in the center comes out clean.

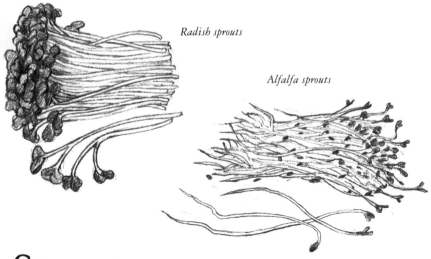

Radish sprouts

Alfalfa sprouts

Sprouts

TECHNICALLY SPEAKING, all sprouts are sprouted seeds, but those types that are grown from tiny
seeds are generally referred to simply as sprouts. Others,
sprouted from larger seeds or beans, are considered bean
sprouts (see Bean Sprouts). Alfalfa sprouts and radish
sprouts are the two most widely available kinds of sprouts.
Crisp and crunchy, with a subtle nutty flavor, sprouts are
prized for their nutritional value and the textural contrast
they provide.

TO SELECT:

Alfalfa sprouts are sold in soft plastic pouches and in sturdier square plastic containers. They may be packaged in a
jumbled heap or in a tidy square that appears to have been
cut and then lifted from the sprouting tray on which they
were grown. Those sold in a square retain their quality
longer and have a fresher flavor. (Alfalfa sprouts are sometimes mixed with red clover sprouts. The resulting flavor is a
bit more peppery, so check the label to determine what
you're buying.)

Radish sprouts are taller and thicker stemmed than
alfalfa sprouts. They also come in plastic pouches and
square containers. Radish sprouts possess a zippy, radishlike
flavor.

When purchasing sprouts, look for fresh, crisp shoots of good color. Check the bottom of the pouch or container for excessive moisture because that is an indication of prolonged storage and probable decay.

TO STORE:　For maximum quality, plan to use sprouts as soon as possible. They may be refrigerated for 5 to 7 days, however, and although they will lose some of their crunchy texture, sprouts store comparatively well when you consider their delicate nature.

TO PREPARE:　Sprouts are grown without soil, fertilizer, and pesticides; consequently, there is no need to wash them. Simply pull apart the required amount and use them as is. Sprouts may be lightly cooked, but the more customary approach is to serve them raw. Scattered over a salad, folded into an omelet, or layered on a sandwich in place of lettuce, sprouts contribute a fresh, clean taste and a crisp, delicate texture.

Sprouts and Fried Rice Salad　　　　SERVES 4

3 tablespoons vegetable oil
2 cups cooked rice
1 tablespoon minced fresh
　ginger
3 tablespoons soy sauce
1 tablespoon honey
1 tablespoon lemon juice
1 garlic clove, pressed
4 ounces alfalfa sprouts
4 green onions, white and
　green portion, sliced
2 ribs celery, sliced
1 tablespoon chopped fresh
　cilantro

Alfalfa sprouts are combined with chilled fried rice, green onions, and celery, then tossed with an Oriental-style dressing. Serve this as a first course or as an accompaniment to fried fish.

1. Heat the oil in a wok or large skillet. Add the cooked rice and ginger and stir constantly over medium heat until the rice is heated through. Transfer to a large mixing bowl. Cover and refrigerate until lightly chilled.

2. In a small bowl, whisk together the soy sauce, honey, lemon juice, and garlic. Cover the bowl and place in the refrigerator.

3. Just before serving, add the alfalfa sprouts, onions, and celery to the rice. Toss to combine. Pour on the soy sauce mixture. Scatter the cilantro over the top and toss gently. Serve at once.

Omelet Rolls with Alfalfa Sprouts

A light egg batter is cooked into small, thin omelets that are rolled around crunchy alfalfa sprouts. Serve for brunch or a late-night supper.

6 large eggs
¼ cup milk
2 tablespoons cold water
½ teaspoon salt
Pinch of cayenne
Vegetable oil
½ cup freshly grated
   Parmesan cheese
4 ounces alfalfa sprouts
Sour cream for garnish
1 tablespoon chopped fresh
   chives for garnish

1. In a small mixing bowl, whisk together the eggs, milk, water, salt, and cayenne.

2. Using a pastry brush, lightly coat the surface of a 6-inch skillet with vegetable oil. Place over medium heat. Measure out 2 tablespoons of the egg mixture and pour it into the pan, tilting to coat the entire surface with a thin layer. Scatter a small amount of Parmesan cheese over the egg mixture, then cook for 30 seconds or until the egg is set. Lift one side of the omelet with a spatula and tilting the pan, slide the omelet onto an ovenproof platter. Place in a low oven to keep warm. Repeat with the remaining batter.

3. Take the omelets from the oven and roll each one around a small bunch of sprouts. Place, seam side down, on a serving plate. Garnish each roll with a dollop of sour cream and scatter the chives over the top. Serve with sliced tomatoes.

Squash: Summer

LIKE WINTER SQUASH, the soft-skinned squash harvested during the summer months are also edible gourds. The major difference between the two is that winter squash is allowed to mature on the vine where it develops large, firm seeds, stringy fibrous tissue, and a tough outer shell; summer squash is picked at an immature stage when the seeds are still small and soft, stringy fibers have not yet developed, and the outer skin is so tender it needn't be removed.

Summer squash used to be easily divided into two groups — yellow and green (see Zucchini). Today, however, this group of vegetables has expanded to include several new varieties. Now there are yellow zucchini, round zucchini, straightneck yellow, crookneck yellow, scallop squash (a pale green, rather flat squash also known as pattypan), and a tiny version of scallop squash called scallopini.

All the summer squash have basically the same nutrients, with slight variations from one type to another. They are all a good source of vitamins A and C.

TO SELECT: The most significant indicator of quality is size. As squash continues to grow in length and width, it becomes less tender and less flavorful. Consequently, the sooner it is harvested, the better it will taste. Look for slender straightneck or crookneck yellow squash about 6 inches long. Supermarkets don't usually offer them much smaller than this, but occasionally you can find 4-inch yellow squash at a farmer's stand. You might even see tiny yellow squash the length of your little finger. Don't pass them by; they're wonderful steamed or sautéed whole. Scallop squash is best when it measures no more than 2 to 3 inches across, and

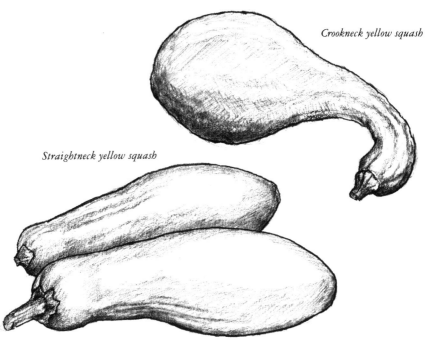

Crookneck yellow squash

Straightneck yellow squash

scallopini should be 1½ to 2 inches in diameter. Summer squash of good quality will feel firm and sleek to the touch and have intensely colored skin. Avoid any with brown blemishes or soft spots. One pound will feed 4 people.

TO STORE: Because the skin of summer squash is fragile, handle it gently. It may look sturdy, but it bruises and the skin breaks easily. Without washing, place unwrapped squash in the refrigerator. It will keep for 3 to 4 days. Summer squash that is stored too long will look wrinkled and turn limp.

TO PREPARE: To retain maximum flavor and nutrients, cook summer squash whole and unpeeled. Steaming, boiling and microwaving are all excellent methods. Depending on their size, summer squash should be steamed for 10 to 12 minutes, boiled for 8 to 10 minutes, or microwaved for 5 to 7 minutes. The squash is cooked when a metal skewer can easily pierce the flesh. When cut into chunks or slices, summer squash may be stir-fried, deep-fried, baked, or grilled. It may be briefly parboiled and then stuffed, or served raw with a dip or dressing.

Scallop squash

Scallopini squash

Yellow Squash Bisque

3 tablespoons butter
1 medium onion, sliced
1½ teaspoons curry powder
½ teaspoon dry mustard
4 cups chicken broth
¼ cup long-grain rice
4 medium-size yellow
   squash, unpeeled and
   sliced
1 cup medium or whipping
   cream
Salt and freshly ground
   white pepper
Unflavored yogurt and
   chives for garnish

Curry powder and dry mustard color this delicious soup a lovely hue.

1. Melt the butter in a large saucepan. Add the onion and toss to coat evenly. Sprinkle on the curry powder and mustard and stir over medium heat until the onion is tender. Pour in the chicken broth. Add the rice and squash. Cover the pan and simmer for 20 to 25 minutes or until the rice and squash are tender.

2. Pour into the container of a blender or processor and whirl until smooth. Transfer to a bowl. Cover the bowl and refrigerate until thoroughly chilled. Just before serving, blend in the cream and season with salt and pepper. Serve in glass bowls set atop crushed ice. Garnish with dollops of yogurt and a sprinkling of chives.

Sautéed Yellow Squash

Julienne strips of yellow squash are cooked until crisp-tender, then tossed with butter and chopped hazelnuts.

4 medium-size yellow
   squash, unpeeled and cut
   into 3-inch lengths
3 tablespoons vegetable oil
¼ cup water
2 tablespoons butter
¼ cup finely chopped
   hazelnuts
Salt and freshly ground
   black pepper

1. Cut each piece of squash lengthwise into thin slices, then cut each slice into julienne strips.

2. Heat the oil in a large skillet or wok. Add the squash and toss to coat evenly. Stir continuously over high heat for 30 seconds. Sprinkle on the water and reduce the heat. Continue stirring for 2 to 3 minutes or until all the liquid is evaporated and the squash is crisp-tender. Add the butter and hazelnuts and toss until the butter is melted. Season with salt and pepper and serve immediately.

Yellow Squash Slices with Goat Cheese

SERVES 4

Tender slices of yellow squash are brushed with melted butter and sprinkled with herbs and crumbled goat cheese.

4 slender yellow squash, unpeeled

4 tablespoons butter, melted

Salt and freshly ground black pepper

1 teaspoon chopped fresh chervil

1 teaspoon chopped fresh thyme

4 ounces soft, unripened goat cheese, such as Montrachet

1. Steam, boil, or microwave the squash whole as described earlier (see TO PREPARE) until tender when pierced. Transfer to a colander and allow to stand.

2. Preheat the oven to 375°. Generously butter a shallow baking dish. When cool enough to handle, trim the ends of the squash and discard. Cut the squash into ½-inch-thick rounds. Arrange the slices in the prepared baking dish in an overlapping fashion. Brush generously with the melted butter and sprinkle with salt and pepper. Scatter the chervil and thyme over the squash and crumble the cheese over the herbs. Bake for 12 to 15 minutes or until the cheese is melted.

Yellow Squash with Bucatini

SERVES 4

4 medium-size yellow squash, unpeeled and cut into 3-inch lengths

3 tablespoons olive oil

3 tablespoons butter

4 green onions, white and green portion, sliced

2 garlic cloves, minced

¼ cup water

1 red bell pepper, cut into julienne strips

1 tablespoon chopped fresh parsley

1 tablespoon chopped fresh savory

½ cup freshly grated Parmesan cheese

12 ounces bucatini, boiled and drained

Salt and freshly ground black pepper

Bucatini are long strands of macaroni, similar to spaghetti except that they are hollow. In this recipe, bucatini are tossed with thin strips of yellow squash and red bell pepper.

1. Cut each piece of squash lengthwise into thin slices, then cut each slice into julienne strips.

2. Heat the oil and butter in a large skillet until the butter is melted. Add the onions and garlic and toss to coat. Stir over medium heat until the onions are tender. Add the squash and sprinkle on the water. Stir in the red bell pepper, parsley, and savory. Continue cooking over medium heat until most of the liquid is evaporated and the squash is crisp-tender. Remove from the heat and scatter the cheese over the mixture to melt.

3. Place the drained bucatini in a large bowl. Sprinkle generously with salt and pepper. Toss the squash mixture to distribute the cheese, then pour over the bucatini. Toss to combine and serve while hot.

Baked Stuffed Scallop Squash

Tiny scallop squash, about 3 inches in diameter, make attractive individual servings when stuffed with a mild cheese and onion filling.

6 small scallop squash
2 tablespoons vegetable oil
2 tablespoons butter
1 medium onion, finely
  chopped
¾ cup chicken broth
1 tablespoon chopped fresh
  chives
Salt and freshly ground
  black pepper
1 small package (3 ounces)
  cream cheese, cut into
  chunks
½ cup freshly grated
  Gruyère cheese

1. Rinse the squash and drop them into a large pot of boiling, salted water. Cook, uncovered, at a gentle bubble for 5 to 8 minutes or until partially tender when pierced. Transfer to a colander and drain. When cool enough to handle, slice off the rounded portion of each squash and set it aside. Using a metal spoon, scoop out the inside of each squash, leaving a shell. Transfer the flesh to a small bowl. Coarsely chop the reserved rounded portions and add to the scooped-out flesh.

2. Preheat the oven to 350°. Generously butter a shallow baking dish. Heat the oil and butter in a large skillet until the butter is melted. Add the onion, tossing to coat. Stir over medium heat until the onion is tender. Pour in the chicken broth and add the chopped squash. Increase the heat and cook, stirring, until most of the liquid is evaporated. Remove from the heat. Stir in the chives, salt, and pepper. Add the cream cheese and return to low heat. Cook, stirring, until the cheese is melted.

3. Spoon the filling into the squash shells, mounding it slightly. Place the filled squash in the prepared baking dish. Scatter the Gruyère cheese over the surface of the filling, dividing it among the 6 squash. Pour in enough water to cover the bottom of the pan and then bake, uncovered, for 30 to 40 minutes or until the squash shells are tender when pierced. Serve immediately.

Yellow Squash Gratiné

SERVES 4

2 tablespoons vegetable oil
2 tablespoons butter
1 medium onion, finely
 chopped
1 garlic clove, minced
4 medium-size yellow
 squash, unpeeled and
 shredded
1 cup heavy cream
Salt and freshly ground
 black pepper
½ cup grated Muenster
 cheese
¼ cup freshly grated
 Parmesan cheese

These are delightful individual casseroles of shredded yellow squash bubbling with melted cheese.

1. Butter 4 individual gratin dishes and set aside. Heat the oil and butter in a large skillet until the butter is melted. Add the onion and garlic and toss to coat. Stir over medium heat until the onion is tender. Add the squash and cook, stirring, until the squash becomes limp. Add the cream and continue stirring until most of the liquid is evaporated.

2. Season with salt and pepper and spoon into the prepared dishes. Distribute the Muenster cheese over the surface of each, then sprinkle with Parmesan cheese. Slide under the broiler and cook until the cheeses are melted and nicely browned.

Yellow Squash Bread

MAKES 1 PAN

1 cup yellow cornmeal
1 cup all-purpose flour
2 teaspoons baking powder
¼ teaspoon ground
 turmeric
½ teaspoon salt
½ cup milk
2 tablespoons honey
4 tablespoons butter
¼ cup freshly grated
 Parmesan cheese
2 large eggs, beaten
1¼ pounds yellow squash,
 unpeeled and shredded

Yellow cornmeal and Parmesan cheese color this bread light yellow and give it a pleasing texture and flavor.

1. Preheat the oven to 350°. Generously grease an 8-inch square pan. Combine the cornmeal, flour, baking powder, turmeric, and salt in a large mixing bowl. Whisk to blend thoroughly.

2. In a small saucepan, heat the milk, honey, and butter until the butter melts. Remove from the heat and stir in the Parmesan cheese. Whisk in the beaten eggs. Add to the dry ingredients and blend well. Stir in the squash. Pour into the prepared pan and bake for 50 minutes to 1 hour or until a wooden pick inserted in the center comes out clean.

Squash: Winter

T HE HARD-SHELLED SQUASH of winter are actually edible gourds. Their tough outer skin and large
seeds are the result of being allowed to ripen on the vine
instead of being harvested at an immature stage, which is
the custom with summer squash. Winter squash include
the familiar acorn and butternut varieties, the large Hubbard, and the relatively new banana squash. Pumpkins
and spaghetti squash are also considered winter squash (see
Pumpkin and Spaghetti Squash).

An excellent source of vitamin A and potassium, all
the various types of winter squash possess pale yellow- to

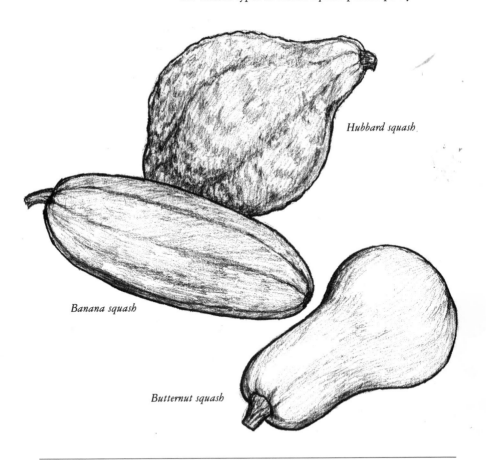

Hubbard squash

Banana squash

Butternut squash

orange-colored flesh. Their flavors and textures are remarkably similar, and therefore they can be used interchangeably in recipes calling for puréed squash. When served unadorned, however, their subtle differences in taste become apparent.

TO SELECT:

Winter squash are sold whole and unwrapped, or cut into portions and covered with clear plastic. When choosing a whole squash, look for rich coloring and a firm skin. In fact, the harder the skin, the better the squash. Quality doesn't depend on size. A large squash tends to be just as good as a small one, but remember that it's easier to cut small squash in half, and an array of small squash will cook faster than a single large one. Winter squash should be free of soft spots and cracks, and the best ones feel heavy for their size. If possible, buy those that have a bit of stem still attached. Figure on ½ pound of whole squash per person.

When purchasing cut portions, select only those pieces that are richly colored and free of spots. One pound of seeded squash will serve 4 people.

TO STORE:

Whole squash keeps exceptionally well and may be stored under maximum conditions until the following spring. Acorn squash is the notable exception; it is more perishable than the others and keeps for a shorter period of time. (Excessive orange coloring on the skin indicates that acorn squash is deteriorating.)

When you bring winter squash home, place it, without washing, in a cool, dry, well-ventilated spot. (Empty net onion bags hung from nails are excellent for this purpose.) Stored at 50° to 55°, winter squash will keep this way for months. At room temperature (approximately 70°), the storage period shortens to several weeks. Do not refrigerate whole winter squash because humidity and extreme cold hasten decay. Cut portions should be refrigerated wrapped and will keep for 3 to 5 days.

TO PREPARE:

One of the major hurdles in preparing a fresh whole squash is cutting it in half. If this has discouraged you from trying winter squash, here's good news. You can partially bake or microwave a whole, unpeeled squash until the skin is soft enough to yield easily to a knife. This is a great shortcut no matter what the final preparation is going to be.

Rinse the squash under cold water and wipe dry. Place in the oven or microwave and cook just until the skin can be broken by the pressure of your thumbnail. By conventional oven, it will take 15 to 20 minutes at 350°; in a microwave, plan on 4 to 5 minutes on high power. Remove the squash and cut in half. Scoop out the seeds and fibrous tissue. Then go on to prepare by whatever method you choose. Unpeeled squash may be baked or grilled; peeled squash may be steamed, boiled (although boiling results in a considerable flavor loss), stir-fried, or deep-fried.

Whole, unpeeled squash can also be baked or microwaved till done without removing the seeds. Depending on the size of the squash, bake or microwave until a metal skewer easily pierces the flesh. Then allow the squash to cool slightly. Cut in half, scoop out the seeds and fibrous tissue, and then peel the squash or spoon out the softened flesh. Cut into chunks, mash, or purée as desired.

Caribbean Squash Soup

SERVES 6

4 tablespoons butter
¼ pound baked ham, coarsely chopped
2 carrots, coarsely chopped
1 medium onion, coarsely chopped
1 tablespoon all-purpose flour
4 cups water
1½ pounds acorn squash, peeled, seeded, and cut into chunks
1 teaspoon dried thyme
1 bay leaf
1 tablespoon tomato paste
⅛ teaspoon ground allspice
Salt and freshly ground pepper
2 cups half-and-half

Ham, sizzled in a small amount of butter, lends extra depth to this full-bodied soup.

1. Melt the butter in a large saucepan. Add the ham and stir over medium heat until the edges begin to curl. Add the carrots and onion and continue stirring over medium heat until the onion is tender. Sprinkle on the flour and stir until the mixture foams. Blend in the water and bring to a boil. Add the squash, thyme, bay leaf, and tomato paste. Reduce the heat and cover the pan. Cook slowly for 30 minutes or until the squash is tender.

2. Pour into the container of a blender or processor and whirl until smooth. Return to the saucepan and stir in the allspice, salt, pepper, and half-and-half. Place over low heat and stir until warmed through, but do not allow the soup to boil. Serve steaming hot.

Grilled Squash Rings

SERVES 4

Rings of acorn squash are brushed with spiced butter, then grilled until lightly browned. Serve with grilled or roast pork.

2 small acorn squash
6 tablespoons butter
2 tablespoons light brown sugar
½ teaspoon ground cinnamon
¼ teaspoon ground ginger
¼ teaspoon ground mace

1. To facilitate slicing, partially bake or microwave the squash whole as described earlier (see TO PREPARE) until the skin can be easily broken by the pressure of your thumbnail. Transfer to a colander and allow to stand.

2. Meanwhile, combine the butter, brown sugar, cinnamon, ginger, and mace in a small saucepan. Stir over medium heat until the sugar is dissolved. Set aside.

3. When the squash is cool enough to handle, cut off the top of each squash and scoop out the seeds and fibrous tissue. Slice the squash into ½-inch-thick rings. Brush the rings generously with the spiced butter and place on a hot grill. Cook, basting frequently, for 5 to 7 minutes or until the squash is tender and lightly browned on both sides.

Butternut Chunks with Gingered Honey

SERVES 4

Chunks of butternut squash tossed with fresh ginger and honey make a wonderful addition to the traditional turkey dinner.

2 medium butternut squash
¼ cup water
¼ cup butter
Salt and freshly ground black pepper
¼ cup honey
1 tablespoon minced fresh ginger

1. To facilitate slicing, partially bake or microwave the squash as described earlier (see TO PREPARE) until the skin can be easily broken by the pressure of your thumbnail. Transfer to a colander and allow to stand.

2. When cool enough to handle, peel the squash with a paring knife or swivel-blade peeler. Cut the squash in half lengthwise and scoop out the seeds and fibrous tissue. Cut the squash into ½-inch cubes and set aside.

3. In a large skillet, combine the water and butter and heat until the butter is melted. Add the squash and toss to coat. Sprinkle with salt and pepper. Cover the pan and simmer for 12 minutes. Stir in the honey and ginger. Increase the heat to medium-high and continue stirring until most of the liquid is evaporated and the squash is tender. Transfer to a serving dish.

Acorn Squash Stuffed with Apples

Tart apple chunks bathed in cinnamon butter create a flavorful stuffing for baked acorn squash.

3 medium acorn squash
3 tart apples, peeled, cored, and cut into small chunks
1 tablespoon all-purpose flour
Salt and freshly ground black pepper
6 tablespoons butter
3 tablespoons light brown sugar
1 teaspoon ground cinnamon

1. To facilitate slicing, partially bake or microwave the squash as described earlier (see TO PREPARE) until the skin can be broken easily by the pressure of your thumbnail. Transfer to a colander and allow to stand.

2. Preheat the oven to 350°. Lightly oil 6 individual baking dishes or a large shallow pan. In a mixing bowl, combine the apples and flour and toss to coat evenly.

3. When the squash is cool enough to handle, cut each one in half lengthwise. Scoop out the seeds and fibrous tissue. Transfer the shells to the prepared baking dish. Spoon the apples into the squash cavities and sprinkle with salt and pepper.

4. In a small saucepan, combine the butter, brown sugar, and cinnamon. Stir over medium heat until the sugar is dissolved. Brush over the exposed flesh of the squash and then drizzle what remains over the apples. Cover with aluminum foil and bake for 20 minutes. Uncover the dish and continue baking for 20 to 30 minutes or until the squash is tender.

Acorn squash

Banana Squash Baked with Hazelnut Praline SERVES 12

A large banana squash cut in half lengthwise and baked is a spectacular addition to a fall buffet. Guests serve themselves by spooning out a portion of squash sprinkled with crunchy hazelnut praline.

1 cup hazelnuts, toasted
¾ cup granulated sugar
2 tablespoons water
1 large banana squash
  (about 5 pounds)
8 tablespoons butter
3 tablespoons light brown
  sugar
⅓ cup hazelnut liqueur,
  such as Frangelico
Salt and freshly ground
  black pepper

1. Generously butter a baking sheet. Transfer the hazelnuts to a coarse kitchen towel while they are still warm, then rub briskly to remove the papery husks. Combine the granulated sugar and water in a wide saucepan and stir to dissolve the sugar. Place over high heat and cook, without stirring, until the mixture is syrupy and light golden in color. Stir in the hazelnuts. When the mixture begins to bubble, pour it onto the buttered baking sheet in a thin layer. Allow it to cool thoroughly.

2. Meanwhile, preheat the oven to 375°. Rinse the banana squash and place it directly on the oven rack. Pierce the top portion of the shell in several places with a metal skewer. Bake for 20 to 30 minutes or until the skin can be easily broken by the pressure of your thumbnail. Transfer to a cooling rack and allow to stand.

3. Lift the cooled praline from the pan, breaking it into small pieces. Place the pieces in the container of a blender or processor and whirl briefly. Stop when a coarse consistency is reached. In a small saucepan, combine the butter, brown sugar, and hazelnut liqueur. Stir over medium heat until the butter is melted and the sugar is dissolved. Remove from the heat and set aside.

4. Lightly grease a baking sheet. When the squash is cool enough to handle, cut it in half lengthwise and scoop out the seeds. Pierce the flesh all over with a fork. Sprinkle with salt and pepper, then brush the flesh with the butter mixture. Scatter on the hazelnut praline. Transfer the squash to the prepared baking sheet and return to a 375° oven. Bake for 25 to 35 minutes or until the squash is tender when pierced.

Squash Date Muffins

2 cups all-purpose flour
2 teaspoons baking powder
1 teaspoon baking soda
½ teaspoon salt
1 teaspoon ground
  cinnamon
½ teaspoon ground ginger
2 large eggs
½ cup buttermilk
¼ cup butter, melted
¾ cup light brown sugar
1 cup fresh squash purée
  (acorn, butternut, or
  Hubbard)
½ cup coarsely chopped
  dates

The secret to using fresh squash purée successfully is to dry it sufficiently. To do this, place the purée in a wide saucepan and stir over low heat until the purée begins to stick to the bottom of the pan.

1. Preheat the oven to 400°. Generously grease 12 muffin tins. Combine the flour, baking powder, soda, salt, cinnamon, and ginger in a large mixing bowl. Whisk to blend thoroughly.

2. In a separate bowl, beat together the eggs and buttermilk. Add the melted butter and brown sugar. Stir in the squash and blend thoroughly. Add to the dry ingredients and mix well. Stir in the dates. Pour into the prepared muffin tins and bake for 20 to 25 minutes or until a wooden pick inserted in the center comes out clean.

Winter Squash Rolls

Flavored with orange juice, these hearty yeast rolls are delicious for breakfast or served with roast pork.

¼ cup orange juice
4 tablespoons butter
⅓ cup golden raisins
2 tablespoons sugar
½ teaspoon salt
1 cup milk
1 large egg, beaten
¼ teaspoon ground
  cinnamon
1 package dry yeast
¼ cup warm water
½ cup puréed winter squash
  (acorn, butternut, or
  Hubbard)
4 to 4½ cups all-purpose
  flour

1. In a small saucepan, combine the orange juice, butter, raisins, sugar, and salt. Heat until the butter is melted. Transfer to a large mixing bowl and stir in the milk. Add the beaten egg and cinnamon. Dissolve the yeast in the warm water and blend in. Stir in the squash.

2. Stir in enough flour to form a stiff dough. Cover the bowl and allow the dough to rise. Generously grease 18 muffin tins.

3. When the dough is doubled in bulk, turn it out onto a floured surface and divide it in half. Roll each half into a 9-inch length. Cut each length into nine 1-inch segments, then form each segment into a small smooth ball. Place in the prepared muffin tins and allow to rise.

4. Meanwhile, preheat the oven to 375°. Using a razor blade, slash the top of each roll 2 times, forming a cross. Bake for 25 to 30 minutes or until nicely browned.

Sweet Potatoes

SWEET POTATOES are frequently referred to as yams, and the interesting point is that, botanically speaking, they are neither potatoes nor yams. Sweet potatoes are the storage roots of a plant belonging to the morning-glory family, a group that is totally unrelated to Irish potatoes, which are of the nightshade family, or to yams, which belong to a group of tropical herbs and shrubs. Sweet potatoes are available all year, but are at their best from October to January. They contain a high percentage of natural sugar and are an excellent source of vitamin A and potassium.

TO SELECT:

Sweet potatoes are elongated tubers with ends that taper to a point, and they bear skins of various colors, including pale yellow, tan, deep red, and copper. Although there are numerous varieties, sweet potatoes can be divided into two

basic types — those that have pale yellow or tan skin and are referred to as Jersey-type sweet potatoes, and those that have red or copper-colored skin and are referred to as the Puerto Rican type. Jersey-type sweet potatoes possess light yellow, mealy textured flesh that cooks up relatively dry and fluffy. They are excellent for baking, steaming, and frying. Puerto-Rican type sweet potatoes exhibit deep yellow or orange flesh that develops a moist, dense consistency when cooked. They are the type that is customarily confused with yams. Look for sweet potatoes with firm, unblemished skin. Wrinkled skin, soft spots, nicks, or bruises are signs of impaired quality. As nearly as possible, select all the same size to facilitate even cooking.

TO STORE:

Sweet potatoes are relatively perishable and their delicate flesh bruises easily. At home, gently transfer them to a dry, well-ventilated area away from strong light. Store them at 55°, if possible, and they will maintain their quality for 2 to 3 weeks; higher temperatures hasten deterioration. Do not refrigerate them because cold temperatures encourage sweet potatoes to soften and spoil.

TO PREPARE:

Scrub sweet potatoes gently with a soft-bristled brush under cold running water , and pat dry. Since the best way to retain the flavor, texture, and nutrients of sweet potatoes is to cook them whole with their skins on, proceed to bake, boil, microwave, or steam them until tender. Sweet potatoes may also be cut into rounds and sautéed, sliced into strips and deep-fried, or shredded and served raw as a salad. Puréed sweet potatoes are often used as the basis for soufflés, flans, pies, biscuits, and many other baked goods.

The exposed flesh of raw sweet potatoes must be immediately covered by acidulated water, a sauce or dressing, or a batter to prevent discoloration. Sweet potatoes, particularly the orange-fleshed Puerto Rican type, can be substituted in any recipe that calls for yams. However, sweet potatoes are seldom used in place of Irish potatoes, because they lack the starch that is essential to the character of most dishes made with Irish potatoes.

Sweet Potato Salad with Honey Vinaigrette

SERVES 6

Julienne strips of crunchy sweet potato, veiled with a honey-flavored dressing, are nested on leaves of Boston lettuce. Coarsely chopped cashews provide an interesting flavor note.

3 medium-size sweet
   potatoes, peeled
4 tablespoons lemon juice
3 tablespoons honey
¼ teaspoon salt
Generous pinch of cayenne
6 tablespoons vegetable oil
1 tablespoon chopped fresh
   cilantro
12 leaves Boston lettuce
½ cup unsalted cashews,
   toasted and coarsely
   chopped

1. Slice the sweet potatoes lengthwise, then cut the slices lengthwise into julienne strips. Immediately submerge the strips in a bowl of cold water. Stir in 1 tablespoon of the lemon juice.

2. Drain the strips of sweet potato in a colander and drop them into a large pot of boiling, salted water. Cook, uncovered, at a gentle bubble for exactly 30 seconds. Drain in a colander set under cold running water. Transfer to absorbent paper and pat dry.

3. In a small bowl, whisk together the remaining 3 tablespoons lemon juice, the honey, salt, and cayenne. Gradually whisk in the oil. Stir in the cilantro. Transfer the strips of sweet potato to a large mixing bowl. Pour on the dressing and toss gently to coat. Cover the bowl and refrigerate until thoroughly chilled.

4. Just before serving, arrange the lettuce leaves on 6 salad plates. Spoon the sweet potato strips into a mound in the center of the leaves and sprinkle on the cashews.

Butter-Steamed Sweet Potatoes

SERVES 4

4 medium-size sweet
   potatoes, peeled
1 tablespoon lemon juice
4 tablespoons butter
¼ cup water
¼ cup orange juice
2 tablespoons Cointreau
Salt and freshly ground
   black pepper

Sweet potatoes cut into thin strips develop a tender, yet crisp texture when cooked briefly in butter over high heat, and then steamed. Orange juice and Cointreau add lively flavor and create a shimmering glaze.

1. Slice the sweet potatoes into ¼-inch-thick rounds, then cut each round into narrow strips. Immediately submerge them in a bowl of cold water. Stir in the lemon juice.

2. Just before cooking, drain the sweet potatoes in a colander. Scatter them over absorbent paper and blot gently to dry. Melt the butter in a large skillet and immediately add the sweet potatoes, tossing to coat. Stir over high heat for 30 seconds. Pour on the water and cover the pan.

(continued)

Reduce the heat to low and cook for 5 to 8 minutes or until the sweet potatoes are crisp-tender.

3. Pour on the orange juice and Cointreau. Season with salt and pepper. Increase the heat to high and stir gently until the liquid evaporates and the sweet potatoes are glazed.

Sweet Potatoes Glazed with Apple Cider

SERVES 4

Slices of sweet potato are sprinkled with cinnamon sugar and baked in cider laced with apple brandy.

1½ cups fresh apple cider
¼ cup apple brandy
4 tablespoons butter
1 teaspoon finely chopped
    fresh ginger
½ cup sugar
1 teaspoon ground
    cinnamon
4 medium-size sweet
    potatoes

1. In a small saucepan, combine the cider, brandy, butter, and ginger. Stir over medium heat until the butter is melted. Set aside.

2. Prepare the cinnamon sugar by thoroughly blending the sugar and cinnamon together in a small bowl.

3. Preheat the oven to 350°. Generously butter a 9-inch round baking dish or casserole. Peel the sweet potatoes and cut into ½-inch-thick rounds. Starting at the outer edge of the dish, arrange the sweet potato slices in overlapping concentric circles. Immediately pour on the cider mixture, brushing it over the slices to completely coat the exposed surfaces. Sprinkle on the cinnamon sugar. Cover the baking dish with aluminum foil and bake for 45 minutes. Baste occasionally during baking. Increase the oven temperature to 400° and remove the foil. Baste and continue baking for 10 to 15 minutes or until the sweet potatoes are tender and beautifully glazed.

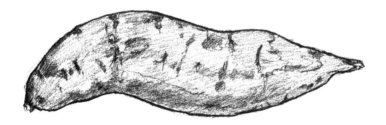

Sweet Potato Medallions with Lime Hollandaise   SERVES 4

Rounds of sweet potato are coated with a gossamer batter and fried. Sauced with Lime Hollandaise, they make an enticing accompaniment for baked or broiled fish.

Lime Hollandaise

Juice of 2 large limes
1 teaspoon finely grated lime zest
1 tablespoon cold water
2 large egg yolks
6 tablespoons cold butter, cut into 24 pieces
Salt and freshly ground white pepper

Medallions

2 large eggs
1 cup cold water
¾ cup plus 2 tablespoons all-purpose flour
½ teaspoon salt
4 medium-size sweet potatoes
Vegetable oil for frying

1. Prepare the Lime Hollandaise by combining the lime juice, lime zest, water, and egg yolks in a nonreactive saucepan. Blend well and place over medium-low heat. Add half the butter and stir with a heat-resistant rubber spatula until completely melted. Reduce the heat to its lowest possible setting. Stirring continuously, add the remaining butter one piece at a time. When one piece is completely melted, stir in the next until all the butter is incorporated and the sauce is thickened. Season with salt and pepper and pour into a bowl. Cover with a clean kitchen towel and set aside at room temperature.

2. For the Medallions, place the eggs in a wide mixing bowl. Whisk in the water until frothy. Add the flour and salt and blend well. The batter will be exceptionally thin. Set aside.

3. Peel the sweet potatoes and cut them into ¼-inch-thick rounds. Meanwhile, heat ½ inch of vegetable oil in a large skillet. When the oil is hot, dip the potato slices into the batter and transfer them to the oil. Cook until lightly browned on both sides. Drain on absorbent paper. Arrange the medallions in an overlapping pattern on a serving plate, spoon on the Lime Hollandaise, and serve.

Sweet Potato and Apple Casserole   SERVES 6

4 medium-size sweet potatoes
½ cup medium or whipping cream
4 tablespoons butter
½ teaspoon freshly grated nutmeg
Salt and freshly ground black pepper
2 tart apples, peeled, cored, and coarsely chopped

Tart apples lend an engaging flavor to this light, airy sweet potato dish.

1. Bake, boil, steam, or microwave the sweet potatoes until tender. Press the cooked flesh through a food mill or ricer, allowing the purée to fall into a large bowl.

2. Preheat the oven to 350°. Generously butter a 1½-quart baking dish or 6 individual ramekins. Combine the cream and butter in a small saucepan and stir over medium heat until the butter is melted.

(continued)

3. Using a wooden spoon, beat the warm cream into the sweet potato purée. Add the nutmeg, salt, and pepper and blend thoroughly. Stir in the apples, then spoon into the prepared baking dish or ramekins. Bake for 20 to 25 minutes (12 to 15 minutes for ramekins) or until slightly puffed. Turn on the broiler and cook for 3 to 4 additional minutes to brown the top.

Baked Stuffed Sweet Potatoes   SERVES 4

A hint of dark rum and a dash of mace give these stuffed sweet potatoes a tropical, exotic flair.

4 medium-size sweet
   potatoes, of uniform size
2 tablespoons medium or
   whipping cream
2 tablespoons honey
2 tablespoons dark rum
4 tablespoons butter
¼ teaspoon ground mace
Salt and freshly ground
   black pepper
½ cup dry-roasted, unsalted
   peanuts, coarsely
   chopped

1. Preheat the oven to 375°. Scrub the sweet potatoes under cool running water and prick in several places with a metal skewer. Bake for 45 minutes to 1 hour or until tender when pierced. (Take special care not to overcook them because the sugar can easily caramelize and create a burned layer of potato next to the skin. Since they go from nearly tender to done in a matter of minutes, watch them closely. It's also important to prick additional holes in the skin during baking because the high sugar content will seal the steam vents closed.)

2. When the potatoes are cool enough to handle, remove a thin slice from the top of each potato with a serrated knife. Scoop out the warm flesh and press it through a food mill or ricer. Reserve the skins.

3. In a small saucepan, combine the cream, honey, rum, and butter. Stir over medium heat until the butter is melted. Blend in the mace, then add to the puréed sweet potatoes. Beat to blend thoroughly. Season with salt and pepper and spoon into the reserved sweet potato skins. Place on an ungreased baking sheet or in a shallow pan. Sprinkle the tops with the peanuts and bake in a 400° oven for 10 minutes. Serve hot.

Sweet Potato Flan

Grated sweet potatoes and orange zest combine to lend a unique flavor to this savory custard. Cut into slim wedges to serve as an accompaniment to roast turkey or game.

3 cups medium or whipping
    cream
3 medium-size sweet
    potatoes, peeled
4 tablespoons butter
4 large eggs
½ cup sugar
2 teaspoons finely grated
    orange zest
1 teaspoon vanilla
½ teaspoon ground
    cinnamon
¼ teaspoon salt

1. Preheat the oven to 325° and generously butter a 9-inch round casserole. Pour the cream into a wide saucepan. Grate the sweet potatoes directly into the cream, then stir to coat evenly. (If you grate them in a processor, immediately combine them with the cream to prevent discoloration.) Add the butter and heat until the butter is melted.

2. In a large mixing bowl, whisk the eggs and sugar until well blended. Stir in the orange zest, vanilla, cinnamon, and salt and gradually blend in the cream mixture.

3. Pour into the prepared casserole and place in a shallow roasting pan lined with a folded kitchen towel. Pour hot water into the roasting pan to a depth of 1 inch and bake for 40 to 50 minutes or until the blade of a knife inserted in the center comes out clean. Transfer to a cooling rack and let stand for 10 minutes. Run the blade of a knife around the perimeter of the pan and invert onto a flat serving plate.

Sweet Potato Rolls

1 cup milk
4 tablespoons butter, cut
    into pieces
¼ cup honey
1 teaspoon salt
1 package dry yeast
¼ cup warm water
1 large egg
1 cup puréed sweet potato
    (2 medium-size sweet
    potatoes)
3 cups whole wheat flour
1 to 1½ cups all-purpose
    flour
Melted butter

These generously sized whole wheat rolls are baked in muffin tins. Exceptionally light and moist, they are a perfect complement to roast chicken or turkey.

1. In a small saucepan, combine the milk, butter, honey, and salt. Place over medium heat and stir until the butter is melted. Remove from the heat.

2. Dissolve the yeast in the water and set aside. In a large mixing bowl, whisk the egg until frothy. Add the sweet potato purée and blend well. Gradually stir in the milk mixture, then add the dissolved yeast. Add the whole wheat flour and beat with a wooden spoon. Stir in enough of the all-purpose flour to form a stiff dough. Turn out onto a floured surface and knead lightly, dusting with additional flour if necessary to prevent sticking. The dough will feel soft and moist. Form into a ball, dust with flour, and place in a greased bowl. Cover the bowl with

plastic wrap and secure with an elastic band. Allow the dough to rise about 1½ hours or until double in bulk.

3. Generously grease 24 muffin cups. Turn the dough out onto a floured surface and roll into a sausage shape, but do not knead. Pressing down with the palms of your hands, continue rolling until the dough measures 12 inches long. Cut the length of dough in half. Working with one length of dough at a time, roll each piece with the palms of your hands until it is 12 inches long. Cut each piece of dough into 12 one-inch slices and form each slice into a ball by pressing and rolling it between the palms of your hands. Place each ball of dough in a greased muffin cup. Cover loosely with plastic wrap and allow the dough to rise for about 1 hour.

4. When double in bulk, bake in a preheated 375° oven for 20 to 25 minutes or until the tops are nicely browned. Immediately brush the tops of the hot rolls with melted butter and tilt them on their sides or transfer to a cooling rack.

Sweet Potato Pancakes with Pecan Butter   MAKES 16 PANCAKES

Serve these beautifully colored pancakes for a special-occasion brunch. Fluffy dollops of rum-flavored Pecan Butter contribute a sophisticated touch of elegance.

2 cups all-purpose flour
3 teaspoons baking powder
½ teaspoon salt
¼ teaspoon ground allspice
3 large eggs
1½ cups milk
1 cup puréed sweet potatoes
  (2 medium-size sweet
  potatoes)
4 tablespoons butter,
  melted
Vegetable oil for frying
Pecan Butter

1. Combine the flour, baking powder, salt, and allspice in a large mixing bowl. Whisk to blend thoroughly. Separate the eggs, setting the whites aside.

2. In another bowl, beat together the egg yolks, milk, sweet potato purée, and melted butter. Add to the dry ingredients and blend well. Whisk the egg whites until soft peaks form, then fold in.

3. Drop by generous spoonfuls onto a hot griddle brushed with vegetable oil. Cook over medium-high heat, turning once. When both sides are nicely browned, transfer to a warmed platter. Serve with Pecan Butter.

4. To make Pecan Butter, beat together ½ cup softened butter and ½ cup light brown sugar. When fluffy, gradually blend in 2 tablespoons medium or whipping cream, 1 tablespoon dark rum, and a pinch of ground allspice. Then gently stir in ½ cup lightly toasted, finely chopped pecans.

Swiss Chard

SWISS CHARD SHOULD really be considered two vegetables in one — the broad red or white center rib, which may be cut into lengths and braised or stir-fried like celery, and the tender green leaves that are prepared as you would spinach. Although Swiss chard is usually recognized for its mild, versatile leaves, many cooks feel that the firm ribs are of equally delicious merit.

TO SELECT: Swiss chard is sold in bunches with stalks that are sometimes loose and other times are attached at the base like celery. The stems should be firm and dry, and the leaves should be glossy, yet slightly crinkled like spinach. Select Swiss chard that feels heavy for its size and has fresh, resilient leaves; pass by any bunches that are limp or wilted.

TO STORE: Place unwashed Swiss chard in a large plastic bag and secure with a wire twist. Refrigerate and use within 3 to 5 days.

TO PREPARE: If the stalks are present, cut them off at the base of the leaves. Plunge the leaves into a basin of cold water and rinse away any sand or dirt. Transfer to a colander and drain.

Using a knife, cut out the center rib of each leaf and set aside. The green leaves may be stuffed and baked in much the same manner as cabbage leaves. They may also be

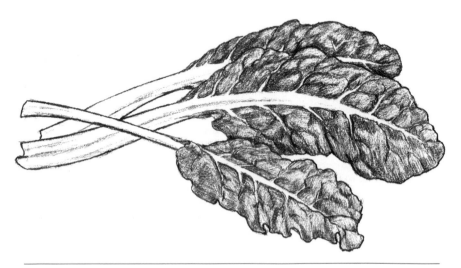

To prepare the center ribs of swiss chard, cut them away from the leafy portion. Insert a knife blade just under the surface of the rib and lift toward you to pull away the fibers.

blanched, steamed, or prepared according to any of the methods used for spinach. In fact, Swiss chard is so mild that it makes an excellent substitute for spinach in all but the most delicate dishes.

To prepare the center ribs, remove the fibers by running a swivel-blade peeler down the length of the rib, or insert the blade of a paring knife directly under the surface of the rib and lift to pull away the fibers. Cut the ribs into 2-inch lengths or slice thinly on the diagonal. Lengths of rib may be braised or prepared au gratin; thin slices are excellent when stir-fried.

Swiss Chard Salad

SERVES 4

A warm salad of wilted Swiss chard leaves dressed with a fat-free blend of reduced beef broth and fresh ginger. Serve as a salad course or as an accompaniment to roast pork.

1½ pounds Swiss chard
1 cup beef broth
Salt and freshly ground black pepper
4 green onions, white and green portion, thinly sliced
1 tablespoon light brown sugar
2 tablespoons rice vinegar
1 tablespoon minced fresh ginger
1 teaspoon crushed red pepper

1. Rinse the Swiss chard and separate the leaves from the stalks, reserving the stalks for another use. Tear the leaves into bite-size pieces and transfer to a large skillet. Pour on the beef broth and stir over high heat for 1 minute or until the leaves are wilted. Drain in a sieve, returning the liquid to the pan.

2. Divide the Swiss chard among 4 salad plates. Season with salt and pepper and scatter the onions over the leaves.

3. Place the skillet over high heat and cook briskly until the liquid is reduced to ⅓ cup. Add the brown sugar and stir until dissolved. Blend in the vinegar, ginger, and red pepper. Boil for 30 seconds, then spoon over the Swiss chard. Serve at once.

Swiss Chard Bundles

Leaves of Swiss chard are wrapped around a filling of chopped Swiss chard stalks to form bundles. Served chilled with olive oil and lemon juice, they make an engaging salad or buffet vegetable dish.

2 pounds Swiss chard
6 tablespoons olive oil
Salt and freshly ground
    black pepper
3 tablespoons lemon juice

1. Rinse the Swiss chard and cut off the stalks at the base of the leaves. Cut the stalks into 2-inch lengths and drop them into a large pot of boiling, salted water. Cook, uncovered, at a gentle bubble for 5 to 8 minutes or until tender. Lift out the stalks with a slotted spoon and transfer to a large bowl of cold water.

2. Drop the leaves into the boiling water and cook, uncovered, at a gentle bubble for 2 minutes or just until limp. Lift out the leaves with a slotted spoon and submerge them in cold water. Select 8 well-formed leaves and place them on absorbent paper. Drain the remaining leaves and the stems in a colander. Chop coarsely and transfer to a large skillet.

3. Set the skillet over high heat and cook, stirring constantly, until all the moisture is evaporated and the Swiss chard begins to stick to the bottom of the pan. Remove from the heat and drizzle on 2 tablespoons of the oil. Stir to coat. Season with salt and pepper.

4. Spoon the chopped Swiss chard onto the reserved leaves and drizzle on 1 tablespoon of the lemon juice. Roll up the leaves, tucking in the sides to form neat bundles. Transfer, seam side down, to a serving platter and refrigerate. When chilled, whisk together the remaining 4 tablespoons oil and 2 tablespoons lemon juice. Pour over the Swiss chard bundles and serve.

Swiss Chard Stalks Au Gratin

SERVES 4

Sharp Kasseri cheese contributes its special flavor to slices of braised Swiss chard stalks.

2 pounds Swiss chard
1½ cups medium or
  whipping cream
6 ounces Kasseri cheese,
  grated
Salt and freshly ground
  white pepper

1. Rinse the Swiss chard and separate the stalks from the leaves, reserving the leaves for another use. Remove the fibers from the stalks as described earlier (see TO PRE-PARE). Slice the stalks thinly on the diagonal.

2. Transfer to a wide saucepan and add enough water to cover by 1 inch. Bring to a boil. Cover the pan and reduce the heat. Simmer for 5 to 8 minutes or until crisp-tender. Drain in a colander.

3. Preheat the oven to 350°. Generously butter a shallow baking dish. In a large mixing bowl, combine the cream and Kasseri cheese. Add the drained stalks and stir to combine. Season with salt and pepper. Pour into the prepared baking dish and bake for 20 minutes or until the surface is nicely browned.

Swiss Chard Quiche

SERVES 6 TO 8

A light crust of Parmesan and feta cheeses tops this lemony Swiss chard tart.

9-inch pastry shell
1 pound Swiss chard
2 tablespoons vegetable oil
4 tablespoons butter
1½ cups sour cream
1 tablespoon all-purpose
  flour
2 large eggs, separated
3 tablespoons lemon juice
1 tablespoon chopped fresh
  chives
Freshly grated nutmeg
½ teaspoon salt
Pinch of cayenne
¼ cup unseasoned bread
  crumbs
¼ cup freshly grated
  Parmesan cheese
¼ cup finely crumbled feta
  cheese

1. Preheat the oven to 375°. Partially bake the pastry shell in a quiche dish. Rinse the Swiss chard and separate the leaves from the stalks, reserving the stalks for another use. Stack the leaves and cut into thin shreds. Heat the oil and 2 tablespoons of the butter in a large skillet. When the butter is melted, add the Swiss chard and stir continuously over high heat until it is limp. Remove from the pan with a slotted spoon and set aside.

2. In a mixing bowl, combine the sour cream, flour, and egg yolks. Blend well. Stir in the lemon juice, chives, nutmeg, salt, and cayenne. Mix in the Swiss chard.

3. Whisk the egg whites until soft peaks form and fold into the Swiss chard mixture. Pour into the prepared pastry shell and set aside.

4. In a small saucepan, melt the remaining 2 table-spoons butter. Stir in the bread crumbs until they are moistened. Mix in the Parmesan and feta cheeses. Sprinkle over the surface of the quiche. Bake for 25 to 30 minutes or until a knife inserted in the center comes out clean.

T

Taro Root (TAH-row)

TARO ROOT IS a finely grained tuber with a consistency and flavor similar to that of mealy potatoes. Grown in the southern regions of the continental United States and in Hawaii, taro root has a starchy texture that is well suited for a variety of preparations.

TO SELECT: Taro roots are irregularly shaped ovals with tough brown skin. Those that are offered for sale are usually about the size of a big potato, although they can grow to be much larger. Purchase taro roots that are firm and unblemished; avoid any with soft spots or cut skin. One pound is enough for 4 servings or for 2 cups of mashed flesh.

TO STORE:

Whole, uncut taro root may be stored in a cool, dry, well-ventilated place, where it will keep for 2 to 3 weeks. Taro root may also be refrigerated, unwrapped, but plan to use it within 5 to 7 days.

TO PREPARE:

Rinse taro root under cool running water, then peel with a swivel-blade peeler or paring knife. Cut or slice the flesh in any of the ways that you would a potato.

Chunks of taro root may be simmered in soups, or boiled until tender and then mashed; thick slices may be microwaved, steamed, or braised; narrow strips may be stir-fried or deep-fried; and thin slices may be deep-fried as chips. Taro root may also be baked in the skin.

The flesh of a taro root is usually white, although varieties with yellow or grey flesh also exist. Don't be surprised if taro root flesh turns pinkish purple when it is cooked. It is a harmless phenomenon.

Taro Chips

SERVES 6

Similar to potato chips in flavor and texture, taro chips usually develop a pinkish purple star-burst pattern while they cook.

3 slender taro roots
Vegetable oil for deep-frying
Freshly ground sea salt

1. Rinse the taro roots and place in a wide saucepan. Add enough water to cover by 1 inch. Bring to a gentle bubble and cook, uncovered, for 40 minutes or until tender when pierced. Drain and pat dry. Refrigerate for 3 hours or until thoroughly chilled.

2. Remove the skin with a paring knife or swivel-blade peeler. Slice as thinly as possible. Heat the oil in a deep-fat fryer to 375°. Submerge the slices of taro root in the hot oil in small batches. Cook until crisp and lightly browned. Drain on absorbent paper and sprinkle with sea salt. Serve as you would potato chips.

Taro Root and Sweet Potatoes

Coconut milk imparts richness and a distinctive flavor to this sweet, yet savory purée. Serve as a vegetable side dish with baked ham or roast turkey.

1 pound taro root, peeled and cut into 1-inch-thick slices
1 pound sweet potatoes, peeled and cut into 1-inch-thick slices
¼ cup light brown sugar
½ teaspoon salt
½ teaspoon ground mace
1 tablespoon cornstarch
1 cup canned or frozen coconut milk
Butter

1. Place the taro root in a large saucepan and add enough water to cover by 1 inch. Bring to a gentle bubble and cook, uncovered, for 10 minutes. Add the sweet potatoes and enough additional water to cover by 1 inch. Bring to a gentle bubble and cook, uncovered, for 20 minutes or until both the taro and the sweet potatoes are tender enough to mash against the side of the pan.

2. Tilt the pan and pour off as much water as possible. Sprinkle on the brown sugar, salt, and mace. Dissolve the cornstarch in the coconut milk and add to the pan. Return to medium heat and beat with a wooden spoon. The mixture should develop the consistency of a rough purée. When heated thoroughly, transfer to a serving dish and place a generous dollop of butter in the center.

Taro Cakes

SERVES 4

These tiny fried rounds are a popular Hawaiian vegetable dish. Serve with grilled pork or chicken.

2 taro roots (about 1 pound)
4 tablespoons butter, melted
3 teaspoons baking powder
1 teaspoon sugar
½ teaspoon salt
Vegetable oil for deep-frying

1. Peel the taro roots and cut into quarters. Place in a large saucepan and add enough water to cover by 1 inch. Bring to a vigorous boil and cook, uncovered, for 5 minutes. Pour the water from the pan and replace with fresh water. Bring to a gentle bubble and cook, uncovered, for 20 to 30 minutes or until very tender when pierced. Drain in a colander, then mash.

2. In a large mixing bowl, combine 2 cups of the mashed taro with the melted butter. Blend well. Stir in the baking powder, sugar, and salt. The batter should be the consistency of biscuit dough.

3. Turn out onto a floured work surface and pat or roll to the thickness of ½ inch. Cut out rounds with a small biscuit cutter. Heat the oil in a deep-fat-fryer to 375°. Submerge the cakes in the hot oil, 5 or 6 at a time. Cook until light brown and crispy. Drain on absorbent paper and serve with additional butter if you wish.

Tomatillos (toe-mah-TEE-yos)

COOKS WHO ARE familiar with decorative plants will immediately note the striking similarity between the appearance of tomatillos and of the fruit of a popular perennial commonly used in dried-flower arrangements. This is more than mere coincidence.

The Chinese lantern plant, which produces an array of papery seed cases shaped like tiny Oriental lanterns, is a member of the *Physalis* family. Its brilliant orange-red lanterns are about 2 inches long, and each contains a small edible berry. Tomatillos also belong to the *Physalis* family, specifically, the group called *Physalis ixocarpa*. But their papery husks are green or tan, and the large berries grow to the size of cherry tomatoes, completely filling their husks, often to the point of bursting.

Tomatillos have a slightly acidic flavor that might be compared with that of a tart apple. It is a distinctive taste, and one which contributes essential character to the cuisines of Mexico and the American Southwest.

TO SELECT: Look for firm, unblemished tomatillos with dry, papery husks. The flesh should be green; yellow tomatillos are those that have been allowed to ripen, and they are not as desirable for use in most recipes.

TO STORE: Without washing or removing the husks, transfer tomatillos to a flat, shallow pan and refrigerate in a single layer. Depending on their condition at the time of purchase, you may be able to keep tomatillos for 1 to 3 weeks.

TO PREPARE: Remove the stems and lift off the husks of the tomatillos. Rinse under cool running water and cut out the small stem patch. Drain and pat dry.

Tomatillos may be sliced or diced, and served raw as a salad ingredient, an appetizer, or a component of a relish. They may also be steamed, roasted, or simmered in liquid, and then puréed. Tomatillos are often coarsely chopped and cooked as part of Mexican-style soups and sauces.

Tomatillo and Jicama Salad
SERVES 4

2 tablespoons lime juice
½ teaspoon sugar
½ teaspoon salt
Pinch of cayenne
6 tablespoons vegetable oil
1 garlic clove, pressed
1 pound tomatillos, thinly sliced
1 medium jicama, shredded
4 ounces Monterey Jack cheese, cut into ¼-inch cubes
1 red bell pepper, coarsely chopped
1 tablespoon chopped fresh cilantro

Cubes of Monterey Jack cheese and coarsely chopped red bell pepper round out this zesty salad.

1. In a small mixing bowl, whisk together the lime juice, sugar, salt, and cayenne. Gradually whisk in the oil and stir in the garlic.

2. In a salad bowl, combine the tomatillos, jicama, cheese, and red bell pepper. Scatter on the cilantro and mix in. Pour on the prepared dressing and toss to combine. Serve immediately.

Grilled Chicken Breasts with Salsa Verde

SERVES 4

Tomatillos are the chief flavor component of this salsa verde, which is delicious paired with grilled chicken. However, it may also be used in any recipe that calls for "green sauce."

2 chicken breasts, boned
  and split
½ cup vegetable oil
Juice of 2 limes
1 pound tomatillos, coarsely
  chopped
¼ cup water
1 medium onion, quartered
1 garlic clove, cut in half
2 green chili peppers, such
  as Jalapeño, seeded
1 tablespoon chopped fresh
  cilantro
½ teaspoon salt
½ cup sour cream

1. Place the chicken breasts in a shallow dish. Pour on the oil and sprinkle with the juice of 1 lime. Turn to coat both sides. Cover the dish and refrigerate for 4 hours, turning occasionally to ensure even marinating.

2. Meanwhile, combine the tomatillos and water in a wide saucepan. Bring to a gentle bubble and cook, uncovered, for 10 minutes or until tender. Increase the heat and cook, stirring, until almost all the liquid is evaporated. Transfer to the container of a blender or processor.

3. Add the onion, garlic, chilies, cilantro, salt, and the juice of the remaining lime. Process until smooth. Transfer to a small bowl and refrigerate.

4. Place the chicken breasts on a hot grill and cook, basting with the oil marinade. When lightly charred, transfer to a serving platter. Spoon a generous dollop of sour cream onto each piece of chicken and spoon on some of the salsa verde.

Plum tomatoes

Tomatoes

Cherry tomatoes

Tomatoes

N O VEGETABLE ELICITS such ecstasy, such un-
bounded sensual joy, as a ripe, juicy tomato. Yet no
other vegetable at the produce stand is the source of so
much disappointment. For nine months of the year, most
of the fresh tomatoes sold in supermarkets are hard, dry,
and tasteless.

Commercially grown tomatoes are a variety especially developed to be durable, so they can be harvested by
machine and shipped long distances. The term "vine-ripe"
is meaningless, because commercial tomatoes are picked
while still green and ripened during shipping by means of
ethylene gas. This causes them to turn pinkish red, but it
certainly doesn't soften them, nor does it improve their
flavor and texture.

There are signs of improvement, however. An increased supply of hydroponically grown, hothouse tomatoes is available year round. They possess a truer, fresher tomato flavor than any of the other wintertime options. Imported tomatoes from Mexico and Israel are also becoming more accessible, although they are not as flavorful as the hydroponic ones.

TO SELECT: The best fresh tomatoes are those that you buy at a farmer's stand during the height of the summer. They are soft and brilliantly red, and you can smell the pungent aroma of the cut vine if you put your nose to the stem cap. Tomatoes like these are what the term vine-ripe is all about. (Some vegetable stands have pick-'em-yourself fields where you can wade through the plants and gather your own. If you can find one, don't pass up the opportunity to experience the lushness of a fresh tomato still warm from the sun.)

Supermarket tomatoes, even at the peak of the season, are a compromise in quality because of storage and handling problems. At best, their quality will be fair to acceptable. Keeping that in mind, look for firm, bright red tomatoes with unblemished skin. They should yield slightly to the pressure of your fingers, but flesh that is softer indicates deterioration in a tomato of this type.

The tiny round tomatoes called cherry tomatoes are good in salads and delicious when sautéed. Plum or pear tomatoes contain a higher proportion of flesh than standard tomatoes; consequently, they are the best choice for preparing sauces and purées. Occasionally you may find yellow pear-shaped tomatoes that make a delicious and unusual treat when served raw or cooked. Green tomatoes are mature, but unripe, standard tomatoes. Purchase those that are firm and bright green with no signs of softness or mold.

TO STORE: Fully ripe summer tomatoes should be kept at room temperature, but don't leave them on a sunny windowsill as a matter of course. Temperatures over 80° cause ripe tomatoes to decay rapidly, so it's important to store them away from direct sunlight. However, it's perfectly okay to give them an hour or so in the sun to bring out their full flavor just before using them.

Tomatoes that are not quite ripe can be kept in a brown paper bag or a domed, plastic bowl with holes in it especially designed for ripening fruit. Natural ethylene gas given off by the tomatoes will circulate inside the bag or bowl and complete the ripening process. Never refrigerate red or yellow tomatoes unless you absolutely must to prevent them from spoiling. Cold temperatures rob tomatoes of their flavor and destroy their texture. Green tomatoes may be refrigerated, but are best if used as soon as possible.

TO PREPARE:

The skin of a fully ripe tomato is often quite tough, and many cooks prefer to remove it. This is a relatively simple task with soft, ripe tomatoes because you can literally lift the skin away with a paring knife. Tomatoes not at the peak of ripeness, however, require a little more attention. Depending on the degree of ripeness, you can pour a pot of boiling water over tomatoes set in the sink and allow it to run down the drain. This is sufficient to loosen the skin of firm, ripe tomatoes. For those that are less ripe, submerge the tomatoes in simmering water for 10 to 30 seconds, then peel while still warm.

Seeding tomatoes is a step that many recipes require you to perform, but it's not nearly as time consuming as it might sound. After removing the skin, cut out the core of the tomato with a serrated grapefruit knife, and slice the tomato into quarters. Then, holding a segment of tomato over a bowl, wiggle your index finger around inside the seed cavity, letting the seeds and juice trickle into the bowl. Strain the juice to drink, if you like. The reason for removing the seeds from tomatoes is to avoid the bitter harshness they can impart during cooking.

Tomatoes may be served raw or cooked in a limitless variety of ways. They may be baked, broiled, fried, and simmered into sauces, purées, and soups. Tomatoes also form the basis for preserves and sorbets.

When seeding a tomato, cut out its core with a serrated grapefruit knife. Slice the tomato into quarters, and use your finger to remove the seeds from each segment.

Tomato Relish

6 large tomatoes, peeled,
  seeded, and chopped
2 medium-size red onions,
  finely chopped
2 ribs celery, finely chopped
1 green bell pepper, finely
  chopped
⅓ cup sugar
1 tablespoon coriander seed
½ teaspoon salt
Freshly ground black
  pepper
½ cup red wine vinegar

A quick and easy relish to serve with cold chicken or to spoon atop grilled hamburgers.

1. Place the chopped tomatoes in a sieve and allow them to drain for 1 hour. Discard the juice or use for another purpose. In a large mixing bowl, combine the tomatoes, onions, celery, and green bell pepper. Sprinkle on the sugar, coriander seed, salt, and pepper. Toss to combine.

2. Pour the vinegar over the mixture and stir to coat evenly. Cover the bowl and refrigerate for 3 days. Stir occasionally during that time to encourage the flavors to meld. The relish will keep in the refrigerator for 5 days.

Gazpacho

2 one-inch-thick slices
  French bread
2 garlic cloves
¼ cup olive oil
¼ cup red wine vinegar
½ teaspoon cumin seed
3 pounds tomatoes, peeled,
  seeded, and chopped
1 medium onion, coarsely
  chopped
3 ribs celery, coarsely
  chopped
1 cucumber, coarsely
  chopped
1 green bell pepper,
  coarsely chopped
1 cup tomato juice
1 cup cold water
1 tablespoon lime juice
½ teaspoon salt
Freshly ground black
  pepper

Because the vegetables in this soup are uncooked, it possesses a fresh, garden-salad taste. Serve only lightly chilled to fully appreciate its blend of flavors.

1. Pull the bread apart into shreds and drop into the container of a blender or processor. Add the garlic, oil, vinegar, and cumin seed and whirl until smooth.

2. Add the tomatoes, onion, celery, cucumber, and green bell pepper. Whirl to incorporate, but do not over-process. The final mixture should have a coarse, grainy consistency. Stir in the tomato juice, water, lime juice, salt, and pepper. Pour into a bowl. Cover and refrigerate until lightly chilled. Serve in glass soup bowls and offer a selection of garnishes, such as finely chopped green bell pepper, finely chopped cucumber, finely chopped onion, toasted croutons, or chopped fresh cilantro.

Fresh Tomato Bisque

SERVES 6

3 tablespoons butter
1 medium onion, coarsely chopped
2 tablespoons all-purpose flour
2 cups water
4 pounds tomatoes, peeled, seeded, and cut into pieces
2 tablespoons light brown sugar
6 whole cloves
1 teaspoon salt
Freshly ground black pepper
1 cup medium or whipping cream

Chunks of fresh tomato contribute textural interest to this clove-spiked soup.

1. Melt the butter in a large saucepan. Add the onion and toss to coat. Stir over medium heat until the onion is tender. Sprinkle on the flour and continue stirring over medium heat until the mixture foams. Stir in the water and bring to a boil. Measure out ¾ cup of the tomato pieces and set aside. Add the remaining tomato pieces to the boiling mixture. Stir in the brown sugar and cloves. Reduce the heat and cook, uncovered, at a gentle bubble for 30 minutes.

2. Transfer to a food mill and force through. Return to the saucepan and stir in the reserved tomato pieces. Blend in the salt, pepper, and cream. Place over medium heat and warm gently, but do not boil.

Tomato Granité

SERVES 6

A granité is a grainy, sherbetlike ice made with a fruit purée and sugar syrup. Tomato granité may be served as a refresher between courses, but it is even nicer, I think, as an adjunct to cold shrimp or a seafood salad.

6 large tomatoes, peeled, seeded, and chopped
2½ cups water
½ cup dry white wine
½ cup white wine vinegar
2 tablespoons chopped fresh basil

1. Combine the tomatoes and ½ cup of the water in a large saucepan. Cook, uncovered, over medium heat. Stir frequently and continue cooking until most of the liquid evaporates and you are left with a chunky purée. Transfer to a bowl and refrigerate for at least 2 hours.

2. Meanwhile, combine the remaining 2 cups water, the wine, and vinegar in a saucepan and cook, uncovered, until reduced by half. Stir in the basil and cook for 1 minute. Transfer to a bowl and refrigerate for at least 2 hours.

3. Combine the tomato purée and the water mixture in the container of an ice cream machine and process according to the manufacturer's instructions. To serve, allow the granité to soften slightly, then spoon it into tomato shells or small glass dishes.

Tomato and Feta Cheese Salad

SERVES 4

4 large tomatoes, peeled
  and sliced
1 shallot, minced
Salt and freshly ground
  black pepper
2 tablespoons red wine
  vinegar
¼ teaspoon sugar
6 tablespoons olive oil
4 ounces feta cheese,
  crumbled
1 tablespoon chopped fresh
  basil
1 tablespoon chopped fresh
  thyme
Sprig of basil for garnish

A simple, yet elegant, salad of sliced tomatoes and feta cheese laced with fresh herbs.

1. Overlapping the tomato slices, arrange them in 2 concentric circles around the perimeter of a large glass plate. Do not include the end slices, but instead chop them coarsely and spoon them into a mound in the center of the plate. Scatter the shallot over the tomatoes and sprinkle on the salt and pepper. Cover with plastic wrap and place in the refrigerator.

2. Just before serving, whisk together the vinegar, sugar, and oil. Pour the dressing over the tomatoes. Scatter the feta cheese over the tomatoes and sprinkle on the basil and thyme. Place a sprig of basil in the mound of chopped tomatoes as a garnish and serve.

Baked Stuffed Tomatoes

SERVES 6

6 large tomatoes
1 can (6½ ounces) tuna,
  packed in oil
1 large egg yolk
1 tablespoon lemon juice
¾ cup unseasoned bread
  crumbs
1 shallot, minced
2 teaspoons capers, drained
6 black oil-cured olives,
  coarsely chopped
4 ounces feta cheese,
  crumbled
2 tablespoons chopped
  fresh parsley
1 tablespoon chopped fresh
  basil
Salt and freshly ground
  black pepper
1 medium head romaine,
  shredded

Cold tomatoes stuffed with tuna salad are a classic summer luncheon dish. Here is a hot version in which the tomatoes are stuffed with tuna and feta cheese, then baked in the oven.

1. Preheat the oven to 375°. Generously butter a shallow baking dish. Cut a small, thin slice from the bottom of each tomato so it will sit upright. Remove the top of each tomato and scoop out the seeds. Invert on absorbent paper to drain.

2. Drain the tuna and reserve the oil. Flake the tuna and set it aside. In a small bowl, whisk together the egg yolk and lemon juice. When slightly thickened, whisk in the reserved tuna oil, a little at a time. Add the bread crumbs and stir to moisten. Mix in the flaked tuna.

3. Add the shallot, capers, olives, feta cheese, parsley, and basil. Stir to combine and season with salt and pepper. Spoon the stuffing into the tomato cavities. Transfer to the prepared baking dish and bake for 30 minutes or until the top of the stuffing is slightly browned. Serve hot, surrounded by shredded romaine.

Grilled Tomatoes with Herbed Cheese

SERVES 4

The best tomatoes to use for grilling are those that are ripe, but not yet soft. Firm-fleshed tomatoes don't disintegrate as quickly when exposed to harsh heat.

4 large, firm tomatoes, unpeeled
2 tablespoons olive oil
Salt and freshly ground black pepper
8 heaping teaspoons herbed Boursin cheese

1. Slice the stem and blossom ends from the tomatoes and discard. Cut them in half horizontally to form 2 thick slices. Using a serrated grapefruit knife, carve out a shallow depression about 1½ inches in diameter in the center of each slice.

2. Brush both sides of each slice generously with oil, then sprinkle with salt and pepper. Place, depression side down, on a hot grill. When the slices soften, turn them over and place a teaspoon-size dollop of Boursin cheese in each depression. Continue grilling until the cheese is soft and hot. Serve immediately.

Sweet and Sour Tomato Sauce

SERVES 4

2 tablespoons olive oil
1 tablespoon butter
1 green bell pepper, cut into narrow strips
3 pounds tomatoes, peeled, seeded, and chopped
1 cup boiling water
2 tablespoons red wine vinegar
1 tablespoon light brown sugar
1 tablespoon honey
Salt and freshly ground black pepper
1 tablespoon chopped fresh cilantro

This lively, fresh tomato sauce is wonderful served hot over fettuccine or cheese-filled tortellini. It is also good when chilled and combined with cold shrimp and pasta shells.

1. Heat the oil and butter in a wide saucepan until the butter is melted. Add the green bell pepper and stir over medium heat until limp.

2. Add the tomatoes, water, vinegar, brown sugar, and honey. Bring to a gentle bubble and cook, uncovered, for 30 minutes or until the tomatoes are reduced to a coarse purée. (Mash them against the side of the pan if necessary to achieve the desired consistency.)

3. Season with salt and pepper and stir in the cilantro. Cook for 5 minutes and spoon over hot, drained pasta. Or transfer to a bowl and refrigerate to serve chilled.

Fresh Tomato Pizza

Slices of fresh tomato take the place of the customary tomato sauce in this up-to-date pizza.

14-inch pizza crust (see p. 208)

Olive oil

4 medium tomatoes, peeled and sliced

Salt and freshly ground black pepper

6 slices smoked ham, cut into ½-inch squares

1 green bell pepper, cut into thin strips

2 ounces herbed Boursin cheese

2 ounces feta cheese, crumbled

1 tablespoon chopped fresh thyme

1. Prepare the pizza crust according to the directions on page 208.

2. Preheat the oven and baking stone to 500°. Generously apply the oil over the surface of the dough with your fingertips.

3. Arrange the tomato slices over the dough in concentric circles, but do not overlap them. Sprinkle generously with salt and pepper. Scatter the ham over the tomatoes and lay on the strips of green bell pepper in an attractive pattern.

4. Drop small dollops of the Boursin cheese over the pepper strips and sprinkle on the feta cheese. Scatter the thyme over the top. Place the pizza on the preheated baking stone in the oven and bake for 12 to 15 minutes or until the crust is lightly browned. Transfer to a cutting board and slice into wedges.

Tomato Herb Bread

2½ cups all-purpose flour

3 teaspoons baking powder

½ teaspoon salt

¼ cup sugar

1 cup quick-cooking oats

6 tablespoons freshly grated Parmesan cheese

2 large eggs

1 cup milk

¼ cup butter, melted

3 tomatoes, peeled, seeded, and chopped (about ½ pound)

1 tablespoon fresh basil

1 tablespoon fresh oregano

Fresh tomatoes and herbs create a moist quick bread with an essence-of-summer flavor.

1. Preheat the oven to 375°. Generously grease a 9x5-inch loaf pan. Combine the flour, baking powder, salt, sugar, oats, and 4 tablespoons of the cheese in a large mixing bowl. Whisk to blend thoroughly.

2. In a separate bowl, beat together the eggs, milk, and melted butter. Stir in the tomatoes, basil, and oregano. Combine with the dry ingredients. Pour into the prepared pan. Sprinkle the surface with the remaining 2 tablespoons Parmesan cheese. Bake for 50 minutes to 1 hour or until a wooden pick inserted in the center comes out clean. Cool on a rack for 10 minutes, then turn out. Serve while warm in thick slices, cut into quarters.

Turnip Greens

TURNIP GREENS, which somewhat resemble collard greens in appearance, are much more assertive in flavor. And because they can hold their own against other strong flavors, turnip greens are often prepared with salt pork, ham, or bacon. These greens are an excellent source of vitamin A.

TO SELECT:

Look for young turnip greens with relatively small, light green leaves. As with most greens, these will be more mildly flavored than the larger, darker leaves. Choose fresh, resilient greens with smooth leaves that show no signs of insect damage. Avoid turnip greens that are limp or wilted.

TO STORE:

Transfer the unwashed turnip greens to a plastic bag and secure with a wire twist. Refrigerate and plan to use them within 1 to 2 days.

TO PREPARE:

Because turnip greens are so strongly flavored, the best method for preparing them consists of simmering the leaves in water, which leaches out some of the harshness from the greens, or in a pork-flavored broth, which imparts a sweet, porky taste.

For best results, remove the tough stem and center rib by folding each leaf in half so that the underside of the rib protrudes slightly. Then gently pull the stem and rib away from the leaf. Plunge the trimmed leaves into a basin of cold water and agitate to wash off any soil. Transfer to a colander and allow to drain. Submerge the turnip greens in a pot of boiling water or broth and cook, uncovered, until tender.

Turnip Greens and Sausage Soup

SERVES 6

3 tablespoons olive oil
2 medium onions, coarsely chopped
2 medium potatoes, peeled and cut into ½-inch cubes
6 cups chicken broth
2 cups water
1 pound turnip greens, stemmed and coarsely chopped
1 pound chorizo, thinly sliced
1½ cups canned cannellini beans, drained
Salt and freshly ground black pepper

Chorizo, a garlic-flavored sausage, adds its spicy character to this hearty soup.

1. Heat the oil in a large saucepan and add the onions. Toss to coat and stir over medium heat until the onions are tender. Stir in the potatoes.

2. Add the chicken broth and water and bring to a boil. Stir in the turnip greens. Add the chorizo and beans. Bring to a gentle bubble and cook, partially covered, for 30 to 40 minutes or until the turnip greens and potatoes are tender. Season with salt and pepper. Ladle into soup bowls and serve piping hot.

Turnip Greens with Bacon

SERVES 4

Turnip greens are served hot with a sprinkling of vinegar and finely chopped raw onion.

3 cups water
½ pound sliced Canadian bacon, cut into julienne strips
1 garlic clove, minced
3 pounds turnip greens, stemmed
1 small onion, minced
Cider vinegar

1. In a large pot, combine the water, bacon, and garlic. Bring to a gentle bubble and cook, uncovered, for 10 minutes.

2. Add the turnip greens, stirring them into the liquid as they wilt. Cook, uncovered, at a gentle bubble for 30 to 40 minutes or until the greens are very tender. Increase the heat and stir constantly until most of the liquid is evaporated. Transfer to a serving dish and scatter the onion over the top. Lightly sprinkle the surface with vinegar.

Turnips

TURNIPS HAVE NEVER been a popular vegetable. Aside from an annual portion on Thanksgiving Day, many Americans don't eat turnips at all. And this is unfortunate, because wisely chosen and carefully prepared, turnips can be a delightful experience.

The secret to enjoying turnips is to buy them in their season. The problem lies in assuming that because turnips are root vegetables, they keep well for long periods of time. That is not exactly so. While it's true that turnips will remain edible for months, it doesn't necessarily mean that they will continue to be delicious.

Turnips grow rapidly and are harvested in cool weather. This means that the peak turnip seasons occur in late spring, when the first crop matures, and then again in early fall, when the second crop is taken in. Turnips purchased at either of these two times will be tender and sweet, and taste totally unlike those that have been held in storage.

TO SELECT:

The turnips most commonly available in supermarkets are the round, white variety with patches of purple at the top of the root, near the leaf base (see also Rutabagas). They are often sold in bunches with their greens still attached. Pick out the smallest turnips on display. If you see some about the size of a golf ball, buy twice as many as you think you need. They'll taste so surprisingly sweet and delicate that people will ask for seconds. Good-quality turnips should feel firm and smooth, and have unblemished skin. If the greens are present, they should be perky and fresh looking. Turnips that have been trimmed should show no signs of sprouting because that indicates prolonged storage. Plan on 1½ pounds of turnips for 4 servings.

TO STORE:

Turnips are much more delicate than commonly believed. They dehydrate quickly, and if stored too long, develop a strong, unpleasant flavor. When you get turnips home, remove the greens if they are present, leaving about 2 inches of stem attached. Without washing, transfer them to a plastic bag, secure with a wire twist, and place the turnips in the vegetable drawer of your refrigerator. For optimum flavor, use the turnips within 4 to 5 days.

TO PREPARE:

Rinse the turnips under cool running water, slice off the taproots, and cut away the remaining stems. (If you have baby turnips, you may want to leave the short stems attached because it looks attractive on the plate.) Young turnips have thin, tender skins, and therefore need not be peeled; the skins of larger turnips should be removed with a swivel-blade peeler. Tiny turnips may be boiled, steamed, or braised whole. Larger turnips are customarily quartered or sliced before cooking. Turnips are also delicious grated and served raw in salads and slaws, or cut into sticks to offer as part of a crudités tray.

Turnip Salad with Mustard Dressing

SERVES 6

⅔ cup mayonnaise,
  preferably homemade
2 tablespoons whole-grain
  Pommery mustard
1 tablespoon lemon juice
1 tablespoon chopped fresh
  chives
2 pounds turnips, peeled
  and shredded
Salt and freshly ground
  black pepper
6 leaves Boston lettuce

Shredded, uncooked turnips create an unexpectedly elegant salad.

1. In a large mixing bowl, combine the mayonnaise, mustard, lemon juice, and chives. Blend well.

2. Add the turnips and toss to combine. Season with salt and pepper and cover the bowl. Refrigerate for 1 to 2 hours or until lightly chilled. Divide the lettuce leaves among 6 salad plates and spoon on the turnip mixture. Serve at once.

Braised Baby Turnips

SERVES 4

Whole baby turnips are cooked slowly in beef broth and sherry, then glazed with heavy cream. If you can't find baby turnips, substitute medium-size turnips cut into quarters.

3 tablespoons butter
1½ pounds whole baby
  turnips, peeled
¾ cup beef broth
¼ cup cream sherry
½ cup heavy cream
Salt and freshly ground
  black pepper
1 tablespoon lemon juice
2 tablespoons finely
  chopped pecans

1. Melt the butter in a wide saucepan. Add the turnips and toss to coat. Stir over medium heat for 1 minute.

2. Pour in the beef broth and sherry. Bring to a boil. Cover the pan and reduce the heat. Simmer for 10 to 15 minutes or until the turnips are tender when pierced.

3. Increase the heat and cook, stirring, until almost all the liquid is evaporated. Remove from the heat and stir in the cream. Season with salt and pepper. Return to medium heat and cook until the cream is reduced to a thick consistency. Remove from the heat. Stir in the lemon juice and transfer to a serving dish. Sprinkle on the chopped pecans.

Turnips Au Gratin

Slices of turnip are baked in a bubbling sauce of Gruyère cheese. Serve as a vegetable side dish with baked ham or roast chicken.

1 pound turnips, peeled and
  thinly sliced
5 tablespoons butter
1 tablespoon all-purpose
  flour
1 cup milk
½ teaspoon salt
Pinch of cayenne
Freshly ground nutmeg
6 ounces Gruyère cheese,
  grated
¼ cup unseasoned bread
  crumbs

1. Preheat the oven to 350°. Generously butter a shallow baking dish. Place the turnip slices in a large saucepan. Add enough water to cover the turnips by 1 inch and set over high heat. Stir frequently. When the water comes to a vigorous boil, immediately drain the turnip slices in a colander set under cold running water. Drain thoroughly and arrange the slices in the prepared baking dish in an overlapping design.

2. Melt 3 tablespoons of the butter in a small saucepan and blend in the flour. When the mixture foams, whisk in the milk. Stir over medium heat until the sauce bubbles and thickens. Blend in the salt, cayenne, nutmeg, and Gruyère cheese. Continue stirring over medium heat until the cheese is melted. Pour the sauce over the turnips.

3. Melt the remaining 2 tablespoons butter in a small skillet. Add the bread crumbs and stir until moistened. Scatter over the sauced turnips. Bake for 20 to 25 minutes or until the turnip slices are tender when pierced.

Turnips Glazed with Apple Cider

Matchstick slices of turnip are veiled with a glossy, apple-flavored glaze.

1½ pounds turnips, cut into
  julienne strips
1 cup apple cider
3 tablespoons butter
2 teaspoons sugar
¼ teaspoon ground allspice
Salt and freshly ground
  black pepper

1. Combine the turnips and cider in a wide saucepan. Pour in enough water to cover the turnips by 1 inch. Bring to a gentle bubble and cook, uncovered, for 10 minutes or until the turnips are crisp-tender.

2. Add the butter, sugar, and allspice. Increase the heat and cook, stirring, until almost all the liquid is evaporated and the turnips are coated with a shiny glaze. Season with salt and pepper and transfer to a serving dish.

Turnip and Pear Purée

SERVES 6

Melted Gorgonzola cheese tops this purée of turnips and pears. Serve as a vegetable side dish with roast veal.

4 tablespoons butter
1 pound turnips, peeled and
 cut into chunks
1 shallot, minced
½ cup water
1 pound pears, peeled,
 cored and cut into
 chunks
Salt and freshly ground
 black pepper
Pinch of freshly grated
 nutmeg
2 tablespoons crumbled
 Gorgonzola cheese

1. Melt the butter in a large skillet. Add the turnips and shallot and toss to coat. Stir over medium heat until the shallot is tender. Pour on the water. Reduce the heat and cover the pan. Simmer for 10 minutes. Stir in the pears. Cover the pan and continue cooking for 10 to 15 minutes or until the turnips and pears are tender. Uncover the pan and increase the heat. Cook, stirring, until all the liquid is evaporated and the turnips begin to stick to the bottom of the pan. Transfer to a blender or food processor and whirl until smooth.

2. Preheat the oven to 350°. Generously butter a casserole dish. Season the purée with salt, pepper, and nutmeg. Pour into the prepared dish and sprinkle on the crumbled Gorgonzola cheese. Bake for 10 minutes or until heated through.

Watercress

WATERCRESS, SO CALLED to distinguish it from other types of cress that take root in dry soil, grows wild in gently flowing streams and at the edge of shallow riverbeds. It is also commercially grown in large shallow pools, where a steady supply of cool, pure water is circulated continuously among the plants. Cultivated watercress is available year round, but because consumer demand is only high in the spring, that's when you're most apt to see it in supermarkets.

Watercress possesses an assertive, yet refreshing, flavor that is often described as "peppery." It may be eaten raw in salads or sandwiches, where its sharp flavor provides a zippy counterpoint to other ingredients. Sprigs of watercress may also be cooked in soups and sauces. The result, however, is a milder, more mellow character because cooking tempers the flavor of this leafy green.

TO SELECT: Watercress is customarily sold in unwrapped bunches tightly secured with string. Look for fresh sprigs of cloverlike leaves with firm, crisp stems. The leaves should be unbruised and bright green. Since thinner stems are more tender, pick out the bunch with the narrowest stem ends. Refuse watercress that is limp or yellow. Part the leaves in the center of the bunch and check for rot. Dark, slimy patches are a sign of deterioration. Smell the leaves; they should have a fresh, appealing fragrance. Decaying watercress will smell offensive.

TO STORE: As soon as you get watercress home, cut the string holding the bunch and separate the sprigs. Pick them over, discarding any that are wilted, yellowed, or decayed. Rinse the sprigs briefly under cool running water, then scatter them over a clean kitchen towel. Pat gently to blot up excess moisture. Transfer the watercress to a plastic bag, secure with a wire twist, and refrigerate. Use within 1 or 2 days. If the leaves get droopy looking, you can refresh them by submerging the sprigs in ice water for 1 to 2 hours.

TO PREPARE: Rinse watercress under cool running water and trim a small portion from the stem ends. Gently pat dry.

Each sprig of watercress consists of 2 or 3 thin leafy stems branching from a thicker main stem. If the main stem seems tough and woody, snap off the thinner branches to use in salads or sandwiches. The thick main stem may be chopped finely and sprinkled over a salad or used as you would any chopped herb. For soups and sauces, the entire sprig may be used as is, or the leaves may be removed and chopped to be added at the last minute for textural and visual interest. Coarsely chopped sprigs may be included as part of a vegetable stir-fry. When presented as a garnish, whole sprigs of watercress are usually arranged in graceful curves or sprightly bundles. Watercress may also be cooked with a small amount of water, then puréed.

Watercress Soup

3 bunches watercress
4 tablespoons butter
2 medium leeks, white and light green portion, thinly sliced
10 green onions, white and light green portion, thinly sliced
6 cups chicken broth
2 medium-size mealy potatoes, peeled and cubed
1 medium head romaine, sliced across into shreds
½ teaspoon salt
Freshly ground white pepper
½ cup heavy cream
Cucumber slices for garnish

Watercress and green onions are the main components of this sprightly soup. Serve for a springtime luncheon garnished with slices of cucumber.

1. Separate the watercress, discarding the thick stems or reserving them for another use. Coarsely chop the leaves and slender stems, then set aside.

2. Melt the butter in a wide saucepan. Add the leeks and onions and toss to coat evenly. Cover the pan and cook over low heat for 20 minutes or until the leeks and onions are tender.

3. Pour in the chicken broth. Add the potatoes, romaine, and watercress. Season with salt and pepper and cook, uncovered, for 15 minutes. Transfer to the container of a blender or processor and whirl until smooth. Return to the saucepan and blend in the cream. Heat gently and serve garnished with cucumber slices.

Watercress and Leek Salad

2 bunches watercress
2 medium leeks, white portion only, sliced lengthwise
1 teaspoon chopped fresh sage
1 teaspoon chopped fresh rosemary
Salt and freshly ground black pepper
2 tablespoons red wine vinegar
1 teaspoon Dijon mustard
6 tablespoons olive oil
1 garlic clove, pressed

Fresh watercress and thin strips of leek are tossed together to create a memorable salad.

1. Rinse the watercress and pull the thin leafy branches away from the main stem. Discard the main stems or reserve them for another use. Pat the watercress dry and tear into small pieces. Transfer to a salad bowl.

2. Thinly slice the leeks crosswise and then separate the slices into half-rings. Add to the watercress and toss to combine. Sprinkle on the sage and rosemary. Season with salt and pepper and refrigerate to chill lightly.

3. Just before serving, combine the vinegar and mustard in a small bowl. Whisk to dissolve the mustard and whisk in the oil. Stir in the garlic and pour over the salad to serve.

Pappardelle with Watercress Sauce

SERVES 4

2 bunches watercress
½ cup olive oil
6 green onions, white portion only, thinly sliced
1 garlic clove, minced
Salt and freshly ground black pepper
½ cup dry white wine
½ cup chopped fresh parsley
1 cup heavy cream
12 ounces pappardelle, boiled and drained
4 tablespoons butter, cut into small pieces
Freshly grated Parmesan cheese

Pappardelle are relatively broad noodles. They are sold both fresh and dried. If you cannot find them, feel free to use fettuccine instead.

1. Rinse the watercress and pull the thin leafy branches away from the main stem. Discard the main stems or reserve them for another use. Coarsely chop the tender branches and leaves. Transfer to a large skillet.

2. Add the oil, onions, and garlic to the watercress and stir over medium heat until the onions are tender. Sprinkle with salt and pepper. Add the wine and parsley. Stir to combine and cook briskly until most of the liquid is evaporated. Stir in the cream and bring to a gentle bubble. Simmer, uncovered, for 3 minutes.

3. Meanwhile, transfer the hot, drained pappardelle to a large bowl. Add the butter and toss to melt, coating each noodle. Pour on the sauce and toss to combine. Serve sprinkled with the grated Parmesan cheese.

Watercress Sauce

MAKES 1½ CUPS

Spoon this beautiful sauce over grilled salmon. Or serve with cold chicken or ham, or sliced hard-boiled eggs.

1 bunch watercress
½ cup mayonnaise, preferably homemade
½ cup sour cream
2 tablespoons lemon juice
2 tablespoons chopped fresh chives
1 tablespoon chopped fresh parsley
Salt and freshly ground white pepper

1. Rinse the watercress and pull the thin leafy branches away from the main stem. Discard the main stems or reserve them for another use. Transfer the tender leafy branches to the container of a blender or processor.

2. Add the mayonnaise, sour cream, lemon juice, chives, and parsley. Whirl until smooth and pale green. Season with salt and pepper and transfer to a bowl. Refrigerate until lightly chilled.

Watercress Biscuits

Finely chopped watercress and green onions lend a nippy accent to these biscuits. Serve with cold ham or chicken salad.

1 bunch watercress
3 green onions, white portion only, finely chopped
2 cups all-purpose flour
3 teaspoons baking powder
½ teaspoon salt
½ teaspoon dry mustard
4 tablespoons butter, cut into small pieces
¾ cup milk

1. Separate the watercress, discarding the thick stems or reserving them for another use. Finely chop the leaves and slender stems. Place in a mixing bowl. Add the onions and toss to combine. Set aside.

2. Preheat the oven to 425°. Generously grease a baking sheet. In a separate bowl, combine the flour, baking powder, salt, and mustard. Whisk to blend thoroughly. Add the butter and cut in until the mixture is crumbly. Add the chopped watercress and onions and toss with a fork to combine.

3. Make a well in the center of the mixture and pour in the milk. Toss with a fork until the dough holds together, then turn out onto a floured surface and knead 20 to 25 times. Roll to ½-inch thickness and cut into 2-inch rounds with a biscuit cutter. Transfer to the prepared baking sheet and bake for 12 to 15 minutes. Serve warm or at room temperature.

Y

Yams

IN CERTAIN PARTS of the United States, particularly the South, it has become a custom to call sweet potatoes "yams." However, even though their flesh is similar in consistency, true yams are an entirely different root vegetable with a distinctly unique appearance (see Sweet Potatoes). Most varieties bear a tough, thick outer covering that resembles the bark of a tree. Yams are shaped like a large, hefty cylinder and may be colored light brown, reddish brown, or dark brown.

A tropical vegetable popular in such cuisines as West Indian and West African, yams possess a white or yellow flesh that is bland and starchy, like that of an Irish potato. The texture of yam flesh, however, is moist and soft, and more nearly resembles that of a sweet potato.

Yams are available year round and are sold mainly in food shops catering to Caribbean, Indian, and African cookery. From a nutritional standpoint, yams are an excellent source of complex carbohydrates.

TO SELECT:

Yams come in a variety of sizes ranging from 8 or 10 ounces to several pounds. You may also find them cut into pieces and sealed in plastic wrap. When buying a whole yam, look for one that weighs no more than a pound. Those with dark brown skin and white flesh are the best choice.

TO STORE:

Treat yams as you would Irish potatoes, storing them in a cool, dry, well-ventilated place. Do not rinse or wrap them. Yams will keep for 2 to 3 weeks.

TO PREPARE:

Yams, unlike sweet potatoes, are toxic if eaten raw. Therefore, yams must always be boiled, baked, grilled, or fried to avoid intestinal discomfort. If not baking the yams, begin to prepare them by removing the tough outer skin with a sharp knife. Then cut the flesh into pieces and cook until tender. Cooked yams are often puréed and flavored with spices and sweet syrups.

Deep-Fried Yam Chips

SERVES 6

Fried in deep fat, thin slices of yam develop a golden hue. Salt lightly and serve as an appetizer.

3 slender yams, peeled
Vegetable oil for deep-
    frying
Freshly ground sea salt

1. Rinse the peeled yams and pat them dry. Cut into thin slices. Distribute the slices over absorbent paper in a single layer and cover with another piece of absorbent paper.

2. Heat the oil in a deep-fat fryer to 325°. Blot the slices of yam and submerge them in the hot oil in small batches. Cook until crisp and lightly browned. Drain on absorbent paper and sprinkle with sea salt. Serve in a napkin-lined basket.

Oven-Roasted Yams

SERVES 4

Spears of yam are roasted in garlic-flavored butter and basted with a sweet-and-sour sauce. Serve with roast beef or chicken.

6 tablespoons butter
1 garlic clove, sliced
2 yams (8 ounces each)
4 tablespoons soy sauce
2 tablespoons red wine
  vinegar
2 teaspoons sugar
⅛ teaspoon Tabasco sauce

1. Melt the butter in a small saucepan. Swirl in the garlic and remove from the heat. Allow to stand for 15 minutes.

2. Preheat the oven to 375°. Peel the yams and cut lengthwise into 8 wedges. Using a slotted spoon, remove the garlic from the butter and discard. Pour the butter into a 9x13-inch baking dish. Add the yams, turning to coat evenly with butter. Bake for 30 minutes.

3. Meanwhile, combine the soy sauce, vinegar, sugar, and Tabasco in a small bowl. Stir until the sugar is dissolved. Brush over the partially cooked yams and continue baking for 15 to 20 minutes or until tender when pierced.

Puréed Yams with Maple Syrup

SERVES 4

Puréed yams flavored with maple syrup bake to a light, puffy consistency. These are particularly good with baked ham.

1½ pounds yams, peeled
  and cut into quarters
⅓ cup maple syrup
4 tablespoons butter
2 large eggs, beaten
½ teaspoon ground mace
Salt and freshly ground
  black pepper

1. Drop the yams into a large pot of boiling, salted water and cook, uncovered, at a gentle bubble for 30 to 40 minutes or until tender when pierced. Drain in a colander. Return the yams to the pan and break them up with a fork. Stir over medium heat until the yams begin to stick to the bottom of the pan. Transfer to a food mill and purée into a large mixing bowl.

2. Preheat the oven to 350°. Generously butter a casserole dish. In a small saucepan, heat the maple syrup and butter until the butter is melted. Add to the puréed yams and blend thoroughly. Beat in the eggs, mace, salt, and pepper and transfer to the prepared baking dish. Bake for 20 minutes or until slightly puffed.

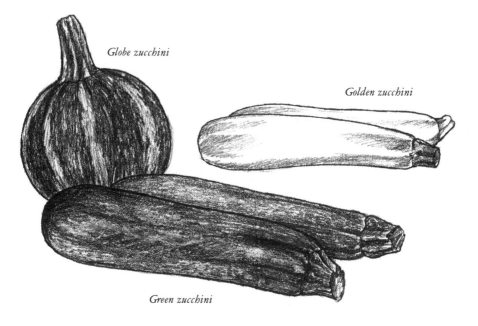

Globe zucchini

Golden zucchini

Green zucchini

Zucchini

CONSIDER THE SUCCESS of zucchini. Only 20 years ago, this vegetable was so unfamiliar in the United States that recipe writers had to define it as "green Italian squash." Today, it is one of the most popular and widely recognized vegetables in the marketplace.

Mild and delicately flavored, zucchini is endlessly versatile. It can be cooked simply and served on its own merit, or stuffed with flavorful fillings. Zucchini can also be stir-fried, deep-fried, or combined with other ingredients to create custards, flans, savory pies, casseroles, and a variety of other dishes. Like other types of summer squash, zucchini is a good source of vitamins A and C.

TO SELECT:	Where once there was one kind, now there are three — golden zucchini, round zucchini, and the familiar green cylindrical zucchini. Golden zucchini, also cylindrical in shape, retains its deep yellow color when cooked and is somewhat milder in taste than its green cousin. Round zucchini, also called globe zucchini, is about the size of a softball. It can be used interchangeably with the others, or best of all, parboiled and stuffed.
	Size is a reliable indicator of quality. Look for slender cylindrical zucchini no more than 6 inches long, or in the case of round zucchini, no more than 3 inches in diameter. The skin should feel firm and be free of cuts and bruises. Occasionally, you'll find baby green zucchini about the size of your little finger. They are a wonderful treat sautéed or steamed whole. Plan on 1 pound of zucchini to serve 4 people.
TO STORE:	Zucchini is a delicate vegetable, so handle it gently. When you get it home, place it in the refrigerator without washing or wrapping. Zucchini stored this way will keep for 3 to 4 days. If it begins to feel limp or wilted, it has begun to deteriorate and should be used immediately.
TO PREPARE:	Rinse briefly under cold running water and pat dry. The skin is delicate and tender, so there's no need to remove it. Zucchini may be cooked whole, cut into chunks, sliced, or shredded. Frequently, a recipe will instruct you to salt the flesh in order to draw off moisture. If you follow this technique, be sure to transfer the salted squash to a sieve and rinse it thoroughly to avoid excessive saltiness in the final dish. Then press down gently on the squash to squeeze out the liquid. A salt-free alternative to this method is to sweat zucchini in a microwave. Place the cut or shredded squash in a glass pie plate. Cover with plastic wrap. Prick a few holes in the wrap and microwave on high for 4 minutes. Allow it to stand at room temperature for 2 minutes, and drain off the liquid that has accumulated in the bottom of the dish.

Zucchini Soup

3 tablespoons butter
2 shallots, finely chopped
4 cups chicken broth
¼ cup long-grain rice
2 pounds small zucchini,
  unpeeled and sliced
2 tablespoons chopped
  fresh chives
Salt to taste
Generous pinch of cayenne
2 tablespoons lemon juice
1 cup medium or whipping
  cream
Freshly chopped savory for
  garnish

*Pale green zucchini soup makes a stunning first course for a
summer evening's meal.*

1. Melt the butter in a large saucepan. Add the
shallots and toss to coat. Cover the pan and cook over low
heat until tender.

2. Pour in the chicken broth. Stir in the rice and
zucchini, then add the chives, salt, and cayenne. Cook
until the rice and zucchini are tender. Transfer to the
container of a blender or processor and whirl until smooth.

3. Return to the saucepan and blend in the lemon
juice. Stir in the cream and heat gently, but do not boil.
Serve hot or cold, garnished with savory leaves.

Zucchini Pickles

1¼ cups water
1¼ cups cider vinegar
1 teaspoon salt
2 teaspoons mustard seed
12 black peppercorns
4 slender zucchini,
  unpeeled and thinly
  sliced
1 medium onion, sliced and
  separated into rings
2 garlic cloves, thinly sliced
1 red bell pepper, cut into
  ½-inch squares
2 tablespoons chopped
  fresh dill leaves

*Crisp slices of zucchini are marinated and chilled to create
these zesty pickles.*

1. In a wide saucepan, combine the water, vinegar,
salt, mustard seed, and peppercorns. Bring to a gentle
bubble and cook, uncovered, for 10 minutes.

2. Meanwhile, combine the zucchini, onion, garlic,
and red bell pepper in a large bowl and toss to combine.
Pour the hot liquid over the vegetables. Scatter on the dill
leaves and stir to mix. Cover the bowl with aluminum foil
and allow to stand at room temperature for 4 hours.
Refrigerate until thoroughly chilled and drain off the liquid to serve.

Zucchini with Minted Vinaigrette

SERVES 4

A light dressing, flavored with fresh mint, veils green-tipped sticks of zucchini in this attractive salad.

2 medium zucchini
2 tablespoons lemon juice
1 teaspoon Dijon mustard
½ teaspoon salt
Pinch of cayenne
6 tablespoons olive oil
1 garlic clove, minced or pressed
1 tablespoon chopped fresh mint
8 sprigs mâche

1. Trim both ends of the zucchini. Slicing down the length of the squash, cut off the rounded portion of the top. Turn the zucchini over and again slice off the rounded upper portion. Then cut the zucchini into ¼-inch-thick slices. Divide these into ¼-inch-wide strips, cutting so that both ends of the strips bear green skin.

2. Drop the strips of zucchini into a large pot of boiling, salted water and cook, uncovered, at a gentle bubble for exactly 1 minute. Drain in a colander set under cold running water. Distribute over absorbent paper and pat dry.

3. In a large mixing bowl, whisk together the lemon juice, mustard, salt, and cayenne. When well blended, whisk in the oil. Stir in the garlic and mint. Add the zucchini and toss to coat evenly. Cover the bowl and refrigerate until thoroughly chilled. Divide the mâche among 4 salad plates and spoon on the zucchini strips, placing them to one side. Serve immediately.

To make these green-tipped strips, begin by trimming the ends from the zucchini. Then, cutting lengthwise, remove the rounded portion of the squash. Turn it over and repeat on the opposite side.

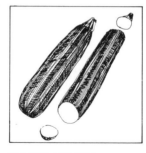

Cut the zucchini into ¼-inch-wide slices, and these slices into ¼-inch-wide strips, making sure that the ends of the strips bear green skin.

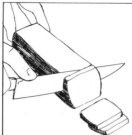

Mushroom Stuffed Zucchini

Small, slender zucchini are sliced lengthwise and then stuffed with a savory mushroom filling.

4 small zucchini, whole
4 tablespoons butter
12 ounces button mushrooms, coarsely chopped
1 shallot, minced
1 garlic clove, minced or pressed
½ cup dry white wine
Salt and freshly ground black pepper
½ teaspoon dried basil
½ teaspoon dried oregano
1 tablespoon lemon juice
½ cup unseasoned bread crumbs
½ cup freshly grated Parmesan cheese

1. Drop the zucchini into a large pot of boiling, salted water and cook, uncovered, at a gentle bubble for 6 to 8 minutes or until a metal skewer can be inserted easily. Lift out the zucchini and allow them to cool.

2. Cut the zucchini in half lengthwise. Scoop out the center with a metal spoon and place, skin side up, on absorbent paper.

3. Preheat the oven to 350°. Generously butter a shallow baking dish. Melt the butter in a large skillet. Add the mushrooms, shallot, and garlic and toss to coat. Stir over high heat until the mushrooms are soft. Pour in the wine. Sprinkle with salt and pepper and stir in the basil and oregano. Cover the pan and reduce the heat. Simmer for 5 minutes. Increase the heat and stir continuously until almost all the liquid is evaporated.

4. Remove from the heat and stir in the lemon juice. Mix in the bread crumbs and Parmesan cheese. Spoon the mixture into the zucchini cavities. Transfer to the prepared baking dish. Cover with aluminum foil and bake for 25 minutes. Uncover and slide under the broiler to crisp the surface of the stuffing. Serve while hot.

Cavatelli with Fresh Zucchini

SERVES 4

3 tablespoons vegetable oil
2 tablespoons butter
4 small zucchini, unpeeled
and diced
1 medium onion, coarsely
chopped
1 green bell pepper,
coarsely chopped
1 red bell pepper, coarsely
chopped
4 large tomatoes, peeled,
seeded, and chopped
1 garlic clove, minced or
pressed
¼ cup chopped fresh
parsley
1 tablespoon chopped fresh
basil
Salt and freshly ground
black pepper
12 ounces cavatelli, boiled
and drained
2 large eggs, beaten
Freshly grated Parmesan
cheese

Beaten eggs create a lightly thickened consistency when this colorful mélange is gently heated.

1. Heat the oil and butter in a large skillet until the butter is melted. Add the zucchini and onion and toss to coat. Stir over medium heat until the onion is tender. Add the green and red bell peppers and continue to stir over medium heat until they are soft. Blend in the tomatoes and garlic. Reduce the heat and simmer, uncovered, for 10 minutes.

2. Stir in the parsley and basil. Season with salt and pepper and remove from the heat. Transfer the hot, drained cavatelli to a large bowl. Pour on the beaten eggs and toss to coat the pasta. Add the cavatelli to the zucchini mixture and toss to combine. Stir over medium heat for 2 to 3 minutes or until slightly thickened and warmed through. Serve with Parmesan cheese.

Grilled Zucchini

SERVES 4

Whole zucchini may be parboiled or microwaved until just crisp-tender and then lightly charred on the grill. They are delicious with grilled lamb steaks.

4 small zucchini, whole
6 tablespoons olive oil
2 tablespoons white wine
vinegar
1 garlic clove, pressed
1 teaspoon dried oregano
½ teaspoon salt

1. Drop the zucchini into a large pot of boiling, salted water and cook, uncovered, at a gentle bubble for 8 to 10 minutes, depending on the thickness of the squash. Lift the zucchini from the water when they are about to become tender, but still feel firm and resilient to the touch. (This precooking step may also be accomplished in a microwave. Wrap each squash in absorbent paper and arrange in a spokelike fashion inside the microwave. Cook

at high power for 2 minutes. Turn and rotate the squash and microwave on high for 2 to 4 more minutes.)

2. In a small bowl, whisk together the oil, vinegar, garlic, oregano, and salt. Brush over the precooked squash. Place on a hot grill and cook for 5 to 8 minutes or until tender when pierced. Turn and baste the zucchini frequently to promote even charring.

Zucchini Frittata

SERVES 4

Thin strips of zucchini combine with Kasseri cheese to create a satisfying open-faced omelet. Serve as a luncheon dish or as a light supper.

4 tablespoons butter
1 pound zucchini, unpeeled and cut into julienne strips
1 medium onion, coarsely chopped
4 large eggs
½ cup light cream
½ cup grated Kasseri cheese
Salt and freshly ground black pepper
¼ cup freshly grated Parmesan cheese

1. Melt the butter in an 8-inch skillet. Add the zucchini and onion and toss to coat. Stir over medium heat until the onion is tender. Remove from the heat and set aside.

2. In a large mixing bowl, whisk together the eggs and cream. Scatter the Kasseri cheese over the zucchini and onion, then season with salt and pepper. Gently pour on the beaten egg mixture.

3. Cover the skillet and place over low heat. Cook for 8 to 10 minutes or until the perimeter is set. Sprinkle on the Parmesan cheese and slide under the broiler. Cook for 2 to 3 minutes or until the center is firm. Slide onto a serving plate and cut into wedges.

Zucchini Corn Bread

MAKES 1 LOAF

1 cup all-purpose flour
1 cup yellow cornmeal
1½ teaspoons baking
  powder
½ teaspoon baking soda
½ teaspoon salt
1 cup buttermilk
1 large egg
¼ cup butter, melted
1 pound zucchini, unpeeled
  and grated
½ cup grated Cheddar
  cheese

Cornmeal contributes a coarse, hearty texture to this cheese-flavored zucchini bread.

1. Preheat the oven to 375°. Generously grease a 9x5-inch loaf pan. Combine the flour, cornmeal, baking powder, soda, and salt in a large mixing bowl. Whisk to blend thoroughly.

2. In a separate bowl, beat together the buttermilk, egg, and melted butter. Add to the dry ingredients and blend well. Stir in the zucchini and cheese. Pour into the prepared pan and bake for 50 minutes to 1 hour or until a wooden pick inserted in the center comes out clean.

Zucchini Cake

MAKES ONE 9X13-INCH CAKE

Shredded zucchini makes a surprisingly moist and rich chocolate cake. Frost with your favorite chocolate icing or spread with Orange Glaze.

½ cup milk
1½ teaspoons lemon juice
2½ cups all-purpose flour
¼ cup unsweetened cocoa
½ teaspoon baking powder
1 teaspoon baking soda
½ teaspoon salt
½ teaspoon ground
  cinnamon
½ teaspoon ground cloves
½ cup butter, softened
½ cup vegetable oil
1¾ cups sugar
2 large eggs
1 teaspoon vanilla
2 cups shredded zucchini
  (about 3 small, unpeeled)
Orange Glaze

1. Preheat the oven to 350°. Grease and flour a 9x13-inch baking pan. In a small bowl, combine the milk and lemon juice and set aside for 10 to 15 minutes or until the milk has soured and become slightly thickened.

2. Meanwhile, in a large mixing bowl, combine the flour, cocoa, baking powder, soda, salt, cinnamon, and cloves. Whisk to blend thoroughly and set aside.

3. In a separate bowl, beat the butter, oil, and sugar until well blended. Add the eggs and vanilla. Gradually beat in the dry ingredients, alternating with the soured milk. Stir in the zucchini. Pour into the prepared pan and bake for 50 minutes to 1 hour or until a wooden pick inserted in the center comes out clean. Allow to cool slightly and then spread with Orange Glaze, if desired.

4. To make Orange Glaze, combine 1 cup sifted confectioners' sugar, 1 tablespoon orange juice, 1 teaspoon grated orange zest, and 1 tablespoon melted butter in a bowl and blend until smooth. Spread over the warm cake.

Mail-Order Sources

THE FOLLOWING LISTING consists of sources you can contact for fresh herbs and specialty food products that may be unobtainable in your local area. The items listed under each source are only those that are referred to in this text. These sources carry a much wider selection than can be listed here, and they will usually send a catalog upon request.

Fox Hill Farm
444 West Michigan Avenue
Box 7
Parma, MI 49269-0007
Telephone (517) 531-3179

Specializes in fresh basil and offers several different varieties, such as dark opal, lemon, and French fine leaf. You may order either fresh-cut or potted basil. A wide selection of other fresh and potted herbs is also available.

Herbs Now
P.O. Box 775
Highland Park, IL 60035
Telephone (312) 432-7711

Offers a wide selection of fresh herbs, both cut and potted. Also specialty produce, such as baby vegetables, long green beans, plantains, and tomatillos.

G.B. Ratto and Company
821 Washington Street
Oakland, CA 94607
Telephone toll free
   1-800-325-3483
   1-800-228-3515
   (in California)

Elephant garlic, fresh shallots, extra-virgin olive oil, Balsamic vinegar, dried pasta, and whole white peppercorns.

Index